Crusader for Freedom

Crusader for Freedom

A Life of Lydia Maria Child

Deborah Pickman Clifford

Beacon Press
BOSTON

Beacon Press
25 Beacon Street
Boston, Massachusetts 02108-2892

Beacon Press books
are published under the auspices of
the Unitarian Universalist Association of Congregations.

99 98 97 96 95 94 93 92 8 7 6 5 4 3 2 1

Text design by Kathleen Szawiola

Frontispiece of Lydia Maria Child
courtesy of the Schlesinger Library, Radcliffe College

Excerpts from the Weston Papers and the Antislavery Collection courtesy of the
Trustees of the Boston Public Library; excerpts from the Lydia Maria Child Papers
courtesy of the Department of Rare Books, Cornell University Library; excerpts
from John Langdon Sibley's private journal by permission of the Harvard University
Archives; excerpts from the Milton E. Ross Collection courtesy of Milton E. Ross;
excerpts from the Ellis Gray Loring Family Papers courtesy of the Schlesinger
Library, Radcliffe College; excerpts from the Beatrice Herford paper and Alfred
Cutting's "Childhood Memories" courtesy of the Wayland Historical Society.

Library of Congress Cataloging-in-Publication Data
Clifford, Deborah Pickman.
Crusader for freedom: a life of Lydia Maria Child/
Deborah Pickman Clifford.
p. cm.
Includes bibliographical references and index.
ISBN 0-8070-7050-5
1. Child, Lydia Maria Francis, 1802–1880. 2. Women social
reformers—United States—Biography. I. Title.
HQ1413.C45C55 1992
303.48′4′092—cd20
[B]   91-33106

To Sally and Upton Brady

Contents

Crusader for Freedom

Introduction

Wherever there was a brave word to be spoken, her voice was heard, and never without effect." So wrote John Greenleaf Whittier after the death of his old friend Lydia Maria Child in 1880. The poet went on to claim "that no man or woman of that period rendered more substantial service to the cause of freedom, or made such a 'great renunciation' in doing it."[1]

More than a hundred years later this generous lover of freedom is remembered, if at all, as the author of the Thanksgiving song which begins, "Over the river and through the wood to grandfather's house we go." In the mid-1800s, however, Lydia Maria Child's name was a household word. To Americans of her day she was known as a tireless crusader for justice and truth who employed a variety of literary forms to forward the many causes she espoused, from the abolition of slavery to the crusade for women's rights.

Child was twenty-three in 1825 when she first captivated the Boston literary world as a promising young novelist. At a time when women writers were few and considered "unsexed," the presence of this witty and learned baker's daughter in the fashionable parlors of Beacon Street was a decided oddity. Ambitious, proud, and independent, this early feminist, who claimed she was George Sand's "twin," spent a lifetime struggling to be a free spirit in an increasingly confining age.

Married in 1828 to an improvident young lawyer and newspa-

1

perman named David Lee Child, Maria, who quickly became the couple's chief breadwinner, began writing successfully for the growing market of women readers. Then, in the 1830s, just when her literary reputation was at its height, she and David joined the band of antislavery reformers organizing under the leadership of William Lloyd Garrison. If Maria's skill as a propagandist was a decided asset to the abolitionist cause, her public support for this unpopular crusade resulted in the loss of both her literary reputation and much-needed income from her writings.

Carolyn Heilbrun has observed that biographies of brilliant women can only tell us how they made the best of what the world gave them, and the world of early-nineteenth-century New England had little to offer a woman like Lydia Maria Child. Not only was she born too early to reap the full benefit of the region's cultural flowering in the 1840s, but as a woman she was denied full acceptance by her peers as a creative, intelligent being. She spent the greater part of a lifetime struggling to find a place where she belonged, a place where she could be respected as a whole woman. There was no script for such a life, and it was easy to distrust her own counsel and divide herself by conforming to the demands of society around her. But there were moments of wholeness and freedom when forces outside her matched her own vision, as when she joined the antislavery movement. "In toiling for the freedom of others," she wrote in 1839, "we shall find our own."[2]

No one had higher expectations for the young American Republic than Lydia Maria Child, and no one worked harder to persuade her countrymen and women to remove the shackles of racism, sexism, and sectarianism which bound them. The truest wisdom, she once wrote, was to "help on each and every good idea of one's age, and yet embrace no one in the spirit of sect or party."[3] Maria Child worked hardest to achieve that end through her writing. Her very idealism made her a stern critic, and she never hesitated to speak out against those members of the American elite who she felt were abusing the power given them by the people.

Lydia Maria Child defies easy categorization. She is both more interesting and more complex than many of her better-known contemporaries. To begin with, she contradicts the popular image of the proper straight-laced Victorian woman. She claimed that nothing annoyed her more than to be forced to sit up straight in her best clothes in some fine lady's parlor. "I had much rather tramp through the forests to the sound of a tambourine, with my baby strapped to my strong shoulders, than to live amid the constrained elegancies of Beacon Street," she wrote in 1846, sounding more like a rebellious young woman of the 1960s than a Victorian middle-aged matron.[4]

Yet Maria was often happiest in the company of a class of people she purported to scorn. Numbered among her closest friends were some of the most cultivated men and women in New England. Indeed, her life is filled with paradoxes. She was famous in her day for her domestic advice books, but privately she considered the duties of a housewife dull and dispiriting. She often spoke longingly of her desire for a permanent home, yet seemed happiest when she was leading the free bohemian life of a boarder. No woman suffered more to advance the antislavery cause than Maria Child, yet she resisted efforts—albeit not always successfully—to draw her into organized reform. She was a profoundly religious woman, yet for most of her life she belonged to no church.

"The world seems to me one great 'Circumlocution Office,' " she wrote in 1857, "conventionally arranged to prevent people from doing anything real, or feeling anything real."[5] The story of Maria Child's life is not only of a struggle for freedom, but also of a struggle to be a whole person in an age of growing divisiveness. The widening gulf between rich and poor, master and slave, employer and employee, that characterized the nineteenth century was matched by deepening divisions between the sexes. It was a man's century, which relegated women to a separate and private sphere, seeking to restrict them to pious and domestic functions. Maria, who once described herself as a having a man's force and power inside a woman's body, longed to find her place in the world as a *person*, not simply as a *woman*.

Lydia Maria Child is only beginning to receive the attention she deserves as a writer and reformer. While three brief biographies of her have been published within the last few decades, none of them makes full use of either her published writings or the letters in her *Collected Correspondence*. Since the originals of these letters are widely scattered in a variety of collections, this microfiche edition makes them easily accessible to scholars. In addition, Milton Meltzer and Patricia Holland edited an excellent selection of Child's letters, published by the University of Massachusetts Press in 1982.

My own interest in Child dates back to the late 1970s, when I was searching about for a new subject for a biography. Lydia Maria Child was suggested to me as someone in need of a full-length study, and I leapt at the challenge. The little I knew of her through my research on Julia Ward Howe brought to mind just the sort of feisty, independent woman I liked. She would, I was certain, be good company.

Over a decade later I am forced to admit that writing this life of Child has proved to be a long, arduous, and often discouraging task. There were many times when the challenge of making sense out of this paradoxical, often maddeningly evasive woman tempted me to lay the whole project aside. But since I share something of Child's stubbornness I persisted, and before long the rewards began to outweigh the difficulties. My efforts to tie her up into a tidy parcel and store her away in various prepackaged nineteenth-century pigeonholes ceased. I learned to listen to her and not to what others said about her. I accepted the paradoxes and began to see through the evasions. Gradually, the woman you will find in these pages emerged.

I do not pretend to have the last word on Lydia Maria Child, but wish simply to reintroduce a woman of great interest who is currently an object of study by a number of other scholars. The book therefore attempts to convey something of the complexity of her character and the variety of her interests and concerns as a writer and reformer, in order that she may resume her rightful place as one of the most important and influential American women of the nineteenth century. It is time for this American heroine to find her way back into America's history books.

The Baker's Daughter

Few in the days of early youth
Trusted like me in love and truth.
—*Lydia Maria Child*

W hen I was quite a little girl," Lydia Maria Francis Child wrote in 1847 to Lucy Osgood, an old childhood friend, "I remember imagining that gypsies had changed me from some other cradle and put me in a place where I did not belong." This description of a poignant daydream is one of the rare references Child made in later life to the years in Medford, where she was born in 1802 and where she lived until after her mother's death in 1814.[1]

By all accounts, except Child's own, life in the Francis family was no worse and perhaps better than most. Her older brother Convers, who has left the most complete description of the Francis household, looked back on his own childhood as a frugal but happy time. His memories of a loving and saintly mother and a stern but honest father stand in sharp contrast to Lydia Maria's severe and spare judgment of her parents.

Lydia—she did not adopt the name Maria until later—was the youngest of seven children born to Convers and Susannah Francis. Both parents had grown up during the hard times accompanying the Revolution and were accustomed to a simple, arduous existence. When asked in later years to explain her own rugged constitution and extraordinary courage, Lydia would reply that she had been "born before nerves came into fashion."[2]

Susannah Francis' family, the Rands, driven from their home in

Charlestown by the flames of the Battle of Bunker Hill, had lost nearly all their possessions. Convers, Lydia's father, had known similar privation in Medford after his father, Benjamin Francis, a weaver by trade, joined the Minute Men at the Battle of Lexington and Concord in the spring of 1775. If Benjamin's wife and children were justly proud of his heroism—Benjamin shot five of the enemy that April day—they suffered great hardship during his five years in the army. With ten children to feed, Lydia Francis—after whom her granddaughter was named—was hard-pressed to find enough to satisfy them and one cold winter day she sent Convers to the grist mill to beg for some meal. The boy arrived to discover that the very last spoonful had been given away and returned home barefoot and empty-handed through the snow. If a neighbor hadn't sent the family some potatoes they might have starved.[3]

Fortunately, Benjamin Francis came home to Medford before the war was over and resumed his weaving. Thanks to the wartime demand for cloth and the decline of foreign imports, his business flourished and the family once more had enough to eat. But the rest of Convers' youth would be spent in hard work. Although the town schoolmaster singled him out as a bright, promising student who deserved a good education, his family could only spare him for a few weeks a year. At fifteen he was apprenticed to a baker, Ebenezer Hall, who drove him relentlessly and treated him roughly. His youngest son, also named Convers, later described his father as "the most intensely industrious man, I think, that I ever knew." He exacted hard labor from his children and was sometimes stern with them, but his son remembered a kind and faithful man under this harsh exterior.

Looking back, Lydia blamed her father's stern pessimism on his religion. He was by nature a gloomy and committed Calvinist who clung firmly to an image of humanity living at the mercy of an angry and righteous God who put people on earth "to toil and suffer" and then hurried them off the scene to burn for all eternity. If the Medford baker was stubbornly opinionated, his youngest son also remembered that he was "a great lover of right and freedom" who "detested slavery with all its apologists in all its forms."[4]

By the time Lydia, the youngest child, was born on February 11, 1802, her father had succeeded in making a comfortable living. His hard work in Ebenezer Hall's bakery brought a promotion to foreman. After holding this position for several years he took his young wife and three small children across the Mystic River to West Cambridge where he established his own bakery. By 1800 the business had succeeded well enough for him to return to Medford, buy out his former employer, and rebuild Hall's old house on the corner of Salem and Ashland streets with a new bakery adjoining. Although the house and shop stood close to the road so the sign could be read from Medford Square, gardens and fields stretched out behind. There the family raised its own meat and fruit. Over the next few years the bakery continued to thrive and expand. Convers Francis' "Medford Crackers" and other breads were in such demand in Boston and elsewhere that, according to his son, "he became a flourishing, and, for those times, a rich mechanic," or, as we would say today, a prosperous businessman who also happened to be a skilled artisan. No baker in the vicinity, Convers remembered, "had so high a reputation" or was more "highly respected."[5]

While the Medford baker had flourished and prospered during the years of struggle which followed his marriage, his wife Susannah apparently had not. Like her husband she had had little education, and like him she had worked hard to keep their growing family fed and clothed. By the time her youngest, Lydia, was born in 1802, the thirty-six-year-old woman had given birth to seven children, five of whom had lived. Worn out by years of childbearing and hard work, Susannah may also have been suffering the first symptoms of tuberculosis.

Young Convers, born six years before Lydia, when Susannah Francis was just thirty and apparently still healthy, had only the happiest memories of his mother. He later recalled the many instances of her "devoted, anxious care," remembering that "if she had but little cultivation, she had what is far better, a simple loving heart and a spirit busy in doing good."[6]

In the few brief and negative references contained in her letters, Lydia dismissed her childhood as cold, uncouth, and uncongenial. Nor did she ever mention her mother by name. Having heaped the full measure of her love on young Convers, Susannah Francis apparently had little left for her youngest daughter. Perhaps the appearance of a stillborn infant in 1799 had led her to think her family was complete, making Lydia's birth three years later an unwelcome surprise. Had this ill and overburdened mother, as historian Margaret Kellow has suggested, resented this late arrival?[7]

Lydia may not have been the easiest child to raise. Less docile and good-humored than her brother Convers, was she consequently less "lovable?" Bright and imaginative, headstrong and curious, Lydia was prone to mischief and would have proved a troublesome charge for a mother whose strength was failing. Whatever the reason, Susannah Francis was either unable or unwilling to lavish on Lydia the same love and attention enjoyed by Convers. For this last of her children she remained a cold and remote figure.[8]

Little is known of Lydia's eldest brother, James, or of her sister Susannah of whom she was particularly fond. Mary, the third surviving child, is a shadowy figure also. But Convers was Lydia's closest companion from infancy. Her earliest memories of him were of a young boy who whenever he had a free moment had his nose in a book. As soon as she could read, Lydia began asking to borrow from her brother's growing library, and when she came home from school she would rush upstairs to Convers' room and throw herself down among his piles of books. She remembered "devouring everything" that came her way. By the time she was ten she was already familiar with Shakespeare and Milton and was eagerly consuming any book she could lay her hands on, even though, as she later admitted, much of what she read "was beyond my childish comprehension."[9]

Convers, for his part, took great pains over his younger sister's education. When she plied him with questions such as, "What does Shakespeare mean by this? What does Milton mean by that?" he would never respond directly but like all good teachers would give her a clue and let her find the answer for herself. She admitted that sometimes he "was roguish" and that when he tried "to bamboozle" her he usually succeeded. Once he persuaded her that the phrase in one of Milton's poems, "raven down of darkness," referred to the fur of a black cat which sparkled when stroked the wrong way. Lydia later wrote that "such developments as my mind has attained, I attribute to the impulse thus early given by his [Convers'] example. Being seven [sic] years my senior, he was qualified to be my leader; but, as my mother had no other children between us, he was my companion also." As long as Convers and her sister Susannah remained at home Lydia had at least two family members whose affection and care she could count on.[10]

Unlike her brothers and sisters, who had shared the hardships of their parents' early married life, Lydia spent her childhood as a member of a respected and prosperous Medford family. Situated on the banks of the Mystic, a meandering tidal river, Medford, at the turn of the nineteenth century, was a quiet country village of some one thousand inhabitants. Comfortable frame houses surrounded by luxuriant flower gardens lined the six major highways that met in the center of town at Medford Square. Until the late eighteenth century the village, with the only bridge spanning the

Mystic River, had been a bustling transportation center. Travelers and traders from as nearby as Salem and as far away as Canada passed through it on their way to Boston. Then in 1787 a new bridge was built across the river in adjacent Charlestown, and Medford turned to rum-making and shipbuilding to maintain its prosperity.

Throughout the eighteenth century the majority of townspeople were of English descent, but as late as 1764 forty-nine blacks had been counted in Medford, many of whom were slaves. At a time when free labor was scarce and costly, chattel slavery, which included Indians as well as blacks, had quietly flourished in New England, particularly in the larger towns near the seacoast. The highest concentration was in Boston, where a census in 1752 counted 1,541 blacks, or 10 percent of the total population. Nearby Cambridge and Charlestown also contained sizable numbers of blacks. According to an early historian of Medford, the town's slaveowners were also its leading citizens, men from families with names like Brooks, Hall, Royall, and Tufts. The old slave quarters in the yard of Isaac Royall's house can still be seen today.[11]

With the coming of the Revolution the number of slaves in and around Boston declined. Some were carried off by wealthy Tories as they fled north to Canada, others went over to the British, while still others joined the American forces and were freed when hostilities ended. Meanwhile, sentiment towards slavery altered significantly as patriots like the Boston historian Jeremy Belknap pointed up the "inconsistency of pleading our own rights and liberties" while encouraging "the subjugation of others." By 1790 slavery had been outlawed in Massachusetts, and some of Medford's citizens had become vigorous opponents of black bondage.[12]

As a small child Lydia Francis would have heard the story of the rescue of the fugitive slave Caesar. In 1798 and again in 1799, Caesar had accompanied his master on several visits north where, besides acquiring a number of good friends in Boston and Medford, he had developed a taste for freedom. In 1805 when Caesar returned with a new owner, a Mr. Ingraham, he tried to escape. But Ingraham caught up with him as he was heading north through Medford to Woburn, buckled him into his carriage, and headed back towards Boston where he planned to stow his slave on board the ship which would carry them back south. As the vehicle was about to cross the Mystic River, Caesar let out a great howl, hoping to catch the attention of his friend Nathan Wait, the blacksmith whose shop abutted the Medford bridge. Wait rushed out to block the carriage and dissuade the Southerner "from carrying a free

man into slavery," but he was ignored. The carriage pushed on
and Caesar was soon securely confined in the ship's hold.

There the story might have ended. But a few days later,
according to an early history of Medford, Ingraham, while calling
on some friends in town, was indiscreet enough to describe Caesar's
whereabouts. The information was passed on to Wait, the blacksmith, who—taking full advantage of his rights as a citizen of the
young American Republic—proceeded to the State House in Boston, where he obtained permission from no less a person than the
governor to rescue the black man. Ingraham made several fruitless
attempts through the Massachusetts courts to recover his slave, but
Caesar remained in the North a free man. For many years Medford
citizens enjoyed boasting that theirs had been the first town in New
England to rescue a fugitive slave.[13]

Nevertheless, Medford in these early years of the Republic was
still ruled by an elite. Here, as elsewhere in New England, the
concentration of wealth and prestige lay in the hands of a small
group of landowners who controlled the town's government as well
as its real estate. The history of Medford's settlement had been
quite different from other towns in the Bay Colony, where groups
of settlers had divided the land obtained by titles from the General
Court. Medford had begun its colonial existence as a private plantation belonging to Matthew Craddock, an English landlord who
never set foot in the New World. His heirs, having no use for the
land, sold it after his death, and in 1656 the plantation was broken
up into eight large parcels. The buyers became the founding fathers
of the town and remained its leading families well into the nineteenth century. The Francises were among the early freeholders
in Medford but were not descended from the eight original landowners.

As an artisan, Benjamin Francis, the weaver, had struggled
hard all his life simply to keep his large family fed and clothed.
His son Convers, however, had known a success far greater than
his father's, and with the income from his flourishing bakery
could now provide his youngest children with material advantages
which the older ones had lacked. The eldest three, James, Susannah, and Mary, apparently received no more than a common
school education. Convers and Lydia, the two youngest, would fare
better.[14]

Both Lydia and Convers began their formal education by attending a dame school run by a woman known affectionately by
her pupils as Ma'am Betty. This elderly spinster taught school in

her bedroom, providing Medford boys and girls from five to seven years old with "an abundance of motherly care, useful knowledge, and salutary discipline," all for twelve cents a week. Ma'am Betty was reputedly rather a shy woman with some surprisingly unlady-like habits: she chewed tobacco, and Dr. John Brooks, one-time governor of Massachusetts, once found her drinking water out of the spout of her tea kettle. Convers, who remembered Ma'am Betty as odd and somewhat untidy, was nevertheless a great friend of hers, and long after he had graduated to the town school he would stop by to fill her water pail, cut her wood, and run her errands. Often during the long winter evenings the old woman and the young boy sat together in her small, messy room whose only distinguishing feature was a set of elaborately embroidered bed curtains. He would read aloud things she liked: storybooks and theological publications. Ma'am Betty was devoted to this kindly, intelligent boy and once claimed that she had two passions in life: Convers and cheese.[15]

Lydia later recalled that Ma'am Betty was among the twenty or thirty "humble friends" of the Francis household who were invited each Thanksgiving Eve into the family's large kitchen for a preliminary celebration of the annual New England holiday. The washerwoman, the berry-woman, the wood sawyer, and the journeyman bakers sat down to enjoy the assorted pies and doughnuts that came from Susannah Francis' oven. Lydia remembered her father plying the guests with crackers and bread when it was time for them to leave, while her mother filled their arms with pies, not forgetting turnovers for their children.[16]

Thanksgiving celebrations remained for Lydia one of the few bright memories in a sober and often lonely childhood. In a household where the long, stern shadows of Puritanism still lingered, and at a time when Christmas and other "popish" holidays were frowned upon, this festive day was a rare and welcome respite. Lydia later put descriptions of these annual feasts in both story and verse, including "The Boy's Thanksgiving Song." Another poem, entitled simply "Thanksgiving Day," describes a thinly disguised Lydia and Convers sharing one of their mother's pies, and recalls affectionately the teasing but close intimacy between them.

> Of me, the rogue took special care,
>   But never failed to have his share
>   Sometimes I thought his mouthful large,
>   And he'd deny the jealous charge;
>   And then perchance, some slight affray

> Would damp the pleasure of the day;
> But he was gentle, good and mild,
> And I was a forgiving child—
> A smile, a kiss would "make all well,"
> And we would funny stories tell.[17]

After two years with Ma'am Betty it was time for Lydia, then seven, to follow in Convers' footsteps and attend the local grammar school. By the turn of the nineteenth century, the education of girls, which had been largely neglected throughout the colonial period, was being treated with greater seriousness, as independence from Great Britain stimulated concern over the need for an educated citizenry. If the young nation was to raise up virtuous republican sons, it needed mothers who themselves were trained in republican principles, or, as Abigail Adams had told her husband, John, in defense of female education, "much depends . . . upon the early education of youth, and the first principles which are instilled take the deepest root."[18] Medford had undertaken the education of girls sooner than most communities in New England, when in 1766 it allowed them to attend the town schools for two hours after the boys had been dismissed. Beginning in 1790 the two sexes were permitted to study together, but only during the summer months. By the time Lydia was ready for grammar school, the red brick schoolhouse behind the Congregational Church had been enlarged to allow the boys and girls to conform to current practice and be taught in separate rooms. Lydia thus experienced for the first time the public acknowledgment that her education was to be different from her brother's.

After a year in the local grammar school, this bright and eager student learned another sad lesson: if you wanted a first-rate education there were decided advantages to being a boy. In 1810, when Convers was fifteen, his father took him aside one day and asked him whether he preferred to learn a trade or to go to college. Taken by surprise at the unexpected question, Convers replied that he would very much like to attend college if his father would let him. "Well then," said the elder Francis, "you shall go to college, and next Monday morning you may begin to attend Dr. Hosmer's academy to be prepared." Convers later remembered how these words had filled him with "an almost trembling gladness." "My strong love of books did much, I suppose, to decide the question," Convers later recalled.[19]

In contrast to Convers' recollection, Lydia later stressed the difficulty her father's friends had in persuading him to send his son to college. She claimed that it had taken a warning from Dr. John Brooks to convince the Medford baker that he would "do very wrong to thwart the inclinations of that boy. He has remarkable powers of mind; and his passion for books is so strong that he will be sure to distinguish himself in learning; whereas, if you try to make anything else of him, he will prove a total failure."[20] In her version of the story Lydia was, perhaps unconsciously, describing her own failure to receive a proper education. After all, as a child she too had shown "remarkable powers of mind," perhaps more remarkable than her brother's. She too had a "passion for books." But women were not welcome at Harvard or any other American college in the early nineteenth century. Lydia was fast discovering that while literacy among women was encouraged, academic learning was not. There was a fear that the classical education designed for young men would actually harm their sisters, would make them vain and self-indulgent, and distract them from their true vocations as wives and mothers.

The elder Convers, in deciding to educate his youngest son, may have recalled a similar attempt made on his behalf by an old schoolmaster, who had unsuccessfully urged his parents to give him a good education. Was the father now fulfilling his own frustrated ambitions by giving his son the very schooling he had lacked? Whatever the case, young Convers duly found his way to Dr. Hosmer's Academy, where as the son of the town baker he felt more than a little out of place. "There was an air of aristocracy about the school," he later recalled. "Sons of rich men from other towns came to it as boarding-scholars; and only 'the better sort' in the town sent their children to it. It was quite a different thing from the common town school, where every Tom, Dick, and Harry, everybody's boys, and everybody's girls, went as a matter of course. The academy was for the *elite*; so that when I, the baker's boy, was transferred from the town school to it, it was a promotion which made me tremble."[21] But Convers was a diligent student and after little more than a year of hard work—he accomplished much of his reading on an overturned barrel in the bakehouse—he was ready, at the age of sixteen, to attend Harvard College.

Lydia never forgot how unhappy she was the day Convers left home. The grief occasioned by such partings would later be convincingly described in stories like "The Cottage Girl," in which the elder of two orphans is separated from his sister. After her brother's departure the little girl "felt as if she were all alone in the world. She did not even like her dog; but would sit moping in a corner, or walk round and round with a troubled look." In Lydia's case the sense of abandonment was heightened by other losses. In 1811, the year Convers left for Cambridge, the family Lydia had known as a small child was breaking up. She said goodbye not only to her youngest brother and closest companion, but also to her favorite sister, Susannah, who married and left home to live in Charlestown. Of the older Francis children only nineteen-year-old Mary was left at home. But Mary would have had little time to spare for her younger sister. Their mother had entered the terminal phase of her illness and was now largely bedridden. The task of running the household probably fell increasingly on Mary's shoulders, leaving Lydia to occupy herself as best she could. No orphan felt more forsaken than nine-year-old Lydia. When she was not moping in a corner, her inquisitive mind was roaming restlessly about in search of knowledge and excitement. Most probably she got into a good deal of trouble, like the willful boys and girls in her stories whose "busy minds" so often lead them "into mischief."[22]

With Convers, her principal tutor, away at college, Lydia's sense of abandonment extended to her education. There was now no member of the Francis household with whom this eager student could share her passion for learning. Her father, while fond of reading and well-informed for a man of limited education, apparently found no time to spare to guide the education of his youngest daughter. Nor did he have much tolerance for her dreamy literary musings. "He is unacquainted with sentiment," Lydia would later write of her father, accusing him rather unfairly of having "a violent prejudice against literature, taste and even the common forms of modern civilized life." As a grown woman Lydia would write a story for children in which she described an ignorant father who told his studious son, Charles, that "*book-learning* would never bring him any good." Unlike Lydia, however, Charles was a boy and had a mother who encouraged his ambitions. She "told him many stories of chimney sweepers who had become mayors of London only by means of their learning." Drawn closer to his mother by such kindness, a kindness Lydia herself apparently never experienced, Charles "was not ashamed to tell her all the thoughts and feelings that were stirring within him." When the boy expressed a wish for more books, this sympathetic parent sold her gold necklace and gave him the proceeds to spend at the bookstore. Unlike Charles' father, this storybook mother understood that "little good" could come "of crossing a boy's inclination." Many years later as a grown woman, Lydia would counsel mothers to keep their daughters always close by to shield them from harm. Was she remembering this time in her childhood when her own vivid imagination had lured her into harboring ambitions considered unsuitable for a young girl whose future was destined to be absorbed by domestic cares?[23]

If home and school provided little in the way of encouragement for an eager student like Lydia Francis, there was one household in Medford where she could count on a warm welcome and where the conversation was certain to be learned as well as lively. This was the family of the Reverend David Osgood, pastor of the Congregational Church. The Osgoods' comfortable frame house was just a short walk from the bakery. Here the minister lived with his wife, Hannah, and their two unmarried daughters, Lucy and Mary. A boy, David, was two years ahead of Convers at Harvard. Unlike his friend and parishioner Mr. Francis, David Osgood had taken special pains to provide all three of his children with an excellent education. The two girls he had taught himself. Both Lucy and Mary had some knowledge of Hebrew, Greek, and Latin and were familiar with modern as well as ancient literature. While Lucy later remembered her scholarly, authoritarian father with a mixture of reverence and awe, she also recalled his encouragement of open and frank discussion among the members of his family.[24]

Of the two Osgood sisters Lucy was Lydia's particular friend. She was considerably her senior—Lucy was twenty-one when Lydia was only nine—and possessed of a rather formidable personality and appearance. She was also exceedingly well-read for a woman of that era. A Medford clergyman who knew her as an old lady recalled that she had the reputation of "talking like a book" and that engaging her in conversation was like listening to a carefully prepared lecture. But she put so much of herself into what she said that you listened gladly to the end. For Lydia Francis, friendship with an educated, gifted, and intellectually disciplined young woman like Lucy Osgood compensated in part for the neglect she suffered at home. To nine-year-old Lydia, Lucy doubtless seemed old enough to be her mother, but, unlike Susannah Francis, this learned lady apparently could provide her young friend with at least some of the affection and understanding so lacking at home. Many years later Lydia Maria Child wrote Lucy that no other house, including her own, was linked to her childhood by so many pleasant memories and associations.[25]

Lucy's father himself must have had a strong influence on young Lydia Francis. From the time she was very small Lydia accompanied her family every Sunday to the services in Medford's First Parish Church. There she heard some of the most forceful preaching in the whole of New England, preaching that had once moved Daniel Webster. Lydia's brother Convers remembered his feeling of "unmingled reverence" whenever the Reverend Osgood stood in the pulpit to preach. "He seemed to me like an apostolic messenger from God. His whitening and at length silvered hair, his dignified look, . . . the whole presence of the man, enhanced the effect of the earnestness, and frequently the awful solemnity, with which he took our souls into the midst of the great truths of eternity."[26]

As a young minister, David Osgood's theology had been sternly orthodox. When first called to preach in Medford in 1774 he had declined the invitation because six of the influential citizens chosen to elect a new minister for the town had strongly objected to his conservative views. Osgood was a firm believer in man's total depravity and subscribed unquestioningly to the Calvinist Confession of Faith of the Westminster Catechism. In the end, despite the opposition to his candidacy, he was persuaded to settle in Medford. There his parishioners soon discovered a chink in their new minister's orthodox armor, which tended to ease the severity of his views. This was Osgood's belief that, corrupt as it was, the human heart had not been entirely deprived of "that freedom which is necessary to moral action." Jesus, he maintained, could pardon and forgive sinners who followed him, despite their innate depravity and unworthiness.[27]

By the time Lydia was old enough to attend church, Osgood's Calvinism had mellowed considerably. "Men are wicked enough," he asserted in the latter part of his life, but only the devil is "*totally* depraved." "Far be it from me," Osgood was heard to say, "to censure any of my brethren, who, after an equally honest and impartial inquiry, think in some respects different from me." For Lydia Francis and the other members of his congregation, such words clearly expressed the responsibility of all people to read and interpret the teachings of Christ for themselves, a responsibility which no orthodox Congregational theologian would have allowed. While David Osgood could never shake off the fear of his own damnation, following his death in 1822 many members of his admiring congregation, including his daughters Mary and Lucy, went over to Unitarianism. There they embraced a theology which not only rejected the awfulness and wrath of God but defined men and women as innately good and free agents, capable of working out their own salvation.[28]

The elder Convers Francis shared his minister's underlying stern Calvinism, remaining convinced, even in old age, that his soul was damned. Little is known of Susannah Francis' personal faith except that she was deeply pious and a devout believer in the Bible as the chief source of religious truth. In "Emily Parker," a story written in the 1820s, Lydia would describe a woman who, like her own mother, died of tuberculosis. Shortly before her death Mrs. Parker calls her young daughter Emily, described as having a "glowing and poetic" imagination, to her bedside and tells her, "There are many things in my heart, which you are not old enough to understand now; but go to the Good Book; that will guide you, whatever may be your trials."[29]

This rather sentimental picture of a dying mother's comforting and pious influence over her daughter is sharply contradicted in another more explicitly autobiographical piece Lydia wrote a few years earlier. "My Mother's Grave" describes a painful incident which had occurred shortly before her mother's death, when Lydia was twelve years old. Susannah Francis had been bedridden for so long by this time that her youngest daughter had "become accustomed to her pale face and weak voice." Although she had been told from the first that her mother would die, when Lydia came home from school each day to find her parent unchanged she soon convinced herself that the dreaded separation would never occur. Then one afternoon, feeling fretful and discouraged after a bad day at school, she returned home to find Susannah Francis looking paler than usual. Absorbed by her own cares, the child took little note of her mother's appearance and when asked to fetch a drink of water "pettishly" asked why the domestic could not do it. Bestowing on Lydia a look of mild reproach, the ailing woman quietly asked, "And will not my daughter bring a glass of water for her poor sick mother?" Lydia then fetched the water but she did not "do it kindly," and setting it down quickly on the table beside her mother's bed she left the room without another word. For the rest of her life Lydia remembered with shame and remorse Susannah Francis' reproachful look. "I would give worlds were they mine to give," she wrote "could my mother but have lived to tell me she forgave my childish ingratitude."[30]

Susannah's death in May 1814 plunged the Francis household into gloom and despair as Convers mourned his wife's passing and feared for her salvation. There would have been little comfort to spare for young Lydia, whose own sorrow was heightened by feelings of shame and guilt and the burden she carried in her own heart that her mother had never forgiven her. Many of Lydia's early stories for children would evoke the keen sense of loss and betrayal which remained with her long after Susannah Francis' death.

One of particular poignancy, published when Lydia was twenty-five, concerns an English orphan named Fanny who was abandoned by her mother at birth. Fortunately for Fanny, she is adopted by the kind parents of a little girl named Maria, who had "no little sister to play with." The two girls, who are six years apart, live and play happily together, and Maria, like Convers, teaches her little sister many of the "good lessons" she learned from her mother. Then one day Maria goes to London for a visit of several weeks. Fanny knows her sister will return soon but she cries "as if her heart would break."

While in London, Maria tries to buy a muff for her mother and is falsely accused of stealing it by the real thief, a poor woman who acts as a witness for the prosecution at Maria's trial. No one, except her own family, believes Maria is innocent; she is sentenced to five years in prison. Heartbroken by the news of her sister's fate, Fanny stands up in the courtroom and offers to go to jail in her place, whereupon the real thief, deeply affected by the little girl's generosity, admits that she stole the muff and lied to protect herself. It then turns out that the thief is really Fanny's mother who had abandoned her as a baby. The woman is sent to prison, where Fanny is very good to her, bringing her little comforts and luxuries. To console her parent she uses words that Lydia probably wished she had been able to say to her mother, who had also deserted her by dying. "Do not cry so. I will come and live with you always and try to love you."[31]

Another echo of these dark months can be found in Lydia's *Mother's Book*, published in the early 1830s, in which she denounces the "associations of grief and terror" with which the Christians of her day surrounded death, observing that the "most pious people are sometimes entirely unable to overcome the dread of death which they received in childhood."[32]

Meanwhile economic worries combined with his recent loss drove Lydia's father to work harder than ever. These were gloomy times not only in the Francis household but everywhere in New England as war with Great Britain brought hardship and misery, particularly to the seacoast towns. The winter before Lydia's mother's death, the federal embargo on all coastwise and foreign trade and the British blockade of the coast from Penobscot Bay to Long Island

Sound had brought business to a standstill. No "Medford Crackers" would get much farther than Boston. That summer, discord and unrest reached a peak as war continued in the name of "free trade and sailors' rights" and the very safety of New England was threatened. All summer and fall two British frigates patrolled the waters between Cape Cod and Cape Ann, and word came from England that land reinforcements were on their way.

But economic losses and the dangers of war would have meant little to Lydia, who watched the familiar world of her childhood rapidly disintegrate. In August 1814, the death of her only remaining grandparent, Susannah Rand, added to an already painful sense of loss. Meanwhile her sister Mary was being courted by a young lawyer from Maine named Warren Preston. The wedding, which took place in September, held little joy for the youngest member of the family, who was losing her only remaining sister to the wilds of Maine. Lydia refused to attend the ceremony. Instead she left the house carrying her kitten with her and wandered down a side lane until the celebrations had ended.[33]

With Mary gone, Lydia was left alone with her father, a singularly uncongenial companion for a girl of twelve. Gloomy even in the best of times and convinced that the world was a hard, cold place, Convers Francis was not likely, in the midst of so much sorrow, to find many cheering words of consolation for his daughter. Nor were their trials over. Six months after Mary's wedding her sister Susannah died, leaving Lydia bereft of all the women nearest and dearest to her, except her friend Lucy Osgood. The pain and losses of these months would haunt her always, leaving bitter memories of her childhood and a hunger for love and acceptance that was never satisfied.

On the Banks of the Kennebec

I always preferred the impetuous grandeur of the
cataract to the gentle meanderings of the rill.
—Lydia Maria Francis to Convers Francis,
1819

After Mary and Warren Preston left for Maine, Lydia was left alone with her father in the big house adjoining the bakery. She would turn thirteen that February, a time in life she was later to describe as one when a girl particularly needs the loving care of her mother. Between the ages of twelve and sixteen, Lydia Maria Child wrote in 1831, a girl's "imagination is all alive," and her "affections are in full vigor." During this important period a mother cannot be too watchful. "As much as possible, she should keep a daughter *under her own eye*; and above all things she should encourage *entire confidence towards herself*. . . . I believe it is extremely natural to choose a mother in preference to all other friends and confidants; but if a daughter, by harshness, indifference, or an unwillingness to make allowance for youthful feeling, is driven from the holy resting place, which nature has provided for her security, the greatest danger is to be apprehended."[1]

Lacking the security and comfort of a confidential and close relationship with her mother even when Susannah Francis was alive, Lydia now found herself dependent entirely on the companionship and guidance of her father, who, in common with other busy parents, may have used the press of duties in the bakery as an excuse for neglecting his last child. In the most autobiographical of her children's stories, "Emily Parker," Lydia later describes a recent widower like Convers Francis. "He was a good man and he meant to be kind—but he was not used to showing tenderness. When he came in from work, he would always inquire what she [his daughter Emily] had done during the day. If she had accomplished a great deal, he would praise her industry; but he did not talk with her during the long winter evenings,—and it was only by the subdued tone of his naturally stern voice, and the prolonged kiss he sometimes gave her, that Emily knew he blessed her in his heart."[2]

While Lydia's father, like Emily's, was always ready to "praise her industry," the twelve-year-old girl's days, apart from the hours in school, were apparently hers to do with as she pleased. Unlike her brother Convers, who had always balanced his studies with a heavy load of chores, Lydia seems to have been given little work to do at home. Convers' later accounts of his childhood describe the many skills he had acquired helping his father in the bakery. By contrast none of Lydia's writings reveal any knowledge of the business. Instead there are countless references to restless, willful, unsupervised little girls who get into trouble.[3] But Lydia was also more than ever devoted to books and reading, and she may at this time have begun composing some of the stories which would later appear in her children's magazine, *The Juvenile Miscellany*, and other publications, putting into writing her youthful dreams, and setting at rest some of the anguish of the past months.

A revealing clue to Lydia's emerging strategy for survival can be found in "Emily Parker," where the heroine, like the author, has a restless, powerful mind and loses her mother to tuberculosis. Like Lydia also, Emily has had "many an enthusiastic hope blighted." But, unlike Lydia, Emily is invariably swayed by what others think of her; she never "examined her own heart," never "judged for herself." Nor does she learn to employ her considerable gifts. Lydia, by contrast, was coming to trust her own mind and heart. She also had an outlet for her talents, "a world of fiction on which to expend" her "glowing and poetic imagination."[4]

Lydia's father was increasingly alarmed by his daughter's passion for literature. It was one thing for a son to be studious: a boy's love of books could be channeled into a respectable career. But of what use was learning for a girl whose future would be burdened with domestic cares? Nonetheless, a recognition that Lydia needed more supervision than he could provide may have prompted him to extend her formal education by enrolling her in a local girl's school.[5]

Miss Hannah Swan's academy in Medford, which Lydia Francis attended for a year, helped to keep her out of mischief but provided little intellectual nourishment. The strong prejudice against learned women discouraged even the fashionable female academies, then springing up all over New England, from offering more than a superficial education. A typical curriculum included a smattering of French and English, together with lessons in drawing, music, and embroidery. One academy graduate later claimed that she had left her school "with a head full of something, tumbled in without order or connection." While Lydia left no record of her experiences in Miss Swan's academy, as a grown woman she had nothing but criticism for such schools, denouncing them for teaching "the *elements* of a thousand sciences" and a "variety of accomplishments" without providing a thorough grounding in any.[6]

Lydia, however, only had to endure a year at Miss Swan's. Sometime early in 1815, after spending several months alone with his daughter, Convers Francis decided that she would be better off living with the Prestons in Maine. Was Lydia, who turned thirteen in February (a notoriously difficult age for girls), proving to be more than her father could handle? Lydia's sister Mary was expecting her first child in May and would welcome an extra pair of hands to help with the housework. How much better for Lydia to make herself useful as a member of a young, growing family than to live alone in Medford with a gloomy, elderly father.

But if Convers Francis had only the best of intentions in sending his daughter to live with the Prestons, Lydia herself was not likely to greet this decision of her father's with much joy. Within little more than a year's time death had claimed her mother, her grandmother, and her sister, and now her father was banishing her from the familiar world of her childhood to live in the wilderness, where she knew only Mary and her husband.

But Lydia had little choice in the matter. The long journey from Medford to Norridgewock was probably made sometime during the summer of 1815 after the ice had melted in the northern rivers and the spring mud coating the highways had dried. In this first summer of peace following the War of 1812 most of the distance could be covered by water: up the coast to Bath and then inland along the Kennebec to Augusta. A bumpy stagecoach ride traversed the last twenty miles from Augusta north to Norridgewock. At the end of the journey Lydia was welcomed by Mary and her husband, Warren, into their roomy frame house just a few steps from the Kennebec River.[7]

Norridgewock, a "pretty, genteel village," as Lydia later described it, was a flourishing community of some one thousand inhabitants when she arrived there in 1815. The war and "Madison's embargo" had barely touched its agricultural economy. Business was brisk, and if currency was in short supply, storekeepers were more than willing to accept muskrat skins or oats and corn in exchange for a length of cloth or some other needed item. In 1809 Norridgewock had been designated the shiretown of Somerset County and since then the population had grown steadily. Among the newcomers were several lawyers and their families, including Warren and Mary Preston, who hoped to profit from the promised prosperity of the newly developed region.

Born in Uxbridge, Massachusetts, in 1782, Warren Preston had graduated from Brown University before taking up the study of law. After practicing for a time in a town near Worcester he decided to move north to the district of Maine. By 1810 he had settled in Norridgewock, where he soon earned a comfortable living buying and selling real estate, enough to build himself a spacious house and to consider acquiring a wife.[8]

This county seat had attracted an unusually large number of educated people and enjoyed a reputation throughout the region as a cultural center. Education was taken seriously there, and the town had early established schools which boys attended in the winter and girls in the summer. Sometimes the teachers were men and women from educated families, sometimes they were recent graduates of Bowdoin College, young men who were hired for a term either by the town or by private individuals whose parlors were turned into classrooms. Unfortunately, we know little of Lydia's education in Norridgewock, except that she attended the local schools.[9]

Lydia's best teacher during these years—apart from her brother Convers, with whom she maintained a regular correspondence—may well have been Warren Preston. By 1814 Preston had established himself as a member of Norridgewock's educated elite and was noted for his "refinement of feeling, cultivation, and liberality." He was a founder of the town's first public library and for a time served as librarian and on the School Visiting Committee. Presumably he gave his children and Lydia the best education Norridgewock had to offer.[10]

But school and studies took up only a part of Lydia's time. Whereas in Medford her domestic responsibilities appear to have been few, in Maine a good part of each day was spent helping Mary both with the housework and with the care of the Prestons' first child, Francis, born in May 1815. In a period when servants were all but unobtainable, particularly in isolated country towns, the help of a young girl in her teens was invaluable. The round of chores was endless, for nearly everything eaten and worn was produced at home. In addition to preparing food and preserving it—hauling water from the well and cooking over an open fireplace—there was cloth to be woven; clothes, candles, and soap to be made; and all the cleaning, washing, and mending to be done.[11]

As Convers had accomplished a good deal of his reading on an overturned barrel in their father's bakehouse, Lydia also learned to combine her studies with an endless round of daily chores. Who but herself is she describing in "Emily Parker" when she boasts that, while her bookish fifteen-year-old heroine "could spin more yarn and weave more cloth, than any girl on the Kennebec," she did not neglect her reading. "Shakespeare and Milton lay open on the loom, and her memory treasured up intellectual stores, while the shuttle was flying from her fingers."[12]

Mary Preston also taught her sister the art of fine sewing, and Lydia forgot little of what she learned. As a young married woman she wrote a very popular little book, *The Frugal Housewife*, a manual filled with recipes, remedies, and household hints, many of which she learned during her years in Norridgewock: a method for testing the temperature of a bake oven; substitutes for coffee; a recipe for green tea made from the "first young leaves of the common currant-bush"; the suggestion that pump handles be kept high in winter and horse blankets thrown over them to prevent freezing.[13]

The winters were long and hard in Maine. One year the snow was so deep that it reached Lydia's second-story bedroom window. For days the household did not see another living thing, "or hear a sound except the crackling of the wood fire." Even the summer of 1816, by a fluke of the weather, was notoriously cold. A heavy snowfall in June was followed by killing frosts in July and August. That year no corn was harvested and flour for bread was scarce.[14]

Strengthened by these hardships, the townsfolk of Norridge-wock prospered. An unusually lively intellectual life characterized this backwoods community, especially during the years following the War of 1812, when people debated the question of Maine's separation from Massachusetts. While Lydia herself makes no mention of politics in the few letters that survive from her years in Norridgewock, the issue of independence was an old one in that northern province. As early as the 1680s, inhabitants of the district had forwarded petitions to King Charles II asking to be delivered from Massachusetts rule. Early drives for separation, however, had met with little support from the people at large. Not until the last months of the War of 1812, when the Federalist government in Boston made it clear that it had no interest in coming to the aid of Maine's occupied towns, did a groundswell of public support build in favor of independence. Ironically, that support came initially not from those towns most badly hurt by the British occupation but rather from the interior. For the time being at least the old seacoast communities remained strongholds of federalism and loyal to Massachusetts rule. It was in more recently developed inland towns like Norridgewock that a sizable portion of the population was coming to favor independence.[15]

Newcomers to the district, young ambitious men like Warren Preston who had settled in the flourishing towns of the interior and had seen the future of Maine as theirs, had come to resent political domination by Boston Federalists. Beginning in the spring of 1816, when the question of independence from Massachusetts was put before the people of Maine in a referendum, heated discussions filled the parlors and public rooms of Norridgewock. While the referendum lost in the town by eighteen votes in May 1816, when the question of separation was put before the townspeople later that year it passed by one vote.[16]

Warren Preston, whose politics were closely allied with those of the leading separationist, William King, supported the referendum. Both he and King were representative of the new wave of settlers who had come to the district to escape the political, religious, and social orthodoxy which reigned in New England's older, more established communities. Impatient with outmoded ways, with entrenched federalism and orthodox Congregationalism, these newcomers wanted power for themselves and the freedom to worship as they pleased. Warren Preston, for example, would become one of the founders of the Unitarian Society when it formed in Norridgewock in 1825.[17]

Discussion of statehood reached a climax in the winter of 1819. On December 6 a constitution was submitted to the people of Maine, who gave it their overwhelming approval. Admission to the Union was now a mere formality, or would have been if Missouri had not picked the same moment to apply for admission as a slave state. The question of Maine's independence from Massachusetts now became embroiled in the controversial issue of whether or not slavery should be permitted in the territory west of the Mississippi. When Henry Clay, the Speaker of the House, insisted on a compromise that would admit the two states together, one slave and one free, many in Maine were dismayed. There were objections that this civilized northern state was being made to serve as "a mere *pack horse* to transport the odious, anti-republican principle of slavery" into Missouri. In the end, however, principle gave way to expediency. If Maine did not become a state now, many argued, she never would. Congress agreed to Clay's Missouri Compromise, and on March 15, 1820, Maine became the Union's twenty-third state.[18]

Lydia probably heard her brother-in-law arguing with his fellow lawyers over these issues. When the county court was in session the attorneys gathered at the Danforth Tavern for lunch. Since the dining room of the inn was just down the hall from the town library, Lydia only needed the excuse of fetching a new book to eavesdrop on any discussion that was taking place. What did she make of these discussions? Did she question the willingness of ambitious young politicians like her brother-in-law to accept a compromise on the issue of slavery in order to gain independence for Maine and power for themselves?[19]

If Lydia's political awakening is hard to trace, so is her spiritual development. After a childhood spent under the stern and sober influence of a father who clung to the old Calvinist dogmas of human depravity and divine omnipotence, how did she respond to the more enlightened atmosphere which prevailed in Norridgewock? Warren Preston, like her brother Convers, had little tolerance for the rigid authoritarianism of the orthodox Congregationalists; the two shared an open-mindedness about religious truth. Nor did Preston's fellow citizens show much interest in traditional New England church fare. When Lydia arrived in Norridgewock in 1815 the town had only recently acquired its first settled minister. But the Reverend Josiah Peet, a young graduate of the rigidly orthodox Andover Seminary north of Boston, had found scant support for the old religion in his new parish. While he had initially roused some interest by leading a revival, in the end his tenure as pastor failed to shake the apathy of the townspeople. During Lydia's five years in Norridgewock only twenty-eight new members were added to Mr. Peet's congregation, and neither Lydia nor the Prestons were among them.[20]

The years Lydia spent in Norridgewock's relatively open society also gave her a taste for freedom. Here, removed from the social constraints characteristic of old New England towns like Medford, she was a person in her own right. Here also she was away from the critical eye of her stern father, who had questioned her passion for reading, and was subject instead to the gentle rule of a scholarly and humane brother-in-law who shared her love of literature.

It was in Maine that Lydia first fell under the spell of the American wilderness and its early inhabitants, the Abenaki and Penobscot Indians. Only a short walk from the Preston house lay the majestic Kennebec, a river whose idyllic grandeur soon captured Lydia's poetic imagination. In places along the shore of the great river, steep banks of tangled shrubbery and clusters of oak, hemlock, and white birch grew right down to the water. In others the hills retreated in gentle slopes exposing cultivated fields, meadows, and orchards.

The Kennebec wound serenely enough through the village of Norridgewock, but a few miles upstream were the Bonebasee Rips, where angry waters swirled around giant rocks. Here near the river's edge lay the site of an old Indian settlement, the original Norridgewock, a village once inhabited by the Abenakis. Vestiges of the old settlement still remained: broken utensils, glass beads, and hatchets, turned up by the white man's plow. To this tranquil spot, where birdsong and the distant sound of rushing water alone disturbed the stillness, Lydia loved to come and ponder the local stories she heard told of the Abenakis and of the Jesuit priest Father Rale, who had built a missionary church in their midst. In 1724, English colonists had destroyed this Indian settlement in a surprise attack, killed all of the inhabitants, including Father Rale, and burnt the church and Indian dwellings to the ground.[21]

Lydia's fascination with Indians carried into her earliest published writings, but actual encounters with them were rare. She never forgot, however, her visit to a Penobscot village somewhere on the banks of the Kennebec. She was introduced to the tribe's chief, Captain Neptune, and his nephew, Etalexis, "a tall, athletic warrior of most graceful proportions." Etalexis, she could see, was "the very dandy of his tribe—with a broad band of shining brass around his hat, a circle of silver on his breast, tied with scarlet ribbons, and a long belt of curiously-wrought wampum hanging to his feet." Recalling the visit many years later, Lydia remembered staring admiringly at the handsome young Indian, while his uncle, Chief Neptune, "stood quietly by, puffing his pipe, undisturbed by the consciousness of wearing a crushed hat and a dirty blanket." Out of curiosity, Lydia picked up one of the heavy wampum tassels and inquired archly of old Neptune why he didn't choose to dress like his nephew. "What for *me* wear ribbons and beads?" the old man had replied, "Me no want to catch'em *squaw*." As he said this,

Lydia could not help noting "the satirical twinkle in his small black eye."[22]

The handful of letters Lydia wrote Convers from Norridgewock make no mention of her meeting with the the Penobscots but do contain spirited discussions about literature. On June 5, 1817, when she was fifteen, Lydia wrote of being "busily engaged" in reading *Paradise Lost*, a work which she could not help but admire for its "astonishing grandeur of description" and "heavenly sublimity of style." She was less taken, however, with the passage where Eve says to Adam,

> My author and disposer, what thou bid'st
> Unargu'd I obey; so God ordained.
> God is thy law, thou mine: to know no more
> Is woman's happiest knowledge, and her praise.[23]

She complained to Convers that Milton was asserting the superiority of the masculine sex "in rather too lordly a manner." "Perhaps you will smile at the freedom with which I express my opinion concerning the books which I have been reading," she added ingenuously, admitting that "it might have the appearance of pedantry, if I were writing to any one but a brother; when I write you, I feel perfectly unrestrained; for I feel satisfied that you will excuse a little freedom of expression from a sister, who willingly acknowledges the superiority of your talents and advantages, and who fully appreciates your condescension and kindness."[24] While Lydia felt comfortable sharing her rather unorthodox opinions with Convers, she was also careful to temper them with conventional clichés.

Whether or not Lydia was aware of it at the time, there was hardly another young man in New England as well equipped as Convers to guide her reading. (Several other distinguished nineteenth-century women, including Elizabeth Blackwell and Emma Willard, were educated by their brothers.) As a divinity student at Harvard and later as pastor of a church in nearby Watertown, Convers was regarded by his fellow clergymen as a brilliant young man with a promising future. But his education at Harvard had not simply trained him for the ministry, it had also encouraged a receptiveness to the new romantic spirit then so prevalent throughout England and Europe, a spirit which was causing writers like Wordsworth and Goethe to turn their backs on the cold certainties of eighteenth-century rationalism and celebrate instead the nobility of the passions. By 1812, the year Convers was a freshman, the old Congregational orthodoxy which had once ruled the college had lost its hold and Harvard was firmly in tolerant Unitarian hands. In such an atmosphere Convers' omnivorous love of learning had room to flourish. He read everything and anything he could lay his hands on. He read history and philosophy and was one of the earliest students of German in America.[25]

When a child in Medford, Lydia had greedily devoured whatever books Convers happened to have in his room, often understanding little of what she read. Now as a young woman in her teens she was familiar enough with the classics to be critical of Shakespeare for his "low attempts at wit" and of Milton for his tone of masculine superiority. At fifteen, Homer's *Iliad* and *Odyssey*, heroic epics replete with war and bloodshed, love and treachery, were her favorites. She assured Convers "every passion that he [Homer] portrayed I felt: I loved, hated and resented just as he inspired me."[26]

Then at nineteen, while staying with friends in Skowhegan, she discovered Sir Walter Scott, whose historical romances filled her mind with visions of rocks and crags and dark blue lakes and made her think for the first time that perhaps she too could write a novel.[27] "I always preferred the impetuous grandeur of the cataract to the gentle meanderings of the rill," she wrote Convers while deep in *Guy Mannering*,

> and spite of all that is said about gentleness, modesty, and timidity in the heroine of a novel or poem, give *me* the mixture of pathos and grandeur exhibited in the character of Meg Merrilies; or the wild dignity of Diana Vernon, with all the freedom of the Highland maiden in her step and in her eye; or the ethereal figure Annot Lyle,—"the lightest and most fairy figure that ever trod the turf by moonlight;" or even the lofty contempt of life and danger which, though not unmixed with ferocity, throws such a peculiar interest around Helen MacGregor.

Lest Convers make too much of his sister's admiration for these wild and free Scottish maidens she was quick to cover her daring by assuring him that "in *life* I am aware that gentleness and modesty form the distinguished ornaments of our sex. But in *description* they cannot captivate the imagination."[28]

Lydia's letters to her brother from Maine are full of questions as well as opinions. "Do not forget that I asked you about the 'flaming cherubims,' the effects of distance, horizontal or perpendicular, 'Orlando Furioso,' and Lord Byron," she reminded him on February 3, 1819. Later that year she was reading Gibbon's *Decline and Fall of the Roman Empire* for an hour every night before going to sleep and wrote Convers that she longed to study Latin so she could read Virgil in his own tongue.[29]

There is a spirited forthrightness in these letters. While she enjoys showing off to this learned elder brother, Lydia does not hesitate to tell him what she thinks. "I perceive that I never shall convert you to my opinions concerning Milton's treatment to our sex," she wrote at fifteen. At the same time, conscious of the limitations of her own quick-wittedness, she assures Convers of his superiority as a trained and disciplined scholar. In a letter written in 1819, this acutely self-aware young woman assessed the workings of her own mind: "I have not enough cultivated habits of thought and reflection upon any subject. The consequence is, my imagination has ripened before my judgment; I have quickness of perception, without profoundness of thought; I can at one glance take in a subject as displayed by another, but I am incapable of investigation."[30]

Lydia's own formal schooling ended when she was sixteen or seventeen, at which time she put her considerable learning to use as a teacher in one of the local schools. By the spring of 1820 she had apparently succeeded well enough to be invited to take a teaching position in the town of Gardiner, some forty miles from Norridgewock. She was then eighteen years old, small but arresting in appearance, with dark hair and deep brown eyes set far apart.

Lydia could not help boasting to Convers in the spring of 1820 that "ever since I entered my nineteenth year I have received nothing but presents and attention." Never in her life had she felt happier, she assured him, and went on to describe her "unbounded elasticity of spirit," her heart vibrating with joy. While she feared she might be lonely in Gardiner among strangers, she was also eager to be on her own. "I hope my dear brother, that you feel as happy as I do. Not that I have formed any high-flown expectations. All I expect is, that, if I am industrious and prudent I shall be *independent.*"[31]

In one of her early stories for children Lydia describes the feelings of a young sailor, Charles Wager, who is about go to sea for the first time. "Thoughts which had hitherto been confined to the narrow bounds of his own home, now roamed abroad over the face of the earth; and his mind swelled and enlarged itself, as if it were desirous to take in the whole creation. An active and restless spirit was busy within him; and he felt a desire to do something in the world, though he could not precisely tell what."[32]

Were these Lydia's secret thoughts as she left Norridgewock for her new life in Gardiner in the spring of 1819? Was she putting feelings into the mind of this fictional sailor boy which had in fact been her own? "Let them be sea captains if they will," Margaret Fuller, her Transcendentalist friend, would daringly proclaim in the 1840s, challenging women to throw over convention and follow their aspirations. But in 1820 naked ambition, "a desire to do something in the world," was a dream which only young men could admit to.

While open admission of an unwomanly ambition would have shocked Lydia's contemporaries, her desire to be independent and self-supporting was less reprehensible. In these early years of the nineteenth century, while most single women looked forward to relying on a husband for support, increasing numbers of them from the middle and upper classes were spurning matrimony, dreaming instead of autonomy and the chance to develop their talents for socially useful purposes.[33] Although professions such as the law, medicine, and the ministry were closed to women, and few writers made a living from their pen, opportunities for women's work outside the home were on the increase in the 1820s. New developments in industrial manufacture began to draw farm girls from all over New England to the mills of Lowell and the factories of Lynn. Meanwhile, common schools, academies, and private seminaries multiplied in these decades, raising the demand for instructors and opening the way for more and more women to enter the teaching profession, at least as a temporary occupation. Although the pay was poor, a living could be made, and the work was more intellectually challenging than most occupations available to women.

Little is known of how Lydia fared in Gardiner in this, her first experiment in independence. A newspaper clipping from the 1890s describing the early schools in that town claims that "teachers were generally selected who possessed muscular power and bull-dog tenacity, rather than because of intellectual ability or refinement in manner."[34] If Lydia Francis was diminutive and scholarly she was also resolute and strong, and she doubtless had little trouble controlling her classes.

In any case Lydia would remain in Gardiner for less than two years. As was the custom for teachers, she probably boarded with the family of one of her pupils or in the home of a fellow teacher. Perhaps it was in Gardiner that Lydia fell in love for the first time. Many years later she recalled her youthful worship for a young man whom she later outgrew. She had women friends as well. On warm summer days their favorite retreat was a "wild shaggy glen" which overlooked a deep gorge near the confluence of the Cobbosseecontee and Kennebec rivers. Here, surrounded by a rich growth of forest and cooled by the sound of waterfalls, the young women had dedicated a bower to the genii of the spot and "were accustomed to take great delight under its pleasing shade."[35]

The beauty as well as the terror of nature were close at hand during Lydia's years in Maine. In Gardiner her love for the "impetuous grandeur" of the northern wilderness, nurtured by the novels of Sir Walter Scott, was reinforced by the poetry of Lord Byron, whose "bold efforts" of genius she likened to the "horrid glare of the lightning amid the terrors of a midnight storm." But for all her love of the heroic and sublime in nature and in literature, Lydia also hungered for the conventional comforts of organized religion. In the spring of 1820 she wrote Convers that she was "more in danger of wrecking on the rocks of skepticism than of stranding on the shoals of fanaticism." Religion, she complained to her brother, was still for her only a beautiful theory which played "round the imagination, but fails to reach the heart," and she longed for a faith in which her heart and understanding could unite, "that amidst the darkest clouds of this life I might ever be cheered with the mild halo of religious consolation."[36]

Lydia had no hesitation about voicing her religious doubts to Convers. He had long ago rejected the simple pietism of his mother and the orthodox Congregationalism of his father for a more rational, open-minded religion. Like most New England children of the time, he and Lydia had been compelled to spend countless hours poring over the Bible and were taught to regard it as the only repository of truth. One of Lydia's earliest memories was of sleeping with the Scriptures under her pillow. Such "Bibliolatry," however, had repelled the young Convers. "If you take away the human element out of a book," he later wrote, "you take away the charm and can give nothing in its place." He remembered that the deepest and most living impressions of religion were made upon him "by some pleasant little story books, or still more by the spontaneous feeling and thoughts that visited my childish heart." In common with other Unitarian scholars who had grown tired of religious disputation and were coming to see the problems of life in other than purely biblical or theological terms, Convers considered literature to be an equally valid source of religious expression, and he undoubtedly encouraged his sister to think accordingly.[37]

Lydia too was eager to reject orthodox Calvinism, with its passive acceptance of God's will and its stifling of individual self-determination. But she was less anxious to part with her early reverence for the Bible and other devotional works. In common with others of her generation, including Ralph Waldo Emerson, Theodore Parker, and Margaret Fuller, she was searching for a faith which had something in it of passion and ecstasy. The religious history of early New England was full of tales of the supernatural: of witches, possessions, and persecutions; of visionaries and utopian dreamers; of people who heard and were guided by voices. But in recent decades the dynamic, mystical piety of the old orthodoxy had been all but smothered by the sober rationality of the theological liberals, who, beginning in the eighteenth century, denounced the heartfelt enthusiasms of revivalism in favor of a religion guided by the understanding, the judgment, and the will.[38]

A product of these two strains of religious history, the rational and the mystical, yet unaware of the new religious fervor that was sweeping through so much of Christianity beyond New England, Lydia Francis at eighteen found herself in a narrow world bounded by a fading orthodoxy and the cautious sobriety of emerging Unitarianism. For a young woman, whose head was filled with visions and dreams, the dry sectarian landscape set before her held little appeal. Yet like other New Englanders both before and after her, young Lydia Francis was torn between the longing to believe that God lived in her heart and in the wonders of nature and the pull of traditional piety, which taught her that her own intuition must be subject to the wisdom of society and her worship of nature must conform to conventional standards of decorum. As a child, she had kept *The Imitation of Christ*, a popular devotional work dating from the fifteenth century, beside the Bible under her pillow, and as a grown woman she would write admiringly of the seventeenth-century French mystic, Madame Guyon. Many years later, John Greenleaf Whittier would describe Lydia Maria Child as a person in whom "mysticism and realism ran in close parallel lines without interfering with each other. With strong rationalist tendencies from education and conviction, she found herself in spiritual accord with the pious introversion of Thomas à Kempis and Madame Guion [sic]. She was fond of Christmas Eve stories, of warnings, signs, and spiritual intimations."[39]

3

A Writer's Beginnings

Know ye the Indian warrior race?
How their light form springs, in strength and
grace,
Like the pine on their native mountain side,
That will not bow in its deathless pride;
Whose rugged limbs of stubborn tone,
No flexuous power of art will own,
But bend to Heaven's red bolt alone!
   —James Wallis Eastburn and
   Robert Sands, "Yamoyden"

By the late summer of 1821, after hardly more than a year in Gardiner, Lydia was back home in Massachusetts living with her brother Convers, now pastor of the First Church in Watertown, a rural village just upriver from Cambridge. No record survives explaining Lydia's decision to move back to her native state. She was nineteen and perhaps had tired of her isolation in the Maine hinterland and was impatient to return to the "real" world. While Gardiner boasted greater social and cultural sophistication than Norridgewock, its amenities paled compared to those offered in towns closer to Boston. Lydia may also have wearied of teaching, an occupation which she would take up again in the course of her life, but never with much enthusiasm. Above all, she surely welcomed the chance to live under the same roof with Convers, her cherished childhood companion and teacher and the one member of her family with whom she could speak, however guardedly, of her dreams and ambitions.[1]

Soon after her return to Massachusetts, Lydia paid a visit to Medford. Her father had sold the bakery and moved to Dorchester. And it may have been partly to please him that she marked this transitional moment in her life by joining her family's old church. Years later she explained her decision to be baptized an orthodox Congregationalist as springing from a yearning for spiritual nourishment. But the only long-lasting effect of her christening appears to have been the taking of the name "Maria." "Lydia" had long had disagreeable associations for her because of an aunt of the same name, and she let it be known that from now on she preferred to be called "Maria" (pronounced with a long *i*).[2]

Once back in Massachusetts, Maria moved into her brother's parsonage, a quaint old saltbox house on Mount Auburn Street in Watertown. She had seen little or nothing of Convers since leaving Medford to live with the Prestons. Her brother, now in his midtwenties, had finished his divinity studies at Harvard in 1818 and a year later had been invited to settle as minister in Watertown, where he was ordained in May 1819. The Reverend David Osgood had come over from Medford to preach the ordination sermon, and President Kirkland of Harvard College had also officiated; so had an old classmate of Convers', John Gorham Palfrey.

The Convers whom Maria found when she moved into the parsonage was in many ways the same bookish, talkative, unaffected brother she had known in Medford. Rarely seen without a volume of the classics in his hands, he was as ready as ever to answer questions and discuss a wide range of subjects. His unpretentious and kindly ways had quickly endeared him to his parishioners, who later credited him with easing their transition to Unitarianism. But Convers, unlike his self-assured younger sister, lacked confidence and was easily swayed by the opinions of others. In private he invariably let loose a rich, uninhibited flow of brilliant talk, but in the pulpit he never veered from his prepared text. While Convers enjoyed scribbling "pshaws," "bahs," and "boshes" on the flyleaves and margins of his books, aloud his objections were invariably expressed in the mildest, most unprovoking manner. He once confided to his diary that before each sermon his mind was "filled and pressed with anxious thoughts," that he felt depressed by his inability to lift his hearers to the heights of religious ecstasy, an ecstasy which he could feel in his own heart.[3]

When Convers was not busy with parish duties he acted as his sister's private tutor. His erudition was legendary in Boston literary circles. One contemporary described him as "a completely furnished and ever-ready guide to the writings and thoughts of others," and as eager to share the information stored in his head as the books lining his study shelves. Many years later Maria wrote

Convers thanking him for his help and spoke of the enlarging and liberalizing effect which his conversation always had on her. "I can say most truly before God," she told him, that "I consider such intellectual culture as I have mainly attributable to your influence."[4]

Maria had the free run of her brother's library, where she acquired her own very thorough, if perhaps unsystematic, liberal education. Here, besides sermons and works of theology, were the Greek and Roman classics. Volumes of history filled many of the shelves, including the chronicles of early New England. Convers believed that God had revealed himself to His people not only in biblical times but throughout history, and that a careful study of the past would improve one's knowledge of Him. Convers' study contained the latest volumes of German philosophy and the writings of the English Romantics, of Coleridge and Wordsworth. Meanwhile, in her brother's parlor Maria was introduced to many of the bright young intellectuals of the day, including Ralph Waldo Emerson, then a student at Harvard. Many years later she remembered long evenings with assorted collegians spent discussing Kant's philosophy. After the young men had left, Maria would retire for the night "without knowing whether or not I had 'hung myself over the chair and put my clothes into bed.' "[5]

Maria's wide reading in Convers' library apparently did little to draw her more closely to the faith of her childhood. Nor did she appear greatly attracted by her brother's more liberal creed. As a member of his household she was a faithful attendant at Sunday services in the First Church of Watertown. She also joined the women of the parish in distributing food, clothing, and other necessities to the town's poor. But Convers' growing attachment to Unitarianism found no echo in her own heart. Instead, not many months after her return to Massachusetts, Maria's attention was drawn to the teachings of Emmanuel Swedenborg, the eighteenth-century Swedish mystic whose "Heavenly Doctrines" were finding a small following, particularly among the students and young graduates of Harvard College. The optimism and sweeping comprehensiveness of Swedenborgianism attracted those, like Maria Francis, who longed to escape the Calvinist doctrines of hell and eternal damnation but found little to satisfy them in the cold rationality of the Unitarians. They desired a faith which made the universe intelligible, yet one which spoke to their hearts as well as their minds.[6]

Maria had first learned of Swedenborg while living in Gardiner, where a small "but highly respectable" Swedenborgian congregation, or Society of the Church of the New Jerusalem, had been formed by 1820. The appearance of the new sect had at least sparked her curiosity, for in May of that year she took pains to assure Convers that she was in no danger of becoming a Swedenborgian.[7] A more likely spur to Maria's interest in the Swedish mystic's doctrines was a lecture given at Harvard commencement in the late summer of 1821 by a recent graduate of the Divinity School named Sampson Reed.

Like Convers Francis, Reed had been trained at Harvard in the commonly accepted psychology of the day, which followed the teachings of John Locke and stressed the limitations of human knowledge, particularly man's inability to grasp his true spiritual nature. But in common with other young theological students, Reed was impatient with the prevailing view at Harvard that all knowledge, including religious sentiment, was acquired through the senses. Inspired by the romantic idealism then prevalent in Europe, which emphasized the value of sentiment over reason and stressed the emotional substance of religion, Reed had come to believe that men and women could grasp religious ideas intuitively, that theological truths could be discovered by each individual within the recesses of his or her own soul.[8]

The old philosophical rules no longer seemed pertinent in the rapidly changing world of early-nineteenth-century America, and when Sampson Reed delivered his "Oration on Genius" on that late summer day in 1821 he was articulating a new line of religious thinking that was shared by several in his audience, including Ralph Waldo Emerson, then a graduating senior. While the speech made no direct mention of Swedenborg, the influence of his thought was clear. According to Reed, divine truth was revealed not in theological pronouncements made by the churches but directly to the human heart from nature. "Nature is full of God," he said, and all those who turn to her have the capacity to understand spiritual truth. The address was both an indictment of the formalism of the liberal church in New England and the articulation of a new faith more suited to the bright promise of the young American nation.[9]

Emerson was so taken with the address that he borrowed Reed's manuscript and treasured the notes he took from it for many years. Copies of the speech were widely circulated among liberal thinkers in Boston and Cambridge, and Sampson Reed became the intermediary through whom these New Englanders were introduced to Swedenborg. Less than one month after Reed delivered his graduation address, he and sixty other men and women signed their names to a declaration of faith in the doctrines espoused by the Swedenborgian Church. Lydia Maria Francis' name was among them, and four months later on February 10, 1822, the records of the Boston Society of the New Jerusalem show that Lydia Maria Francis had been admitted a member of the Society.[10]

Emmanuel Swedenborg believed that God had revealed directly to him the true meaning of the Bible, which saw all of creation as a unified, harmonious whole. He described this revelation through his doctrine of correspondences, which taught that everything in the natural world, including man, is the expression of, and corresponds to, some higher spiritual reality. Words themselves became symbols of universal ideas which the purified heart could understand without benefit of church or clergy. Thus the whole universe was explained in a new way. The old orthodoxy with its controversies, its pessimistic emphasis on the enduring conflict between good and evil, was replaced by an optimistic faith which stressed the innate goodness of man and the harmonious relation between the natural and the spiritual world.[11]

Many years later Maria remembered that when she first discovered Swedenborg, "all he said seemed to me a direct revelation to his soul, from the angels. His doctrine of Correspondences seemed a golden key to unlock the massive gate between the external and spiritual world. I then *experienced religion*;' and for a long time lived in a mansion of glories."[12]

Maria also welcomed a faith which exalted what was then seen as the peculiarly feminine gift of sensibility. She lived in an age when a woman's emotional and moral superiority were invariably stressed at the expense of her intellectual abilities, and here was a religion which exalted the heart over the mind as a surer, purer path to divine truth than intellectualism. Describing true religion as a "delightful state of internal resignation" to God's will, which exalted "every feeling into the region of pure, ethereal tranquility," leaving "no void in the heart," Maria insisted that true wisdom was not learning but piety. "Good books," she would write in 1827, "may assist in gaining this wisdom, . . . but they are not necessary to it. A life according to the precepts of the Gospel is the surest way to obtain true and lasting faith. . . . The heart should be watched,—it should be kept pure and quiet."[13]

The same year that Maria joined the Swedenborgian Church, her brother Convers acquired both a wife and a new house. "There has been nothing here this three months but painting floors, making carpets, filling feather beds, putting up crockery," Maria wrote her sister Mary Preston from Watertown in May 1822. Two weeks earlier, following Convers' marriage to Abigail Allyn, the three had set up housekeeping in the new, handsome brick parsonage on the corner of what are now Riverside and North Beacon Streets. Convers' parishioners had shown their approval of his marriage by providing him with a new horse, a sofa, two lamps, and various household articles. Maria liked her new sister-in-law and assured Mary that Abby's "sweet, unassuming" character combined with her intelligence and breadth of learning would make her a good wife for Convers. Furthermore, Abby, the daughter of a minister, was well acquainted with the duties expected of a pastor's wife.[14]

In her own room in the new parsonage, sometime early in 1824, Maria Francis began writing her first novel, *Hobomok*. During the quiet interval between morning and afternoon services at Convers' church, while glancing through a back issue of the *North American Review*, the most respected literary periodical of the day, she came upon a review by Convers' friend John Gorham Palfrey. The subject was "Yamoyden,"a long narrative poem by James Wallis Eastburn and Robert Sands on King Philip's War, the most devastating of the hostilities between Indians and New England settlers in the seventeenth century. Palfrey praised the poem for its use of early Puritan history. "We are glad," Palfrey wrote, "that somebody has at last found out the unequalled fitness of our early history for the purposes of a work of fiction. For ourselves we know not the country or age which has such capacities in this view as New England in its early day; nor do we suppose it easy to imagine any element of the sublime, the wonderful, the picturesque and the pathetic, which is not to be found here." The stern, romantic character of the Puritans reminded Palfrey of the novels of Sir Walter Scott.[15]

Maria must have thought Palfrey was speaking directly to her. During her years in Norridgewock she had been caught up in the romance of early American history and the story of the Abenaki Indians who had flourished there until their destruction by the English colonists in the early eighteenth century. Then, she had discovered Sir Walter Scott and, inspired by the "pathos and grandeur" of his historical romances, had thought for the first time of writing a novel herself. Now here was a noted critic and friend of her brother's suggesting that the New England past, with whose history she was also familiar, was an ideal subject for a work of fiction.[16]

The germ of a story must have already occurred to her, for no sooner had she finished reading Palfrey's review than she put pen to paper, and before it was time to go to afternoon service she had completed a chapter. Later, when she showed it to Convers, she was flattered to hear him exclaim, "But Maria did you *really* write this? Do you *mean* what you say, that it is entirely your own?"[17] *Hobomok, A Tale of Early Times* was finished in six weeks and published in May 1824. It has the distinction of being the first New England historical novel, and although Maria, like other English and American women writers of the nineteenth century, did not disclose her identity, it was not long before everyone knew the book had been written by the younger sister of the Reverend Convers Francis.

Hobomok is a story of the early Puritan settlement in Salem, Massachusetts. Mary Conant, a young aristocratic Englishwoman—her grandfather is an earl—has recently crossed the Atlantic to help care for her dying mother. Shortly after her arrival she falls in love with a fellow countryman, Charles Brown, also a newcomer to Salem. Brown, a confirmed Anglican, makes the mistake of proselytizing for his faith among the colonists and is forced into exile by the town elders, who include Mary's father, a stern, uncompromising Puritan. A year or so after Brown's banishment, Mary, who is secretly betrothed to him, learns that he has been lost at sea, and in desperation she turns for comfort to a noble young Indian, Hobomok, who loves her. The two elope to Plymouth. When Mary's father, who fears his daughter has drowned, hears that she is alive but married to a red man, he is filled with grief and outrage. "I had made up my mind to her watery grave, but to have her lie in the bosom of a savage, and mingle her prayers with a heathen who knoweth not God, is hard for a father's heart to endure."[18] In due course Mary bears Hobomok a son, and the three manage to live reasonably contentedly in their wigwam. Then, one day, Hobomok is out hunting in the woods when he is surprised by the appearance of Mary's fiancé, Charles Brown, who was presumed dead. Unaware of her marriage to the Indian, he has returned to claim her. Hobomok, knowing that Mary has never ceased to love Charles, nobly relinquishes her and vanishes into the forest. The story ends happily for everyone but Hobomok. Mary and Charles are married, and little Hobomok, eventually educated at Harvard as well as in England, soon becomes indistinguishable from any other Englishman.

Maria Francis in this first novel is looking at early New England history from a feminine point of view. Instead of concentrating her story on the deeds of the Puritan elders, she focuses instead on ordinary settlers, particularly the women. From this vantage point the history appears in a very different light. Compared to the stern, contentious Puritan men, whose concern is the need for theological purity, their wives and daughters are determined to maintain a humane and civilized existence in the harsh surroundings of the New England wilderness. Much as Susannah Francis sought to temper the elder Convers' rigid orthodoxy with her gentle piety, so Mrs. Conant does her best to ease the effects of her husband's harshness on their daughter, Mary.[19]

There are even traces of Maria's recent conversion to Swedenborgianism in this first novel, as when she compares spiritual light to that of the "natural sun." It "shines from one source and shines alike upon all; but is reflected and absorbed in almost infinite variety; and in the moral, as well as the natural world, the diversity of the rays is occasioned by the nature of the recipient."[20]

Hobomok would seem crude to most twentieth-century readers. The plot is uneven and the style suffers from sentimentality and pretentiousness. But despite these flaws the book is of considerable interest. Many years later, Thomas Wentworth Higginson, a noted writer and reformer, attributed the success of *Hobomok* to the fact that it "marked the very dawn of American imaginative literature."[21] In 1824 Boston was still in its infancy as a literary center, and the great writers and thinkers who would emerge in the 1830s and 1840s had not yet made names for themselves; Emerson was only twenty-one in 1824, Hawthorne twenty, and Thoreau a boy of seven. Maria Francis was twenty-two.

Like many first novels, *Hobomok* reveals much about its young author, exposing her dreams and ambitions along with the pains and sorrows of her early life. Brought up in England by a doting, cultivated grandfather, Mary Conant is given the kind of upbringing Maria wished she had had, an upbringing which gently and lovingly nurtured her intellectual gifts and artistic sensibilities. Within the marble halls of Lord Rivers' house, Mary Conant had "become familiar with much that was beautiful in painting, and lovely in sculpture, as well as all that was elegant in . . . poetry." The kindly old gentleman had reared her "like some fair and tender blossom in his gardens." In time this gifted, elegant young woman became the "little idol of a brilliant circle . . . covetous of mental riches" and ready to worship "at the shrine of genius."[22]

Mary Conant's ideal childhood comes to an abrupt end, however, once she is shipped off to the desolate little settlement on the edge of the American wilderness to help care for her dying mother. Here she is exposed to poverty, hardship, and loss. In other words, this aristocratic, fictional heroine endures many of the same privations and losses her less gently bred creator experienced. Mary Conant like Maria Francis has suffered, and like her she has been strengthened by that suffering.

> Indeed it seemed as if the chilling storms, which had lowered over the young life of Mary Conant, had not only served to call forth the fervid hues of feeling in their full perfection, but had likewise strengthened her native elegance of mind. The intellectual, like the natural sun, sheds its own bright and beautiful lustre on the surrounding gloom, till every object on which it shines seems glowing into life; and amid all the dreariness of poverty, and the weight of affliction (the heavier, that it was borne far from the knowledge and sympathy of the world), Mary found much to excite the native fervor of her imagination. [23]

Like young Lydia at the time of her mother's death, Mary Conant finds herself bereft of all kindred souls. Her mother has died; her fiancé is lost at sea; her best friend has married and moved away. But unlike twelve-year-old Lydia Francis, Mary Conant is old enough to take charge of her own destiny. While Lydia was sent away to live with her sister in Maine, the heroine of *Hobomok* banishes herself by marrying an Indian and moving to Plymouth. Mary Conant also has the best of both worlds. During her brief union with Hobomok she satisfies a longing for the freedom of the untamed wilderness. Then, when she is restored to the arms of the well-born and cultured Charles Brown, she gratifies an equally strong need for intellectual stimulation and the amenities of civilized life.[24]

If *Hobomok* shows a certain daring in its evocation of a heroine "covetous of mental riches," its true boldness lies in its portrayal of an interracial marriage. According to critic Leslie Fiedler, the novel was the first in America to fictionalize miscegenation.[25] Maria's declared intention, however, is not to shock her readers but to educate them, to tell them something of Indian manners and customs, and above all to criticize her fellow white Americans for their prejudicial treatment of a primitive but noble people. She is also careful to allow Mary Conant to escape from her socially stigmatized union by divorcing Hobomok and marrying her white suitor. Still, no other writer had had the nerve to speak approvingly of marriage between an Indian and a white woman—even the subject of divorce was taboo—and for a young, unmarried woman to discuss these subjects was regarded as most improper. But Maria Francis had little reverence for social taboos, or for the hierarchies of race, class, and sex which absorbed the attention of so many of her contemporaries. She simply took it for granted that in a truly egalitarian society, in the harmonious universe described by Swedenborg, the mingling of the races would be both good and acceptable.

If writing *Hobomok* was relatively painless, publishing it was not. The very idea of a woman wishing to see her writing in print was a potentially revolutionary act in early nineteenth-century America, where the creation of culture was considered a traditionally public and male preserve. Caroline Howard Gilman, a popular novelist of the 1830s and 1840s, was horrified when, as a young girl in 1810, she discovered that a member of her family had sent one of her poems to a Boston newspaper. "When I heard of it I cried half the night with a kind of shame," she recalled later, comparing her alarm at being published to being "detected in man's apparel." As literary historian Mary Kelley has pointed out, "with a presumed destiny that was private, not public, and a role that called for the support of others, women could become receptors of culture. . . . But to go beyond that, to envision themselves as contributors to culture was problematical for those who, in a sense, looked to a culturally invisible past." For women to think of themselves as legitimate creators of culture "would have required a leap of vision that could only have drawn upon a confidence and a faith in their own ability and power to create and shape their own lives."[26]

For a woman of her time, Maria may have possessed unusual confidence in her abilities as a writer, but persuading a publisher of them would have been another matter. The best-known woman novelist of the 1820s was Catharine Maria Sedgwick, a native of Stockbridge, Massachusetts, who wrote suitably domestic tales with morally uplifting themes. The questionable subject matter of Maria Francis' own book may have been one reason why she agreed to publish it anonymously. Added to this problem was that in the 1820s the American book publishing industry was still in its infancy, and writers were responsible for the cost of printing as well as distributing their works. Furthermore, the chances of earning a significant profit or reaching a large audience were remote for any author, but particularly so for a woman. Despite these handicaps, Maria found a willing publisher, Cummings, Hilliard, & Co., and the $495 required to print one thousand copies of *Hobomok*. Perhaps her father lent her the money. In any case, the slim volume in its brown cloth binding began appearing in bookstores in the summer of 1824 at a cost of seventy-five cents.[27]

Sales of the novel proceeded slowly at first, thanks largely to a critical notice in the *North American Review*. Although the reviewer maintained that the excellencies of the book outweighed its faults, he denounced Mary Conant's marriage to her noble savage as "not only unnatural, but revolting . . . to every feeling of delicacy." Nearly a year after its publication only half of the first edition of one thousand copies had been sold. Maria was understandably discouraged by the poor reception and felt that she had been "too severely punished" for her rashness in treating an indelicate subject. Her spirits were lifted, however, when she learned in March 1825 that George Ticknor, a powerful voice in New England literary circles, had been overheard making "flattering observations" about *Hobomok*.[28]

At the age of thirty-four, George Ticknor already ruled the Boston literary world. Back in 1819 this intensely serious young man had returned from four years of study and travel in Europe, where he had trained himself as a professional man of letters in the great German universities. His keen wit and learning, combined with the manners and polish of a European aristocrat and intellectual, ensured Ticknor a warm welcome in Boston's most elegant parlors, and he rose quickly to become a powerful social arbiter. By the time Maria Francis published *Hobomok*, the Harvard professor's blessing on a young writer acted as a kind of open sesame, guaranteeing acceptance into Boston's elite social world. Many years later the radical Unitarian Theodore Parker commented wryly that "no man could consider himself of any account in the world if he was not admitted to Mr. Ticknor's study."[29]

Luckily, Convers was one of these fortunate men, and it was this connection which prompted Maria to ask for Ticknor's help in promoting the sale of her book. On March 29, 1825, she wrote George Ticknor a letter urging him to use his influence on her behalf, an influence, she was careful to point out, which was very great in the literary and fashionable world. Asking him to say a few words in support of her novel, she argued confidently that a good notice from him would induce many people to buy the book "who otherwise regard the subject with indifference."

This sort of influence is all that I wish, and more than I expect. Indeed my vanity would hardly have formed such a *wish*, had you not voluntarily praised my trifling production. I am aware that it is almost unpardonable to obtrude myself upon you, amid all the cares that unavoidably wait upon a station like yours; but I am certain it will afford you some pleasure to revive the hopes of a young and disappointed author. Regard for my brother's feelings has induced me to keep him in ignorance of this presumptuous action.[30]

Such temerity on the part of an obscure woman writer was, to say the least, remarkable. Even prominent literary women like Catharine Sedgwick genteelly mouthed their preference for obscurity. But Maria Francis, when she had an object in mind, was never one to be daunted by conventionalities. Nor had fear of rejection ever held her back. What mattered was that her book wasn't selling well, and if she didn't do something to promote it herself she would remain "a young and disappointed author."

Fortunately, her courage was soon rewarded. In July 1825 a second and much longer notice of *Hobomok* appeared in the *North American Review*, written by none other than the editor, Jared Sparks, a respected historian and friend of Ticknor's. In his review Sparks agreed with those who considered the novel to be in bad taste but forgave the young author, who, he insisted, was guilty of little more than too great a devotion to historical accuracy. "If our ancestors were more sternly virtuous," Sparks told his readers, "they were certainly without much of the delicacy and refinement of the present generation." He went on to praise the author's delineations of the Indian character, commended the "feeling of pathos" surrounding the death bed scenes, and concluded by saying, "We think this book has suffered much from the general prejudice against the catastrophe of the story, and that its animated descriptions of scenes and persons, its agreeable style, and the acquaintance with the history and the spirit of the times which it evinces, have not received the credit due to them."[31]

In the months following Sparks' review the sales of *Hobomok* improved considerably. But an equally important result of Ticknor's efforts on behalf of the novel's author was the entree it provided Maria Francis into Ticknor's literary and social circles. "The Boston fashionables took me up and made a 'little wee bit' of a lion out of me," she later recalled.[32] Maria was suddenly transported from the sober, frugal world of her childhood into a glittering one of riches and luxury, where the intellectual fare promised to be as abundant as the material.

A Wee Bit of a Lion

*Intellect has a still greater triumph, when genius
born in poverty and nurtured in seclusion, sees
wealth and rank with all their gilded trappings,
shrink to their own nothingness and pay reluctant
homage where Heaven has set its own high impress
of nobility.*
— *Lydia Maria Child,* The Rebels

B oston in the 1820s still resembled a provincial English town,
with its narrow streets, its Common dotted with cows, its
clapboard houses ringed with flower gardens. But the city's
appearance had recently been enhanced by the graceful federal
architecture of Charles Bulfinch, whose private houses and public
buildings, crowned by the imposing State House on Beacon Hill,
reflected the sober and refined taste of its leading citizens.

It was on the whole a clean, orderly city. Josiah Quincy, who
had been elected the second mayor of the newly incorporated
metropolis in 1824, had seen to that. The streets were swept, trash
was removed, and a recently appointed police force kept order.
Blacks and poor immigrants, not yet confined to ghettos, were
scattered about the city in neighborhoods like "Nigger Hill." With
new bridges and causeways connecting what had once been an
isolated peninsula to the mainland, any overflow could spill easily
into the surrounding countryside.[1]

The decades following the War of 1812 were generally prosperous ones for this largest New England city. Although trade with
the agricultural hinterland was shrinking, the industrial growth of
nearby towns like Lowell and Lynn compensated for this loss as
the great fortunes of the china trade merchants were invested in
the manufacture of shoes and textiles. By 1830 Boston would rival

46

New York as a banking and financial center. The city was also growing fast—not as fast as New York perhaps, but in the fifty years between 1790 and 1840 the population expanded from eighteen thousand to ninety-three thousand, as newcomers poured in from the New England countryside in search of work. These Yankee immigrants blended almost invisibly into the local population. A similar uniformity extended to the city's leadership. While New York attracted men of wealth, power, and status from all over the country, Boston's elite were New Englanders. From 1820 until the Civil War an increasingly tightly knit group of interrelated families dominated the city's economic, political, and cultural life.[2]

The 1820s were a time of great optimism in Boston, as elsewhere in the United States. The hard times of war with Great Britain had been forgotten and Americans everywhere were working to create a dynamic and prosperous society. In Boston this ebullient confidence included a dream of the city as a cultural capital, a modern Athens. One Bostonian, Edward Everett Hale, later recalled the determination of the city's "best people" to make Boston a "model city." "They had Dr. Channing preaching the perfectibility of human nature; they had Dr. Joseph Tuckerman determined that the gospel of Jesus should work its miracles among all sorts and conditions of men; they had a system of public education which they meant to press to its very best; and they had all the money which was needed for anything good. These men subscribed their money with the greatest promptness for any enterprise which promised the elevation of human society."[3]

In no other American city were the worlds of business and culture so closely allied. Here wealthy traders, bankers, and industrialists, men making handsome profits in finance, commerce, or the newly burgeoning textile industry, invested generously in institutions supporting education, literature, and the arts. At a time when libraries of any kind were rare in the United States, the collections of the Boston Athenaeum, a private library founded in 1807, were growing so rapidly that a new building was needed to house them. Harvard College and the highly respected literary periodical the *North American Review* also benefited greatly in these years from the patronage of wealthy Bostonians.[4]

Unlike New York, where literary society was regarded as bohemian, Boston honored its scholars and writers. The elite's high respect for culture assured the prominence of intellectuals like George Ticknor and helps in part to explain Maria's sudden popularity. In the autumn of 1825, after the second review of *Hobomok* appeared in the *North American Review*, Maria Francis, once an obscure young novelist, was suddenly a celebrity, sought after by some of the best families as George Ticknor's personal protegée.

Maria found herself welcomed overnight into a world of gilded luxury, into parlors furnished with treasures from the east, where Persian carpets, Chinese hangings of silk, and exotic carvings of jade and teakwood formed the background for lavish hospitality. Boston society was in transition the year Maria was introduced to the "fashionables," as she called them. The old federalist leadership dominated by families like the Brookes and Otises was giving way to a new order of wealthy merchant industrialists, men with names like Lowell and Appleton, who would later form the backbone of the Whig party. Nathan Appleton, the textile magnate and future congressman, had built himself a grand house at 39 Beacon Street, with French wallpaper lining the vestibule and a hall floor tiled in black and white marble. His brother Samuel lived next door at number 37 where he gave frequent dinners for up-and-coming political figures like Daniel Webster.[5]

A satirical portrait of Boston society in these years conveys the impression of a moneyed aristocracy bent on amusement and display. The author, Samuel Knapp, careful to hide his identity under a pseudonym, describes a large social gathering where the men concentrate all their attention on the few belles of the evening, leaving the rest of the women to entertain themselves. While Knapp admitted that Boston women were lively and handsome—if rather gaudily overdressed—he found them "conspicuously deficient" intellectually. "Even the current literature of the day," he noted, "is too much for them—excepting always *poetry* and *novels*." According to Knapp, who may have been describing his own frustrating attempts at conversation with fashionable women, if a young man tried to introduce a serious literary or historical subject he could expect to hear such ejaculations as "Oh my! he is so pedantic, or tedious, or so impertinent that I can't bear him."[6]

More to Maria's taste would have been a dinner at the Ticknors, where she could expect a meal of venison or roast chicken and brown bread washed down with a whiskey punch made from Sir Walter Scott's recipe. Here she would have been introduced to an intimate circle of friends who measured themselves against the literary lights of Edinburgh and included Daniel Webster, Dr. William Ellery Channing, and the Everett brothers, Edward and Alexander. Ticknor and his wife, Anna, presided over these occasions with dignity and grace, guiding the conversation skillfully, she with her pungent humor, he with his vast store of anecdotes and quotations. Ticknor was clearly proud of his latest discovery, the learned and witty Maria Francis: a match for any man when it came to poking holes in an argument or telling a good story. She was a compelling presence, this diminutive young woman whose fresh and delicate complexion flushed so easily with every emotion. Her dark eyes were equally expressive, glowing with passion or indignation one minute and childlike merriment the next.[7]

Maria was a curiosity in Boston society. While cultivated men of humble background had found ready acceptance among the city's elite, it was another story for an obscure, learned woman to be so favorably treated. The historian Hannah Adams, reputedly the first American woman to support herself by her pen, lived in Boston. But this author of religious histories, who was also a lacemaker, had once remarked that weaving lace "was much more profitable than writing books." Now an elderly recluse, timid and unworldly, Miss Adams was remembered chiefly for her eccentricities. Maria befriended the old woman in her last years and was in the habit of carrying her bunches of fresh violets. As the two talked the younger could not help observing the elder's diffidence and timidity, her "troublesome consciousness of being unlike other people." The only other contemporary woman writer of any prominence in the mid-1820s was Catharine Maria Sedgwick, and she lived more than a hundred miles west of Boston in Stockbridge.[8]

Maria herself was very aware of the peculiarity of her position. She had been warned before she published *Hobomok* that female writers were considered "unsexed," and she certainly had little wish to model herself after Hannah Adams. But fear for her reputation would never prevent Maria from doing anything she was determined to do. In later life she described for Convers this unconsciousness of danger: "I know not how it is, but my natural temperament is such that when I wish to do anything I seem to have an instinctive faith that I can do it." The success of *Hobomok* convinced her that she could earn enough to be independent.[9]

Writing as a profession was still very much in its infancy in America. Only Washington Irving and James Fenimore Cooper had made the important discovery that people would buy their books as fast as they could write them. Most of the books published in the early nineteenth century were religious, educational, or practical, and what fiction appeared was more likely to be the work of English than American authors. It would be another decade before Hawthorne's "mob of scribbling women" would begin to flood the market with their sentimental novels. Meanwhile, this promising American woman novelist excited a good deal of interest in the Boston literary world. Thomas Wentworth Higginson, the Unitarian author and reformer, was only a boy at the time, but he later recalled how Maria Francis was courted in these years. He spoke of her as "almost a fashionable lion," comparing her to the English novelist Fanny Burney, while admitting that the literary lights of Boston were "rather reduced copies of Burke and Johnson."[10]

For a time it seemed to Maria as if her brightest dreams were to be fulfilled, that, as she later put it, her native genius, "born in poverty and nurtured in seclusion," had "set its own high impress of nobility," and she was gaining the recognition she deserved. Later, in an essay entitled "The First and Last Book," she would describe how "restless insatiable ambition" had filled her "like a fiery charm," how everything she saw and did seemed to partake of the "brightness and boundlessness" of her own hopes. She found the whole world fascinating and was sure it returned the compliment. Furthermore, in her pride she relished "the honest independence, which every highly-gifted and well-balanced mind may feel towards those who possess merely the accidental advantages of rank and fortune."[11]

In June 1825 General Lafayette, who had been making a triumphal tour of the United States, came to Boston to help celebrate the fiftieth anniversary of the Battle of Bunker Hill. It was his second visit within the year. Late the summer before, at the start of his tour, a jubilant citizenry had welcomed the Revolutionary War hero; their deafening hurrahs echoed through the streets to the accompaniment of bells and cannon while he rode by in an open barouche drawn by four white horses. No one had been so lavishly honored since George Washington's visit back in 1789. Twelve hundred people had joined the French general for dinner under a tent on the Common where a chorus of school children had sung the "Marseillaise." Maria had not been included in this first round of festivities, but when Lafayette returned the following June her reputation as a young novelist brought her an invitation from the governor to attend a reception in the general's honor. According to one account Maria received a kiss from Lafayette on her hand, which she vowed should "never be washed off."[12]

That winter Maria moved into Boston, where she boarded at an academy for young ladies at 4 Somerset Street. Run by Monsieur and Madame Canda, the school offered daily lessons in French, as well as instruction in Latin, English, music, drawing, and needlework. Maria, who would have been considerably older than the other pupils, attended the school principally to learn French and drawing. For the next six months she divided her time between studying, writing, and a whirl of social activities.[13]

Among the boarders at the school was the beautiful Emily Marshall. Five years younger than Maria, Emily was apparently a faultless creature, as charming in manner as she was in looks, and as friendly to women as she was to men. She was an intelligent, even brilliant girl, and totally unaffected. One of her sisters once asked Emily if she realized how ravishing she was and received the ingenuous response, "Yes, I know that I am beautiful, but I do not understand why people act so unwisely about it." When Emily visited Philadelphia, schoolgirls were dismissed from class to watch her drive by; in New York people crowded the lobby of her hotel to catch a glimpse of her; and at home in Boston all the young men were in love with her. On one occasion, when she attended the theater on the same night as Daniel Webster, it was Emily and not the famous statesman who received a standing ovation. Maria and Emily quickly became such close friends that when a young man wished to impress Emily Marshall with his devotion he would send Maria Francis a bouquet.[14]

Maria had admirers of her own, however, including a popular and successful young artist, Francis Alexander, who had insisted on painting her portrait. The likeness now hangs in the Medford Historical Society and, while poorly restored, catches something of the vitality and charm which so easily infused Maria's rather plain features. Characteristically, she found the portrait much too flattering and accused Alexander of trying to "make a Sappho of me, and to pour over my very ugly face the full tide of inspiration."[15]

Another admirer from these years was Nathaniel P. Willis, who had won celebrity as a poet while still an undergraduate at Yale. An aspiring journalist who became editor of the *American Monthly Magazine*, young Willis prided himself on being a dandy and an aesthete. Maria later recalled, with a certain irony perhaps, the walks the two took together over the Common's broad meadow: his tall handsome figure attired in the very latest fashion complete with white top hat, buff vest, and new light-colored French gloves, looking down on her "slender shortness," as he dreamed aloud of "the high position he meant to conquer for himself."[16]

To the degree that she enjoyed being in the company of educated people with a taste for literature and the arts, Maria Francis relished being made much of by Boston's elite. Yet there are indications that she was not entirely comfortable with her position. The Boston social world was small, increasingly competitive, and tightly knit, and in this world women were expected to hide respectfully in the shadows of their husbands and fathers, to speak in generalities and not have ideas of their own. Yet at the age of twenty-three, Maria not only conversed more eloquently than most men but had published a book, and a shocking one at that. In her second novel, *The Rebels*, which appeared in 1825, a heroine named Lucretia, having been accustomed to the "republican simplicities" of pre-revolutionary Boston, suddenly finds herself thrust into fashionable London society where wealth is looked upon as a "glittering and much coveted bauble." Lucretia is miserable. She often retires to her room "to think of Boston" and weep tears that "start up from the fountain of bitterness." "What do I care for Turkey carpets, Parisian mirrors, and Chinese vases," she complains to her friends back home, "when every being around me is as chilling as the tessellated marble of our grand saloon."[17] In her impassioned defense of "republican simplicities" had Maria perhaps forgotten that Mary Conant, the heroine of *Hobomok*, was an earl's granddaughter?

An even more revealing story is "Harriet Bruce," written after Maria's initial delight in her own popularity and success had cooled. Harriet, the tale's overpowering, ambitious, and erudite heroine, is enchanted by her own genius. "Power, power! and, above all, intellectual power! was the constant dream of her wild ambition. To have been sure of Madame de Staël's reputation, she would have renounced human sympathy, and lived unloving & unbeloved in this wide world of social happiness—there was such magnificence in the idea of sending one's genius abroad, like a spark of electricity, to be active and eternal,—defying calculation in its form, duration and power!"[18]

So enamored is Harriet with her own genius that she dismisses any suggestion that she might become a victim of romantic love. "On this subject she often philosophized, and always laughed. 'Who' said she scornfully, 'who that has felt the gush and thrill attendant upon fame, would be foolish enough to exchange dominion over many for despotism of one?' " But then Harriet is introduced at a party to a charming, intelligent Harvard student from Virginia, George Macdonough. The two exchange pleasantries until Harriet, observing his interest in a lovely girl who has entered the room, reproaches "him teasingly that beauty is his idol." Embarrassed, even annoyed, George replies that he "did not think Miss Bruce had observed my character sufficiently to form any conclusion with regard to my taste." This rouses "the pride of the proudest girl in Christendom," and Harriet laughingly assures him that she thinks him "quite a specimen" in his way. "Society is such a bag of polished marbles," she quips, that anything odd is a valuable study. Taken aback by this unladylike display of sarcasm, George tries to make amends by pronouncing her "the most singular girl" he has ever met. Unabashed, she rejoins, "When a compliment is doubtful, Chesterfield says one should always take it, therefore I am obliged to you Mr. Macdonough."

While Harriet disguises her true feelings behind such displays of "*extreme* nonchalance," she is nonetheless clearly smitten with George. But "the proud Virginian," with his "love of dazzling beauty" and obvious distrust of clever women, in the end looks elsewhere for a wife. "The fact is," as Maria had written in an earlier story, "mental superiority is borne with less patience than any other; and those whom successful talent has rendered celebrated, cannot fail to arouse enemies in their path, however kind their disposition; however noble and generous their feelings."

Whether or not Maria Francis was ever spurned by an aristocratic lover like George MacDonough, she relished displaying her cleverness and often as not "the harmless arrow of playful wit" was mistaken "for the poisoned darts of sarcasm." She was also reprimanded on occasion for failing to show proper reverence towards established literary lions. Once, after listening to a speech in Plymouth by the celebrated orator Edward Everett, "while all around me were praising his eloquence," Maria, unmoved, remained silent. When her friends insisted on hearing her opinion of the lecture, she unequivocally dismissed it as "rhetoric, not eloquence. It plays round the head, but not a syllable of it reaches the heart." She later remembered this declaration had been "deemed heretical, and somewhat presumptuous."[19]

In a letter to her sister Mary, written in June 1826 just before she left Boston to return to Watertown, Maria admits that all had not been smooth for her in her new role as a celebrity: "Just in proportion to my conspicuousness I have had enemies as well as friends,—and I have deserved them both. Oh, how often I have wanted you to fly to, for advice and assistance. If people knew half the extent of my vehement and impetuous temperament, they would give me credit for governing myself as well as I do."

There is at the same time a sad, wistful tone in the reference to herself as "a poor isolated spinster." Maria was convinced she would never find a husband, that she was too plain, too learned, too outspoken, and too self-sufficient for any man to wish her for his wife.

Still, Maria couldn't help boasting to her sister a bit about all the attention she was getting: "With all absence of vanity be it spoken—the slightest movement of mine, now, goes to the four winds of heaven. . . . It is sufficiently amusing that *strangers* should lay by a fragment of my hand-writing as a choice relic, and be fearful of writing to me—Oh, how much I have had to smile at and be vain of!"[20]

But, attracted as Maria was by the cultivated gentility of New England's urban aristocracy, her free spirit found its "stiffened elegance and cold formality" stifling. Looking back years later she remembered only her distaste for the Boston social world. "In such company I am like a butterfly under a gilded glass tumbler; I can do nothing but pant despairingly, or beat all the feathers off my wings, thumping against the glittering walls of limitations."[21] Like the Indian or African chieftains whom wealthy eighteenth-century Britishers had enjoyed displaying before their peers as exotic curiosities, Maria had been trotted out for the amusement, even the admiration, of people who had no intention of accepting this wild, free creature as one of their own.

A story Maria published in 1827 comes close to conveying this feeling of confinement. In "George and Georgiana," two children, raised among the natives of Pitcairn Island, are brought to live in a grand house in New York City. Unused "to sitting upright, or moving according to rule," they particularly object when visitors come to call and they are made to dress up in their finest clothes. Then, Maria observes sympathetically, they feel "as uncomfortable as little birds do, when they are first taken from the green woods, and shut up in a gilded cage. It is vain to feed them with luxuries, or to dress their cages in flowers. The little things want to fly freely abroad in the air, and sing when and where they choose." Years later Maria confessed to her old childhood friend Lucy Osgood how much she disliked "sitting up straight in the midst of people with my best clothes on." In such surroundings she invariably felt like a square peg in a round hole. "My lines are all *straight*," she admitted to a friend in 1859, "and they run against a great many corners which graceful sinuosities would avoid."[22]

While suffering the constraints of polite society, Maria worked if anything harder than ever on her writing. Within six months of the publication of *Hobomok* she had written a book for children called *Evenings in New England*, followed twelve months later by her second novel, *The Rebels*, which she dedicated to George Ticknor. *Evenings in New England* announced in its preface that it contained both American scenes and American characters. Maria was echoing the conviction of other educators and writers of the time that the youth of the United States must no longer be forced to depend on English models of good conduct, but needed a literature of their own. As a pioneer writer of children's books she felt she was filling a void.[23]

This first of Maria's writings for children comprises a series of educational conversations between Aunt Maria and two children, Robert and Lucy. Here can be found discussions of history and literature, slaves and Indians, botany and other sciences. Stories and fables illuminate the lessons Aunt Maria is teaching, and when Lucy complains that history is boring and that all she remembers is "a jumble of battles and revolutions,—of kings murdered and princes poisoned," her aunt suggests that she has not been studying properly and that after reading about the reign of a particular king or queen she should then read a novel or play immediately connected with it. "By this means you will no longer feel as if you had only *heard* of the characters, but as if you had actually *seen* and *talked* with them."[24] Maria Francis had not forgotten the profound impression literature had made on her as a young girl, how deeply she had felt every passion portrayed by Homer, how the vividness of Walter Scott's descriptions had brought the wild Scottish landscape into the room in which she sat.

When Lucy reminds Aunt Maria that many people consider it "wicked to read novels and plays," her aunt replies, "It is, no doubt, wrong to read such books very frequently,—and very unprofitable to read them at all, without much discrimination; but everything is valuable according to its *use*; and when the lighter kinds of reading serve to impress something more valuable upon our minds, they answer an exceedingly good purpose."[25]

In this passage Maria conveniently draws a veil over her own childhood passion for reading everything that came her way and gives lip service instead to the received wisdom of the day that literature's only justified function was to instruct. As a contemporary expressed it, the first aim of fiction was "to present models of good conduct for imitation and bad examples to be shunned, to explain and enforce the highest principles of moral duty." Maria was learning how to write what would sell, and her published views on the function of children's literature would change very little over the years. In 1873 she wrote the then popular poet Lucy

Larcom that stories for children "should be written with a view to bring the moral emotions into *activity*; such emotions as tenderness towards the aged, kindness towards animals, compassion for the poor and suffering, brotherly feeling towards all races of men, and all religions."[26]

"Brotherly feeling towards all races of men" is also a theme in *Evenings in New England.* Here Maria's early views on the slavery question are first revealed. In a conversation between Robert and his Aunt Maria, the boy begins the discussion by observing that Southerners "must be very cruel or they would not keep slaves as they do." Aunt Maria, instead of agreeing, scolds him for being "very unjust:"

> Every man who possesses any national pride must indeed regret that the indelible stain of slavery is fastened upon our country; and every one that has a single particle of human kindness could not but rejoice to see the Africans released from a state of servitude and oppression. But it is not right to conclude that our southern brethren have not as good feelings as ourselves, merely because they keep slaves. . . . I regard slavery rather as their misfortune than their fault. Many of their best men would gladly be rid of it; and some time or other, I have no doubt they will.[27]

Aunt Maria's guarded little speech concludes by cautioning her nephew that the great evil of slavery is too fixed a habit to be done away with easily. She expresses the hope, however, that someday Southerners will come to scorn slave labor and accept only those services "such as freemen render to freemen for honorable hire."[28] No objections appear to have been raised to this moderate denunciation of slavery by the author of *Hobomok.* The views Aunt Maria expressed conformed to the prevailing view among Northerners, who regarded the institution as deplorable but insisted it was a Southern problem.

Meanwhile, *The Rebels*, published in 1825, centered on Boston before the Revolution. Like many second novels, it was overambitious. Unfocused and unconvincing as a piece of historical fiction, the book was not a favorite with critics. The *North American Review* depicted the author as overwhelmed by "the richness of her inventive powers" and accused her of crowding "into a short volume, a sufficient quantity of incidents to form the ground work of half a dozen novels."[29] Yet in the public mind her gifts as a historian were powerful enough for two imaginary speeches, one by George Whitfield, the evangelical preacher, the other by James Otis, the patriot, to find their way into school readers where they were memorized by young scholars as genuine pieces of revolutionary eloquence.

Much as *Hobomok* sees early Puritan history through the eyes of the women settlers, *The Rebels* observes prerevolutionary Boston from the perspective of two woman patriots, Grace Osborne and Lucretia Fitzherbert. Grace, true to her name, is a gently pious and virtuous young woman, who normally shuns all talk of politics but is forced to admit that "in these times" it is fitting that women should act. "If John Dudley and all the honest farmers in the country, can refrain from mutton," Grace declares in a fit of feminine revolutionary fervor, "I surely can dispense with the petty luxury of tea."[30]

But the truly free spirit in this story is the impetuous, imaginative Lucretia, who like her creator "possessed a large share of that freedom of thought, that boldness of investigation, which renders exalted talents a peculiarly dangerous gift." Lucretia makes the great mistake of glorifying such brilliance in herself and others, heedless of whether or not "it stood on the firm pedestal of virtue." Upon discovering she is the heiress to a large English fortune, Lucretia is easily taken in by fortune-hunters' flattery. Fortunately for this bedazzled heroine, at the end of the book she discovers to her dismay that she is not a child of privilege but rather the granddaughter of a lowborn witch. Not only does Lucretia (now Gertrude Wilson) survive the "fiery trials" which accompany this dismaying revelation, but she learns to place her hopes of happiness on a firm foundation and is rewarded with marriage to Grace Osborne's virtuous and cultivated brother, Henry, who had long loved her.[31]

Perhaps because of *The Rebels'* poor reception from critics and the reading public, Maria would not publish another novel for ten years. Her efforts to stay solvent through her writing were proving more difficult than she had anticipated. Receipts from the sale of her books were modest, thanks in part to the primitive state of the American publishing industry. Unsophisticated marketing techniques and distribution hampered by limited and hazardous transportation meant that books published in Boston were not likely to be available outside the regional market served by local booksellers. Furthermore, publishers did little to push sales; authors were expected to promote their own books. Maria's eagerness to have George Ticknor endorse *Hobomok* was simply smart business practice. Added to these difficulties were those faced by women writers, who were not only treated as curiosities but were also often badly underpaid by their publishers.[32]

In the summer of 1826 Maria returned to Watertown to live with Convers and Abby. There, in an effort to augment her income, she and a friend, Martha Robbins, opened a school for the older girls of the town, offering them lessons in French, drawing, and gentle manners. The expenses incurred by spending a winter in Boston had proved too great for Maria's small budget, but she wrote Mary Preston that she was not looking forward to the prospect of moving back into the Watertown parsonage: "I do not like it, very much; but this winter's campaign has cost me a good deal, and I must earn something immediately. . . . Relations ought never to live together, unless they keep debt and credit like strangers." The truth of the matter was that Maria was not getting along very well with her sister-in-law. Abby "is jealous of every compliment paid to my talents, of every attention I receive, even from my brother," she told Mary.[33]

By the fall of 1826 Maria was too busy to give much thought to the hazards of being a celebrity. She now spent six hours of every day in her Watertown school. In addition to her teaching duties she had agreed to edit a new periodical designed especially for children. She wrote Mary that two publishers had asked her to undertake the work and she had refused, but in the end "some Boston ladies finally persuaded me into it." Who the Boston ladies were she does not say, but *The Juvenile Miscellany*, the first children's magazine to be published in the United States, proved both popular and lucrative. The first number came out in September 1826, a paperbound volume measuring three inches by five, its hundred or so pages of text relieved now and again by a modest engraving. In less than five months the little bimonthly had eight hundred and fifty subscribers, and Maria could count on a small but steady income from its sale. "Children's books are more profitable than any others," she wrote Mary, "and I am American enough to prefer money to fame—Especially as I having [sic] reasonable prospects of being always single."[34]

One subscriber to the *Miscellany* later remembered the eagerness with which she and her friends awaited delivery of the latest issue: "The children sat on the stone steps of their house doors (including the author) all the way up and down Chestnut Street in Boston, waiting for the carrier (it always came on Saturday). He used to cross the street, going from door to door in zig zag fashion; and the fortunate possessor of the first copy found a crowd of little ones hanging over her shoulder from the steps above."[35]

The early issues of the *Miscellany* include stories and poems, history and biography, puzzles and conundrums. Here are happy tales recalling the simple pleasures of Maria's years in Maine, including descriptions of the Indians she came to know there. Here also are fairy tales, thought at the time to hinder moral growth. Stories describing the miseries suffered by the idle rich are set off by tales of thrifty, industrious poor children who achieve both prosperity and happiness. In her introduction to the first issue Maria spoke of the "anxious tenderness" she felt concerning the education, the temper, and the morals of the children she saw around her. "Yes," she insists, "children can act from good principle, as well as gentlemen and ladies." As in *Evenings in New England*, Maria was anxious not simply to amuse her young readers but to educate them, to teach them how to be good as well as happy, to be honest and generous as well as successful.[36]

The Juvenile Miscellany, and *Evenings in New England*, like all the children's literature of the time, were strongly didactic in tone. Catharine Sedgwick voiced a widespread concern when she declared it to be a truth "that cannot be too assiduously taught" that "the safety of the republic depends on the virtue of the people."[37] Americans of the day mixed an exaggerated hope in the young nation's democratic future with an anxiety about the prevalence of lawlessness, ignorance, and immorality among their fellow citizens. It followed naturally that an obvious way to counteract the dangers and encourage the virtues of the republic was through the education of its children.

The education of children absorbed most of Maria's time and talents. Subscriptions to the *Miscellany* continued to grow, and the school in Watertown prospered. It is not known what salary she received for her teaching, but she could now count on $300 a year as editor of the *Miscellany*, as well as additional income from her other writings. For a woman trying to make a living on her own she was managing very well. Maria's friendships prospered also. When she moved back to Watertown in 1826 she had feared that the rich and fashionable world would confine her to oblivion. But to her surprise her Boston friends continued to be as attentive as ever.[38]

Meanwhile she made new friends in Cambridge as well. One of these was the young Margaret Fuller, whose intellect would someday challenge the best minds of New England. In 1826, when the two met, Margaret was only sixteen, a plump and awkward adolescent with a breadth of learning that was extraordinary for a young woman at that time. She had just returned from two years in a seminary in Groton and was living in her father's house in Cambridge, devoting her days to the study of language and literature. Margaret was delighted to discover another woman who shared her zeal for learning. In the winter of 1827 she wrote an old teacher that she and Maria Francis were thinking of reading Locke "as an introductory to a course of English metaphysics" and of following that with Mme de Staël's *De l'Allemagne*. Margaret then expressed her delight in her new friend, "this most interesting woman," Maria Francis: "She is a natural person,—a most rare thing in this age of cant and pretension. Her conversation is charming,—she brings all her power to bear upon it; her style is varied, and she has a very pleasant and spirited way of thinking. I should judge, too, that she possesses peculiar purity of mind."[39]

This description of Maria Francis is one of the few which survive from these brief, mostly happy years when she was an independent and successful young author, editor, and schoolteacher. There is another, written nearly twenty years later by her Medford friend, Lucy Osgood, who upon reading Maria's recently published *Letters from New York* was surprised to discover "that the L.M. Francis of 1826 is the identical L.M. Child of 1843—the editor of the Anti-Slavery Standard, Madame Canda's pupil, and the youthful schoolmistress of Watertown, making baskets for May day; brushing the morning dew, & writing poetical compliments to accompany her flowers, are but one & the same person; with the same aspirations after good, the same impatience of wrong, the same independence, originality & honesty."[40]

Maria's "Knight of Chivalry"

Domestic love is the only rose we have left of paradise.
—*Lydia Maria Child*, Good Wives

O ne evening in early December 1824, Convers and Abby Francis invited the nephew of a Watertown lawyer and neighbor to dine with them at the parsonage. David Lee Child had been two classes below Convers at Harvard. Now a kindly, ascetically handsome man of thirty, he had recently returned from abroad after taking part in the Spanish army's abortive 1823 rebellion against the incompetent rule of King Ferdinand VII. David had a way of attaching himself to ill-fated noble schemes. When asked why he had supported this failed revolution, he spoke of his duty to secure and defend liberty. At this first meeting, Maria was aware only of David's intelligence, idealism, and lack of conceit, characteristics which endeared him to her from the start. Since his return from Spain, he had taken up the study of law with his uncle, Tyler Bigelow, and no doubt dreamed of serving his own country with the same romantic fervor he had given the Spanish rebels. The conversation that evening centered on Europe. When David spoke of the slow advance of technology in Spain and Italy, Maria was surprised to learn that Italian farmers still used the very plows Virgil had described. She was impressed by the immense store of knowledge David had acquired in the course of his travels and even more by his lack of what she referred to as "the traveler's vanity."[1]

Six weeks later Maria was invited to meet David again by her friend and neighbor Lois Curtis. Mrs. Curtis was a widow with two

61

sons. The younger of the boys, George, was only twelve at the time but later recalled that David Child and Maria Francis met frequently at his mother's house. After this second meeting in late January 1825, Maria confided to her diary that David Child was "the most gallant man that has lived since the sixteenth century and needs nothing but helmet, shield, and chain armor to make him a complete knight of chivalry." Four months later she couldn't decide which to admire more, the "vigor of his understanding or the ready sparkle of his wit."[2]

David in turn was thoroughly enchanted with the "ethereal, high-souled-high-reaching" Maria Francis, and confided to his journal that he knew of "no mind with which it seems to me my soul could hold such sweet converse as with the elegant, susceptible, sweet and brilliant spirit which animate the form of Maria. I could love her dearly if the fates were not averse to it. She is the only lady in Watertown who has made any impression on me of a serious and enduring kind i.e. to say of *a tender kind.*"[3]

If Maria Francis and David Child were already in love they did their best to hide it. Young George Curtis, observing the behavior of the couple and listening to their mutual teasing and criticism, was convinced they disliked one another. Wiser observers, however, were less easily deceived, including George's maiden aunt, who pronounced prophetically, "Those two people will end by marrying."[4]

David's reluctance to show his true feelings for Maria probably reflected sincere doubts that he could win such a successful and independent woman for his wife. Maria, for her part, had good reason to question the wisdom of such a match. Attracted though she was by David's apparent goodness and intelligence, she must have wondered why this man of thirty had yet to settle into a proper career. Among his friends, Child was respected for his learning, for his fluency in several languages, including Latin and Greek, as well as for his thorough understanding of American politics, history, and law. But those who knew him well would not have praised him for his good sense. On the contrary, they would have described him as both vague and hopelessly impractical, qualities which might have been dismissed as humorous if they had not so often proved his undoing. He was one of those people who never seem to learn from their mistakes but take up one quixotic scheme after another with unbounded enthusiasm.

In addition to any doubts she may have had about David as a prospective husband, Maria must also have questioned her own readiness for marriage. Having successfully carved out a literary career for herself, did she really want to give up this independence for a life of domesticity? If she planned to defy convention, which decreed that once married a woman must renounce all other professions and remain in her husband's shadow, she was nonetheless very conscious of the demands which marriage entailed. The years spent with the Prestons in Norridgewock had exposed her to the endless labor which was the housewife's lot. Until there were children to care for, she might have a few hours each day to write and continue editing the *Miscellany*, but once the babies started arriving there would be little time for her own pursuits.

However, while marriage might mean the loss of the independence Maria sought, it also promised a haven from her anomalous and often uncomfortable position as a self-supporting woman writer. Her youthful dream of herself as a woman of genius invading the high masculine realm of literary culture had proved illusory. Like the heroine of her story "Harriet Bruce," she had found herself treated as less than a woman yet not a man. She would later describe the "social atmosphere" of places like Beacon Street as pressing "heavily upon women," inhibiting the development of their faculties and feelings.[5]

Marriage to David, who, unlike most of the men she had met, was enamored of her mind as well as her person, would enable her to escape the "constrained elegancies of Beacon Street." But more importantly it would also satisfy a deep craving for affection; Maria now found herself having to decide which mattered most: her longing for independence or her longing for love. The mock battles witnessed by George Curtis, his mother, and maiden aunt in their Cambridge parlor, like those of Beatrice and Benedick in Shakespeare's *Much Ado About Nothing*, probably reflected more accurately a war Maria was fighting with herself than any dislike she bore for David Lee Child.[6]

Maria was given plenty of time to ponder the possible loss of her independence. David was an inveterate procrastinator, and two years passed before he asked her to be his wife. Meanwhile he completed his law apprenticeship and began to carve out a career in politics. Maria probably heard about the ardently patriotic address David gave in Watertown on March 4, 1825, at a dinner honoring the inauguration of President John Quincy Adams. David's speech glowed with admiration for the new president. Noting "the pictures fancy has drawn" of the nation's "growing greatness and accumulating glory," he assured his fellow dinner guests that with Adams in the White House those dreams had become a "substantial and almost miraculous reality."[7]

As a recognized supporter of John Quincy Adams and the National Republicans, David was chosen to edit the *Massachusetts Journal*, a triweekly newspaper supported by such distinguished Bay State politicians as Daniel Webster and Edward Everett. The editorship had already been turned down by Caleb Cushing, a Harvard classmate of David's with political aspirations. Cushing was wisely apprehensive about the financial risks he would have had to assume as both editor and proprietor of the newspaper. But David Child, undaunted by such pecuniary responsibilities, readily accepted the position.[8]

When regular publication of the *Massachusetts Journal* began in the summer of 1826 the popularity of President John Quincy Adams, never great outside New York and New England, had reached its national nadir. Adams was an old-style politician: intelligent, honest, but diffident and detached. From the start of his administration he had shown himself a strong nationalist, favoring tariffs and internal improvements to facilitate industry and commerce. With the air of a haughty aristocrat he had set about molding the nation to his own design, hoping to infuse it with a strong moral purpose. But if Adams' intentions were good, his tactics failed miserably, and during the off-year elections of 1826 the administration was soundly defeated by the opposition, which won control of both houses of Congress and a majority of the state governments.

The leader of this opposition was Andrew Jackson, the hero of the Battle of New Orleans and a new kind of politician. Imperious, adventurous, and ambitious for power, Jackson possessed a charisma which, in keeping with the nationalistic fervor of the age, appealed to a broadened electorate in search of new idols. His political (as opposed to military) career was so far undistinguished, but, unlike Adams, he saw himself as a party leader, and his convictions were elastic enough to appeal to voters in different sections of the country. Nonetheless, in Massachusetts, where Federalists and Republicans had formed a broad "union" coalition behind the Adams administration, support for Jackson was scattered and insignificant. His common touch, more representative of the New England frontier, was repellant to New England aristocrats. As editor of the *Massachusetts Journal*, David Child made little effort to hide his aristocratic sympathies or his scorn, not only for Jackson, whom he denounced as a political demagogue, but for the growing partisan spirit which he saw emerging in support of the hero of New Orleans.[9]

On October 19, 1826, David wrote an editorial defending his paper's political stand. "We believe the present administration is too strong in honesty, ability, and in the confidence and attachment of the people, to need the services of political *Hotspurs,*—of men who swear fealty to a patron and protector, and devote themselves soul and body to his cause, right or wrong." David feared above all that the tendencies of societies and governments to focus on people and parties rather than on principles and conduct would lead to despotism.[10]

Apparently Daniel Webster was pleased enough with the tone of the *Massachusetts Journal* to recommend it to his friends, and for the time being at least the paper prospered. Meanwhile David was elected a member of the Massachusetts General Assembly. Thanks to his reputation as a firm administration supporter he was asked in April 1827 to address a meeting in Fanueil Hall in support of a union ticket favoring Adams over Andrew Jackson in the election of 1828. William Lloyd Garrison, then editor of the Newburyport *Free Press*, was among those who heard David denounce the Jacksonians. While Garrison praised the "strong and pungent language" of the speech, he couldn't help remarking on the "harsh and stubborn" manner of the delivery, on the way David's voice, when raised, grated painfully on the ear. Nevertheless, Garrison praised his fellow editor for his "candor, good sense and sterling independence." David's prospects as a rising young politician, while perhaps not brilliant, were at least promising. By the fall of 1827 he had completed his law studies, won a seat in the Massachusetts House, joined the Masons, and was the respected editor of a political journal. David's future at last seemed secure, secure enough to ask Maria Francis to be his wife.[11]

Accounts differ as to the exact manner in which David pressed his suit. According to an excerpt from David's journal later copied by Maria, he proposed by letter and was accepted by return mail. However, George Curtis' version of the proposal seems more in character. Maria was staying with the Curtises, who had recently moved to Cambridge from Watertown, when David's letter arrived in the mail. George, whose interest in the behavior of the two lovers had not slackened, remembered that David's letter had not produced the desired response. Not one to be easily discouraged, the rejected suitor had decided to try persuasion in person. One evening David rode out from Boston on horseback. Having tied his horse by the reins to a post at the bottom of the Curtises' front steps, he was admitted to the house where he found Maria waiting for him in the parlor. Lois Curtis had tactfully retired upstairs and ordered her son George, then fifteen, to go to bed also. But George had been observing the progress of this romance for two years and was not going to miss out on the denouement. Settling himself in the upstairs hall he could imagine the gist of the conversation taking place behind the parlor door. "The lady was a long time in making up her mind," he later recalled. Hours passed and David's horse impatiently stamped his feet on the wooden steps to gain his master's attention. Once or twice David emerged from the parlor to pacify the animal. Finally as the clock struck one David came out for the last time. As the sound of the horse's hooves died away Maria rushed upstairs to tell Mrs. Curtis that she was engaged to marry Mr. Child.[12]

In a letter to Mary Preston telling of her engagement, Maria described the cloak of witty disputation which she and David had manufactured to disguise their true feelings. "We have both been playing hide and seek, for various idle reasons," she confessed, "but it is all over now,—and I am happier than ever any woman was in reciprocated affection."[13]

David could hardly believe his good fortune and wrote his mother describing himself as "the luckiest dog that ever lived" and Maria as "one of the brightest and best of beings . . . who possesses the intellect of Johnson, the goodness and learning of Lady Jane Gray; and the gentleness and attractions of Aspasia." With characteristic vagueness he almost forgot to mention his fiancée's name, tagging it on to the letter in a postscript.[14]

Unfortunately, Maria's father did not share her enthusiasm over her choice of a husband. Word must have reached Convers Francis that David Child was not a promising breadwinner, for he warned Maria that her fiancé's effectiveness with respect to business matters was about equal to "cutting stones with a razor." Maria's father would also have been disturbed by what he learned of David's upbringing. His parents, Zachariah and Lydia Child, had raised their twelve children on a hardscrabble farm in the village of West Boylston, northeast of Worcester. Unlike Convers Francis, who had worked his way from poverty to relative affluence through hard manual labor, Zachariah Child had paid little attention to the business of earning a living, preferring to devote his time to intellectual matters. With his head in the clouds he spent his whole life struggling ineffectively against financial difficulties. His wife, Lydia, was an educated woman from a prominent Worcester family, the Bigelows, but with twelve children, an improvident husband, and a house and farm to care for, she would have had little leisure for reading. Basic necessities were often lacking in the Child household, including water, which David and his brothers and sisters would be sent to the neighbors' to fetch, lugging it back across the fields in great heavy pails.[15]

Of all the children David was apparently the most like his father. His powers of concentration were legendary among family and friends. He would become so absorbed by whatever he was doing that he would forget to eat or sleep. This fixed attentiveness was matched by a fierce stubbornness which made him reckless, even foolhardy, in pursuit of whatever object was at hand. Like a horse wearing blinders, he saw neither to the right nor to the left and, undaunted by obstacles of any sort, he was constantly getting himself into scrapes. His mother worried about him even after he was grown. In 1819, when David had turned twenty-five and was teaching at the Boston Latin School, she received a letter from a Mr. Noah implying that her son was incapable of taking care of himself. She urged David to return home to West Boylston where she could keep an eye on him, but he spurned her counsel, declaring firmly that "hitherto my fortune has been of my own making, I expect it will be so hereafter. I ought therefore to be as free from interference and dictation of pretended friends as any man whatever. . . . Permit me only to say, that I can never be called home and put under the wing to keep me out of danger."[16]

David's recklessness was particularly evident when it came to money. What little he was given or earned disappeared as quickly as it reached his pocket. At age thirty he was still writing home for funds to pay his room and board, unconscious of the inappropriateness of a grown able-bodied son begging financial assistance from impoverished and elderly parents. In one letter to Zachariah he expressed the wish that after his father had provided "for the comfort of Mother and yourself & sisters my wants may rank next and be attended to *for all my old debts*."[17]

The prospect of a daughter marrying such an improvident, impractical man as David Child would have been disturbing to any sensible father, but for Convers Francis it was an unmitigated disaster. The Medford baker had never had much faith in book learning as a profession, and here was Maria engaged to this visionary who could speak untold languages and quote the classics but who had not the faintest notion how to keep bread on the table for himself, much less for a wife. It mattered little to the elder Convers that Maria's proven practicality and self-reliance more than made up for her fiancé's failings in that regard. Once the two started a family his daughter would find little if any time for writing. Furthermore, in an age when a wife's property legally belonged to her husband, she would certainly be at the mercy of David Child's capriciousness, if not of his avariciousness.

If Convers Francis' objections to his daughter's choice of a husband raised doubts in her own mind there is no record of it. Maria was as stubborn as her father; the very fact that he opposed the match would have made her more determined than ever to go through with it. Yet for all David's deficiencies as a breadwinner, he was in many respects a happy choice for Maria. Most men of the time expected their future wives to be docile and domestic. David, by contrast, spoke admiringly of Maria's talents and success as a writer. Before their engagement he had included flattering reviews of her books and published some of her stories in the columns of the *Massachusetts Journal*. The *Juvenile Miscellany* was recommended "to all parents who wish their children to cultivate virtuous principles, kind feelings and useful knowledge." On April 5, 1827, he proudly announced that "L. M. Francis of Watertown had won a Gold Medal valued at $20, for an 'Essay on the Cultivation of the Intellect.' " Learned women were no threat to David Child. At least so he convinced his Maria.[18]

But what endeared David to Maria far more than his support for her writing career were his idealism, kindly intentions, and affectionate endearments. At last she had found someone who would cherish her as she had never before been cherished, a large-souled man who would prove a moral anchor and a spiritual refuge. These qualities, for a young woman in love, seemed a sure guarantee of future happiness.

David and Maria were engaged for over a year, during which time she continued to write stories and edit the *Miscellany*. Soon after the engagement was announced she moved into Boston to Madame Canda's, which was conveniently located just up the street from David's own boarding house. In December she and David went to West Boylston so she could meet his family. Maria became particularly intimate with David's invalid sister, Lydia, with whom she conducted a regular correspondence about books, sewing projects, and home remedies.

All proceeded smoothly with plans for an October wedding, until the spring of 1828 when David and his newspaper were plunged into serious legal and financial difficulties. Two libel suits were brought against David as editor of the *Journal*, the first of which concerned an overseer at the Massachusetts State prison whom David had charged with fraud. The second suit was brought by a Jacksonian state senator from Concord named John Keyes who was running for reelection. In an editorial published on March 29, 1828, David had accused Keyes of agreeing to the illegal employment of an avowedly Jacksonian firm as state printer.[19]

An equally serious problem for David was the financial health of his newspaper. On June 24, 1828, a letter signed by such eminent Boston merchants and industrialists as Thomas Handasyd Perkins and Abbott Lawrence was published in the *Journal* urging support and encouragement for the paper from its readers. Citing the editor's "upright and undeviating course," and praising Child for his "zeal," "talents," and "honest patriotism," they defended his muckraking, claiming that no "republic can flourish without a constant reference to the political character of those who aspire to office." This was simply the first of several efforts to rescue the *Journal* and keep it afloat. The only problem was that, since David was the sole proprietor of the paper, the debts were his responsibility to repay. By the end of 1828 David was at least $15,000 in arrears, owing money to a whole assortment of people, including Daniel Webster, Abbott Lawrence, and the richest man in Massachusetts, Peter Brooks. Even his prospective father-in-law, Convers Francis, had generously contributed $1000.[20]

No fiscal records of the *Journal* explaining its financial troubles have survived. But David's notorious lack of business sense probably contributed. When he broke the news to Maria she temporarily convinced him to put off their marriage at least until the following spring. But he soon brought her round to agreeing to an October wedding. Maria wrote her future sister-in-law, Lydia, that she was reluctant to start married life in a boardinghouse but would do so if necessary. She described David as "working like a very carthorse," but observed that his heart was "perilously open to good and pure influences." She feared that in his desire to "relieve all the distress in the world" he had "done himself wrong." "I love him the better for it," she assured Lydia, "but it makes me look forward to the expenses of housekeeping with anxiety and fear."[21]

Lydia Maria Francis and David Lee Child were married in Watertown at eight o'clock in the evening on Sunday, October 19, 1828. Maria had purchased thirty-five pounds of cake for the occasion, enough to feed a large number of wedding guests, and she hired a dressmaker to provide her with a gown of India muslin trimmed with white satin. David's niece Clarissa Bigelow was the only bridesmaid.

After the wedding the Childs drove to a tiny house they had rented on Harvard Street in Boston. "A proper little martin box, furnished with very plain gentility," was the way Maria described her new home to her sister Mary, who had been unable to make the long journey from Maine for the festivities. The spare furnishings, which Maria had purchased with money saved from her earnings, were enhanced by a number of wedding presents, including a pair of silver-plated candlesticks and another of stellar lamps. Young George Curtis was among the first guests whom the couple entertained, and he remembered that Maria produced a very frugal meal of mutton pie, baked potatoes, and Indian pudding. The only drink provided was plain water. Such, according to Curtis, "was the beginning of the married life of a woman of genius."[22]

6

"Le Paradis des Pauvres"

*Since vice and folly are sometimes triumphant in
this world, and goodness is sometimes depressed,
we should learn to look for reward where alone it
is always certain to be found—within our own
hearts.*

—*Lydia Maria Child,*
"The Bold and Beautiful Convict"

ompany,—company,—company,—all the time; and domestics changed three times!" was the way Maria Child described the first weeks of her married life in November
1828. She was finding little time to write and even less time to read
but hoped that things would settle down now that their friends had
"most done coming ceremoniously." David left early each morning
either for the office of the *Massachusetts Journal* at 34 Congress
Street or for his law office on Court Street, often not returning
until nine o'clock at night. Meanwhile, Maria was discovering the
difficulties of pursuing her career amid household demands. "Literary women are not usually domestic," she would write in 1831,
"not because they cannot easily be so—but because they early acquired the habit of attending to literary things, and of neglecting
others." As a boarder at Mme Canda's she had been free to spend
hours over her writing and her books, but now all the washing,
cleaning, ironing, sewing, cooking, and baking were her responsibility. The Childs' meager budget only allowed for the cheapest
household help: either a single girl or an elderly widow, whose sole
compensation was room and board. For the time being, however,
Maria tried to be cheerful about her new life, assuring her mother-
in-law that she was "as willing to be useful in one way as in another."[1]
Meanwhile, David's affairs appeared to be prospering. Political

71

allies praised his editorship of the *Massachusetts Journal*, while friends assured him that the Keyes libel suit would be decided in his favor. The only cloud on the horizon was the all but certain prospect of a Jackson victory in the upcoming presidential election. Maria apparently shared David's distrust of the Democratic candidate, regarding him as little more than a demagogue bent on hoodwinking the people. She refused to believe that the American electorate was "corrupt enough to choose by fair and honest votes, such a blot on humanity as Andrew Jackson." Nonetheless, by November 18, two weeks after the election, Jackson's victory seemed certain. David was forced to admit reluctantly in the *Journal* that "the People" were defeated.[2]

By January the Childs' frugal honeymoon in their little "martin box" on Harvard Street, a short block from Boston Harbor, was over. Despite all her household economies Maria was not managing to make ends meet. She had thought that her income from the *Miscellany* plus David's earnings would be sufficient to cover their expenses. Now she discovered to her shock and dismay that David was mired in financial difficulties, some stemming from poor investments, others from a vast array of old debts, still others from the legal fees connected with his pending libel suits. Even if David won his case with Keyes, legal fees would cost him $300, a sizable portion of their expected yearly income. Maria wrote her sister-in-law that she was trying "to be as saving as possible—I certainly have denied myself every superfluity, I have dropped *all* my acquaintance. I neither visit, nor receive visits. . . . It seems queer to me,—I used to go about so much, but after all I am happier than I ever was," she added, trying to put a good face on things.[3]

Maria was discovering how quickly the freedom and independence she had known and cherished as a single woman could evaporate. As David's wife neither her time, her money, nor her person were her own. When she married she had not only taken David's name but had accepted his legal and financial protection as well. Like other nineteenth-century wives her identity was now subsumed in her husband's. Her personal property, including her earnings from her writings and the clothes on her back, were now legally his. She could neither sue nor be sued; nor could she sign a contract or a will without David's consent.

Yet from the start of their marriage David proved incapable of providing even for his own welfare, and Maria quickly learned she must play the role of breadwinner as well as wife. In later life she claimed that almost from the beginning she had paid all the household expenses from her own earnings. Meanwhile, David made full use not only of his wife's money but of her literary talents. Maria often contributed stories and articles to the *Massachusetts Journal.* Three months after the wedding she began editing a literary column for the paper.[4]

Then, on January 12, 1829, David was arraigned before the Supreme Judicial Court of Massachusetts, charged with publishing a "false, scandalous and malicious libel" against State Senator John Keyes. Unfortunately for David, the judge presiding over the trial, Marcus Morton, was a firm supporter of the Jacksonian Republicans. A champion of the underdog, Judge Morton, who had twice been put forward as a candidate for governor, was convinced that democracy's archenemy was the "powerful monied aristocracy." "The danger most to be feared," he had written his friend in Washington, John C. Calhoun, "is the encroachment by the powerful upon the weak—by the rich upon the poor."[5]

Morton made no secret of his partisan sympathies, and from a political point of view David Child, the editor of an opposition newspaper endorsed by powerful Boston industrialists, was on the side of the enemy, the rich. Nor is it likely that the Jacksonian judge entertained much sympathy for David Child's brand of detached elitism, which claimed to be opposed to political parties while engaging in the most blatantly partisan attacks on supposed political enemies.

The trial lasted for three days and was of particular interest to newspaper editors for its treatment of the libel issue and the larger question of freedom of the press. The defense based its case on two grounds. First, that David's charge was substantially true, that Senator Keyes, as a member of the Legislative Committee of Accounts, had agreed to employ True & Greene as state printers even though their bid for the job was $500 higher than anyone else's. Second, that even if the charge were not true, "it was published without malice, from good motives and justifiable ends." The defendant, having received his information from a reliable source, had every reason to believe his accusation was well-founded.[6]

The prosecution took a different view. David L. Child was presented to the jury as a man of "malicious disposition who had wickedly intended to injure and vilify the good name, [and] fame" of John Keyes. According to the prosecution lawyer, all that was needed to convict the defendant of libel was to prove the falsehood of his charge. Malice, and therefore libel, was to be inferred from the falsehood itself.[7]

Judge Morton, in his final summation of the case to the jury on January 15, agreed with the prosecution that "if the defendant fails to establish the truth of his charge, he fails in his defense." But he went even further and insisted that the defense had to prove not simply that Keyes had used favoritism in his application of public funds but that he had done so in a deliberately corrupt manner. Morton could find little evidence of such corrupt conduct from the trial. Therefore the publication was false and libelous. The jury heeded Morton's advice and returned the following morning with a verdict of guilty. David was sentenced to prison but obtained a temporary reprieve by appealing the decision to the state supreme court.[8]

A verdict of guilty was also prescribed in the libel suit brought against David by Samuel R. Johnson, a supervisor of the stone-cutting department of the Massachusetts state prison, whom he had accused of fraud. This second trial took place only four days after the first, and David escaped with a modest fine of $25. Despite these judgments against him and consequent loss of time and money, David made it clear in the columns of his paper that he was not going to be browbeaten into silence by his political enemies. In an article published on January 29, 1829, he assured his readers that "the mere *name* and *proclamation* of libel *actions* and *indictment*" would not put down his paper.[9]

Among some Bostonians David was fast earning the sobriquet David L(ibel) Child. But a good many editors, decrying particularly the decision in the Keyes case, rallied to his side. The Boston *Advertiser* summed up their objections:

> We care not how strictly the publishers of the journals are called to account for any aspersion of the character of individuals, public or private, from a feeling of personal hostility or from mere wantonness and indifference to the injury they do; but when the character and conduct of public officers, and candidates for office, are discussed, the welfare of the public, and the spirit of our government require that a favourable construction should be put on the motives of a publisher, and that he should not be punished where there is no appearance of a malicious intention, and where no injury is done, other than what results from the publication of the truth.[10]

Maria of course agreed with David's supporters that he had done a great service to the state of Massachusetts by his exposure of political fraud and corruption. She too cherished her husband's reputation for "manly, bold and fearless intrepidity."[11] At the same time, however, she was discovering that David's dogged and enthusiastic labors on behalf of noble causes had a way of plunging him further and further into debt. Her money, which he controlled, was fast disappearing.

Added to the costs arising from David's two libel suits were the expenses he incurred in his legal practice. Although he did not complete his law studies with his uncle Tyler Bigelow until the end of 1827 and was not admitted to the Massachusetts bar until 1828, the *Boston Annual Advertiser* for 1826 lists David L. Child as a legal counselor sharing an office with Sherman Leland at 93 Court Street. David brought the same fearless intrepidity and impracticality to his legal career that he applied to all his other endeavors. Commercial law, which would have netted him a decent income and helped pay off his mounting debts, held no interest for him. Instead he used his talents defending the derelict and downtrodden, often refusing to send bills to his poorer clients.[12]

Soon the future of the *Massachusetts Journal* was again in jeopardy. David's characteristic response to impending failure was to throw himself with greater vigor than ever into his work as editor. He now published three editions of the newspaper: a daily, a triweekly, and a weekly, hoping to gain more subscribers. Unflaggingly optimistic, he seemed unconscious of the precariousness of his finances. In a letter to Daniel Webster on January 3, 1829, David denied that Jackson's election had affected sales of the *Journal*, boasting instead that his thirteen hundred subscribers were "*all good men.*" He made the sanguine prediction that income from the *Journal* would soon exceed expenses and hoped that Webster would continue his support. Only the year before, the senator from Massachusetts had generously lent David over fifteen hundred dollars. But this time he refused further help.[13]

While David remained stubbornly optimistic about the future of his paper, Maria was so anxious she could neither eat nor sleep. She wrote an old friend and supporter of David's, Henry Dearborn, who had also been very generous to the paper, that "with regard to the prospects of the Journal, I have had many wretched hours. It will be a shame, as well as a pity, if such a good paper as that is allowed to go down, while a dozen paltry papers are enabled to stand beside it—and that too, after it has just got well established, after such monstrous labor."[14]

Desperate to find some way to keep the *Journal* afloat and collect some of the money demanded by her husband's creditors, Maria swallowed her pride and asked George Ticknor for "an advance of one thousand dollars on her furniture and books." Contrary to

David's boast to Webster that Jackson's election had not affected sales of the *Journal*, Maria informed Ticknor that two or three hundred subscriptions had been canceled "at the first news of the election." She described the "annoying tricks" resorted to by Jackson's supporters, who teased David's creditors with rumors that the paper was sure to fail.[15]

No record survives of Ticknor's response to Maria's plea for help. Somehow the paper managed to stay afloat. Meanwhile Maria determined to earn as much as possible from her own writing. Given the extent of David's debts there was little likelihood that the few hundred dollars she earned yearly could pay them off, but at least she might stem the tide.

While an effort to bring out a collection of her stories failed, and a book for children describing the subjugation of the Massachusetts Indians, *The First Settlers of New England*, received little notice, Maria did succeed in producing a genuine best-seller in 1829. *The Frugal Housewife*, a compendium of practical advice for women, resembled other domestic manuals of the time in furnishing recipes and remedies and other directives for the householder. Most of the existing manuals, however, were English in origin. In her notice of one such book entitled *Domestic Duties*, Maria complained that "few ladies in this country need to be cautioned against keeping so many servants." Her *Frugal Housewife*, she announced in the pages of the *Journal*, was intended for Americans, and "suited to the common wants of common people."[16]

Maria had obviously drawn much of the practical information found in *The Frugal Housewife* from her own experience. As a young girl in Norridgewock she had been trained by her sister Mary in the many skills required of the New England housewife. Now as a young married woman struggling to make ends meet in the little house on Harvard Street, Maria put these frugal tips to use. What better way to make some extra income than by gathering all this household lore into a small volume and publishing it?

Inside the covers of *The Frugal Housewife* can be found instructions for the care of furniture and clothing, a remedy for exterminating bed bugs, others for dysentery and worms. Such New England staples as rum, molasses, and potash appear frequently in remedies as well as recipes. Maria suggests that pokeroot boiled in water with a good quantity of molasses will kill cockroaches, and she recommends New England rum as an excellent shampoo. A cure for cancer uses potash boiled down to the consistency of molasses and covered with plaster of tar. Until the middle of the nineteenth century, when stoves came into general use, most house-wives continued to prepare food over an open hearth, so in a long section on cooking she recommends boiling or roasting nearly everything from beef to Indian pudding.

But *The Frugal Housewife* was more than a collection of practical tips for the American homemaker. Maria had a moral message as well. "The greatest evil of the day," she declared in her introductory chapter, "is the extravagance of all classes of people. We shall never be prosperous till we make pride and vanity yield to the dictates of honesty and prudence." The underlying cause of this extravagance could, she believed, be traced to the upbringing of American girls, who instead of being told to cherish domestic life as "the gathering place of the deepest and purest affections; as the sphere of woman's *enjoyments* as well as of her *duties*," are taught to look for happiness where it can never be found: "in the absence of all occupation, or the unsatisfactory and ruinous excitement of fashionable competition."[17]

Young girls, instead of being allowed to waste their time dreaming about marriage, should learn to be useful. They should spend two or three years with their mothers helping with the household chores and the care of the other children. *The Frugal Housewife* made it clear that educating a girl at home is far more valuable than sending her to school, where time is wasted "in acquiring the *elements* of a thousand sciences" or "a variety of accomplishments of a very doubtful sort" and "where no feminine employments, no domestic habits can be learned." In one of her children's stories written about this time Maria describes a French girl, entirely educated by her mother, who "could speak Italian as well as she could make pies" and whose "music was as good as her puddings."[18] For Maria the ideal education combined book learning and domestic training.

The Frugal Housewife, written in an era when such occupations as the law and medicine were becoming increasingly professionalized, was an early attempt to raise domesticity to a level of professional competence equal to that of other skilled trades. By stressing the value of intelligent household management Maria Child was showing how women could make a valuable contribution to the well-being of the nation. "Let them prove by the exertion of ingenuity and economy, that neatness, and good taste, and gentility are attainable without great expense." "A republic without industry, economy and integrity," she warned her readers, "is Samson shorn of his locks."[19]

The success of *The Frugal Housewife*—it sold six thousand copies in the first year and ran to thirty-three editions in America, as well as twelve in England and Scotland—showed Maria how profitable it could be to write for the growing American audience of women readers. Her *Mother's Book*, published in 1831, is directed at the same market. Intended as a manual for housewives, it contains advice on rearing children, particularly girls, whose education, as Maria had pointed out in *The Frugal Housewife*, left much to be desired. Recalling her own lonely and unsupervised childhood in Medford, she insists that a girl is much better off under the watchful eye of her mother until her character has been sufficiently molded to withstand worldly temptations and her knowledge of domestic skills sufficiently ingrained to guarantee her proficiency as a housewife. Is the author of *The Mother's Book* forgetting, as she gives this advice, how much her own character has been strengthened by solitude and lack of supervision? Or, as seems more likely, is she writing what she thinks her audience wanted to read?[20]

In her counsel to mothers with marriageable daughters, Maria reveals something of her own difficulties with matrimony. A young woman, she warns, must be prepared realistically for this new state and its "new and arduous duties," for it will likely "form a violent contrast to her previous mode of life." Marriage "should not be entered into, except at a mature age, and with great certainty that affection is strong enough to endure such trials."[21]

Despite all her emphasis on domestic training for girls, Maria does not overlook the need for literary studies. She insists that a love of reading is "the greatest blessing" education can provide a woman. It "cheers so many hours of illness and seclusion" and "gives the mind something to interest itself about, instead of the concerns of one's neighbors and the changes of fashion." The enjoyment of literature also increases the wife's sympathy with an intelligent husband and provides the mother with "materials for furnishing the minds of her children." She even goes so far as to encourage women to study the classics. "I do not mean that they should study Latin and Greek. I merely mean that they should have general information of the government, customs, religion, etc. of the ancients; and the reason I think this is desirable is, that they cannot understand the allusions in good English books without such knowledge."[22]

But Maria is equally strong in warning of the dangers of indiscriminate reading. Girls in particular, she insists, should be guided by their mothers to a love of literature, which springs from a "thirst for information" rather than a "love of pleasing excitement." Presaging modern diatribes against television, Maria warns that too much fiction "tends to destroy a relish for anything more solid, and less exciting." But, perhaps recalling her father's alarm over her own passion for books, she is equally vehement that novels should not be entirely forbidden: "this always produces a fidgetty desire to read them; and unless the principles are very strong, they will be read by stealth."[23]

Among those works which Maria recommends as suitably "pure in spirit and language" for young readers are the novels of Catharine Sedgwick. The author of *Hope Leslie*, a popular historical romance published in 1827, Sedgwick like Maria Child was a pioneer in the movement to forge a native American literature. Combining homely and realistic detail with an overdose of pathos and coincidence, her novels and stories were universally praised for their high moral purpose. She had never planned to become a professional writer, but in 1830, despite her womanly reluctance to obtrude herself "upon the notice of the world," Catharine Sedgwick had the distinction of being the most widely read novelist of her sex in the United States.[24]

In a letter written in the summer of 1830, Sedgwick, doubtless having learned of the great success of *The Frugal Housewife* but not of David's debts, assured Maria, "I have rejoiced in all your prosperity & felt something like an elder sister's interest in you and yours." But the older woman also expressed surprise at her fellow novelist's "condescension" in taking up this "new department of writing" and urged Maria not to abandon the novel, "the department for which the rich gifts of nature so eminently qualify you" and a "fortunate vehicle for the highest communication of one mind to another."[25]

This was not the last time that Maria would be chastised for compromising her literary standards in order to appeal to a wider audience. And while she may have agreed with her friend in Stockbridge that novels were a high form of literary art, she also knew they were risky ventures in the publishing world of the 1820s and 1830s, particularly for women writers. For someone in straitened circumstances like herself, a steadier income could be gained by less ambitious forms of writing, including cookbooks, short pieces for magazines, and contributions to the currently popular annuals and giftbooks. Maria, along with other women novelists of the time, suffered from the stinginess of publishers. This is confirmed by the husband of Caroline Gilman, a popular novelist of the 1830s. "I hear of the booksellers' liberality sometimes," Samuel Gilman wrote in 1838, "but for a popular author, Mrs. G. has experienced as little of it as Child used to."[26]

Maria was also discovering that the "restless, insatiable ambition" she had known at the outset of her literary career had been tempered by financial constraints. As the twenty-two-year-old author of *Hobomok* she had been certain that genius was accessible to all who earnestly sought after it. Now as a matron of twenty-eight she had learned that "the eye may be fastened on the sun but the weary wing can never reach it." Fame no longer had the same power to "kindle" her "into enthusiastic energy." Instead, the cares of the world pressed heavily on her spirit, while the printer's boy stood at her elbow waiting for copy. "We look to the bookseller's accounts for inspiration," she told the readers of the *Journal* in 1830, "hunt for pearls because we have promised to furnish them, and string glass beads because they will sell better than diamonds."[27]

In her search for profitable material, Maria had discovered a new and potentially wide market in the growing audience of literate American women, a group whose numbers doubled between 1790 and 1840. Like writing for children, writing for women was an acceptable endeavor. It conformed to society's image of what women writers were best at and was less likely to encounter the scorn of male literary critics. Furthermore, literature intended for women readers served a real need. "The situation and prospects of a country may be justly estimated by the character of its women," Maria had noted in *The Frugal Housewife*, voicing a belief shared by many Americans since the early years of the republic that the new nation needed citizens, not fashion plates, that women as well as men should learn to be disciplined and self-reliant. During her years of being courted by George Ticknor and his friends, Maria had seen at first hand the lives of leisured, well-to-do women who had few duties and much time to waste. She was extremely critical of what she called the clubbing and social mania among those of her sex and accused them of sacrificing the improvement of themselves and their families to promote association. Nor did she approve of most of the literature directed at women, dismissing it as "flat, stale and unprofitable." Nevertheless, when Sarah Josepha Hale first published her *Ladies' Magazine* in January 1828, Maria praised the new publication for its "good sense, piety, naivete, and honest patriotism."[28]

Although Maria Child's books were selling well—*The Frugal*

Housewife probably netted her $2000 in its first two years of pub-
lication—her earnings failed to keep pace with David's growing
indebtedness. "I have kept thinking the darkest time had come,
and that the clouds must break away," she wrote her sister-in-law
in February 1830, "but still a darker one would come." David's
appeal of the Keyes case had failed and in March he would begin
a term of several months in jail. Meanwhile Maria was desperately
looking for ways to increase their income. She had taken in two
boarders that winter, but this had meant losing precious hours at
her desk. She had even considered opening her own school but
concluded that it would be several years before such a venture
would pay off.[29]

When David went to prison in the spring of 1830, Maria gave
up the house on Harvard Street and moved in with friends. For a
time she boarded in Boston with Emily Marshall's family in Franklin
Place. The Marshalls had always welcomed her, and their generosity
extended to other lengths as well. When, in the winter of 1829,
Maria was too poor to afford any new clothes, Emily saw to it that
she had a pretty and serviceable woolen dress to wear.[30]

Other close friends who were happy to make room for the homeless Childs were Louisa and Ellis Loring, who had a commodious
house in Boston at 671 Washington Street. Ten years younger than
David, Ellis Gray Loring was already launched as a successful young
lawyer. Gentle and amiable, Ellis inspired respect as well as affection. His wife, Louisa, was a witty, generous woman whose company
Maria particularly enjoyed. Once, when the Lorings had left town,
Maria wrote Louisa that she didn't believe she could have missed
anybody so much. "I go past your gate feeling like a poor little
kitten in a deserted house."[31]

Living with friends had the advantage of freeing Maria from
her usual household cares, but she had more than enough work
and worry to fill her time. With David in jail, she was now responsible for the editorship of the *Journal*. She was also expected to
bring her husband his meals. Many years later a neighbor remembered the sight of the celebrated Mrs. Child hurrying down the
street three times each day with David's dinner pail swinging on
her arm.[32]

Despite this cheerful portrait, one can imagine Maria's conflict-
ing emotions as she saw her husband going off to prison: first,
deep sorrow at the thought of David alone behind bars in a dank
cell; second, anger at the unfairness of the sentence; and, finally,
worry about their bleak future. Did she think bitterly of all the

compromises she had had to make to earn more money from her writings? Since David seemed to lose her earnings as fast as they came in, she must have wondered, as she later expressed it, if she wasn't simply pouring water into a sieve. David's fecklessness, his irresponsibility as a breadwinner, his blind refusal to face up to their mounting debts were deeply troubling matters. But perhaps Maria was already learning how pointless it was to dwell on her husband's failings. She knew that in his own way David loved her deeply. He respected her intelligence and took pride in her accomplishments. What other man in Boston would so happily tolerate a literary wife?

In any case Maria had too much work to do to spend much time worrying. Besides her duties at the *Journal*, she had her *Miscellany* to put together. Although no book came out under her name in 1830, she did begin collecting children's games and puzzles for a small volume to be called *The Girl's Own Book*. In addition, she and a number of other prominent Boston matrons, led by Sarah Josepha Hale, had formed a subscription committee to raise funds for a Revolutionary War monument to be erected on the summit of Bunker Hill.[33]

Two months after David went to jail, Maria received an offer to teach in a girl's academy in Dorchester Heights where her father lived. She had never particularly enjoyed teaching, but pecuniary anxieties forced her to accept the position. This time, however, the added responsibility proved too much even for her iron constitution.[34]

When Maria collapsed with exhaustion in July, the Marshalls came to her rescue and sent her off to the seaside to recuperate. Meanwhile, David, having been released from prison, was back on the editorial treadmill. From a farmhouse by the ocean in Lynn, north of Boston, Maria wrote him a funny, loving letter. She told him how much she pined for his kindly affection, his foolish endearments. She doubted if she could stand being separated for a whole week. It was "nonsense," she declared, for her to go "pleasuring" without him. At the same time, however, she was clearly enjoying herself in her rustic surroundings.

> Here I am in a snug little old fashioned parlour, at a round table, in a rocking chair writing to you; and the greatest comfort I have is the pen-knife *you* sharpened for me just before I came away—As you tell *me* sometimes (I don't believe you, though) it makes my heart leap to see anything which you have touched. The house here is real old-fashioned, neat, comfortable, rural and quiet. There is a home-

spun striped carpet, very much like the one at West Boylston,—two profiles over the mantelpiece, one of them a soldier placed in the frame rather one-sided, with a white shirt-ruffle, a white plume, and a white epaulette;—a vase of flowers done in water colours, looking considerable sickly, and straggling about as if they were only neighbors in law;—and Ophelia with a quantity of carroty hair, which must have cost oceans of bear's grease,—(which hair is thrown over three or four rheumatic trees,—) and one foot ankle deep in water, as if she were going to see which she liked best, hanging, or drowning.

While Maria ridiculed the primitive portraits on the parlor walls, the simple, kindly ways of the farmer and his wife delighted her. She told David that the only sign of affectation anywhere on the place was "a hen that sidled up to her [rooster] husband and then ran off in a great fright when he came near." In the quiet of the evening she could hear the sea washing on the beach. Only that morning she had walked down to a little cove, taken off her shoes and stockings and "let the saucy waves come dashing and sparkling" into her lap.[35]

The end of the summer found the Childs back together in Boston, still without a home of their own. Maria continued her writing and editing, and early that fall David made a tour of New England collecting materials for a series of articles on Daniel Webster. He wrote Maria telling her how homesick he was. "I had need to be absent to learn how necessary you are to me. . . . You cannot imagine how often I have thought of your bright and affectionate face looking up so kindly and confidingly in mine. It makes my heart melt and the tears come to think how sweetly you have borne yourself to me in the severe trials which I have brought upon you."[36]

The reality of her own uncertain future was spelled out with ironic clarity in the spring of 1831 when Maria and David were invited to Emily Marshall's wedding. After turning down a succession of eager suitors, Boston's most sought-after belle was marrying William Foster Otis, the son of Mayor Harrison Gray Otis, a man who for many decades had dominated the city's Federalist politics. As Maria stood among the well-dressed Bostonians who filled the Marshalls' parlor on that May evening, listening to them praising Emily for her beauty and unaffectedness as a bride, she surely noted the wide separation which existed between the world which her friend had chosen as the wife of William Otis and her own as the wife of David Child. By marrying David, Maria had indeed removed herself from the suffocating conformity and idle vanity of the rich, fashionable world, but she had also committed herself to a life of poverty, with little time to pursue her literary ambitions.

Several weeks after the wedding Maria wrote her mother-in-law that David was "in a perpetual drive making speeches, reports, etc." In this same letter she spoke of her longing to be a mother; although she admitted this was more "for my husband's sake, than for my own." With suspicious candor she described being "a little fidgety, because I want to go into housekeeping so much, . . . but when I fidget my husband only looks sad and says, 'It *is* a shame such a good creature as you can't have everything you want.' "[37]

If Maria resented this remark from the husband she was doing her best to support, she made no mention of it. As for children, while she naturally yearned for them, she must also have wondered how she could possibly take care of even one baby when she and David couldn't keep a roof over their own heads. Still, the couple's continued barrenness was troubling. Years later Maria spoke of the "childlike" nature of her and David's lovemaking. What exactly did she mean by this? Was David impotent? While there are no clear answers to these questions, there are indications that, despite David's genuine love for Maria, he may have failed to satisfy her sexually. Affectionate and kindly as he was when the two were together, no hint of passion is evident in his behavior towards her, and when the two were apart he often forgot her existence. It is significant that until Maria came into his life David does not appear to have shown much interest in women. Nor is there any evidence that his affections wandered during the long years of their marriage. His surviving correspondence shows a man intent mainly on the task at hand. David's passion went into his work. While he loved Maria, admired her, found her a lively and amusing companion, he did not apparently desire her.

By contrast, a naive yearning for an idealized marriage is revealed in a letter Maria wrote David in October 1831 from Lancaster, a town north of Worcester where she had gone to oversee a printing job. "It has been in my heart more than once to leave the printing here to take care of itself, jump into the stage, and come right back home; but alas, I *have* no home to come to—no corner in which to fix up my things for the winter. Oh, how I do long to be settled! I will have everything so snug and bright when you come home. Your slippers and stockings warm by the fire; and I with 'a whole Iliad in my face,' and Paradise Regained in my heart."[38]

That winter, however, the prospect of a home of their own seemed further off than ever, for in February 1832 the *Massachusetts Journal* folded and David was thrown back on the practice of law as his only source of income. Given his altruistic preference for serving clients who could not afford to pay fees, the future was not very promising.

Meanwhile Maria was also discovering how cut off from society she had become. With writing and editing consuming most of her waking hours, there was little time left over for visiting and no money to spare for entertaining. In the fall of 1832 she admitted to her sister-in-law that she was "almost as much out of the way of hearing any [news] as you are at W[est] B[oylston]. It is nearly two years since I left off going anywhere, and now people have left off coming to see me; for which I am thankful—I grow more and more fond of entire, perfect solitude; and I have it to my heart's content at present. . . . Were not my occupations different from most women, I should no doubt be lonely."[39]

After three years of marriage, Maria was learning what enormous inner resources were required for her to maintain a cheerful demeanor, not only around David but around others as well. She was finding it easier to stay home and write, to cultivate a certain reclusiveness, than to expose herself to the scrutiny, perhaps even the pity, of her rich, fashionable friends.

Maria's published writings from the early years of her marriage reveal little of these personal trials and disappointments. On the contrary, the five volumes of *The Ladies Family Library*, which appeared between 1832 and 1835 and were designed for the substantial market of middle-class American women readers, idealize marriage and domesticity. If Maria was restless and unhappy in her union with David, there is no hint of it here. Any radical ideas which she harbored about woman's proper place she kept to herself. She desperately needed to earn money and probably knew from experience that it was more profitable, particularly for a woman, to mouth current pieties than to preach radical doctrines.

The first three volumes of *The Ladies Family Library* contain long and short sketches of notable women, each exemplifying the ideal of republican womanhood. In her introduction to *Good Wives*, the third volume in the series, she assures her readers that all individuals, women as well as men, affect the destiny and character of the American nation and that women as well as men must cultivate those republican virtues so ably demonstrated by the courageous and compassionate wives of history.

Without exception, all the women described in *Good Wives* are commended for their piety, their courage, and their patriotism. They placed their ultimate happiness in domestic affection and subscribe to "the only politics which belong to a woman—viz. loyalty to her husband." While several of the wives were blessed with unusual learning and talent, these gifts were invariably subordinated to their spouses' needs. Ann Flaxman, the wife of the British sculptor John Flaxman, was herself an accomplished woman with a "taste for art and literature" and some knowledge of Greek. But first and foremost she was an "enthusiastic admirer" of her husband's genius; "she cheered and encouraged him in his moments of despondency" and "regulated modestly and prudently his domestic economy." "She was none of those knowing dames who hold their lords in a sort of invisible vassalage, or with submission on their lips, and rebellion in their hearts, make the victim walk as suits their sovereign will and pleasure. NO—they loved each other truly—they read the same books—thought the same thoughts—prized the same friends—and, like bones of the same bosom, were at peace with each other, and had no wish to be separated."[40]

Perhaps the most submissive of these women was the wife of John Howard, an English philanthropist, whom Maria describes uncritically as "a great friend of subordination in families." Fortunately for her husband, Mrs. Howard was an "amiable, affectionate and benevolent" woman who apparently did everything she was told and reminded Maria of the "beautiful image of Milton's Eve, 'God is thy law, thou mine.' " Was the now-married author of this sketch forgetting her own youthful critique of this same passage, when, as a girl of seventeen, she had accused the English poet of "asserting the superiority of his own sex in rather too lordly a manner?" Or, as seems more likely, was she publicly endorsing women's assigned role as pious and submissive helpmeets?[41]

The subordination of a wife's talents and aspirations to those of her husband is also an important theme in "The Biography of Madame Roland," one of the longer sketches contained in *The Ladies Family Library*. Manon Jeanne Roland, a heroine of the French Revolution, who by most accounts dominated both her husband and the Girondist Party, is here portrayed as the epitome of the selfless woman devoting her intellectual talents entirely to the service of France and her husband's political career. While Maria described the Rolands' salon in Paris as an important rendezvous for leaders of the Revolution, she minimized Madame Roland's participation in the discussions that took place there, leaving the reader with a picture of a discreet wife who knew her place.[42]

The only maverick among the saintly women portrayed in the *The Ladies Family Library* was Madame de Staël, a figure Maria greatly admired but whom she had a hard time fitting into her prescription for self-effacing and discreetly feminine behavior. Germaine de Staël, a supremely gifted woman of unbounded ambition, was a recognized force in the intellectual and political circles of the French Revolution. No other literary figure of the time exerted a more profound influence on the women writers of the nineteenth century. Her novel *Corinne*, with its freedom-loving genius of a heroine, seemed to reflect the thoughts and feelings of exceptional young women all over Europe and America. Certainly Maria herself was under de Staël's spell and did her best in her biography to smooth over the Frenchwoman's less than admirable qualities. "If there is much to forgive in de Staël," she wrote in the concluding pages, "her excesses, her eagerness for all kinds of distinction—there is more to admire." Like Maria Child, Germaine de Staël combined a passionate nature with a probing rational mind as analytical as any man's. Like Maria, too, she was both fearless and fiercely independent. The two also shared a love for history and agreed that literature was primarily a tool to serve a moral and a social end.[43]

Placed side by side in the first volume of *The Ladies Family Library*, the portraits of Germaine de Staël and Manon Roland represent the clash between Maria's own longing to be an independent artist and the pull of the more conventional calling of dutiful wife and citizen. That true happiness comes from fulfilling one's duty to family and country is the lesson of the life of Madame Roland, but Maria, like Madame de Staël, also yearned for beauty and fame and envied the Frenchwoman's genius, her "irresistible inspiration."[44]

While Maria was completing her biography of de Staël, another Frenchwoman of genius was writing a novel which would bring her instant fame. George Sand, the author of *Indiana*, the story of a woman who abandons her husband for a young lover, was two years younger than Child. A romantic idealist whose imagination carried her aloft into mystical reveries, dreams of boundless love, and quests for eternal truth, Sand created heroines of Byronic stature and asserted unequivocally her belief that women had an equal right to freedom and justice. Known for her preference for mannish attire and her open advocacy of free love, Sand scandalized most of her conventional contemporaries. But bolder and more progressive spirits admired her greatly; she was articulating many things they themselves believed but didn't have the courage to come out and say.[45]

Although there is no record of when Maria first encountered

the writings of George Sand, later in life she confessed that when she did read the novels of this notorious Frenchwoman, who defied all the conventions of womanly behavior, she was immediately conscious of her affinity with Sand. In 1858 she wrote her old Medford friend, Lucy Osgood:

> It is curious how you have found me out. I have always known that George Sand was my twin sister; but I never mentioned it to anybody but Mr. Child. When I say that she is my twin sister, I mean with allowance for the difference occasioned by one of us being born in France, and the other in New England; and I, by no means, presume to claim such close affinity with her remarkable *genius*. But the grain of the wood is the same in both of us. This consciousness of her being my double has given her works an irresistible fascination for me. They often provoke me; sometimes shock me; but I am constrained to acknowledge, "Thus in all probability, should *I* have written had I been brought up in France." I never read a book of hers without continually stumbling on things that seem to have been written by myself. You are perfectly right. She *is* my double; and if the external influences of our lives had been the same, I should doubtless have been like her, faults and all.

As with Madame de Staël, Maria was unwilling to believe that Sand was really a "wanton woman." If she had faults, they were those of her society. "The affections in her nature are too strong for her intellect, and they have befooled her. Don't I know how to sympathize with *that*? She has lived in a very artificial and corrupt state of society; while I, thank God, was born in New England."[46]

What this letter reveals is that despite Maria's willingness to subscribe to all the current pieties about proper womanly behavior, to write and publish books like *Good Wives*, underneath she was still the same impulsive, ambitious, independent young woman who had dared to chastise Milton and publish *Hobomok*. Had she perhaps been frightened by her own rebelliousness and early fame? By marrying David she had chosen to do what society expected of her. Now her responsibility as a good New England woman was to make the best of this marriage, to play the properly dutiful wife, to care for her husband, allowing her ambitions to take second place to his needs.

In 1831, Maria wrote a revealing story for the *Miscellany*. "William Burton" describes a studious, dutiful boy suddenly overtaken by a longing to become a sailor. While his parents are distressed at the prospect of their son leaving on a long sea voyage, and although William's conscience tells him that "it was wrong to indulge his own inclinations at the expense of giving others pain," in the end his love of adventure conquers "his love of home," and for two years he is marooned on an island in the Pacific. William eventually returns home only to discover that his mother has died of grief. "Oh, do you think I killed her?" he asks his fiancée, Mary. Mary assures him that he did not, that while his mother had constantly talked of him, she never had spoken a word of reproach. But William is not comforted: "to think I broke a heart that loved me so!"[47] Unlike her earlier story, "Charles Wager," where the seafaring hero is rewarded for his ambition and adventuresomeness by bringing prosperity to his family, in "William Burton," Maria, as a married woman, is extolling duty over ambition and domestic satisfactions over professional rewards.

In these early years of her marriage, Maria was publicly scornful of all talk of women's rights, dismissing it as a dangerous subject espoused by a radical fringe of European and American thinkers. In the summer of 1829, Frances Wright, the Scottish-born free-thinker and promoter of female emancipation, had given a public lecture in Boston. Maria expressed surprise in the pages of the *Journal* that so many had gone to hear Wright but insisted that this exhibition of Boston degeneracy was nothing to be alarmed about. People, she told her readers, "were weary of going to the museum, and they were as thankful to Miss Wright for giving them something new to talk about, as they would have been to a Boa-Constrictor, or a caravan of monkeys." Maria, however, was less forgiving of Miss Wright herself. She spoke darkly of the "baneful inferences" of this reformer's "vague premises" and warned that "she represents all that is bad about the infidelism of the French Revolution."[48] Maria Child had been raised to believe that true happiness lay not in following one's own inclinations but in doing one's duty to God, one's family, and society. Life with David might be hard and discouraging, the domestic satisfactions few, but he was her husband, and her foremost duty was to him.

The future brightened up a bit for the Childs in 1833. Sometime that year they acquired a little house in Cottage Place off Washington Street on the Neck in Roxbury. How they found the money to pay the rent is not known, but at long last they were able to forego the well-worn hospitality of friends and live once more on their own. Maria later remembered with pleasure the small cozy cottage which sat right on the edge of the water, commanding a view of Dorchester and Brookline. "An arm of the bay flowed up under the eastern window of the little parlor, from which it was separated only by a plank walk, two or three feet wide. We slept in the chamber above, where our waking eyes were refreshed by gold-sparkles on the water from the rising sun." Although ships were visible in the distance, the cottage was too far from the commercial part of Boston to "be defiled with wharves, or disturbed by the rattling of drays." In front of the house was a patch of ground the size of a dining-room table and here Maria grew a mass of flowers which bloomed from early spring to late autumn. The couple christened the house "Le Paradis des Pauvres."[49]

"Exciting Warfare"

I am fully aware of the unpopularity of the task I
have undertaken; but though I expect *ridicule*
and censure, it is not in my nature to fear *them.*
—*Lydia Maria Child,* An Appeal

At a Fourth of July celebration in 1829 the speaker at the
Park Street Church was a balding, bespectacled young
newspaperman named William Lloyd Garrison. Attired in
black, with a white linen collar draped over his waistcoat, Garrison,
with trembling knees, mounted the pulpit to deliver his address.
At first his words were so faint the audience strained to hear him,
but gradually Garrison's earnest manner overcame his nervousness
as he launched into a forceful attack on the institution of slavery.
Calling on the clergy, newspaper editors, and women to mount an
organized crusade against the evil, he assured them that the cause
was "worth the desperate struggle of a thousand years."[1]

William Lloyd Garrison, a native of Newburyport, was no
stranger to David Child, who had employed him as a typesetter
back in 1827. Both men shared the same political views, having
supported Adams over Jackson in 1828. Like David, Garrison was
fearless and determined in his pursuit of truth and justice as he
saw it. As editor of the Bennington, Vermont, *Journal of the Times*,
he had declared that he would "be trammelled by no interest, biased
by no sect, awed by no power."[2]

It was as editor of the *Journal of the Times* that Garrison met
Benjamin Lundy, the Quaker reformer from Baltimore, whose
monthly, *The Genius of Universal Emancipation*, had impressed the
Bennington editor with its vigorous antislavery stand. Lundy

shared Garrison's antislavery sympathies and for some months had been urging his young colleague to come to Baltimore and help edit the *Genius*. In August 1829 Garrison accepted his offer and made his way south.

Garrison marked his debut on Lundy's paper with a critical editorial questioning the gradualist nature of antislavery reform as it then existed in the United States. Since 1817 the chief force behind the effort to end slavery had been the American Colonization Society, which encouraged voluntary emancipation and proposed returning the freed blacks to Africa. Most supporters of colonization regarded slavery as an anomaly in a free republic, a dangerous and economically unsound institution. They warned that if the system was not abolished peacefully and gradually it would end of its own accord in violence and insurrection. But the colonizationists also saw the degraded condition of the free black population in the North as a threat to social order and proposed transporting all manumitted slaves to the free colony of Liberia on the west coast of Africa.

Garrison in his editorial unequivocally denounced these cautious and conservative goals. He claimed that "the slaves are entitled to immediate and complete emancipation" and that, once freed, they should be "at liberty to choose their own dwelling place, and we possess no right to use coercive measures in their removal."[3]

Although Lundy, a firm supporter of colonization and gradual emancipation, disagreed with his new editor's position, he nevertheless encouraged him to state his opinions freely. Then in November Garrison published an abusive attack on a Yankee shipowner whom he accused of amassing a fortune in the slave trade. This led to an outcry from the paper's readers, who rushed to cancel their subscriptions to the *Genius*. Garrison was charged with libel and sent to jail. By the time he was released in June 1830 the *Genius* had folded. Two days later, buoyed up rather than discouraged by opposition to his cause, the editor-turned-reformer made his way back to Boston more determined than ever to have his antislavery message heard. It must have been shortly after his return that Garrison called on the Childs to discuss with David the prospects for publishing an antislavery paper in Boston. Many years later Maria remembered that her husband, whose own position, like Lundy's, favored the colonizationists, had nonetheless given his immediate support to the idea, but she had hesitated, finding the fiery young reformer "too rash" and "too ultra."[4]

Garrison's paper, the *Liberator*, made its first appearance on the streets of Boston on New Year's Day 1831. The editor and his assistant had worked hastily all through the night in a small, dark, and dingy room under the eaves of Merchants Hall to set the borrowed type. The following morning a handful of subscribers received an unimpressive looking sheet consisting of four small pages, for which the charge was two dollars per year. While the *Liberator's* physical appearance was unassuming, its message was not. Garrison took pains to warn his readers that he did not wish to "think, or speak, or write with moderation." He promised that on the subject of slavery he would be "harsh as truth, and as uncompromising as justice. . . . I am in earnest—I will not equivocate—I will not excuse—I will not retreat a single inch—AND I WILL BE HEARD."[5]

Garrison's impassioned cry for attention was barely heeded by white Bostonians. For the first few years subscribers were mostly free northern blacks. Nonetheless, publication of the *Liberator* marked a new phase in the American antislavery movement: an abandonment of the moderation and gradualism which had characterized earlier efforts in favor of a radical call for immediate abolition. White Southerners began paying attention to the paper long before white Northerners did, thanks largely to the publicity Garrison gave to an insurrection led by a young slave named Nat Turner in the late summer of 1831. For six weeks, until Turner's capture and execution, the *Liberator* reported at great length every detail of the uprising and its aftermath. Comparing the rebel slaves to Greek, Polish, and American patriots, Garrison claimed that the slaves themselves were not responsible for their violent actions. Rather it was the American people who, by permitting the institution of slavery to exist, were guilty.[6]

Southerners were outraged by this publicity and accused Garrison of actually fomenting the Turner uprising. In Columbia, South Carolina, a $1500 reward was offered for any white person convicted of circulating copies of the *Liberator*. By October 21, David Child was referring to Garrison in the *Journal* as "the Lion of the Day at the South" and warning that any effort by the press to silence him was "as idle an attempt, as that to turn the wind by blowing against it. He has vowed to fight for the entire and *immediate* emancipation of the blacks—and we know him well enough to know that he will not cease while his life lasts." David insisted that Garrison had no part in inspiring Nat Turner's rebellion; the *Liberator's* publicity had excited the whites far more than the blacks. But the editor of the *Journal* had a few words of warning for the editor of the *Liberator*: "We cannot but think that his object might have been pursued with more *judgment*—though it could not be with more *zeal*."[7]

David Child was not yet ready to go as far as Garrison, who by now was denouncing the Colonization Society as a proslavery plot to remove free Negroes from the South, but he no longer approved of the Society's scheme to resettle freed blacks in Liberia. In 1827 the *Journal* had enthusiastically applauded the restoration of "the African to his country of origin," where he could introduce "civilization into a region not yet emerged from barbarism." By 1831, however, it had become clear to David and other erstwhile supporters that the colonization scheme was both ineffective—only 1,420 blacks had been transported to Liberia during the previous decade—and unpopular; free blacks themselves vehemently opposed African colonization. They declared the United States to be their home and were determined to remain and work there for both the abolition of slavery and political recognition for their people. David Child's change of heart on the question is evident in an article he wrote late in 1831, "The Slave Question." After declaring his loyalty to the Colonization Society itself he went on to denounce the scheme of returning blacks to Liberia as a "worthless" method for reducing the black population in America and a "wicked" one "if used as a means for *compelling* by force the emigration of free blacks." Child's growing interest in the abolitionist cause did not escape the attention of his readers. A letter to the editor on October 31, 1831, cited the paper as one of the few "which does not shrink from hearing honest testimony in regard to the criminality and dangers of slavery."[8]

Maria's interest in the slavery question predated her marriage. In *Evenings in New England*, published in 1824, she had denounced the institution as a great evil. Other critical mentions of slavery can be found among her early writings, but "Jumbo and Zairee," published in January 1831, is her first story about black bondage in America. In it two children of an African prince are captured and carried off in a slave ship to America, the country which boasts "that men are born free and equal." Jumbo and Zairee are sold together upon arriving in the United States, where "nobody abused them." While forced to work hard, they are comfortably clothed and fed. In a footnote Maria maintained that "this is usually the case with slaves at the South," but she cautioned that "the *principle* is wrong, even if there are nine hundred and ninety-nine good masters out of a thousand." While the two children are separated for a time, in the end a kind plantation owner buys them both and sends them home to their parents in Africa. This story is remarkable for its passionate indictment of slavery and the slave trade.[9]

Equally close to Maria's heart in the years immediately following her marriage was the plight of the Indian. Her long-standing interest in Native Americans was now heightened by a growing national concern over President Jackson's policy supporting the removal of Indians from land desired by the mounting flood of settlers on the frontier. A crisis had been reached in Georgia, where the Creeks and Cherokees were putting up a strong resistance to the fraudulent treaties imposed by the white man. Whereas President Adams had shown his sympathy for the Indians by repudiating a treaty depriving the Creeks of all their land in the state, Andrew Jackson not only favored removing the Indians but openly supported the less than worthy methods—including bribery and threats—used to persuade the tribes to move away. Maria responded to the crisis in Georgia by writing *The First Settlers of New England*, a small volume directed particularly at young girls. Set in the form of a dialogue between a mother and her two daughters, the book addresses itself only in passing to the removal question in Georgia and focuses instead on the Indian wars of seventeenth-century New England. As in *Hobomok*, Maria blames the white settlers' inhuman treatment of the Indians on their religious bigotry. By concentrating on New England she demonstrates once again that all white Americans are guilty of racial prejudice, an argument she would use a few years later when describing whites' attitudes towards blacks. According to Maria it was the Puritan religion with its Judaic concept of a chosen people which nursed such prejudice. The early settlers saw themselves as the elect, superior to all other races and creeds, and assured one another that their "vindictive and unjust" God had authorized them to punish the Indians, who were "born to suffer."[10]

Maria's singling out of Puritan religion to explain brutal treatment of the Indians seems an oversimplification of the removal question. It is unlikely that there were many Puritans in Georgia in the 1820s, and greed and rapacity were largely responsible for the illegal and often cruel methods used to rob the Cherokees and other tribes of their land. But Maria's approach to the issue does reflect her impatience with institutional Protestantism and with the endless theological wrangling which continued to occupy church leaders in the 1820s. Like other Christian liberals of her day, she was coming to see the true Christian church as one that emphasized deeds not doctrines.

The First Settlers of New England is a remarkably radical book for its time. Here the cautious sanction of racial intermarriage in *Hobomok* is transformed into a courageous endorsement. Miscegenation would have been good, she claims, for both races. "The primitive simplicity, hospitality, and generosity of the Indians, would gradually have improved and softened the stern and morose feelings" of the Puritans, while "our arts and sciences would have imparted to the Indians new light and vigour," and Christianity, particularly the example of Jesus, would have helped to subdue "the wayward passions and evil propensities" of the natives. Whatever objections people might make to the idea of intermarriage between the races, Maria reminds them that God "has made of one blood all nations of men, that they may dwell together" and suggests that such intermingling, by reducing racial hatred, might actually diminish the amount of crime and violence in the world.[11]

Although *The First Settlers of New England* was published in 1829, it received no notice from the press or the public. Even the journals that usually reviewed Child's work failed to mention it. Did Maria, as Carolyn Karcher has suggested, deliberately refrain from promoting the book for fear its radicalism would destroy her career? It had been a financially disastrous year for the Childs, redeemed only by the publication of *The Frugal Housewife*. Moreover, Garrison's extremist views on the slavery question had yet to disturb the complacency of his fellow New Englanders. For whatever reason, *The First Settlers of New England* vanished with hardly a trace.

Meanwhile, the little band of antislavery reformers allied with William Lloyd Garrison began to organize themselves. On a miserable January day in 1832, while the wind from a raging northeaster whipped snow and sleet through the streets of Boston, David Child, Garrison, Ellis Gray Loring, and a dozen or so other white antislavery sympathizers groped their way up the back side of Beacon Hill, known as "Nigger Hill," to the basement of the African Baptist Church. In a schoolroom for black children these men discussed a constitution and preamble for a proposed New England Anti-Slavery Society. While David had originally helped to draw up the documents, he, together with Loring and another lawyer, Samuel Sewall, refused to accept the wording of the new preamble, which declared immediate emancipation to be a fundamental doctrine of the new society. In the end the three lawyers were outvoted and the New England Anti-Slavery Society was organized without them.[12]

David and his fellow lawyers, it appeared, were still reluctant to renounce the gradualist approach of the Colonization Society, which saw slavery as a social and economic problem, in favor of the Garrisonian view that slavery was a sin which must be immediately eradicated. In the last few issues of the *Journal*, before it folded in February 1832, David commended Garrison's *Liberator* for lifting up "the voice of remonstrance against the unchristian and sinful character of slavery." At the same time he refused to turn his back completely on the Colonization Society, calling it a "humane and patriotic institution."[13]

By 1833 David was firmly in Garrison's camp. Maria's conversion is harder to pinpoint. Many years later, as a woman in her seventies, she remembered "very distinctly" the first time she saw Garrison. "I little thought then that the whole pattern of my life-web would be changed by that introduction. I was then all absorbed in poetry and painting,—soaring aloft, on Psyche-wings, into the ethereal regions of mysticism. He got hold of the strings of my conscience, and pulled me into Reforms. It is of no use to imagine what might have been, if I had never met him. Old dreams vanished, old associates departed, and all things became new."[14]

Was Maria perhaps recalling Garrison's visit to the house on Harvard Street in June 1830 when he had come to consult David about publishing the *Liberator*? She had then dismissed his methods as too extreme. But Garrison could be charmingly persuasive when he chose. In the company of close friends and colleagues this radical reformer was mild and gentle; a "lion in the arena," he was a "lamb at home." Furthermore, his views on the slavery question matched Maria's own. Later she claimed that Garrison's "blunt strong language" describing the evils of slavery had won her over to abolitionism. Perhaps his personal warmth had worked on her as well. Few reformers were as adept as Garrison at making his followers feel loved and respected.[15]

In any event, Maria's conversion was neither sudden nor surprising. She had long been a champion of freedom and an enemy of oppression. Beginning with *Hobomok*, her writings on the Indians had denounced northern prejudice and bigotry. Abolitionism also met a spiritual need. In the years immediately following her conversion to Swedenborgianism, the Church of the New Jerusalem had been a new and vibrant sect, seemingly free of institutional and theological constraints. But now Maria was coming to fear that even this church was too preoccupied with doctrinal niceties. To make matters worse, she discovered that her own parish and pastor were so "bitterly pro-slavery and so intensely bigoted, that I doubted whether *such* a church could have come down from heaven."[16]

Meanwhile her brother Convers' good friend, the saintly Unitarian minister William Ellery Channing, had been preaching since the early 1820s an old but neglected message that virtue was the true end of human life and government, that deeds, not words, were the essence of the Christian message. To be truly virtuous, Channing believed, all that was needed was a rejuvenated conscience and a commitment to a life of Christian benevolence. Church, government, and other external controls would vanish in the millennium. Such views accorded perfectly with Maria's own. Impatient with sectarian constraints and impelled by a fierce love of freedom, she shared this radical vision. She longed to rid the world of tyranny and oppression; and what better way than by abolishing slavery.

Shortly before her death in 1880 Maria wrote an old abolitionist friend, Theodore Dwight Weld, a nostalgic letter recalling the bracing moral atmosphere of the early antislavery days:

> The Holy Spirit *did* actually descend upon men and women in tongues of flame. Political and theological prejudices, and personal ambitions, were forgotten in sympathy for the wrongs of the helpless, and in the enthusiasm to keep the fire of freedom from being extinguished on our national altar. *All* suppression of selfishness makes the moment great; and mortals were never so sublimely forgetful of self, than were the abolitionists in those early days. . . . Ah, my friend, that is the *only* true church organization, when heads and hearts unite in working for the welfare of the human-race.[17]

As a committed abolitionist, Maria now found herself a member of a small, dedicated band of reformers which included women as well as men. From the start Garrison had made it clear that he wished both sexes to take an active role in promoting the reform. Early issues of the *Liberator* contained a "Ladies Department," which not only urged its readers to heed the plight of their slave sisters in the South, who were "exposed to all the violence of lust and passion—and treated with more indelicacy and cruelty than cattle," but begged them "to weep, and speak, and act" in their behalf. A few Boston women had taken up Garrison's challenge and were lending their talents to the crusade. Ellis Loring's wife, Louisa, was one. Henrietta Sargent, destined to be a life-long friend of Maria's, was another. But the most magnetic was Maria Weston Chapman, a woman whose influence over the Boston circle of antislavery reformers would in some respects rival Garrison's own. Dazzlingly handsome and serenely aristocratic, with "swift eyes of clear steel blue," Maria Chapman was self-assured to the point of arrogance. Yet no other Garrison supporter worked harder for the cause or showed him a greater personal loyalty.[18] Most of the women who joined the abolitionist movement preferred to remain out of the public eye and concentrate on fund-raising. Maria Child would eventually do her share of such work, but, for the time being, as a respected writer with a national reputation, she put her literary talents to work for the cause.

David Child had marked his conversion to abolitionism by giving a lengthy address at the first anniversary meeting of the New England Anti-Slavery Society on January 16, 1833. Boylston Hall was crowded that Wednesday evening with people curious if not eager to hear speeches on what the *Liberator* described as "the all absorbing topics of Slavery and Colonization." David's talk focused on the evils of slavery in America and began by echoing his wife's denunciation of racism among white people in the North as well as the South. "The most obvious and universal of those peculiar hardships, under which the colored race labor in this country," he told his audience, "is the inveterate, cruel, and . . . ferocious prejudice against their skins." The people of Massachusetts, David declared, were as guilty of racism as the citizens of any other state.[19]

Sometime after her conversion to abolitionism, Maria began working on a small volume destined to be the first scholarly American overview of the history of slavery and the condition of the Negro. Other biographers of Maria Child have maintained that she did most of her research for this book in the Boston Athenaeum, whose trustees voted in 1832 that she be allowed to take out books at no charge. But an examination of the list of books she did check out shows that only a few were related to the subject of slavery. Either she read the necessary books in the library itself, borrowed them from David, or obtained them from some other source.[20]

An Appeal in Favor of that Class of Americans Called Africans was published in August 1833 by Allen & Ticknor, the new owners of Maria's old publisher, Carter and Hendee. William D. Ticknor, a cousin of Maria's mentor, George Ticknor, was hardly sympathetic to abolitionist principles. He was, however, an admirer of Maria Child's writings and apparently had no hesitation in bringing out the book.[21]

Garrison's recounting of the evils of slavery had helped to pull Maria into the abolitionist crusade. She hoped that a similar exposition of the facts would convert the readers of her *Appeal.* In the preface she implores them not to throw the volume down as soon as they have looked at the title, urging them instead to read the book "for the very truth's sake." She insists that she is fully aware of the unpopularity of the task she has undertaken; "but though I *expect* ridicule and censure, it is not in my nature to *fear* them." Should her book "be the means for advancing, even one single hour, the inevitable progress of truth and justice," she concludes, "I would not exchange the consciousness for all of Rothchild's [sic] wealth, or Sir Walter [Scott]'s fame."[22]

Maria's *Appeal* opens with a brief history of slavery. She describes its evil effects on all whom it touches, from the inhabitants of Africa, to the white seamen who carried the captive blacks across the horrors of the Middle Passage, and finally to the slaveholders themselves. The history of the Negro "is written in blood," she announces unequivocally at the start. After recounting several "detestable anecdotes" of slaves being tortured to death, she warns her readers not to allow their "nerves to be more tender than their consciences." Nor does Maria shrink from discussing what was then considered a grossly indelicate subject—the sexual oppression of slave women. "The Negro woman," she tells her readers, "is unprotected either by law or public opinion. She is the property of her master, and her daughters are his property. They are allowed to have no conscientious scruples, no sense of shame, no regard for the feelings of husband or parent; they must be entirely subservient to the will of their owner, on pain of being whipped as near unto death as will comport with his interest, or quite to death, if it suit his pleasure."[23]

Maria blames Northerners as well as Southerners for the continuation of the slave system. Her excoriation of her countrymen spares no one. Above all, she denounces the Colonization Society for its conciliatory attitude towards the Southern slaveholder and its acceptance of slavery as a necessary evil. Even northern prejudice against free blacks, which the colonizationists claim is ineradicable, even this, she insists, can be removed. "Let us no longer act upon the narrow-minded idea, that we must always continue to do wrong, because we have so long been in the habit of doing it." Furthermore, she maintains, the facts show that antiblack sentiment is not endemic. The English, for one, have largely done away with such prejudice.[24]

Maria then defends the abolitionist cause. She explains that she and her fellow reformers support immediate emancipation, first, because it is in keeping with God's law and, second, because it provides the only true guarantee of safety for the white population. She denies slaveowners' claims that blacks are happy in their bondage and displays her talent for exposing false reasoning by repeating a recent conversation with an old Boston acquaintance. The man, who had been brought up in the South, began by insisting that the slaves were perfectly content; they loved their masters and their masters loved them. "The less people know the merrier they are," he assured Maria. Reminding him of his plans for educating his son, she asked, "If knowledge brings wretchedness, why do you not keep him in happy ignorance?", which elicited the lame reply that "the fashion of the time requires some information." At this point a woman who had recently visited South Carolina joined the conversation. She described the fear aroused by rumors of slave uprisings in that state, only to be told by the ex-Southerner that there was no need for alarm as a fort had been built as protection against precisely such an eventuality. "So," Maria observes with a certain relish, "they have built a *citadel* to protect them from their happy and contented servants."[25]

Slavery, Maria assures the readers of her *Appeal*, is the cause of insurrections and emancipation their cure. She cites the example of Haiti, which a quarter of a century earlier had become the first black republic in the western hemisphere. A political and economic success, Haiti was enjoying a profitable trade with the United States in the 1830s. But this impressive record of black self-rule had yet to bring official recognition from Washington. The power of southern politicians, Maria claims, had prevented it, and northern representatives resisted acknowledging Haiti's independence "because a colored ambassador would be so disagreeable to our prejudices."[26]

Two chapters of the *Appeal* are devoted to countering the charge that Negroes are naturally inferior both morally and intellectually to whites. First, Maria points to the number of advanced civilizations which had existed in Africa. Second, she blames slavery itself for the brutish and immoral behavior attributed to many blacks. Finally, she effectively demolishes the reasoning of those who attempted to turn "the wrongs of the oppressed" into "an argument against them." "We first debase the nature of man by making him a slave, and then very coolly tell him that he must always remain a slave because he does not know how to use freedom. We first crush people to the earth, and then claim the right of trampling on them for ever because they are prostrate. Truly, human selfishness never invented a rule which worked so charmingly both ways!"[27]

The final chapter is directed particularly at her fellow New Englanders, whom she implicates as deeply as any other Americans in perpetuating the subjugation of the Negro race. "Our prejudice against colored people is even more inveterate than it is at the South," she charges her Northern readers, echoing the observations of Alexis de Toqueville, who in his travels through the United States in the early 1830s had noted that "prejudice of race appears to be stronger in the states that have abolished slavery than in those where it still exists."[28]

As Maria points out, the social and economic condition of the blacks in Massachusetts was deplorable. In the city of Boston they were largely confined to two neighborhoods, "Nigger Hill" and "New Guinea." Jim Crow sections segregated them in stagecoaches and omnibuses, in theaters and lecture halls. Many churches had "nigger pews." Maria notes that those black children who attended public school are "subject to many discouragements and difficulties" and that private schools will not admit them. Her tone changes somewhat when she pokes fun at the state law forbidding intermarriage between whites and blacks, facetiously noting that so much was made of the repugnance between the two races, being "founded in the laws of *nature*, methinks there is small reason to dread their frequency."[29]

In the last paragraph of this courageous and powerful book Maria expresses her satisfaction at having put her "mite into the treasury." She has made her contribution to the antislavery cause. And while she is pained by the "expectation of displeasing all classes," she maintains it to be "a duty to fulfill this task," declaring that "worldly considerations should never stifle the voice of conscience."[30]

Although Garrison was in England at the time the *Appeal* was published, the *Liberator* wasted little time in printing a favorable notice of the book. "A thousand thanks to Mrs. Child for this admirable work! It must—it will be extensively read; and that heart must be harder than the nether mill-stone which can remain unaffected by the solemn truths which it contains." The reviewer dubbed the book's author a true believer. "Mrs. Child is an abolitionist. . . . She avows herself an opponent of the Colonization Society, and a friend of the Anti-Slavery Society. . . . We intend hereafter to enrich our columns with extracts from this work."[31]

In private, the abolitionists expressed astonishment as well as delight over the strength and vigor of Maria Child's attack on slavery. This respected and popular woman writer had been a great catch for their obscure little antislavery society. But as Samuel May, one of its founders, later recalled, few had suspected that she possessed either the power or the courage "to strike so heavy a blow." For a woman to speak her mind on any public issue was daring enough, but for one to publish an unequivocal attack on a taboo subject like slavery was heroism indeed.[32]

Scholars credit Maria Child's *Appeal* with converting more men and women to abolitionism than any other publication. Contemporary sources attested to its power. At an antislavery meeting in Utica, New York, the Reverend Ludlow claimed that "Mrs. Child had done more to wake up the people to effort in this cause of God and humanity than all the men that went before her in this country." With less hyperbole, James Forten, a black abolitionist, called the *Appeal* one of the best productions on the subject he had ever read. A manager of the American Bible Society refused to read the volume for fear it might convince him to join the abolitionists. Meanwhile, back home in Boston, William Ellery Channing had walked to Cottage Place from his own home on Beacon Hill to discuss the book with Maria.[33]

Channing's aristocratic parishioners, however, showed little enthusiasm for the *Appeal*. Only a month before its appearance, the *North American Review* had printed a long essay on Maria's published writings, claiming that few could outrank her as a lady who "has long been before the public as an author with much success" and promising that if Mrs. Child "will continue her useful labors . . . we have no doubt that they will be received with constantly increasing favors."[34] Maria must surely have wondered as she read these words of praise whether the editors of the *North American Review* would have been so effusive had they read her latest book.

Samuel May, the fellow abolitionist to whom she had dedicated her *Appeal*, later recalled how quickly she was denounced. Old admirers lost no time in pointing out that there were "some very indelicate things in her book." Politicians and other civic leaders spoke with disdain of this woman who "presumed to criticize so freely the constitution and government of her country." Even the clergy were heard to talk gravely of "the evil and ruin" which would befall the nation "if women generally should follow Mrs. Child's bad example and neglect their domestic duties to attend to the affairs of state."[35]

Edward Everett Hale was a boy of eleven when he heard his

parents criticize the *Appeal*. Later, when he saw the book displayed
in the window of the Old Corner Book Store, he was tempted to
throw a stone at it. Sales of nearly all of Maria's books fell sharply.
Her friend John Greenleaf Whittier claimed that "no woman in
this country . . . sacrificed so much for principles as Mrs. Child. . . .
She found no market for her books and essays and her praises
were suddenly silenced."[36]

If Maria's conversion to abolitionism had, as she later claimed,
changed her life, the appearance of this volume brought home with
glaring clarity the full significance of her commitment to such an
unpopular cause. The *North American Review*, which had earlier
been so fulsome in its praises of Maria's writings, voiced regret in
July 1835 "that a writer capable of being so agreeable, and at the
same time so useful, should have departed from that line of authorship in which she has justly acquired a high reputation."[37] The
editors of this respected journal had apparently forgotten *Hobomok*
and remembered only Maria's more conventional writings published since her marriage.

Before 1833 few in the North paid much attention to the abolitionists. When Nat Turner led his slave uprising in Virginia in
August 1831, Southerners had written Boston's mayor, Harrison
Gray Otis, urging him to silence Garrison and his "incendiary"
paper. Otis, however, responded with indifference to these demands, insisting that no one in Boston had ever heard of the *Liberator* and that Garrison's followers consisted only of a "very few
insignificant persons of all colors."[38]

But Bostonians soon began paying attention to William Lloyd
Garrison and his little band of reformers. The abolitionist editor's
growing notoriety in the South spread north with the publication
of his *Thoughts on African Colonization* in May 1832. This direct attack
on the American Colonization Society was in effect a condemnation
of the racial prejudice Garrison saw all around him in the North.
"Of this I am sure," he wrote, "no man, who is truly willing to
admit people of color to an equality with himself, can see any
insuperable difficulty in effecting their elevation."[39]

Few white Bostonians, however, were willing to grant equality
to people of color. As long as the abolitionists confined their attacks
to the South, no one in Boston took much notice. But as soon as
they spoke of eradicating Northern prejudice as well, a storm of
protest arose. By the time Maria Child's *Appeal* appeared in the
bookstores in August 1833 suspicion of the abolitionists among

proper Bostonians was rife. Thus, when admirers of Maria's earlier writings recognized in her latest book echoes of Mr. Garrison's plea for racial equality, they were ready to disown her.

In later years, Maria admitted that her literary prospects had been greatly injured by her espousal of the abolitionist cause; "the respectables, who had condescended to patronize me, forthwith sent me to 'Coventry.' ". At the same time she remembered how the antislavery movement had introduced her "to the noblest and best of the land, intellectually and morally, and knit us together in that firm friendship which grows out of sympathy in a good but unpopular cause." In the 1850s she would write Whittier extolling "those noble self-forgetting days! when love to our fellow-men was the basis of all our ethics, and willing obedience to the God of love was the broad basis of our creed!"[40]

The only surviving hint that Maria had any second thoughts about the unpopular course she had set for herself can be found in a poem published in the *Liberator* in October 1833, two months after the appearance of her *Appeal*. The subject of the poem is John Vanderlyn's then-famous painting, "Marius seated amid the ruins of Carthage."

> Pillars are fallen at thy feet,
>   Fanes quiver in the air,
> A prostrate city is thy seat,—
>   And thou alone are there.
>
> No change comes o'er thy noble brow,
>   Though ruin is around thee
> Thine eye beam burns as proudly now,
>   As when the laurel crowned thee.
>
> It cannot bend thy lofty soul
>   Though friends and fame depart;
> The car of fate may o'er thee roll,
>   Nor crush thy Roman heart.
>
> And Genius that electric power
>   Which earth can never tame;
> Bright suns may scorch, and dark clouds lower,
>   Its flush is still the same.
>
> The dreams we loved in early life,
>   May melt like mist away,
> High thoughts may seem, 'mid passion's strife,
>   Like Carthage in decay.

And proud hopes in the human heart
  May be to ruin hurled,
Like moulding monuments of art
  Heaped on a sleeping world.

Yet there is something will not die,
  Where life hath once been fair;
Some towering thoughts still rear on high,
  Some Romans linger there![41]

The reception accorded Maria's *Appeal* made it unmistakably clear that there was now no turning back. By the close of 1834, canceled subscriptions forced her to relinquish the editorship of the *Juvenile Miscellany*, which for nearly a decade had guaranteed her a regular if modest income. The following spring, she received a note from the trustees of the Athenaeum revoking her library privileges. When several of her friends, including Maria Chapman, tried to buy her a share in the institution they were apparently rebuffed.[42]

At the same time George Ticknor and his literary friends were adding their words to the tide of abuse which swept over her. Maria was neither the first nor the last nonconformist whom Ticknor would punish with ostracism. Many years later he defended his efforts to protect the elite from what he saw as dangerous elements within Boston society by declaring that "the principles of that society are right, and its severity towards disorganizers, and social democracy in all its forms, is just and wise. It keeps our standard of public morals where it should be. . . ." In common with other Unitarians, including Edward Everett, Ticknor feared the disruptive tendencies of abolitionism. Never again would Maria hear his name without making some sneering comment. In 1860, she rebuffed a compliment Ticknor sent through a friend, dismissing him as a "smooth-tongued hypocritical pecksniff."[43]

By 1835 Maria had adjusted to the idea of belonging to a band of outcasts and could take comfort in the realization that "they who take the first and most difficult steps are always reviled and persecuted; for principles of divine truth can never go out into the midst of a perverse generation, without exciting warfare."[44] Although the loss of so many friends and admirers was a bitter blow, Maria had the consolation of knowing that the small band of antislavery crusaders was pleased with her work.

In the antislavery crusade, Maria Child found what she had long been looking for: a religion uncorrupted by theology and controversy, which allowed her to perform the supremely creative act of disseminating heavenly truths to humanity; a holy cause that fulfilled her youthful dreams of romance, heroism, and faith and to which she could consecrate the privation and self-denial of her life with David. Here among Garrison's abolitionist crusaders was a community of believers, women as well as men, who shared her passion for truth and freedom and with whom she could labor and prove her faith by her works. The past with all its burdens and cares was put behind her. Like a slave relieved of her chains, she was now released from the encumbrances of orthodoxy and respectability. She felt free at last.

8

Mob Year

*We have fallen on evil times. But He who led the
Israelites safely through the land of the Philistines
is with us, a cloud by day, a pillar of fire by night.*
—*Lydia Maria Child, 1835*

B y the end of 1833 organized antislavery had expanded from
four local societies in two states to forty-seven in ten states.
In December of that year abolitionists gathered in Philadelphia to form a national organization, the American Anti-Slavery
Society (AASS). Pledged to promote immediate emancipation by
circulating tracts and newspapers and establishing societies in every
town and village, the AASS dedicated itself to "the destruction of
error by the potency of truth—the overthrow of prejudice by the
power of love—the abolition of slavery by the spirit of repentance."[1]

Although four women—all Quakers—attended this first meeting of the national society, membership was restricted to men.
Women supporters of the movement were expected to organize
separate auxiliaries. In early October 1833 Garrison returned from
a trip to England with glowing accounts of women's antislavery
activities in that country. Thanks to their efforts, Garrison claimed,
800,000 antislavery petitions had been sent to Parliament demanding the emancipation of slaves in the British West Indies. "We
cannot believe that our ladies are less philanthropic or less influential," he announced in an article in the *Liberator*. "In their hands
is the destiny of the slave."[2] Within weeks of the publication of this
challenge, Maria Chapman and twelve other women, including her
three sisters, Caroline, Anne, and Deborah, had established the
Boston Female Anti-Slavery Society (BFASS).

For a time Maria Child resisted joining the BFASS. Her "rabid individualism," as she called it, made her uncomfortable with the machinery of organizations. She also questioned the need for separate women's societies. But repeated persuasion by the leaders of the BFASS, combined with a growing realization that perhaps by not joining she was keeping others away, finally won her reluctant consent. "The plain truth is," she wrote Charlotte Phelps, the president, early in 1834, "my sympathies do not, and never have, moved freely on this project; but this is no reason why others may not effect a great deal of good by it, and do it in all sincerity. I am willing to pay my subscription, and to increase it by donations, as soon as we have fewer pecuniary difficulties to struggle with; but I had much rather not, in any way be connected with the government."[3]

Once a member of the BFASS, however, Maria found it difficult to remain quietly in the background. Her recognized skills were too valuable to be wasted. No sooner had she joined the Society than she and Louisa Loring drew up plans for a bazaar to raise funds for the New England Anti-Slavery Society. According to one account, while Louisa provided the needed money to run the sale, Maria did most of the organizing and solicited homemade goods from antislavery friends.[4]

The bazaar opened on a cold day in mid-December in the New England Society's headquarters at 46 Washington Street. Banners carrying antislavery slogans greeted visitors as they entered the hall set aside for the sale. "Remember them that are in bonds, as bound with them," read one. "We trust in the power of truth, the truth shall make us free," read another. Tables covered with merchandise filled the room, each table presided over by a member of the BFASS. Next to a plate of cookies a sign read: "Sugar not made by slaves."

Sarah Southwick and her sister had been driven by their father all the way from Peabody to attend the bazaar. Each sister had contributed a few homemade articles, and Sarah, once an avid reader of the *Juvenile Miscellany*, was most anxious to meet Maria Child, so, upon spotting her own needlebook on Mrs. Child's table, she asked her for the price. To Sarah's mortification, the editor of the *Miscellany* first scrutinized the childish piece of handiwork and then replied, "It is marked fifty cents, but it is not well made and you may have it for two shillings."[5]

Despite the uneven quality of the merchandise on display, this first antislavery bazaar surprised its organizers by raising $300. Word quickly spread of the Boston women's success, and the idea of a Christmas sale to raise money for antislavery work caught on in towns all over the North. Meanwhile, the Boston bazaar became an annual event, putting more money each year into the coffers of the Society while at the same time attracting new converts to the cause.

Maria Child helped to raise funds for another project of interest to the BFASS, the Samaritan Asylum for Colored Orphans, which occupied a small house on Poplar Street. Here thirteen black children were cared for by a group of Boston women whom Maria described as forsaking the comforts of home in order that they might "preserve a few unfortunate children from the contaminating influence of vicious example, and the helplessness of ignorance."[6]

In addition to her work for the BFASS, Maria was active behind the scenes, first in the New England Anti-Slavery Society, and later in its successor, the Massachusetts Anti-Slavery Society (MASS). Samuel May, a leading abolitionist, recalled years later how Maria Child and Maria Chapman had in a "private way been the presiding geniuses in all our councils and public meetings, often proposing the wisest measures and suggesting the most weighty thoughts, pertinent facts [and] apt illustrations." This mild-mannered Unitarian minister remembered that he had often prefaced an antislavery speech with the words "Hear me as the mouthpiece of Mrs. Child or Mrs. Chapman" and convulsed his audience with a joke or electrified them with a "flash of eloquence."[7]

David and Maria were welcome visitors in the Chapmans' parlor, which served as a central meeting place for the circle of Garrison supporters familiarly known as the Boston Clique. Near both the Garrisons' and the Lorings', the house belonging to Maria Chapman and her wealthy merchant husband, Henry, was a pleasant refuge from the hostile world outside. Here a refreshing cup of tea could be had in the comforting presence of loyal co-workers in the antislavery cause. Maria Chapman's sisters were likely to be there, as were Garrison, Ellis Gray Loring, and Samuel Sewall. From behind her tea table the handsome and aristocratic Maria Chapman presided over this gathering of outcasts as if she were the recognized arbiter of fashionable society.

While both Childs enjoyed stopping by the Chapmans for an afternoon of good talk, the couple's somewhat erratic participation in the activities of the Boston Clique prevented their being counted as full-fledged members.[8] David's absorption in his own projects, together with Maria's skittishness with respect to organizations, partly explained their aloofness. But poverty also kept them apart. Unlike most of the other women in the Clique, Maria had to work for a living. With her writing, antislavery work, and caring for David, there was little time to spare for tea parties.

The years between 1833 and 1838 were among the most productive of Maria's career. The list of her publications includes stories and poems, advice books and antislavery tracts, as well as her most ambitious work to date, *The History of the Condition of Women, in Various Ages and Nations.* This completed her *Ladies Family Library* and contained in its two volumes a wealth of information about women from ancient times to the present. Meanwhile some of her earlier works were beginning to sell well in England. But despite the impressiveness of her literary output the Childs' financial situation remained as desperate as ever. Plummeting sales of Maria's books at home did not help. Nor did David's legal ownership of all copyrights. Whatever she earned continued to be swallowed up to pay his debts. Only the generosity of Maria's father, Convers Francis, saved the couple from financial disaster. By 1836 the retired Medford baker had lent them so much money that Maria would insist that the copyrights to her works be put in his name instead of David's.[9]

Among Maria's publications from this period is a small volume modeled on the then-popular gift book annuals brought out each fall for the Christmas trade. *The Oasis,* published in October 1834, contains stories, poems, and articles all related in some way to the antislavery cause. Although Maria herself was the author of most of the selections, she persuaded her husband and several friends, including the Quaker poet John Greenleaf Whittier, to contribute as well. The book was intended for the general reader, and its purpose, as Child stated simply and succinctly in the preface, was to "familiarize the public mind with the idea that colored people are *human beings*—elevated or degraded by the same circumstances that elevate or degrade other men."[10]

The countering of northern racial prejudice is the gift book's underlying theme, but Maria is very careful to point out that she has no intention of forcing her views on anyone. "Even if you would *allow* me to exert the power of persuasion against the perfect freedom of your own conclusions," she insists, "I would have no wish to avail myself of that power." She simply asks her readers to "examine candidly and judge in freedom" what she has to say. As she explained to a new friend, Sarah Shaw, she was "so great an advocate of individual freedom" that she would "have everything done voluntarily, nothing by persuasion."[11]

The issue of prejudice was, as Maria knew only too well, hardly a popular one with her intended readership. "Bear with me," she urges them, much as she had in her *Appeal*, "while I again come before you with an unwelcome message." She also makes it clear from the start that she has no intention of idealizing blacks as a class. They are, she contends, "what any people would be, who had so long been trampled upon by the iron hell of contemptuous tyranny." Exposing her own middle-class squeamishness about mingling with "the vicious element in society," Maria is careful to assure her readers that she hasn't "the slightest wish to do violence to the distinctions of society by forcing the rude and illiterate into the presence of the learned and refined." The abolitionists, she maintains, "merely wish that colored people should have the same opportunities for instruction, the same civil treatment at public places, the same chance to enlarge their sphere of usefulness, that is enjoyed by the lowest and most ignorant white man in America."[12]

In Boston, as elsewhere in the North, the social mingling of blacks and whites was all but unheard of, particularly in the middle and upper ranks of society. Maria herself had known few blacks before she joined the antislavery movement, and, while women of color had been admitted almost from the beginning as members of the BFASS, the role of black men in the deliberations of the state and national societies was less clear. Charles Follen, a Harvard professor who lost his job when he joined the abolitionists, expressed the ambivalence of many of his colleagues when he reported to the MASS that they had been advised "not unnecessarily to shock the feelings, though they were but prejudices, of the white people, by admitting colored persons to our Anti-Slavery meetings and societies."[13] Despite such warnings, blacks continued to be welcome at abolitionist gatherings in Boston, relegated, however, to their own section of the hall.

If Maria had done her best in *The Oasis* to avoid offending the sensibilities of proper Bostonians, whom she hoped would buy and read her book, she was less cautious in a story she wrote for children in one of the final issues of the *Miscellany*, whose subscriptions were already paid for. "Mary French and Susan Easton," a tale which calls to mind John Howard Griffith's novel *Black Like Me*, concerns two little girls who live on neighboring farms in a sparsely settled region west of the Mississippi. Mary is white and Susan is black, but apart from the color of their skins there is little difference between them. One day while the two are out playing they are captured by an itinerant pedlar, who ties and gags them, intending to sell them both as slaves. Mary's fair complexion is no protection, for the pedlar simply cuts off her hair and curls it, then rubs her body with soot and grease until she is even blacker than her friend Susan. Mary quickly learns what it feels like to be a slave. Following their captor down the road, the two children pass a white man, to whom Mary calls out, hoping he will rescue her, but when the pedlar tells the stranger that the girls are "only a couple of young slaves who are so refractory I can't keep 'em still," the man replies that the pedlar should "give 'em a touch of the whip; that will quiet their tongues." The pedlar then carries the girls off into the woods and beats them with his shoe.

Mary is sold to a plantation owner and given over to the care of Dinah, a kindly old slave, who does not believe the little girl when she tells her "again and again, that she was a white child." Dinah knows only too well how many lies she herself has told to avoid a whipping. Not until she gives Mary a bath does the old woman discover the little girl is telling the truth. But even with the black soot removed, Mary is not treated any differently from the other slaves on the plantation. Once, while working in the fields, she innocently turns to look at a little bird perched on the stump of an old tree, only to find herself struck "smartly across the shoulders" by the slave driver.

Eventually Mary's master discovers he has been cheated by the pedlar, and the girl is allowed to return home. But Susan Easton is never freed. Her father "was afraid to go in search of *his* child, because," as Maria explains to her young readers, "a free colored man travelling was liable to be taken up and sold, or shot through the head for a runaway slave." The little black girl's parents therefore "wept without hope." "They never could gain any tidings of their lost child. She is no doubt a slave, compelled to labor without receiving any wages for her hard work, and whipped whenever she dares to say that she has a right to be free. Yet the only difference between Mary French and Susan Easton is, that the black color could be rubbed off from Mary's skin, while from Susan's it could not."[14]

The fictional little girl, Mary French, had not known what it meant to be prejudiced against blacks until she and Susan were captured by the pedlar. Here Maria echoes an observation she had made in her *Appeal*, namely that much of the discomfort that she and other Northerners felt in the presence of blacks stemmed from the lack of contact between the two races. If whites knew more about black people, saw more of them, and understood better what they had suffered, this prejudice might go away. "It would seem natural," she had told the readers of her *Appeal*, "that those who were more accustomed to the sight of dark faces would find their aversion diminished, rather than increased."[15]

According to Harriet Martineau, the English writer and reformer who paid a long visit to the United States beginning in 1834, quite a stir was created when rumors circulated that the Childs had entertained colored people in their own home. One winter afternoon in 1834 a black couple had called at the house in Cottage Place seeking legal advice. The visit was a long one and as the tea hour approached Maria went into the kitchen to put on the kettle. When she returned with the tea things, she found that the visitors had left, not wishing to embarrass their hosts by sharing a meal with them. Word quickly spread that David and Maria Child "had given an invitation to colored people" and, according to Martineau, the story prompted laughter and ridicule in aristocratic parlors. The event was even remarked upon in abolitionist circles. Caroline Weston reported hearing from a friend that "Mrs. Child has had a party lately and invited colored persons."[16]

Eyebrows were raised again the following winter when David rushed to the defense of a crew of pirates. Back in 1832 an American brig, the *Mexican*, out of Salem, had suffered an unprovoked attack on the high seas from the Spanish *Panda*. One of the survivors told a horrifying tale of theft, arson, and murder, but the culprits had escaped unharmed. Two years later, however, a British man-of-war intercepted the *Panda* and delivered the twelve members of the crew over to law enforcement authorities in Boston. In the eyes of the public the dozen men, five of whom were described as "men of color," were unquestionably guilty and deserved to be hung. But David Child, who had been closely following the affair, was certain that important evidence proving the crew's guilt was lacking. The men had been apprehended apart from their ship with no proof, only suspicion, that they were the true culprits. Ready as ever to take up the cause of the underdog, David offered to defend the pirates at no charge.

The crew's reputation as a disreputable, foul-mouthed gang did not make David's job as their counselor an easy one, but he nonetheless succeeded in removing the charges for five out of the twelve. On December 16, 1834, after what was later described by some as an unfair trial, the remaining seven were sentenced to be hung. Only a presidential pardon could now save them. David, who characteristically could not rest until everything possible had been done for his clients, would have gone to Washington himself to plead with President Jackson on their behalf but decided to remain in Boston to protect the condemned men from threatened mob violence. Maria therefore agreed to go in his place.[17]

Sometime in February 1835, Maria journeyed south to the nation's capital by boat and stagecoach, a courageous venture for any woman alone, but particularly for one of known abolitionist sympathies. By the twenty-fifth she was in Washington, staying at the home of Attorney General Benjamin Butler. In the end her efforts to obtain a pardon for the pirates proved futile, since David had sent her away with no documents to support her case. Without a formal document requesting a reprieve from either the judge or the jury in the case—neither of which David had been able to obtain—a presidential pardon was unlikely. By February 28 Maria had left Washington and was in New York, where, grasping at straws, she sent Butler one final plea asking him to extend the date of execution. Were she certain the accused were indeed guilty of piracy, she assured the Attorney General, she would feel no mercy. "But when I think of the seven men, six of whom are husbands and fathers, being hung first, and proved innocent afterward, it seems as if I could go to the ends of the earth to prevent it."[18]

Perhaps it was thanks to Maria's efforts that the last of the condemned men did not swing from the gallows until September, but she could claim no credit for the fact that one of the seven went free. While her own protestations on behalf of the prisoners had gone unheeded by Jackson, the tearful pleas of the beautiful young wife of the *Panda's* first mate struck a more responsive chord in the President, who pardoned her husband. Years later the abolitionist orator Wendell Phillips praised Maria's efforts in the *Panda* affair, claiming that "it was she as much as her lionhearted husband who, at their own cost, saved Boston from the crime and infamy of murdering twelve pirates before they had even a mockery of a trial."[19]

Unfortunately, David's admirable defense of the *Panda's* crew did little to improve his reputation as a supporter of law and order. Among Bostonians a conviction was growing that the Childs and their abolitionist friends were conspiring to force disreputable people into their midst. By the summer of 1835 fear and hatred of the Negro had erupted into mob violence in Boston and elsewhere in the North as "gentlemen of property and standing" rose up against the organized antislavery movement.

Public suspicion of the menacing power of abolitionist sentiment had been mounting since the previous summer, when Garrison had returned from a tour of England with the news that the British had denounced the principle of colonization as an effective antislavery tactic. While abroad, the editor of the *Liberator* had befriended George Thompson, the renowned British antislavery agitator. Garrison had been so impressed by the professional skill with which Thompson debated the cause that he invited him to come and tour the Northeastern states and share his reform tactics with American abolitionists.

George Thompson's American tour, which began in the fall of 1834, had done little to quiet the rising storm of opposition to Garrison and his followers. If anything, the presence of this "foreign agent" seemed to further polarize opinions on the slavery question. In lecture after lecture—he gave some three hundred in all—Thompson denounced the slaveholders, the colonizationists, even the American clergy, and implied that if any people in this world had a right to take up arms to secure their own freedom the slaves of the United States did.[20] Thompson's reputation as an antislavery agitator had preceded his arrival on American soil, and from the time he landed in New York in the fall of 1834 until his clandestine departure from Nova Scotia in November 1835 his presence seemed to generate an atmosphere of excitement and violence.

Yet by all accounts the British abolitionist, like his friend Garrison, was as gentle and kindly in private as he was outspoken and uncompromising in public. The Childs, who had probably been introduced to Thompson shortly after his arrival in Boston in December 1834, found themselves quickly drawn to this eloquent Englishman with his easy manner and extraordinary gift for grasping the essentials of any argument. As one admirer described him, "Mr. Thompson is never vehement, never impassioned, except in cases where truth—from its strength, and fact from its atrocity . . . require it; and then and only then is he energetic—powerful—overwhelming—almost oppressive."[21] Maria delighted as well in the private Thompson, in his playful moods and nimble wit. Over the course of the next twelve months she and David developed a deep attachment to the British reformer.

Both Childs were in Julian Hall on the first of August 1835, when Thompson delivered an address commemorating the first anniversary of the British emancipation of the West Indies. As Maria waited for the meeting to open, she picked out a number of Southerners standing at the back of the hall dressed in fine broadcloth. She also noticed "a dozen or more stout red-faced truckmen in shirt sleeves." Closer to the front, she spotted "an ill-looking fellow, whose bloated countenance, so furious and so sensual, seemed a perfect embodiment of the French Revolution. A genteel-looking young man, with nice gloves, and white fur hat, held frequent whispered consultations with this vile-looking personage. It seemed to me a strange alliance. I inquired who the white hat was, and was told that it was Mr. Stetson, bar-keeper of the Tremont [House]."

When Thompson entered the hall Maria watched as one of the Southerners pointed significantly in the Englishman's direction. Her heart beat violently, she later recalled, as she observed preparations being made for a savage mob. Thompson, apparently unperturbed, proceeded to let loose "burning torrents of eloquence." His address, by Maria's recounting, contained "nothing vulgar or vindictive, but it had scorched like lightening." Following the lecture a palpable tension filled the air. The stairway and front entrance were reportedly blocked by "desperate-looking fellows, brandishing clubs and cart-whips." Determined to protect her hero, Maria moved toward the lecture platform and joined a group of women forming a dense circle around the speaker. While engaging Thompson in conversation, the group gradually approached a small door at the rear of the platform. Then, as Maria described it, "the circle opened—the door opened—" followed by a "volley of oaths" from the truckmen, and "a deafening roar down the front stairs." But a carriage with fast horses and a Negro driver was waiting at the back entrance to convey Thompson to safety.[22]

Whether or not it was Thompson's idea to send both Childs to England as antislavery agents, he clearly had a part in the scheme. His lecture tour in the United States had been fully publicized back home, providing his countrymen with unprecedented coverage of American antislavery efforts. The Garrisonians were concerned, however, that their own case was being misrepresented by the British press, and in the spring of 1835 they drew up plans to send several agents abroad to represent their views. The Childs seemed an appropriate choice for this mission.[23]

From their point of view the timing could not have been better. David's law practice had failed and the income from Maria's books was at an all-time low. On top of their salary as agents, Maria believed she could earn more money from her writing in England where, unlike in the United States, her books were selling well. Thankful for this solution to their difficulties, the Childs prepared to leave the country for an indefinite period. On August 6 an auction of their household furnishings was held at Cottage Place.[24] Now the only obstacle to their departure was a pending suit against David connected with his editorship of the *Massachusetts Journal.* But for the time being at least it did not hinder their plans.

Much was made of the Childs during these days as they prepared to leave for New York to await passage to England. In gratitude for Maria's services to the antislavery cause, the Lynn and Salem Female Anti-Slavery Society had pooled its resources and presented her with a gold watch. On August 8 the Childs were given a farewell party by the Lorings. Meanwhile, antiabolitionist riots had erupted all over the North, sending people into the streets to denounce the Garrisonians and their foreign allies. George Thompson's friends, alarmed for his safety, slipped Thompson away with the Childs when they left Boston on August 10. After stopping in Newport to visit David's brother John, the three found a relatively safe haven in Brooklyn at the home of a British abolitionist and his wife. But, as Maria wrote Louisa Loring on the day after their arrival, the atmosphere in New York was no friendlier than that of Boston. "I have not ventured into the city, nor does one of us dare to go to church today, so great is the excitement here. You can form no conception of it—'Tis like the times of the French Revolution, when no man dared trust his neighbor. Private assassins from N[ew] Orleans are lurking at the corners of the streets . . . and very large sums are offered for any one who will convey Mr. Thompson into the slave states." Maria admitted to Louisa that she had "started and trembled and wept like a child" for fear that he would be discovered. Thompson returned to Boston the following day.[25]

Had all gone according to plan the Childs would themselves have been safely en route to England on August 16. But David's legal entanglements had followed him to New York. Hours before they were to sail, he was arrested on the dock for nonpayment of a debt owed to his ex-law partner, George Snelling, one of the financial backers of the defunct *Massachusetts Journal.* Maria is reputed to have sat down right there on the dock and wept when she heard the news. Later David would claim that an antiabolitionist conspiracy in Boston was behind the arrest; nor was he alone in ascribing malicious intent to it.[26]

A few days after his arrest, David returned to Boston to settle the charges against him. Maria, hoping the date for their departure had simply been postponed, remained behind. Not wanting their Brooklyn hosts to incur risks on her account she rented a room in a seaside hotel. "Never before or since," she later recalled, "have I experienced such utter desolation, as I did the few days I remained there." With no friends in New York, it seemed "as if anti-slavery had cut me off from all the sympathies of my kind." She consoled herself by watching the surging ocean and writing a poem for George Thompson. By August 25 she had found more congenial lodgings, boarding with the family of Joseph Carpenter, a Quaker farmer, whose house had long served as a station on the Underground Railroad and more recently had sheltered persecuted abolitionists.[27]

David, his affairs still unsettled, returned from Boston at the end of the month bringing word of Mayor Otis' denunciation of the abolitionists before a cheering crowd in Fanueil Hall on August 21. A new date, October 1, was now set for the departure for England, and in the interval Maria accompanied David on a trip to Philadelphia.

News that the respected Boston author and abolitionist was in town brought Maria an invitation from the members of the Philadelphia Female Anti-Slavery Society to attend one of their monthly meetings. Here for the first time she met the eloquent Quaker preacher and crusader for women's rights, Lucretia Mott. Here also she was introduced to a new convert to abolitionism, Angelina Grimké. In 1829, Angelina, repelled by the system of slavery in her native Charleston, South Carolina, had taken a bold step for a well-born Southern woman and migrated north to join her sister Sarah, also unmarried, then living in Philadelphia. Deeply religious, both sisters had joined the Quakers and were devoting themselves to a life of piety and good works. In the spring of 1835, moved in part by the oratory of George Thompson, Angelina had joined the abolitionists. Maria was delighted with this spirited Southerner. She enjoyed particularly Angelina's apt response when a member of the Philadelphia Society cautiously suggested that the time was not yet ripe for the overthrow of slavery: "If thou wert a slave, toiling in the fields of Carolina," Angelina had assured the woman, "I apprehend thou wouldst think the time had *fully* come."[28]

Maria and David returned to New Rochelle only to resume their uncertain existence. October 1 came and went but no ship carried them to England. Meanwhile Maria did her best to profit from living in a household where blacks and whites mingled freely with one another. Shortly after the Childs' arrival in the small Quaker community surrounding the Carpenter farm, rumors began circulating that the Boston abolitionists objected to sitting at the same table with colored people. In fact, quite the reverse was true, and Maria wrote Ellis Loring that "it was a solid satisfaction to see prejudice so entirely forgotten." "At *our* table," she boasted, "the blacks, domestics and all, have a majority of one."[29]

Three of these blacks were the children of a poor widow. Maria had persuaded the Carpenters to take them in as boarders so they could attend a nearby school where the teacher was ready to welcome colored scholars. But even in this Quaker district of New Rochelle the sight of blacks and whites mingling freely was unusual enough for Maria to be stopped by a local farmer as she accompanied her three charges to school on their first morning. He was curious, he explained, to find out "what little white girl that was with three colored children walking with her."[30]

As it turned out Maria had plenty of opportunity to bask in the egalitarian atmosphere of the Carpenter household—she would remain there for more than six months. While David looked for work, Maria took advantage of the peace and quiet of her new surroundings to attend to her writing. When a mob of angry Bostonians stormed a meeting of the BFASS on October 21, 1835, and dragged Garrison through the streets of the city, she was far away from all the excitement and danger. Did she miss it? Perhaps. But she was also feeling confined by her new career as a reformer and longed to get back to literature."[31]

9

A Reluctant Reformer

*There have been seasons when my soul felt restless
in this bondage.*
　　　　　　　—*Lydia Maria Child*, Philothea

By early 1836 the Childs had withdrawn from their proposed
mission to England. A new and more adventurous scheme
had captured David's fancy: the opportunity to join Benjamin Lundy's free-labor settlement in Matamoros, Mexico. Lundy,
who had once employed Garrison as co-editor of his reformist
newspaper, *The Universal Emancipator*, planned to demonstrate in
his proposed colony that racial inferiority was a myth and that
whites and free blacks could work and live comfortably side by side.
He also hoped to stimulate the free produce movement by em-
ploying blacks to raise such traditionally slave-made staples as cotton and sugar. This last aspect of the scheme particularly appealed
to David Child.[1]

Lundy was delighted that such a respected antislavery supporter
as Child was interested in joining his experimental colony. But
David's enthusiasm for the project was not shared by his wife or
his friends. They quite rightly regarded the whole scheme as an
outlandish and extremely risky venture.[2] Since the Mexican government had abolished slavery in 1829, American settlers in Matamoros had been fighting to establish an independent proslavery
republic there. Throughout the summer and fall of 1835 armed
clashes between Texan colonists and Mexican troops had been
mounting, rendering the political situation there extremely volatile.

Such dangers were no obstacle to David. Never one to be deterred once he'd made up his mind, he spent the autumn trying to convince Maria that the project made sense. In late January 1836, after months of "anxious deliberation," she finally gave in, and, in a letter to Ellis and Louisa Loring, did her best to sound cheerful about the privations and difficulties which now faced her. Reflecting that no other practical solution to their indebtedness had materialized, she hoped the Lorings would "see the necessity of our going into *some* new country." At least she had the satisfaction of knowing that by living in a free-labor colony she could be "extensively useful to the oppressed."[3]

Maria confessed in this same letter that she was tired: tired of poverty and chronic homelessness; tired of having her hopes raised when some new solution to hers and David's future arose, only to have them dashed when the prospect fell through. She admitted that "the state of *inaction* and *uncertainty*" which she had suffered for the last few months had proved a "severe trial. I have not always borne it as a Christian should," she conceded, but comforted herself with the reminder that "such seasons are useful to teach us how habitually we lean upon the world, and how little we trust in God. I have been nearer to losing all faith and hope in Divine Providence than I remember ever to have experienced."[4]

The writing of *Philothea*, her first novel since *The Rebels*, proved a source of comfort in these months of isolation and uncertainty in New Rochelle. For the past several years Maria had seized the rare idle moment to begin composing a romance set in ancient Greece. But only here in this quiet Quaker farmhouse, where most of her domestic needs were cared for, would she find the time to finish the story. For perhaps a few hours each day, when her writing for the antislavery papers was done and David's wants attended to, she was free to wander unimpeded in a romantic and idealistic region of her own making. She describes this sense of release in the preface to the first edition of the novel:

> The hope of extended usefulness has hitherto induced a strong effort to throw myself into the spirit of the times; which is prone to neglect beautiful and fragrant flowers, unless their roots answer for vegetables, and their leaves for herbs. But there have been seasons when my soul felt restless in this bondage,—like the Pegasus of Greek fable, chained to a plodding ox, and offered in the market; and as that rash steed, when he caught a glimpse of the far blue-sky, snapped the chain that bound him, spread his wings, and left the earth beneath him—so I, for awhile, bid adieu to the substantial fields of utility, to float on clouds of romance.[5]

The heroine of this escapist venture, Philothea, is a creature of unsurpassed beauty and virtue. She is Maria's ideal woman: wise, serene, and otherworldly, neither distracted by earthly concerns nor torn by earthly passions. Philothea's intense love of beauty lends a poetic excitement to even the most ordinary occupations of her life, and she thus greatly prefers a quiet domestic existence to the pleasures and vanities which flourish outside her father's house. This "gentle recluse," as Maria describes her, who "listens to the whisperings of the gods in the stillness of her own heart," eventually marries an equally virtuous and spiritual young man named Paralus. Shortly before the wedding Paralus is stricken with a debilitating illness and the marriage is never consummated. Philothea, perfectly content with this state of things, passes her wedding night dreaming of holding "free communion with Paralus in that beautiful spirit-land," where his soul was already "wandering before its time." In the short span of their earthly life together, Philothea devotes herself unstintingly to caring for her "tall infant," as she calls Paralus, who like Maria's own husband is more of a child than a man. After her husband's death, Philothea mourns not his passing but her "own widowed lot." She longs, above all, for their spirits to be reunited in heaven, and her prayers are soon answered.[6] At the end of the story, the reader is left wondering if Philothea's creator is not expressing an unconscious desire for her own husband's death.

Philothea may be set in ancient Athens, but the political and philosophical preoccupations of its major characters are more reminiscent of nineteenth-century Bostonians. Here we find Pericles, the Athenian statesman, bearing an uncanny resemblance to David Child's idea of a Jacksonian tyrant. He deems honesty "excellent in theory" but "policy safe in practice" and proceeds to deprive his enemies of power by reviving ancient laws which lead to the decline of democracy and the growth of intolerance. Here also is the good republican, Anaxagoras (Philothea's father) who distrusts democratic rule and refuses "to believe that a man who is governed by ten thousand masters has more freedom than he who is governed by one."[7]

But *Philothea* is, above all, a fictional exploration of the connection between the material and the spiritual world. Combining Swedenborgianism and Platonic idealism with the newly emerging philosophy of Transcendentalism, Maria has created a heroine who is perfectly in tune with nature and the Divine Mind. She herself has seen the "Spirit of Beauty, that glides through the universe, breathing the invisible through visible forms, in such mysterious harmony."[8] Philothea knows better than anyone except her husband, Paralus, that spirit is the substance of reality and that matter is merely its shadow.

In her preface to *Philothea*, Maria observes that, while most readers might consider her book "romance of the wildest kind," there are a "few kindred spirits, prone to people space 'with life and mystical predominance,' " who will "perceive a light *within* the Grecian temple."[9] One such kindred spirit was Ralph Waldo Emerson, whose long essay *Nature* would appear in Boston bookstores only a few weeks after *Philothea*. Emerson, now in his early thirties, had quit the Unitarian pulpit in 1832. Since then he had been writing essays and giving lectures which were attracting a growing number of young men and women. Many of the themes first aired in these lectures and essays were now gathered between the covers of his first book. *Nature* begins by calling on Americans to embrace a new faith, one more in tune with the progressive spirit of the age. Why, Emerson asks, "should we grope among the dry bones of the past," when we have before us "new lands, new men, new thoughts"? To find this new religion, he suggests, men and women must be in harmony with nature, for it is through nature and not through tradition that God speaks to us. Nature's secrets, however, must be grasped intuitively, and they are so faint and dim that only the quiet and pure can hear them. But, Emerson asks his readers, "Who can set bounds to the possibilities of man?" Once purified and attuned to nature's language, human souls will have access to the entire mind of God and will themselves become creators.[10]

Emerson had presented a copy of *Nature* to his friend Convers Francis, knowing that he would be sympathetic to the idealistic views of man and nature contained there. Back in 1832 Maria's brother had openly declared his sympathy for the emerging philosophy of Transcendentalism when he spoke of the human soul as "a particle of the Divine Mind," and in 1836, the "Annus Mirabilis" of Transcendentalism, he rejoiced to see "spiritualists" like his friend Waldo and his sister Maria "taking the field in force."[11] Knowing that Convers would be one of her more indulgent readers, Maria had dedicated *Philothea* to him.

The novel was ready for the printers by the spring of 1836, but it was late summer before it appeared in the bookstores. A letter from Caroline Weston to her sister Anne suggests that unnamed persons were trying to prevent its publication. Once out, however,

Philothea received wide notice and was generally acclaimed as Maria Child's most distinguished literary work to date. The *North American Review*, which had spoken so harshly of her *Appeal*, predicted that *Philothea* would "take a permanent place in our elegant literature." Edgar Allen Poe declared the novel, with its lucid evocation of the "distantly antique," to be "an honor to our country and a signal triumph for our country-women." While no record survives of Emerson's response to *Philothea*, young Henry Thoreau, then a senior at Harvard, liked it enough to copy two pages of extracts into a notebook.[12]

But sales of Maria's new novel did not match the attention it received from the critics. Perhaps Sarah Joseph Hale summed up the problem when she noted in her review of *Philothea* that "the bitter feelings engendered by the [antislavery] strife have prevented the merits of this remarkable book from being appreciated as they deserve." Maria's other publishing efforts were not much more successful. While she was earning some money from her *History of the Condition of Women*, antislavery articles she had been commissioned to write for the New York commercial and political newspapers were either ignored or rejected.[13]

The Childs' future remained uncertain. In May 1836 Maria informed Louisa Loring that David had grown "somewhat disheartened and unsettled" by events in Texas and feared war might break out there between Mexico and the United States. The Matamoros venture was thankfully off. Meanwhile a letter had come from George Thompson urging them to reconsider emigrating to England, where the friends of abolition wished them to edit a periodical. While they waited to hear further news from Thompson, the couple spent the early part of the summer in West Boylston with David's parents. There, according to one report, David occupied his time ploughing while Maria sewed.[14] In July, Maria, needing a quiet place to write, left her in-laws and moved in with her father, who now lived in South Natick.

Within days of leaving West Boylston, Maria responded to a sad letter from David with deliberate cheerfulness, as if to reassure herself as much as him about their marriage and their future prospects. "Do not be discouraged," she wrote on July 28. " 'Better days are coming'—even in *this* world. And for another, who can tell with how much gratitude we may hereafter look back upon the fiery trials sent to purge away the gold?" Few men, she assured him, "have done more good in the world than you have done. Few are more *truly* respected, though thousands are more popular." She tried to console him by insisting that the mistakes he had made were not "willful wrongs" but only "errors of judgment."[15]

For every five letters Maria wrote David during the ensuing weeks she received only one from him. Admitting that she was perhaps foolishly sentimental to write so often, she explained how important it was that she busy herself about something that concerned him. In one letter she enclosed a love poem, the last two verses of which echoed her idealization of love in *Philothea*:

> And think not now that *any* power
> Can burst the magic chain,
> Begun by love in youthful hour,
> And strengthened since by pain!
>
> No! death itself can ne'er destroy
> What love and time have done—
> He will but purify our joy,
> And make us *truly* one.[16]

Occasionally, during the weeks she lived with her father, Maria slipped into Boston for a visit, staying either with the Lorings or Henrietta Sargent. Early in August she learned from her antislavery friends that a Bostonian, Thompson Aves, was holding a very young slave girl named Med captive in his house on Pinkney Street. The child belonged to his daughter, a Mrs. Slater of New Orleans, and the abolitionists wanted to make certain that Med never returned south with her mistress. A delegation of antislavery women, including Maria Child, succeeded in gaining admittance to Aves' house, where they tried to persuade him to set the little girl free. But Aves refused, later claiming that the women had entered his house under false pretenses by pretending to be Sunday school teachers looking for pupils. Maria and her friends did not leave the premises, however, until they had made certain that Med was indeed a slave and that her mistress intended to carry her back to New Orleans. A writ of habeas corpus was then secured against Aves for his detention of Med. When the trial opened on August 18, Maria was in the courtroom, marveling at the "sophistry and eloquence" employed by the southern counsel as they attempted to persuade the Court of a slaveowner's right to retain his slaves on visits to the North. She later told a friend that one of the lawyers had actually shed tears over the possibility that "mistaken benevolence" might separate Med from her slave mother. But this pathos was undercut when Ellis Loring produced evidence obtained by the BFASS that Mrs. Slaughter planned to sell the child on her return to New Orleans. In the end, Chief Justice Lemuel Shaw in an unprecedented decision ruled in Med's favor. He declared that a slave carried temporarily into a free state had a right to remain there.[17]

Maria was back in South Natick following the successful outcome of the trial when word came that her old friend, Emily Marshall Otis, had died in childbirth. The two had not seen much of one another in recent years, and Maria had resisted the impulse to call on the Otises the previous spring for fear of embarrassing Emily and her family. But the sad news of her friend's passing flooded her mind with memories: "The various scenes of gayety and sorrow in which we two had been together; her uniform kindness to me; the deep tenderness I always felt for her, the gradual estrangement which took place from no estrangement of feeling, but because our paths in life diverged from each other."[18]

September found David and Maria in New York together, staying with Dr. Abraham Coxe on Broome Street while they awaited confirmation of their sailing date for England. Then came the news that David had lost his lawsuit to his ex-partner, George Snelling, and owed that gentleman the enormous sum of $9,750. To repay his now considerable debts, David probably felt that he needed more lucrative employment than that offered by his English friends. For some time he had been captivated by the possibilities of yet another scheme, the chance several wealthy Philadelphians offered him to learn the process of beet sugar manufacture.

Sugar beet production was all the rage in the mid-1830s. Manufacturers in France were demonstrating that sugar made from beets could be competitive with cane sugar. By learning the new process David could satisfy his long-standing interest in contributing to the free-produce movement and to the eventual boycott of slave-made goods. But no sooner had he agreed to accept the Philadelphians' offer than it was withdrawn. "Then all was afloat again," as Maria wrote her mother-in-law. In the end, thanks to the generosity of antislavery friends, David was persuaded to go abroad on his own to study beet sugar manufacture. On October 17, 1836, Maria was on the docks waving goodbye as her husband's ship, following innumerable delays, finally sailed for England.[19]

David's departure alone meant the end of a dream for Maria. In a letter to her mother-in-law, she admitted resignedly that her poverty and not her will had "consented to remaining behind, while one I loved so much was going where I so much wished to go."[20] She could not afford to accompany David, and, while she would not admit this to his mother, she surely resented the fact that in being sent abroad he was getting what by all rights should have been hers. Her books were selling well in England, and she had welcomed an opportunity to recoup her literary fortunes in what she imagined would be more congenial surrounding for an abolitionist. The disappointment was a bitter blow from which she never entirely recovered.

At first Maria planned to spend the winter in Boston, where she could more easily find the books she needed for her writing. But by the end of November she had decided that it would be cheaper to live in South Natick with her father. In a determined effort to receive no more charity from anyone, she had obtained Convers Francis' reluctant consent to accept one dollar per week for her board and the cost of her own firewood.[21]

Apart from an occasional trip to Boston or New York on antislavery society business, Maria rarely left her father's house. The months of David's absence proved a sad and lonely time. After one rather brisk letter from him in mid-January telling of his safe arrival in England, she heard no more for two months. All that winter and spring she indulged in gloomy fantasies that her husband was "pleasuring away in Europe forgetful of his old wife." She admitted to Louisa Loring that she had been "out of sorts with matrimony," but that repeated disappointments and discouragements had perhaps prompted these "querulous and unreasonable thoughts." Added to David's long silence was her father's unremitting melancholy. "To contend with his gloom and my own too, has sometimes seemed a hopeless task," she told her sister-in-law Lydia Child after finally receiving another letter from her husband in late March. Nor was she sanguine about David's prospects once he returned. "I have a sort of superstition customary bad luck will follow him in everything," she observed resignedly. "The fact is, I no longer have any hope concerning these matters"[22]

Maria's anxiety about the future redoubled her need to make money from her writing, but she was finding it more difficult than ever to publish her work. In the years between 1836 and 1842 only two small books were printed: the third volume of her *Authentic Anecdotes of American Slavery* and a sequel to *The Frugal Housewife*, entitled *The Family Nurse*. Occasionally a periodical would take her poems and stories. *The Maine Monthly* brought out a poem in February 1837 called "Pleasant Valley," and that same year *The Boston Book* published an earlier story, "The Fountain of Beauty."[23] But by 1838 only the antislavery press seemed willing to publish her writing, and theirs was not a lucrative market.

With no printers at her back demanding copy, Maria began composing a long work of abolitionist fiction; the book was never finished, however, and the manuscript is now lost. Perhaps the appearance of a pioneer antislavery novel, *The Slave; or, Memoirs of Archie Moore*, by Richard Hildreth early in 1837 discouraged her. Maria greatly admired this story of a runaway slave told with "all the eloquence of genius," but she also realized that "anything that took the *same* ground as Archy Moore would seem utterly tame in comparison."[24]

Not surprisingly perhaps, Maria's Boston friends noticed a change in her that winter. The old enthusiasm for antislavery society work had subsided, and she seemed to prefer hibernating with her cranky father in South Natick to forwarding the abolitionist cause in the company of good friends in Boston. When Louisa and Ellis remarked critically on this growing reclusiveness, Maria replied that the "bustling world" had become "inconceivably irksome" to her "wearied spirit." Broke, discouraged, abandoned by her husband, and unable to publish her writings, she had no need to defend herself. She told the Lorings she was tired of being "polished marble, without any obtruding corners to jostle other polished marbles," particularly when her own future was so uncertain. "With all the busy machinery of society, I have nought to do. The puppets, and those that move them, are all strangers to me; and I cannot find any reasons why I should seek to make acquaintance with them."[25]

One such "puppet," in Maria's eyes, was the revered Unitarian minister William Ellery Channing. Back in 1833 this small, frail but powerful preacher, whom Emerson referred to as "our bishop," had been so greatly impressed by Maria Child's *Appeal* that, despite his ill health, he had walked the mile and a half from his house on Mount Vernon Street to Cottage Place to discuss the issue of slavery. During their three-hour conversation Channing had credited Maria Child with rousing his conscience to speak out on the question, but he had also cautioned her against overzealousness.[26]

Channing was no abolitionist, which he made very clear in a pamphlet entitled *Slavery* published in 1835. Distancing himself from reformers like Garrison and George Thompson, whose "fierce, bitter and abusive" language he blamed for inciting mob violence and courting social upheaval, he spoke instead of the need to bring an end to slavery in a "calm, self-controlled, benevolent" Christian spirit. Channing's reluctance to embrace abolitionism was hardly surprising for a clergyman of his stature. Even his normally admiring parishioners were so outraged by the measured antislavery views expressed in his pamphlet that they cut him on the street. But Channing's moderation infuriated the Garrisonians, including Maria. After reading *Slavery* she sat down and wrote the author a long letter defending abolitionist principles, including immediate emancipation, which she claimed had given their doctrines "a purifying and energizing power. It leaves no escape for the startled conscience," she told Channing. "It says '*Now* is the time; and *thou* art the man.' " Had the abolitionists held back "until the wise and prudent of this world were ready to act with them," no effort to abolish slavery would ever have been made. Like the guests invited to the feast in St. Luke's Gospel they all had excuses: "Judicious politicians wanted Southern votes; judicious manufacturers were making negro cloths; and therefore could not come. Sober deacons had daughters wedded to slaveholders; sober ministers had married a slaveholding wife; and therefore they could not come."[27]

For all her denunciation of Channing's tepidness, Maria remained one of the few abolitionists with whom this influential Boston minister was willing to discuss the antislavery cause. But the role of propagandist to the "respectables" was becoming irksome to her. She complained to Louisa Loring in July 1836 that "for the sake of abolition" she had endured interviews with Channing she would not willingly have undertaken for any other cause, insisting sharply that she had "suffered many a shivering ague-fit in attempting to melt, or batter away the glaciers of his prejudice." The Lorings, however, who knew how persuasive their friend could be on the issue, showed little sympathy for such diffidence. Thus, when Maria paid a long visit to them in late October 1836, Ellis lectured her on "the absolute *necessity* of . . . mixing with people of the world—for the want of which," he told her, she "was growing intolerant and unsocial." He insisted that she must call on Channing both for politeness' sake and "as a duty to abolition."[28]

Fortunately, Maria's reluctant act of courtesy was amply rewarded. As she climbed Mt. Vernon Street to pay her intended call she met Channing himself coming down Beacon Hill. The minister was so delighted to see his abolitionist friend that he insisted on turning back to his house with her. As soon as the two were comfortably settled in Channing's parlor the conversation quickly turned to antislavery. "I could see that he had progressed (as we Yankees say) considerably since I last conversed with him," Maria reported with smug satisfaction to Henrietta Sargent, being careful to note, however, that "he still betrayed his characteristic timidity." Channing readily agreed with her that the antislavery movement and Christianity shared similar principles. The reformers' methods were what concerned him. Promoting a cause as intertwined with "politics, prejudice and interest" as antislavery was demanded good judgment and tact, he insisted. He doubted whether the seventy abolitionist agents recently sent into the field by the AASS possessed these qualities. Maria then asked whether the seventy missionaries appointed by Jesus' apostles to convert the heathen had been so very wise and prudent, at which point their argument was interrupted by several Beacon Hill ladies paying a call. One look at these visitors was enough to persuade Maria to keep silent on the issue of antislavery, until Channing himself asked her to describe the progress of the cause. Believing as always that the facts spoke for themselves, she remarked that a good number of Southerners had stopped by the headquarters of the AASS in New York to "inquire for the best books on abolition." She also told of a slaveholder's anonymous donation of fifty dollars to the Society, which had been inscribed as "The *Master's* mite toward the relief of those in bondage." This interview with Channing and his Beacon Hill friends boosted Maria's spirits for a time, especially since she later learned that her gentle adversary's name had headed a Boston petition calling for the abolition of slavery in the District of Columbia. She was quick to assure her friend Henrietta that on her next trip to Boston "the busy *mouse* will again go to work gnawing away the network, which aristocratic family and friends are all the time weaving around the *lion*."[29]

After three weeks in Boston Maria returned to South Natick, where she was soon hard at work "writing, pasting, sewing and knitting—sometimes for myself, sometimes for the [antislavery] Fair." Mid-December found her back in the city putting the final touches on an antislavery scrapbook to be displayed at the annual bazaar. According to Henrietta Sargent, who admired her friend's persistence, Maria had spent most of these cold, early winter days poring through the shelves of unheated bookstores to find a suitable illustration for the antislavery motto, "As the hart panteth for the water brook, so panteth the slave for liberty." Henrietta marveled at the hundreds of books Maria searched through in vain, the collections of engravings she pored over. When "at last the right one was found she expressed a pleasure no cruel sportsman can ever know." On the day of the fair Maria stood behind one of the many tables piled high with goods for sale, noting with pleasure that the crowded room contained "not a few of the wives and daughters of 'gentlemen of property and standing.' "[30]

For many antislavery women, who enjoyed the middle- and upper-class benefits of money and leisure, such activities as attending meetings and planning fairs provided a welcome distraction from domestic cares, a chance to work with other women, and an opportunity to feel useful to the cause. Maria lacked these benefits, and, as she later expressed it, preferred to work on her "own hook" and in her own way. She nonetheless welcomed women's expanding public mission on behalf of the slave.[31]

Maria's views on the function of women in society had been spelled out most recently in her two-volume *History of the Condition of Women*, published in 1835. This ambitious work, which completed *The Ladies Family Library*, describes the place of women in various cultures from biblical times to the present. As in her other writings in this series, Maria was careful to avoid offending her readers by speaking directly to feminist issues. Yet beneath the rather dry descriptions of the customs and laws which had affected women throughout history, there emerges the clear message that a society which respects women and gives them perfect freedom to develop and use their talents will be both virtuous and prosperous. Contradicting the charge that women who move out of their domestic sphere invariably develop masculine traits, Maria claims that if they "had perfect freedom to exercise their faculties and feelings unobstructed by partial laws or false customs," they would retain a feminine character no matter what their occupation. Over and over again she shows how woman's influence has been beneficial within a given culture, how her labor has contributed to economic welfare, her learning to moral stature, her softening influence to the enhancement of manners and the arts. When she makes the (erroneous) claim that Greek women once had the vote and that when it was taken away from them "the outward forms of decency were less scrupulously observed," she appears to be justifying women's suffrage.[32]

In her discussion of nineteenth-century American women, Maria dismisses the "many silly things" that "have been written and are now written concerning the equality of the sexes." At the same time she willingly admits that American laws and customs degrade women. As a solution to women's inferior status she offers, not a demand for equal rights, but the encouragement of "true and perfect companionship" between the sexes. Maria herself had experienced such harmony while working with Garrison and the other male members of the Boston Clique. A sketch of Garrison she wrote in later life for the *Atlantic* recalled that "no tinge of that odious thing called gallantry" had marred their behavior. The men had "consulted with anti-slavery women, and listened to their suggestions with the same respectful interest that they listened to each other." Such "true and perfect companionship," she insisted, "gives both man and woman complete freedom in their places, without a restless desire to go out of them."[33]

The respect accorded Maria Child by Garrison and his friends, their willingness to have her work side by side with them, only confirmed her already strong conviction that men and women could labor more effectively together than apart. But her sister reformers in Boston and Philadelphia were more supportive than she of a commitment to separateness. Wishing to capitalize on the proliferation of female antislavery societies in towns all over the North, they were determined to augment, not diminish, this growing solidarity among antislavery women. These female societies had been particularly effective in collecting signatures to antislavery petitions; Maria herself had assisted in this effort. By the spring of 1837, the scope and intensity of this petition drive led to a call for a Woman's Anti-Slavery Convention to be held in New York City in May. By coordinating petition work, it was hoped that over a million signatures could be obtained urging the federal government to end the interstate slave trade and to abolish slavery in the District of Columbia and the territories. The subject was discussed at the April meeting of the BFASS which Maria attended. And when the time came to choose delegates to represent the Society she was among those elected.

At first, to the consternation of her fellow reformers, Maria obstinately refused to attend the convention. Once back in South Natick, however, feeling a bit guilty about her coolness towards the project, she wrote Henrietta Sargent asking if she was wrong not to go. "If so, tell me frankly," she urged her friend, admitting that she had "various misgivings" and that her reluctance to go was so great that it might blind her "to perceptions of duty." The struggle over whether or not to conform to someone else's idea of what she should do continued. A few weeks later she was still dodging "all solicitations or inquiries about going to the great Female Convention." In the end, however, persuasion finally won her over and she agreed to be a delegate.[34]

When the convention opened in the Third Free Church in New York City on the afternoon of May 9, the large gathering of women struck some observers as ludicrous: the New York *Commercial Advertiser* dismissed it as an "Amazonian farce," attended by a "Monstrous Regiment of women." Nor were all antislavery men, even those supporting the convention, convinced that the women could carry it off. Theodore Weld, the New York abolitionist, implied as much to one of the delegates from Philadelphia, Angelina Grimké, offering her his advice and counsel. But Angelina reported that the Philadelphia and Boston women, whom she described as particularly well-versed in business, had been quite mortified to have Mr. Weld (whom she later married) suggest that they could not work effectively except under his direction.[35]

As if to prove Angelina right, Maria Child, despite her reservations about the whole affair, accepted the considerable responsibilities imposed on her at the convention and performed her duties efficiently and well. Besides being elected a vice-president, she helped draw up resolutions to be acted upon by the delegates. One such resolution urged that colored women be "seated promiscuously in all our congregations." This apparently passed without discussion. But another, criticizing the clergy for responding inadequately to the issue of slavery, was actively debated. In the end it too passed, but not unanimously.[36]

The resolution that provoked the most controversy, however, was offered by Angelina Grimké. Maintaining that "certain rights and duties are common to all moral beings," she called on women to break away from "the circumscribed limits in which corrupt custom and a perverted application of scripture" had encircled them, and to do all they could with their voices, their pens, their purses, and their example to bring an end to slavery. In a speech defending these enlarged rights and duties, Angelina challenged her sisters in "the nominally free states to break free of the bonds of womanhood" and aid the female slaves. *"They are our sisters,"* she maintained, "and to us as women, they have a right to look for sympathy with their sorrows, and effort and prayer for their rescue."[37]

Some delegates felt Angelina was going too far both in urging such an expanded public function on women and in suggesting that white women ought to help black women rather than slaves generally. These delegates refused to endorse the resolution as written. While Maria was not among those abstaining, and likely agreed with everything Angelina said, she was apparently concerned that such a radical public pronouncement might do the antislavery cause more harm than good. On the third day of the convention, she showed her willingness to compromise by moving that Angelina's resolution be reconsidered. The majority of delegates, however, did not share her concern and after some discussion the motion was lost."[38]

If Angelina had antagonized some of her fellow delegates with her radical ideas about public roles for women, the members of the BFASS who attended the convention were impressed enough with her eloquence on the subject of slavery to ask her to come to New England and speak to the women's societies there. Angelina and her sister Sarah arrived in Boston in late May, and their talks— particularly Angelina's—immediately drew large enthusiastic audiences of women. Between public lectures there were parlor meetings where the sisters addressed leading abolitionists. After an evening at the Chapmans, Angelina was pleased to report that the women present had agreed that it was time "our fetters were broken." She noted particularly that Child and Maria Chapman strongly supported this view.[39]

Within two weeks of the start of their lecture tour, the Grimkés' talks were arousing so much interest that men began attending them, and before long the sisters were speaking regularly to mixed audiences. Since most sects, except Quakers, objected to women speaking in public, there was soon a clerical outcry protesting the unladylike behavior of the two women. They were chastised both for stepping outside their sex's accepted bounds and for doing so in the name of antislavery. In late June 1837, the Congregational General Association of Massachusetts issued its annual pastoral letter which, without mentioning the Grimké sisters by name, denounced women's public appearances as lecturers and reformers: "The appropriate duties and influence of women are clearly stated in the New Testament. Those duties and that influence are unobtrusive and private, but the sources of mighty power.... We cannot, therefore, but regret the mistaken conduct of those who encourage females to bear an obtrusive and ostentatious part in measures for reform and countenance any of that sex who so far forget themselves as to itinerate in the character of public lecturers and teachers."[40]

While the Grimkés were naturally taken aback by the vehemence of this clerical attack, the president of the BFASS, Mary Parker, sent word that the Boston women would stand by them even "if everyone else forsook them." Heartened by such support, the sisters continued their speaking tour, which before it ended would carry them to more than sixty-seven towns in New England.[41]

Maria, meanwhile, spent the remainder of the summer awaiting David's return from Europe. She'd been told to expect him around the last of May. But punctuality had never been one of her husband's virtues, and it was late that fall before he finally appeared. As yet uncertain of where they would finally settle, the couple rented rooms on Washington Street in Boston, and while David looked for someone to underwrite his beet sugar business, Maria resigned herself to accepting whatever the future might bring. She felt strengthened, if not cheered, by the growing conviction that there was a "deep and eternal meaning in the symbol of the cross." She announced stoically in January 1838 that she was ready "to follow any path of usefulness." Wherever David's business took him, she would go, even "if it be to the log cabins of the West."[42]

As the winter months passed, without David finding any financial support for his beet sugar business, excitement in abolitionist circles erupted yet again over the woman question. Angelina Grimké had agreed to address a special committee of the Massachusetts Legislature on the question of antislavery petitions, and not everyone thought it a good idea. For a woman to speak at antislavery meetings was one thing, but to expose herself publicly in the halls of government was going too far. David Child was among the few, besides the women of the BFASS, to give Angelina his full support. In a letter dated February 12, assuring her of his and his wife's approval, he spoke of the encouragement he and others had given Maria to pursue a similar course, insisting that he would "feel ashamed now and forever after" if he prevented his wife from performing this or any other service "to which her judgment and the full feeling of her generous heart may impel her in behalf of the tortured and despairing innocent; and I am persuaded that if the time shall come, when the internal monitor shall indicate that way as the most useful for her to walk, she will not in any event be disobedient to the commandment."[43]

Maria herself never showed the slightest inclination to mount the lecture platform, but she and the other women of the BFASS were in the State House on February 21 to cheer Angelina on. The hall was crowded with legislators and observers. Recalling the event many years later Maria described how thin and pale Angelina had seemed when she first stood up to speak, how, at first, her voice had trembled, but soon steadied, allowing her to be heard distinctly by every person in the hall. "There was a mobility of expression, both in her countenance and her voice. . . . The whole speech was characterized by good sense, and there were passages of genuine eloquence. Knowing as I did the struggle which this conscientious effort had cost her, I looked upon her moral heroism with admiration amounting to reverence; and such I believe was the feeling of hundreds who were present."[44]

Angelina spoke twice more before the members of the Massachusetts legislature, most of whom were ready to praise the dignity and grace of her manner and the surprising cogency of her arguments. Then, before leaving Boston for good in late April, the Grimké sisters gave a series of weekly antislavery lectures at the Odeon Theater on the corner of Franklin and Federal Streets. Maria was in the audience when Angelina spoke for two hours in early April, and she could not help comparing the sight of the crowd of three thousand attentive listeners to an earlier meeting sponsored by the BFASS when a few brave women "were mobbed in their small room at 46 [Washington Street.]!"

Maria described this heartening scene in a letter to her mother-in-law which also announced that she and David would soon be moving to central Massachusetts. The Northampton Sugar Beet Company, formed in 1837, had agreed to employ David, she told Lydia Child, "on terms that will give us a comfortable living."[45] If she was hardly elated at the prospect of leaving Boston, she had the satisfaction of knowing that in following her husband to Northampton she would be doing her duty.

10

The "Iron-bound Valley of the Connecticut"

> *Great* labors do but strengthen the intellect
> of a well-balanced character, but these mil-
> lion Lilliputian cords [of domesticity] tie
> down the stoutest Gulliver that ever wrestled
> in their miserable entanglement.
> —*Lydia Maria Child to Convers Francis,*
> *1840*

Northampton, Massachusetts, was justly celebrated as an
"Eden of Loveliness" when David and Maria first went
there to live in May 1838. Picturesquely set in the Connecticut River Valley, surrounded by the most fertile farmland in
New England, the town, with its handsome, comfortable houses
and well-kept gardens, was looking its best in the bright green of
full spring. As the Childs approached Northampton from the east
Maria must have delighted in the rich, brown, newly ploughed
fields. Surely in such soil David's sugar beets would flourish.

Upon their arrival the couple rented a room in one of the houses
lining Northampton's elm-shaded streets. Their landlord, Enos
Clark, was a respected citizen. He owned a large farm and orchard,
was a deacon of the Congregational Church and a founder of the
local Anti-Slavery Society. Clark and his family were glad to welcome these distinguished new tenants. Maria's reputation as an
author and antislavery reformer had preceded her, and David's
plans for manufacturing beet sugar had already aroused considerable interest among the townsfolk. The Beet Sugar Company of
Northampton, which had promised to underwrite David's experiment and pay him a decent salary, had been founded back in 1837;
earlier in the spring of 1838 David himself had come to Northamp-

ton to lecture on the manufacturing process which he hoped to employ in his projected factory. Unable to afford a farm or factory of his own until the experiment had proved successful, David began by leasing an acre or so of rich alluvial soil and planting a small crop of sugar beets. Maria wrote Louisa Loring that they would often get up before dawn and go out together to weed the rows of beet plants when "all the world, except the birds, are asleep."[1]

For a time the beauty of the scenery and the prospect, however distant, of eventually having a place of their own filled Maria with a sense of domestic contentment. She told Louisa that she had "more of a home feeling than I have had since we left Cottage Place." She even found the stern Calvinism of their landlord, Enos Clark, and the "quiet religious refinement" of his family reassuring. She and David had rented a pew in the Unitarian Church where the pastor, Mr. Stearns, was both a good preacher and a member of the Northampton Anti-Slavery Society.[2]

The first weeks passed pleasantly enough. David went out to his field several times a day to weed and Maria often accompanied him. The remainder of her time she devoted to keeping David's clothes in order (she was making him a frock coat) and promoting the antislavery cause. At first, the Childs were warmly welcomed by the citizenry of the town, most of whom were of old Yankee stock. Northampton's reputation as one of the most beautiful spots in New England had attracted a number of retired business and professional people who contributed to its refined and cultivated tone. Maria was amused by the ease with which she befriended these gentlefolk. "Once more," she wrote Louisa, "I have it in my power to be the favorite of the class denominated first."[3]

One Northampton woman who seemed "the very embodiment of aristocracy" was Anne Lyman, the wife of the sheriff of Hampshire County. The Lymans occupied the adjoining pew in the Unitarian Church, and Maria felt instantly drawn to this learned woman who, like herself, was outspoken and firm in her convictions and with whom she could indulge the "poetical" side of her nature. Anne Lyman's opinions on most subjects ran strictly counter to Maria's. Nonetheless, the two spent many happy hours together. "I like her notwithstanding her distorted view of men and things," wrote Maria somewhat patronizingly of her new friend. "If she can manage to like me, anti-slavery, rights-of-woman, and all, it must be because she respects the daring freedom of speech which she practices."[4] Maria hoped to convert both Anne Lyman and her husband to abolitionism. She never succeeded, but the two women remained firm friends. Years later Maria described their relationship to Anne's daughter, Susan Lesley: "Both of us were as direct and energetic as a loco-motive under high pressure of steam; and, coming full tilt from opposite directions, we sometimes ran against each other with a clash. But no bones were ever broken. We laughed and shook hands after such encounters, and indulged in a little playful raillery at each others' impetuosity."

Underneath all their high-spirited disputatiousness these two friends understood one another. Aristocratic as Anne Lyman was, Maria remembered with delight the "lofty disdain" with which she rebuffed any sign of social pretension. She recalled particularly Anne's account of a visit she once paid to a very wealthy family whose members were "exceedingly careful of their dignity." During the course of her visit, Anne was informed that "a friendship of questionable gentility" had formed between one of the relatives of this family and Maria Child. "Mrs. Child is an abolitionist, you know," the rich folk informed their guest, "and she does not belong to the circle of our visitors." At this Anne Lyman exploded: "Visit *you* indeed! I should like to have you try to get her here! Send a carriage and six horses, and see if you can *get* her here!"[5]

Although the Childs had been led to believe that Northampton was a stronghold of antislavery, they soon observed that all but a few reputed sympathizers kept it wonderfully to themselves. Maria reported back to her Boston friends that Christian orthodoxy "has clothed most of the community in her straitlaced garments." If the Childs witnessed plenty of praying and preaching and concern with saving souls, they could discern little of what they considered true charity among the townspeople. After living in Northampton for two months they were only willing to claim two people as "real abolitionists."[6]

Northampton's conservatism on the slavery question was buttressed by the arrival each summer of a number of prominent Southern families. The Childs' closest neighbor, for example, was Thomas Napier, a former slave auctioneer from Charleston, South Carolina. Maria and David quickly discovered that despite his shameful profession, Napier was a respected member of the Northampton community. Like their landlord, Enos Clark, Napier was a deacon of the Congregational Church. He also taught Sunday school, informing the children under his charge that God had officially consigned the blacks to perpetual slavery.[7]

Disagreeable as it was to live so near someone who had made his living "trafficking in human beings," even more irritating to

David and Maria were the pious posturings of this man who called himself a Christian. It happened that the south wall of Napier's house rose only a few feet from the Childs' single window, and on warm summer evenings the sound of the man's prayers carried easily into their room. David did his best to drown out the offensive noise by singing and playing his accordion.[8]

Anne Lyman asked Maria soon after her arrival in Northampton if she had made the acquaintance of her Southern neighbor. When Maria observed that a slave auctioneer and an abolitionist were not "likely to find much pleasure in each other's society," Anne Lyman accused her of being as bigoted as Napier himself. Maria responded by insisting that it was one thing for Mrs. Lyman to disagree with the tactics of the abolitionists and quite another for Mr. Napier to promote his slave-trading as a God-given good. There was a difference, she insisted, "between errors of opinion and sins in actual practice."[9]

If Maria found it hard to tolerate the "fiery irascible" Mr. Napier, she had better luck befriending some of the other Southerners in town. Challenged by the opportunity to try her argumentative skills on genuine slaveholders, she willingly sought them out and, with what she described as a careful mixture of "candour and courtesy," spent many hours in hotel lobbies and private parlors discussing the issue of slavery. At first Maria was encouraged by the Southerners' friendliness and hoped her powers of persuasion would convince them of the sinfulness of the "peculiar institution" and of the need to regard Negroes as fellow human beings. But she quickly discovered her job would not be an easy one: "By education and habit they have so long thought and spoken of the colored man as a mere article of *property*, that it is impossible for them to recognize him as a *man*, and reason concerning him as a *brother*, on equal terms with the rest of the human family. If, by great effort, you make them acknowledge the brotherhood of the human race, as a sacred and eternal principle,—in ten minutes, their arguments, assertions and proposed schemes, all show that they have returned to the old habit of regarding the slave as a '*chattel personal*.' "[10]

Relations between Maria Child and Northampton's Southern visitors cooled visibly when it became clear that she and David not only opposed slavery in theory but were actively pursuing its extinction. Thomas Napier was particularly annoyed by their proselytizing and countered with missionary tactics of his own. Thus in July when his sister from South Carolina arrived for a visit accompanied by her slave Rosa, he urged Rosa to befriend Mrs. Child and show this Yankee woman how well slavery agreed with her. The colored woman passed frequently under Maria's window, looking sleek and contented. When engaged in conversation she would "boast of her happy slavery" and laugh at Maria's efforts to persuade her to take her freedom. Maria, refusing to be taken in by such subterfuges, sent Rosa's mistress a long letter decrying the evils of slavery and comparing the happiness of slaves "to that of well-fed pigs" and their destiny to dogs who were sold to one buyer while their puppies went to another. Accompanying the letter were several antislavery tracts.

If Maria hoped this barrage of antislavery literature would convince Rosa's mistress of the error of her ways she was sadly mistaken. Within two hours the letter was angrily returned, followed shortly by an indignant Rosa. The Napiers had informed their slave that their abolitionist neighbor had called her a pig and her children puppies. Maria quickly set matters straight by reading Rosa a copy of the letter, and, encouraged by this Yankee woman's sympathetic manner, Rosa was soon disclosing her life's story. Although she'd been promised her freedom by a previous owner, the document granting it had been lost. Maria, who feared that once back in the South Rosa would lose all chance of obtaining her freedom, tried to persuade the woman to remain in Northampton. But Rosa could not bear the thought of living apart from her children and other close relatives and friends, and in the end she returned home with her mistress. Maria's failure to coax Rosa into remaining in the North was a source of delight to Mr. Napier and his family, who boasted that for all of Mrs. Child's efforts to persuade Rosa to take her freedom she had preferred to stay with her beloved mistress. Here was positive proof that slavery was a benevolent institution after all.[11]

More discouraging than the intransigence of Southerners was the behavior of Northampton's Yankee natives, who showed more concern with not offending those in their midst who were proslavery than in combating Northern prejudice against Negroes. The owner of the Mansion House, a favorite resort for Southern travelers, became very annoyed with Maria when she asked a colored man staying in the hotel if he were free. "I dislike slavery as much as you do," the hotel keeper assured her, "but then I get my living by slave-holders." Maria also discovered that Margaret Dwight, the principal of the Gothic Seminary for Young Ladies, five or six of whose pupils were Southerners, was strongly prejudiced against the abolitionists. By the end of her first year in Northampton Maria was even upbraiding the tenants in her own boardinghouse for their "narrow and bigoted spirit."[12]

Most disheartening of all was the attitude of the clergy, whom Maria accused of valuing the peace of the church more than moral principle and sectarian doctrines more than the brotherhood of man. She reported to her abolitionist friends in Boston that Mr. Mitchell, the pastor of the Congregational Church, would not permit antislavery lectures in his meetinghouse for fear of driving Mr. Napier out of town. From her observation post next door she watched as almost every day baskets of fruits and vegetables were carried from Napier's garden to Mr. Mitchell's rectory and dismissed this neighborly generosity as "part of the price for which the Judas betrays his master."[13]

During this first year in Northampton both Childs were active in the organized antislavery efforts of Hampshire County. In addition to the tedious and often unpleasant ordeal of obtaining signatures to congressional petitions, they also faithfully attended antislavery meetings. Once, having traveled twenty miles to Greenfield for a Franklin County antislavery convention, Maria found the atmosphere considerably chillier than Northampton's. As she seated herself among the delegates she was at first unaware that her presence was causing any uneasiness, and she ignored the implicit hostility in the announcement that all the *gentlemen* present were welcome to join the convention. Then she overheard one man whisper to another, while gesturing in her direction, "I hope she doesn't come to introduce Boston notions. . . . I trust she is not going to advocate women's rights!"[14]

By autumn Maria was deeply discouraged with the progress of antislavery reform in what she described as "this iron-bound valley of the Connecticut." To have found lukewarm public opinion in what was reputed to be an abolitionist town was opening her eyes to certain realities which she and the other followers of William Lloyd Garrison had been unable or unwilling to face. First, many so-called antislavery sympathizers, while declaring their opposition to the "peculiar institution" in principle, willingly tolerated it in practice. Second, these same sympathizers were often very prejudiced against the Negro. On November 18 she confessed to Henrietta Sargent that she had

> ceased to believe that public opinion will ever be sincerely reformed on the question, till long after emancipation has taken place. I mean that, for generations to come, there will be a very large minority

hostile to the claims of colored people; and the majority will be largely composed of individuals, who are found on that side from any and every motive, rather than hearty sympathy with the down-trodden race. . . . The abolition of slavery in this country will certainly come; but I despair of a regenerated public sentiment, till God has brought about the event in his own way."[15]

Maria was equally pessimistic about the prospects of using moral suasion to convert the Southern slaveholder. "I do not believe the South will voluntarily relinquish her slaves, so long as the world stands," she wrote in October 1838. "It [emancipation] must come through violence. I would it might be averted; but I am convinced it cannot be."[16]

At the end of six months little of Maria's initial optimism about the move to Northampton remained. Her discouragement, combined with the mounting hostility of the townspeople, did not make the prospect of the coming winter a cheerful one. She longed for the "good, warm abolition-sympathy" to be found in Boston and dreaded the thought of the long, lonely months that lay ahead. Now that the beet crop had been harvested, David spent his days and evenings toiling in his sugar factory on Masonic Street. In earlier years she would have welcomed such solitude for her writing, but, although some of her earlier books, notably *The Frugal Housewife*, were continuing to bring in royalties, publishers were not taking any of her new work. In April 1839, particularly desperate for money, she wrote the editor of *The Token*, a magazine she had contributed to a few years earlier, asking if she could do some editing, writing, or compiling for him. Apparently nothing came of this inquiry.[17]

Meanwhile, she was growing increasingly depressed by the dreariness of her surroundings. The northern exposure of their chamber, which in summer had been refreshingly cool, now proved cold and gloomy. Not a gleam of pale sunshine penetrated the room's single window, and frost had killed the flowers which in warmer weather she had picked to add a touch of beauty to their spare furnishings. When Louisa Loring sent her some little pictures for a New Year's present, Maria wrote of the pleasure they had given her. "Three or four times a day I sit and contemplate them . . . and my soul seems to drink in beauty at long draughts."[18]

To swamp Maria's depressed spirits, in late winter David's sugar business, which until then had seemed so promising, was in severe financial trouble. The summer's beet crop had been harvested and David was successfully manufacturing his first batch of sugar when news reached them that some up-to-date machinery, bought while David was in Europe, had been lying for several months rusting on the docks in New York awaiting payment for its release. The Illinois Company, which had originally underwritten David's business but then backed off, had refused to pay the bill of more than $300, and the Childs were now being forced to come up with a sum they didn't have. Maria's father had kindly helped by sending them $100, but that left another $200 still to be found.[19]

Reluctantly, Maria wrote Ellis Loring asking for a loan to be repayed with royalties from her writing. Meanwhile George Snelling, David's old partner, was once again harassing him for nonpayment of debts connected with the *Massachusetts Journal*. Just as planting season was under way, Snelling's lawyer called David down to New York City. Threatened with another jail sentence if he didn't pay up, David finally got away with a plea of insolvency and a partial payment of $150. When he finally returned to Northampton several weeks later, Maria was nearly frantic with worry. She wrote Louisa that she would willingly try anything to earn some money if she could only figure out what to do. She would consider starting a school except for the danger of being called away "to follow Mr. Child's fortunes." For a while she even thought of making candy out of the beet sugar. In the end she decided to leave Northampton and return to Boston to find employment.[20]

By June 1839 Maria was in the city staying with friends. She expected David to follow soon, but it was October before he joined her. While looking for a place to live the couple discovered that their little house on Cottage Place was available, but, unable to afford the rent, they hired two cheap furnished rooms instead. With some honesty this time, Maria wrote her sister-in-law that "even this humble imitation of a home is exceedingly pleasant, after our long wanderings and separations."[21]

Given David's propensity for disaster, Maria was learning to take happiness in small doses and to laugh at her husband's foibles even when they made her miserable. One wet, dreary day in February 1840 the Childs were setting out to visit Maria's father in South Natick. A boy had promised to carry their bags to the train, but after waiting in vain for him until the last minute, the couple finally made their own way to the station. David rushed ahead with the luggage, leaving Maria, bootless, to pick her way along the wet, icy streets. Where the road dipped into a hollow, a puddle of water hid the treacherous ice underneath on which Maria slipped and fell. David, who by this time was far ahead, turned to see her fall, but, instead of running back to help, simply stood looking wistfully, first at her and then at the train (which with loud snorting and puffing was about to start) and crying "Oh, dear me! what *shall* I do?" Maria's shoes and cloak were soaked with icy water and her elbow hurt, but she saw soon enough that she had better scramble up as best she could. As she caught up with David he remarked bemusedly that it had all happened so quickly he thought she'd been capering for public amusement. Suppressing tears of exasperation and rage, Maria said nothing, but as they clambered onto the train she recalled Emerson's prudent advice: "A wise man sits at home with might and main."[22]

During the year she spent in Boston, much of Maria's time was taken up with antislavery affairs. From their outpost in Northampton she and David had observed with mounting concern new symptoms of division in the ranks of antislavery reformers. What had begun in 1837 as a clerical appeal to curtail women's public activity in the movement had grown by early 1839 into a more generalized attack on Garrison and his supporters. Increasingly, the columns of the *Liberator* were filled with articles endorsing a variety of radical causes from anticlericalism and women's rights to perfectionism and pacifism. According to Garrison, all religious and political institutions were fundamentally coercive, and he insisted that such traditional voices of authority as the government and the church must be challenged if sins like the enslavement of Negroes and the subjection of women were to be abolished.[23]

This airing of radical doctrines annoyed more conservative reformers, who charged Garrison with encouraging the public to identify these causes with abolitionism, thereby distracting them from the principal goal of freeing the slaves. Maria Child herself was of two minds about the new tone of the *Liberator*. On the one hand she strongly supported Garrison's crusade for universal reform, believing as he did that "a struggle for the advancement of any principle of freedom would inevitably tend to advance *all* free principles." At the same time, she both doubted the wisdom of pretending to live in the millennium when there was still so much wickedness in the world, and feared that this airing of "isms" in the *Liberator* was turning readers away rather than attracting them. Her months of working with antislavery reformers in Northampton had taught her that there was "a large class of sincere friends of emancipation" who strongly disapproved of Garrison. Ultimately, however, it was less Garrison's promotion of radical causes and more the wrangling over differences that bothered Maria. She ex-

pressed this attitude best in a letter she and David sent to the
Liberator on January 15, 1839. "Shall we stop to settle creeds," the
two inquired of their fellow reformers, "while our brother lies
wounded and bleeding by the wayside?" As Maria had said in defense of her own reluctance to speak out on the woman question:
"It is best not to *talk* about our rights, but simply go forward and
do whatsoever we deem a duty. In toiling for the freedom of others
we shall find our own."[24]

This division in abolitionist ranks was intensified further as a
movement grew among some of Garrison's opponents to press for
more political action to bring an end to slavery. By the late 1830s,
while opposition to slavery and the South was widespread, the
original hope of converting the nation by purely moral means had
largely faded. Younger antislavery crusaders were now turning to
political action as a more promising tactic. At a meeting of the
MASS in March 1839, James G. Birney, a leader of the Ohio antislavery movement, spoke of the need for all abolitionists to exercise their right to vote. Two months later at the AASS Annual
Meeting in New York, Lewis Tappan introduced a resolution making voting a condition of membership. The measure failed when
the delegates from Massachusetts insisted that antislavery societies
had no business passing on moral questions other than slavery.

Garrison and his supporters had long valued politics as a means
of agitating the slavery question. They favored petitioning legis-
latures and questioning candidates and presumed that fellow reformers who did vote would choose only recognized abolitionists.
But Garrison himself did not vote. For some time the editor of the
Liberator had believed that the Constitution, by legalizing and protecting slavery, violated human rights and Christian principles. He
distrusted politicians on the slavery question. Even if the government did succeed in legally abolishing slavery, such political coercion, he was certain, would not change the hearts of the people.
Moral suasion, not compulsion, remained the best antislavery tactic.[25]

"My sympathies go with the Mass. [MASS]," Maria wrote in April
1839, "because I think they are jealous *for* freedom, and the others
against it." While she personally supported Garrison's antigovern-
ment, nonresistant views, she had no objection to others voting but
felt strongly that forcing people to go to the polls violated "an
obvious principle of freedom." What was said on the subject in the
Liberator was Garrison's opinion on the question and no one else's.
Furthermore, she insisted, nonresistant members of the MASS were

few in number and careful not to raise the issue at antislavery meetings. Nor did they insist that their opponents withdraw from the Society "because they *do* go to the polls," while these same opponents "wish to expel them because they do *not* go."[26]

Maria used similar arguments to defend the Society for its attitude towards the woman question. She claimed her sex had been actively working for the abolitionist cause since the beginning, and, in their "strong sympathy for the slave," women had not bothered to inquire about "each other's religious opinions or appropriate spheres." Nor had anyone objected to their activities until the Grimkés began their public lecturing in the summer of 1837. Besides, she knew that several of the men now speaking out most strongly against women's expanded role in the movement had once urged their full participation. She particularly recalled an antislavery meeting called by Lewis Tappan in New York in 1836. No one had come to the meeting prepared to speak, and, after several embarrassing intervals of silence, Tappan had approached her to address the audience. When she declined on the grounds of never before having spoken in public, he had insisted that she must try. "You will doubtless recover from your embarrassment in a few moments," he had assured her, adding that it was her duty to overcome her reluctance. "Reflect how much good you can do, and how much the audience will be interested, if you allow me to announce that Mrs. Child of Boston is about to address them." Maria had persisted in her refusal, yet she now marveled at the inconsistent behavior of this man who had once accused her of neglecting her duty by *not* giving a public speech and was now calling it sinful if other women did.[27]

So certain was Maria of the correctness of the position taken by the MASS on the woman question and other issues that she accused those who lacked this certainty of blindness. What she failed to see was that both sides clung to principles apart from the drive to free the slave. Garrison's supporters were idealists who dreamt of the future reign of human brotherhood and believed this dream could be fulfilled if righteous people would only listen to their consciences. By contrast many of Garrison's opponents found these utopian dreams both unrealistic and dangerous. They insisted that social, political, and religious institutions were essential to maintain order in a less-than-perfect world.

Maria arrived in Boston in May 1839, just in time to witness the first open split between the two antislavery factions. On the twenty-eighth the annual New England Anti-Slavery Convention opened in the Chardon Street Chapel. The previous year women had been invited, over the objections of a small minority of delegates, to take full part in the proceedings. This year a resolution to restrict full participation to men had been brought forward by the antiwoman faction, but once again they were outvoted and a countermotion inviting all abolitionists present to serve as full-fledged members was approved. Maria Child and Maria Chapman were then both elected to the business committee, but not before the disappointed minority had withdrawn to form their own organization, the Massachusetts Abolition Society.[28]

Meanwhile the meetings of the BFASS had disintegrated into a bitter power struggle, wherein a conservative majority was attempting to wrest control of the organization away from Chapman and the other Garrisonians. Ever since the summer of 1837, when the orthodox clergy had denounced the public appearance of women as antislavery lecturers, a wide difference of opinion had developed within the society "as to the merits and manner of conducting" their crusade. That year in her annual report of the BFASS, Chapman had insisted that women as moral beings were obliged to oppose slavery and speak freely against it at every opportunity. But more conservative members, afraid of overstepping the bounds of womanly modesty and decency, objected strongly to encouraging such autonomous behavior. When, at the April 1839 quarterly meeting, someone had proposed that the Society no longer subscribe to the *Liberator* and suggested that the funds raised at the annual fair be sent to the AASS instead of to the MASS, Chapman, according to one report, had "roared like a female bull" in support of both the *Liberator* and the MASS. In the end, however, she and her followers were outvoted.[29]

From her outpost in western Massachusetts, Maria Child had faulted Maria Chapman for being too zealous in her eagerness to maintain control of the BFASS, and she arrived in Boston determined to be "cool and unbiassed," even though her sympathies were with the Garrisonians. Meanwhile, the attention of the abolitionist women had been diverted from their own infighting by preparations for the third National Anti-Slavery Convention of American Women to be held in New York in mid-May. The meeting the previous year in Philadelphia had ended in violence when angry mobs had threatened the women and burned Pennsylvania Hall behind them. Maria had missed all this excitement, having successfully resisted pressure to serve as a delegate, and she was no more enthusiastic about attending the convention in 1839. As she told Lucretia Mott, she simply had no interest in going. "I never have entered very earnestly into the plan of female conventions and societies," she explained, adding that they had always seemed to her "like half a pair of scissors." Nor did she think the meetings had been worth the trouble and expense. "For the freedom of women, they have probably done something," she grudgingly conceded, "but in every other point of view, I think their influence has been very slight." The recent admission of women to full participation in the men's societies only confirmed her outlook. If women could now openly work and share power within the larger male organization, what need was there for a separate female society?[30]

Maria had found it easy to remain cool, detached, and reasonable about the woman question from afar, but as soon as she reached Boston such objectivity was harder to maintain. Her coolness had vanished entirely by October when a succession of BFASS meetings proved how effectively the conservatives were denying the Garrisonians a voice. While admitting that "the scenes in our Female Anti-Slavery meetings" were "disgusting and painful," Maria was soon defending the "Old Organization" (the MASS) with as much vehemence as Maria Chapman. For the next six months the BFASS was torn by dissension as both factions sought to gain control. Meetings dissolved into shouting matches. That year, two antislavery fairs were held, one in October, managed by the Chapmanites for the benefit of the MASS, and the official BFASS fair in December for the benefit of the AASS. Although the October fair netted a far greater profit, the conservatives refused to concede any power to their rivals. In a letter published in the *Liberator* on April 3, 1840, Maria defended the Chapmanites' position. "They believe that the old society has never departed from its original integrity; has never sought to saddle anti-slavery with foreign topics; is now, and has ever been, a true, generous uncompromising friend of the slave."[31] The final split came on April 8 when the conservatives declared the BFASS dissolved. But the minority, refusing to concede defeat, called a rump session of the Society on April 14. Maria Child, who had been elected president pro tem, presided over this meeting, where action was taken to continue the BFASS under its old name.

For all her pronounced hatred of factionalism, Maria expressed considerable relief at the departure of the anti-Garrisonians from both the MASS and the BFASS. "This division is painful to me," she wrote after the split had occurred, "but since we were divided in spirit, I am glad they have gone from us. For a long time past they have spoiled our meetings and hindered the free action of our souls."[32] The possibility that the opposition was feeling equally hamstrung by the Garrisonians seems never to have occurred to her. The final rupture in the movement as a whole came in May 1840 at the annual meeting of the AASS in New York. But by that time the Childs were back in Northampton, where David had resumed his cultivation of beets.

David left Boston in time for the spring planting, while Maria remained behind until he called for her to join him. Once again there were grounds for optimism about the beet sugar business, at least from David's point of view. Back in December he had won a premium of $100 from the Massachusetts Agricultural Society for his initial batch of the sweetener, which was acclaimed as the best and largest ever produced in the United States. Meanwhile, the old Northampton Sugar Beet Company was promising renewed financial support for his venture. Finally, and most concretely, Maria's father, then in his mid-seventies, had decided to join the Childs in Northampton. The old gentleman was proposing to buy a farm where they could all live and where David could raise his beets and manufacture his sugar. This was a remarkable offer from a man who had once referred to his son-in-law's effectiveness in business matters as equal to "cutting stones with a razor."[33]

The farm was not bought until early June. Meanwhile, needing land on which to plant his beets, David leased twenty acres of an abandoned silk farm in what is now the town of Florence but was then the hilly outskirts of Northampton. He also found a house for rent across the street from his fields that was large enough to accommodate his wife and father-in-law until their own farmhouse was ready to move into. Convers Francis arrived in Northampton before his daughter and for a brief time shared the housekeeping with David. Two days before she was due to leave Boston for Northampton, Maria received an urgent letter from David asking her to come immediately as her father had severely bruised himself by a fall from a wagon. Maria arrived to find her overwrought husband, ailing parent, and "a stout Irish laborer" installed in an unfamiliar house all but empty of furniture. Without pausing for breath, she was soon overwhelmed with domestic chores. Besides the work of cooking, cleaning, washing, and mending for three men, in a house without beds and tables and other housekeeping necessities, she had to dress her father's bruise at least twice daily. When the furniture did at last arrive it was "tumbled in heaps on the floor" and left to her to arrange. All this was done without help of any kind.[34]

Had Convers Francis settled into the household comfortably, Maria might have withstood the ensuing months with at least the satisfaction of knowing she was making him happy. But he continued gloomy and cross, and all her efforts to please him only met with criticism and complaints. Even after his leg had healed and he was no longer confined to a chair his temper showed no improvement. Particularly annoying to this stern Calvinist was David's conduct around Maria: his habit of patting her head and calling her by some silly nickname, like "Carum Caput," or treating her to a purposeless stream of loving banter, all of which the old gentleman dismissed as "childish folly." Maria, acutely sensitive about their rather awkward "pecuniary connection" with her father, did her best to smooth over the relations between the two. She wrote Louisa Loring of her frustration with her parent's behavior. "The old gentleman means to do us a kindness; but he is unacquainted with sentiment, and has a violent prejudice against literature, taste and even the common forms of modern civilized life."[35]

Nor was Maria cheered by David's prospects. In 1839 a severe depression was gripping the nation, making it a particularly bad time to start a new business. Money was in short supply, and that year the Northampton silk industry went bankrupt, taking with it the capital David was counting on to underwrite his beet business.[36] If Maria, quite properly, was sick with worry, her husband remained undaunted by these difficulties. His brother John, who had a successful business in nearby Springfield, had provided him with two oxen, two horses, and one cow and was paying for the two men who now helped him in the fields. At least there was an abundance of food. But there were also many mouths to feed, and Maria spent most of her time preparing meals.

For all Maria's desire for a home of her own, she was quick to observe how completely total immersion in domestic cares atrophies the brain. "Thank God that you are not a woman!" she wrote her brother Convers after six months on the farm. "*Great* labors strengthen the intellect of the well-balanced character; but these million Lilliputian cords tie down the stoutest Gulliver that ever wrestled in their miserable entanglement." Her first weeks of domestic drudgery brought on an acute attack of depression. She was soon close to despair: all energy, all hope, had vanished. When the worst was over she told Convers that never had "circumstances so mastered my soul, as during this present year. Unavailing efforts to overcome father's habitual restlessness and gloom, with the fretting, conscience-stricken feeling that I should fail in filial duty unless I continued to renew my efforts, combined to produce a disastrous state of feeling, in which God seemed a tyrant and this life a dungeon."[37]

The arrival in July of Nora, a cheerful, hardworking Irish woman, brought some relief. Maria told Convers that a "whole boys' school" had been let loose in her brain, "kicking up heels, throwing up caps, haraaing, chasing butterflies—everything in short except drowning kittens." She now had a little time each day to read, and to think, and was finding peace and contentment in being close to "the swallows and the flowers." Above all, she told her brother, she wanted to "keep still, out of sight and hearing of the bustling world." Meanwhile, friends in Boston did their best to cheer her. She especially enjoyed corresponding with 'Nony,' the Lorings young daughter Anna, whom she regarded almost as her own child. She could tell Anna the kind of stories she used to enjoy writing for the *Miscellany*: cheerful stories about the swallows who lived inside the arched doorway of the house, or funny ones about a terrified Nora chasing crickets with the stove shovel.[38]

As always when the "fiery trials" of this world threatened to overwhelm her, Maria sought comfort in contemplating the spiritual delights of the next. If her husband and father showed little interest in such mystical musings, there were others who did. A visit from her brother Convers in midsummer helped to nourish her starved spirit. So did her correspondence with a a young woman named Maria White, whom she had befriended the previous winter in Boston. At barely nineteen years of age, Maria White was regarded in youthful literary circles as a high-souled, angelic creature, who translated German and recited poetry in a low, musical voice. The two Marias had come to know one another at Margaret Fuller's "Conversations," which, beginning in November 1839, had been held each Saturday morning at Elizabeth Peabody's bookshop on West Street. These gatherings were attended by twenty-five or so Boston women, including Louisa Loring and Emerson's wife, Lidian, and they were presided over by a now-dazzling Margaret, who conducted lively discussions on topics ranging from Greek mythology and art to ethics and women's rights. What Maria Child thought of her old friend's virtuoso performances at these meetings is lost to history, but she seems to have made no effort at this time to renew Margaret's acquaintance. More to her taste, perhaps, especially in these months when she felt so depressed and careworn, were the gentle mystical musings of Maria White, who shared her interest in Swedenborg's doctrine of correspondences and enjoyed meditating on such questions as the spiritual meaning of moss.[39]

Such mystical preoccupations were further stimulated by a friendship with the newly ordained pastor of Northampton's Unitarian Church, John Sullivan Dwight. Dwight was a bashful, dreamy Transcendentalist, who was just beginning to make a name for himself as a translator of the poetry of Goethe and Schiller. He had a profound love of music, though he had no training, and his mind was often so distracted by the melodies of Mozart and Beethoven that he would forget to write his sermons. Maria delighted in the company of this slender young cleric, whom she described to Louisa Loring as a "ministering angel sent by God, in this, the darkest hour of our lives."[40]

Dwight's sermons and their conversations together nourished Maria's already strong love of music. Both agreed it was the true language of the soul, the connecting link between the spiritual and the natural worlds. Unfortunately, the Reverend Dwight found little satisfaction in his ministerial calling, and by winter he had left his parish in Northampton to live at Brook Farm, the famous cooperative community in West Roxbury. Maria wrote Convers that she was now entirely cut off from all spiritual and intellectual companionship except what came to her from nature or "directly from the World of Spirits." With little opportunity to indulge her love of music, she humored the artistic side of her nature by occasionally laying down her dishcloth or her broom to contemplate a little plaster caryatid figure which she claimed acted on her spirits "like a magician's spell."[41]

For all her absorption in household matters and her desire not to mingle in the "bustling world," Maria had not lost interest in the antislavery crusade. She was therefore very hurt to learn that Maria Chapman and her sisters were accusing her of indifference to the cause. Anne Weston wrote her sister Deborah that she thought it a "pity that one who really lives so very much in the *outward* should so perseveringly think she lives in the inward." Maria Child did her best to assure these friends of her continued loyalty and support. "My detestations of the mean, vile treachery deepens daily," she wrote Chapman in late August, but she conceded that the pressure of domestic duties had nourished in her an "increasing love of stealing away into secluded, poetic nooks of thought." When Chapman's sister Caroline Weston offered to send a carriage to Northampton to bring Maria to Boston for the annual antislavery fair, she excused herself on the grounds that her father was in too feeble a state of health for her to leave him and furthermore she had quilts and comforters to make for the beds, stout woolen trousers and shirts to make for David and the hired man, together with "various quidities to keep father warm."[42]

The long winter proved all but unendurable. Confined indoors for weeks on end, father and daughter got more and more on each other's nerves. When Maria sought relief from her chores in novels and poetry, her father objected that "literature always leads to beggary." Nor could he abide David reading aloud, as was his custom in the evening. Nothing they did seemed to please the old gentleman. Maria wrote Louisa Loring in February 1841 that she wished George Ripley had started Brook Farm "before we came here, to this Desert where no water is." The prospect of shared housekeeping offered by such a community had its appeal. Meanwhile, she disliked Northampton and its surroundings more with every passing week. "Calvinism sits here enthroned, with high ears, blue nose, thin lips and griping fist. I would I had lived in an age when the gaunt spectre had *done* his mission."[43]

By late winter it had become clear that Convers Francis would have to move elsewhere. While the old man's eventual departure would lighten Maria's workload, it also further strained the Childs' already shaky finances. Convers Francis, needing money for a place of his own, would have less to give Maria. When she and David moved to their own farm in May they would have to make do with a two-room shanty already on the property instead of building themselves the new house they had planned.[44]

To add to their troubles, David's sugar business was not prospering as he had hoped. Compared to the rich acre of alluvial soil on which he had planted his first crop in 1838, this larger parcel in the hills was of poor quality. Whatever nourishment these twenty acres once contained had long since been devoured by the silk farmer's mulberry bushes. Ever the optimist, David now talked of the good crop they would grow on their own hundred acres, which as it happened was another abandoned silk farm with worn-out soil. To add to his earlier debts, David now owed his brother John for a loan to replace the rusted French beet sugar machinery. Meanwhile, no sugar had been manufactured the previous winter.[45]

By April, Maria felt so desperately in need of money that she was prepared to leave home and take up schoolteaching. Then came word that she and David had been appointed by the AASS to edit its official weekly newspaper, the *National Anti-Slavery Standard*, at a salary of $1000 a year. This meant moving to New York, and for a time both resisted the offer. David was reluctant to leave his sugar business and Maria clearly thought her duty was to remain near him in Northampton. She must have felt that if she were to leave her husband, the house would become a pigsty, he wouldn't eat properly, there'd be new harebrained schemes for him to invest in, and she wouldn't be around to keep an eye on him. Furthermore, society frowned on wives who left home to pursue careers. A woman's husband was supposed to be the breadwinner. But what if he were incapable of winning that bread? What should the wife do then? So the offer must have been hard to resist. Although Maria doubtless realized that life as a woman editor alone in New York City would not be easy, surely it would be better than ossifying in Northampton. If she had been ready to leave home to teach— poorly paid work which she'd never particularly liked—why should she hesitate to take a well-paid job of a kind she both enjoyed and was good at?

In the end, pressure from friends combined with the tempting salary persuaded the Childs to accept the appointment on the condition that David would spend as little time as possible in New York and Maria would bear the brunt of the editorial responsibilities. Their names would appear together on the paper's masthead. An encouraging letter from Ellis Loring, whose advice Maria always took to heart, urged them to accept the assignment and devote themselves once more to the antislavery movement. "Such is your fitness for it, that I am quite sure the cause cannot release either of you, till Slavery or you have both left the world." This letter decided it. After tidying up the little shack on the farm and seeing that David's clothes were in order, Maria was ready to leave for New York.[46]

Editor in Harness

My business is not to please the abolitionists but to convince the people.
—Lydia Maria Child, 1842

A fter a journey delayed by floods and other hazards, Maria arrived in New York City on May 11, 1841, just as the AASS anniversary meeting was drawing to a close. Edmund Quincy, a delegate from Boston, described her as in good spirits and "resolved to hold up the flag to the breeze."[1] Radical changes had occurred in the antislavery movement during Maria's year of domestic confinement in Northampton. The final rupture between the two abolitionist camps had taken place at the anniversary meeting a year earlier when opponents of Garrison's radicalism and supporters of political action had walked out of the convention to form their own organization, the American and Foreign Anti-Slavery Society. The remaining AASS delegates had then regrouped themselves and elected three women to the executive committee: Maria Chapman and Maria Child, who were both absent, and Lucretia Mott. Meanwhile, Child, Chapman, Abby Kelley, and others had been chosen to represent the MASS at the World Anti-Slavery Convention to be held in London that June. But all these efforts to draw Maria Child back into a more active role in the movement had failed until the post as editor of the *Standard* was offered to her.

When Garrison's opponents withdrew from the AASS they took with them the official organ of the national society, the *Emancipator*. This weekly antislavery newspaper, edited by the New York abolitionists, had manifested little sympathy for the *Liberator*'s radicalism. Its editorials favored political action and the ballot box as the best weapons against slavery. In the summer of 1840 the AASS, now under the unchallenged control of the Garrisonians, began publishing the *National Anti-Slavery Standard* as its new official weekly. Nathanial P. Rogers had been editor until being forced to resign for publishing his own nonresistant views as official AASS policy. The Childs' considerable editorial experience had made them the obvious choice as his successor.

Upon reaching New York, Maria was given little time to adjust to her new surroundings. Isaac T. Hopper, a Quaker abolitionist who lived at 110 Eldridge Street on the Lower East Side, had agreed to take her into his family as a boarder, and she had no sooner settled her few belongings there before she plunged into her work as editor. While the offices of the *Standard* were some distance away at 134 Nassau Street down near the Battery, Maria preferred to do most of her work at the table provided in her sunny bedroom at the Hoppers'.

It did not take Maria long to discover that her new position would not be an easy one. In addition to her editorial responsibilities, she, together with James Gibbons, the managing editor of the *Standard*, had been elected to serve on the executive committee of the AASS, which shared offices with the newspaper. Since real control of the national Society rested in the hands of Garrison and his colleagues on the MASS board, the New York committee had little actual power. Besides publishing the *Standard*, its members were expected to raise funds for the Society and to recruit the agents who were sent into the field to spread the antislavery gospel.[2]

Maria's most demanding duties were editorial. The day-to-day work of writing and soliciting articles, of poring over legislative documents, reports, and other newspapers to find suitable material to reprint, was unrelenting. Nor was it easy to be the first woman editor of a journal of public policy, which happened also to have an abolitionist slant. Maria complained to Ellis Loring that she was treated like a "black sheep" by the other members of the New York press. Even the booksellers refused her the common courtesy of providing the *Standard* with their latest publications, and she was forced to rely on her landlord, Isaac Hopper, and his son John to obtain the volumes she needed.[3]

Maria's greatest challenge as an editor was to make a success of the *Standard*. To begin with she discovered that both the paper and the AASS were deeply in debt. The funds which had once poured into the coffers of the Society were drying up, and there was almost no cash on hand to pay her or any of her staff. Within a week of her arrival she attended her first meeting of the AASS executive committee, where two black members, who doubtless resented having to pay a salary to a woman editor, urged her to take a pay cut, telling her "they earned their money too hard to spend it so lavishly." That night, back in her room at the Hoppers', Maria wept tears of frustration. On the one hand was her own desperate need for money to pay off David's debts, on the other her reluctance to take any money from the antislavery cause.[4]

An even more vexing problem was the challenge of maintaining her independence as an editor while satisfying the often contradictory demands of her fellow abolitionists. While Maria promised to adhere to the principles of the Garrisonian Old Organization, she made it clear from the start that under her editorship the *Standard* would not adopt the harsh, aggressive tone of the *Liberator* but find a middle ground between the latter's uncompromising radicalism and the more conservative political spirit of the New Organization papers. Rather than cultivating a readership already converted to abolitionist principles, her aim was to edit a family newspaper which would bring new adherents to the cause. Above all, Maria was determined to avoid controversy. The sectarianism she so abhorred was already undermining the antislavery crusade, and she hoped to avoid discussing issues that might contribute to further discord. Finally, Maria made it clear that the opinions she expressed in the columns of the paper would be strictly editorial and would not necessarily reflect her personal views. Her first editorial on May 20, 1841, stressed this determination to maintain her independence: "I am here—ready to work, according to my conscience and my ability; promising nothing, but diligence and fidelity; refusing the shadow of a fetter on my free expression of opinion, from any man, or body of men; and equally careful to respect the freedom of others, whether as individuals or societies."[5]

During her first months as editor of the *Standard* Maria addressed many issues of current interest to the friends of antislavery. While refusing to oppose political action as such, she readily denounced the antislavery Liberty Party, formed back in 1840. Speaking both for herself and as editor she maintained in true Garrisonian style that the only effective way to bring an end to slavery was to change the moral sentiment of the nation and its rulers. "You can do better than *be* a politician," she argued, "you can *move* politicians." She also went out of her way to defend the policies of the Old Organization, particularly its refusal "to apply any test to the opinions of its members, except on the one subject of slavery."[6]

On the whole the members of the Old Organization were satisfied with their new woman editor. Garrison wrote a friend in England that "Mrs. Child is now at the head of the Standard and everything looks well." In Philadelphia, Lucretia Mott claimed that Maria was advancing the cause of women as well as antislavery "by acquitting herself so nobly in the editorial chair." A few doctrinaire Garrisonians, however, were less enthusiastic. Oliver Johnson wished the paper would have in it "more of the Liberator fire." He complained that not enough space was given to exposing the corruptions of the church and that the paper's very "agreeableness" was attracting the support of some "half-and-half milk-and-water sort of abolitionists." Furthermore, it didn't seem right to him that the Standard was "often complimented at the Liberator's expense."[7]

Although the response to her editorship was largely favorable, Maria herself had little confidence that she was doing a good job. In August she complained to Ellis Loring that the only encouragement she had received in recent weeks had come from Gerrit Smith, a member of the New Organization, who told of his delight with "the ability that sustained it [the Standard], and the kind spirit that breathed through it." She added that she needed an encouraging voice to wind her up at least once a week.[8]

By the end of September Maria's spirits had risen somewhat. Words of praise and encouragement were now reaching her from many quarters. The subscription list was increasing steadily, and she had hopes that if this trend continued for a year the society would be out of debt. While she complained to Ellis that Garrison seemed to take little or no interest in the Standard, she was more disturbed by a warning from Maria Chapman that some future controversy might challenge her independence as an editor and bring her "into rough water." For the time being, however, harmony prevailed between the leaders of the AASS in Boston and New York, and Maria resigned herself to being "chained to the oar two or three years at least."[9]

The first threat to her independence came in November 1841 when the managers of the Pennsylvania Freeman, the organ of the Philadelphia Anti-Slavery Society, suggested uniting their paper with the Standard. Maria, knowing how difficult it would be to keep both the Bostonians and the Philadelphians happy, was not pleased with the idea and expressed her reluctance in a letter to Ellis Loring:

"The Freeman," she wrote, "is filled with twaddling articles without intellectual life and spirit, generally; and moreover, it is always betwixt & between on points of principle. It holds out a hand to both organizations, and gives encouraging glances to 3d party." But Maria was also aware of the financial benefits to be gained by acquiring the *Freeman*'s subscription list. She therefore reluctantly agreed to accept articles from Philadelphia, on the condition that they receive the same editorial scrutiny as other material sent to the *Standard*. She further warned the Philadelphians that she could not yet be certain whether their policy would conflict with hers, "for I cannot clearly ascertain what Pennsylvania policy *is*. My dislike of 3d party and N[ew]. Organization is too strong and settled, to admit of anything like accommodation with them."[10]

From a financial point of view the merger of the two papers was a success. Subscriptions to the *Standard*, which had risen steadily if slowly during the first months of Maria's editorship, now climbed sharply. By May 1842 the paper had a circulation of four thousand, an increase of over two thousand since January 1841. Thanks to careful economizing, something Maria had a good deal of experience with, the vast debt she had inherited when she took over the paper was slowly but surely being paid off. In another year, presuming no further demands were made on its income, the AASS should be free of all its old obligations and ready to think about expanding its activities.[11]

But new demands were made. In an effort to stimulate greater public support for the AASS, delegates to the anniversary meeting in May 1842 voted to add to the number of paid antislavery agents out in the field. Experience had shown Maria and her colleagues at AASS headquarters in New York that an increase in the number of agents would mean a further drain on the Society's already overtaxed resources. They were quickly proved right. No sooner was the expansion policy in place than the expenses of the agents were exceeding their income by $100 a week, leaving the Society to make up the difference.[12]

In October Maria wrote a desperate letter to Ellis Loring complaining that there was not enough money to meet the salaries of her employees. She herself had not taken a cent for the last three months and was in great need of some decent winter clothing. Her call for help went unheeded. In December she laid down an ultimatum: that the Society choose between supporting the work of the agents or the work of the *Standard*. While her threats were ignored, sufficient funds were sent from friends in Boston and

Philadelphia to cover the rent and the printers' bill and part of Maria's salary. One contributor, Samuel May, could not bear the thought "that Mrs. Child, who has sacrificed so much, and toiled so untiringly in the cause," was in such straitened circumstances. Others on the MASS board, particularly Maria Chapman, upheld the benevolent principle that people should work for the antislavery cause for love not money.[13]

Meanwhile Maria was turning the *Standard* into a first-rate newspaper. There was something for everyone in its pages. David contributed articles on politics and foreign affairs. In addition to extensive coverage of antislavery matters, there were weekly editorials on such issues of current interest as capital punishment, temperance, and women's rights. Under the heading "Letters from New York," Maria described various sights in and around the city and gave her views on a wide variety of social questions. Some of the "Letters" described the latest methods of treating criminals and the insane. Still others discussed Transcendentalism, Fourierism, Puseyism, and the Quakers. For less intellectually minded readers there was a column written for housekeepers and farmers.[14]

In a letter to Caroline Weston, Maria compared the strategy she used in all her writings when dealing with opponents to a theologian attacking bigotry with "a troop of horse shod with felt." Gentle and logical persuasion was her preferred approach.[15] Some of Maria's most successful antislavery writing in the *Standard* took the form of imaginary dialogues between people of opposing views. This was an old device she had successfully employed in her early writing for children, and she now found it helpful in clarifying the controversies which plagued the antislavery movement. For example, on July 7, 1842, she published a fictional conversation between a Liberty party supporter and a member of the AASS. The latter argued that the presence of a third party took away any incentive for members of the two major parties to please the abolitionists. If there were no Liberty party, the AASS member explains, "men of strong party predilections, favorably inclined to anti-slavery, might be induced to act openly in its favor, if they had the two-fold object of obeying their own consciences, and of gaining all the strength of the abolitionist voters who were inclined to the same party. But when a distinct abolitionist party is formed, this stimulus is taken away."[16]

Garrison liked "Talk about Third Party" enough to reprint it in the columns of the *Liberator*, and when a fellow editor had the gall to ridicule the piece Garrison rallied to Maria's defense, praising the "good sense, clear discrimination, and catholic spirit which usually characterize the writings of this estimable woman."[17]

Clearly the *Standard* was meeting a need. By 1842 its circulation had doubled that of the *Liberator*. One correspondent, who signed himself "O," claimed that there were thousands of readers like himself who regarded it as the best political paper in the United States. Even Abby Kelley, one of Maria's severest critics, had to admit that the *Standard* was convincing good numbers of people in New York State to join the AASS. In April 1842, when she had been at the helm less than a year, Maria herself estimated that each issue of the paper reached at least sixteen thousand people. According to James S. Gibbons, letters of approval were flooding the offices of the *Standard*.[18]

As the months passed, however, Maria found it increasingly difficult to satisfy the demands of her fellow abolitionists. As early as March 1842, she complained of feeling "fettered" by the editorship of the *Standard*. Her determination to remain impartial required a precarious balancing act. She gave offense to the Philadelphians if she refused to publish Liberty Party notices and was rebuked by the Garrisonians for not printing the resolutions passed at a meeting of nonresistants, who declared it a sin to uphold manmade law.[19] Furthermore, she was coming to realize that what she had always hailed as the broad-mindedness of the AASS—its refusal to be an umpire in the mounting controversies among the abolitionists—was degenerating into narrow sectarianism. The bickering and the personal denunciations now indulged in by both sides repelled her.

She was also fed up with the "wild spirit of ultraism," which the Garrisonians encouraged, and which she felt was driving the antislavery cause to its ruin. Since 1840, fanatics like Stephen Foster, Parker Pillsbury, and Nathaniel P. Rogers, upset by the failure of the churches to denounce slavery, had been going about New England interrupting Sunday services and lecturing startled congregations on the evils of slavery. Such behavior was outrageous enough, but even more annoying was Maria Chapman's insistence that the *Standard* support the efforts of these "come-outers" as they were called.[20]

Maria, who at the outset of her editorship had given wholehearted support to the work of the antislavery societies, was less than a year later beginning to think they had outlived their usefulness. She cited the lack of vitality in the associations themselves and the growing interest of the people as a whole in the abolitionist cause. The only way to "cast out the demon of sectarianism," she told the readers of the *Standard*, is by "the calm but earnest promulgation of the truth."[21]

In an editorial published on November 3, 1842, Maria cited as proof of her lack of bias the fact that she received complaints from all quarters for her editorial policy.[22] And for the first few months this policy had met with general approval from Garrison and other members of the Old Organization, who like Maria had defended free exercise of opinion on any issue. Since the split in antislavery ranks in 1840, however, there were indications that the Garrisonians themselves were moving to establish their own tests for membership in the AASS and quite naturally wanted the *Standard*, as the official organ, to support them. Garrison's attempt at the annual meeting in May 1842 to have the AASS endorse a policy calling for the overthrow of the Union was an early manifestation of this tendency.

In January 1842, ex-president John Quincy Adams, now a congressman from Massachusetts, presented a petition signed by the citizens of Haverhill calling for the dissolution of the Union in protest against the Gag Rule, which forbade any discussion of slavery in the halls of Congress. Adams was censured and eventually forced to withdraw his resolution. Encouraged by Adams' initiative in defying the power of the slaveholders in Washington, both the *Liberator* and the *Standard* published editorials favoring disunion. Claiming that recent events in Congress, from the institution of the Gag Rule to secret efforts to annex Texas, threatened "the very existence of our civil liberty," Maria declared that repeal of the Union was the only way "for the free states to clear themselves of being accomplices in [the] tremendous guilt" of slavery. But while Maria supported the idea of petitioning Congress for disunion she urged caution in the wording of such petitions. "With the institutions or customs of the southern states, we have no right to interfere, except with . . . weapons of argument and wit."[23]

A month later Maria wrote a second article on the same subject in which she accused the South of protecting and extending its own interests at the expense of those of the North. "To keep up the appearance of union, the American people are fast becoming accustomed to the relinquishment of those real principles, on which free institutions *must* rest, if they exist at all." While she readily admitted that the Union was "a sham," she could not support Garrison in urging abolitionists to break all ties with their government. For many, she argued, this would seem a dereliction of their civil and social duties. It was also important, she insisted, to remain sensitive to the impression such an action might have on "the friends and enemies of liberty," who are "looking anxiously upon our great experiment of republican institutions." A better solution would be an amendment to the Constitution which would loosen the North's ties with the South and "absolve us . . . from *direct* partnership in slavery." But here too she cautioned restraint, reminding her readers that the North must bear its own share of the guilt. The free states have, "for half a century, been accomplices with the South in slave trading and slaveholding" and for the sake of both master and slave "we ought to strive, as long as there is hope," to take the South "*out* of the condition *into* which we have helped to bring her." Finally, she reiterated her strong objection "to the application of tests or rules" on members of the society. Each individual must be free to follow his or her own conscience in this matter.[24]

Maria's cautionary words fell on deaf ears. By mid-April 1842 a number of Massachusetts antislavery societies loyal to Garrison had passed disunion resolutions, leading the Boston editor to decide that the time had arrived for the national Society to address the question. In an editorial in the *Liberator*, Garrison urged a large attendance at the May anniversary meeting in New York's Broadway Tabernacle and suggested that the most important issue to be discussed would be the duty of abolitionists to demand either the abolition of slavery or the repeal of the Union.[25]

Within days the New York press had pounced gleefully on these treasonable words and put pressure on the city authorities to prevent Garrison and his "motley crew of traitors" from meeting in the Tabernacle. Antislavery was not a popular cause in the city. Irish Catholic laborers, for example, feared that, once freed, the slaves would come north and take away their jobs. Warnings from the press that mobs might disrupt the meeting alarmed Maria and other New York officers of the AASS. To ward off this threatened unrest they sent an official disclaimer to the papers declaring that the principle of dissolving the Union was "entirely foreign to the purpose" of the AASS and that the Society itself had never at any time authorized the promotion of such an object. The disclaimer went on to assure the public that the Society would employ no means for the abolition of slavery "but such as are strictly consistent with morality and the rights of citizenship."[26]

In Boston, Garrison voiced dismay that his friends in New York had even suggested that his views conflicted with the Society's principles. He insisted that, far from wanting to threaten anyone with his disunionist sentiments, he had merely desired to point out that abolitionists had a moral obligation to clear their garments from "pollution," their souls from "blood-guiltiness." Anxious that the Society should feel free to discuss and take action on the issue without pressure from him, Garrison resolved not to go to New York.[27] Fortunately, the threatened mob never materialized and, although the delegates discussed disunionism at length, to Maria's relief they refrained from acting on the issue. In her report on the meeting, Maria told the readers of the *Standard* how the delegates had voiced their unanimous conviction that "the North could not continue her present connection with the South, without being a direct partner in the guilt of slaveholding," and that the duty of abolitionists both as individuals and as a society required them to "use all moral means to deepen and strengthen this conviction."[28] For the time being at least, the AASS, while sympathetic to the principle of disunionism, was loath to make support for it part of its official policy.

The reluctance of Maria and other members of the AASS in New York to act on the issue of disunionism was influenced in part by its unpopularity among the very people whom they were hoping to convert to the cause. Cries of treason from the New York press were proof enough of the danger of adopting such a tactic. But Maria had other objections. In an editorial published less than a month after the anniversary meeting, she made it clear that, as she understood it, the Society continued to stand on its old platform with the single objective of abolishing slavery. She stated firmly that the AASS "established no religious or political test." Nor did it prescribe any particular sphere of action. "It says to each and all, 'Work with us, according to your own conscience, and your own reason.'" Another article in the same issue reiterated her editorial policy. "Our object has been, and is, to make the Standard a good *family* newspaper. Therefore, we offer something for the young and the old, the politician and the moralist, the religious and the economical, the literary and the uneducated." She felt confident that this policy was effective and that the cause had the "ear of the nation as never before."[29]

The very popularity of the *Standard* was part of the problem, however. John Collins, the general agent of the MASS, blamed the tone of the *Standard* for his failure to raise money for the AASS. Its moderate tone, he maintained, discouraged people from joining and supporting the national Society with its radical reputation.

James Gibbons, who had little use for Collins' effectiveness as an agent, suggested that he was trying to blame the *Standard* for his own failings. But there may have been some truth to Collins' assertion. Maria Chapman warned David Child in April 1842 that the paper was displeasing the cause's best friends—the AASS— while at the same time "gratifying and serving their worst enemies."[30]

Maria realized that the conflict of her editorial policies with those of the AASS placed her in a false position. In the fall of 1842 she tendered an informal resignation to the MASS board; she would stay on only until the following spring. The pressure to descend into what she called "the narrow and crooked path of personal and party controversy" had been more than she could bear, and she wrote Ellis Loring that she had lost all interest in the paper.[31]

The Garrisonians were both relieved and annoyed by Maria's resignation. No one could deny that the *Standard* commanded a wide readership. At the same time, Maria's intransigence over the publication of controversial matters—she was accused by some of interfering with the freedom of the press—and her sensitivity to the mounting criticism from the MASS board was making it difficult for the leadership to work with her.[32]

Having announced her intention to resign, Maria felt relieved of a great burden. In a letter to Ellis Loring she described how impossible it was to heed advice forced upon her in so many forms and from so many different directions. She stayed on until early May and in her farewell editorial defended her policy for the last time. "If I have seemed proud and lofty in my undeviating course, it was because I felt the *necessity* of relying upon myself, and never looking outward for stimulus or guidance. . . . He who turns from the light of his *own* judgment, and the convictions of his *own* conscience, has neither rudder nor pilot in the storm. . . . The freedom of my own spirit makes it absolutely necessary for me to retire. I am too distinctly and decidedly an individual, to edit the organ of any association."[33]

The Boston leadership denied that any official attempt had been made to interfere with Maria's editorial freedom. In an article in the *Liberator* published after her retirement, Garrison insisted that Mrs. Child had been entirely free to edit the *Standard* "precisely as her own taste and judgment dictated, and as independently as though she acted on her own responsibility." He admitted that she had not pleased everyone, but what editor does?[34]

On May 1, 1843, after her last number of the *Standard* had gone to press, Maria slipped out of New York to join David, who by that time was back in Northampton. She was anxious to be out of the city before Garrison and his friends arrived from Boston for the anniversary meeting. She wanted nothing more to do with the AASS or any other society. On May 19 she wrote requesting that her name be removed from the membership roll, cutting her ties with the organized antislavery movement.[35]

12

Letters from New York

*Therefore blame me not, if I turn wearily aside
from the dusty road of reforming duty, to gather
flowers in sheltered nooks, or play with gems in
hidden grottoes. The Practical has striven hard to
suffocate the Ideal within me; but it is immortal
and cannot die. It needs but a glance of beauty
from earth or sky, and it starts into blooming life,
like the aloe touched by a fairy wand.*
—*Lydia Maria Child*, Letters from New York

During the two years she worked for the *Standard* Maria gradually grew accustomed to life in New York. The Hopper house at 110 Eldridge Street lay just east of the Bowery, one of the busiest thoroughfares in the city. Here, amid a confusion of activity, the strident calls of hawkers were matched by the ceaseless clatter of iron wheels and hooves on the pavement. New York was a noisy, dirty, crowded, and ill-governed city.

Inside the Hopper house, however, all was serene and orderly. Hannah Hopper, Isaac's second wife and the mother and stepmother of a large family, was a modest, kindly, and reserved Quaker woman who went about dressed in the old-fashioned bonnet and drab-colored dress characteristic of her sect. She welcomed Maria Child as a member of the family, making sure she had a clean and comfortable room to work and sleep in.

Hannah's husband, Isaac, who bore an uncanny resemblance to Napoleon, was equally welcoming. Although many years older than his wife, he seemed sprightly by comparison, with a trim figure and firm elastic step that belied his seventy-two years. Maria reported seeing the old gentleman springing off the Bowery horsecars with the agility of a boy of fourteen. She noted also the care he took with his personal appearance, dressing in old-fashioned breeches buckled at the knee and long stockings which displayed to advantage "his finely formed limbs."[1]

In 1829 the Hoppers had moved to New York from Philadelphia, where Isaac had been known as a friend and legal advisor to the colored people of the city. Once settled in New York he opened a Quaker bookstore on Pearl Street. For a time, until its location became too well known, Hopper's store served as a station on the Underground Railroad, where escaped slaves, arriving by boat from Philadelphia, were aided on their journey north to Canada and freedom. By the time Maria came to live with the Hoppers the market for Quaker books had diminished, and Isaac had sold his shop and gone to work as an agent for the AASS and a contributor to the *Standard*.

Although Hopper's devotion to the antislavery cause was firmly rooted in his Quaker beliefs, his support for the reform was not shared by many New York Friends who had strong business ties to the cotton-producing South. Shortly before Maria joined the Hopper household, these proslavery Quakers had arraigned her landlord, and two other Friends who worked for the *Standard*, before the Rose Street Meeting and accused them of "being concerned in the support and publication of a paper which has a tendency to excite discord and disunity among us." After months of wrangling among Friends on both sides of the Atlantic the three were officially disowned—the Quaker equivalent of excommunication. According to one of Hopper's biographers, the whole affair awakened the Quakers to the "dangers of fighting among themselves over slavery."[2]

Maria could readily sympathize with someone who was suffering from religious intolerance. Isaac Hopper and his new boarder soon became fast friends. In a biography of the Quaker abolitionist written shortly after his death, Maria spoke of Hopper as one of the few genuine democrats she had ever met, so completely did he "ignore all artificial distinctions" of race, creed, or class.[3] The admiration and love she felt for this Quaker crusader were returned. When Isaac Hopper was on his deathbed in the spring of 1852, he asked particularly to see Maria Child and she made the long journey down from Massachusetts for one last visit with this old friend.

For all the warmth of the Hopper household, and for all her relief at being away from Northampton and the farm, Maria missed David. Their last weeks in Northampton, after her father's departure, had been a happy time and she had done her best to leave the little two-room shanty as comfortable as possible.[4] Now, finding herself alone amid the roar and bustle of New York, Maria felt overwhelmed by the responsibility and the singularity of her new position as a woman editor living apart from her husband. In addition to fretting about David's ability to care for himself alone, she doubtless also had qualms about the effect of such a long separation on their marriage. When he had been abroad studying beet sugar manufacture in 1836, Maria had rarely heard from him, and the letters she had received were strangely cool and indifferent. At the time she had despaired for the future of their marriage, and she must now have feared that a similar coolness on his part, fed by a long separation, would divide them forever.

One member of the Hopper family went out of his way to dispel the loneliness of Maria's first weeks in New York. Isaac and Hannah's son John—then a drug salesman in his mid-twenties—was clearly enraptured by the family's new boarder. He offered to fetch the books she needed for her editing and often came to her room in the evening to read or talk. Maria, for her part, basked in the warmth of these kindly attentions. The young man and the middle-aged woman had much to talk about. They shared a love of literature and the arts, subjects of little interest to David and other members of their respective families. Isaac Hopper, like Maria's father, ridiculed such preoccupations as a waste of time. Music, he insisted, was nothing more than a "spiritual brandy" which only served to "intoxicate people."[5]

John Hopper was also a welcome escort for Maria in a city where respectable women rarely ventured out alone. On warm spring evenings when the day's work was done, she and John often took long walks. Passing along narrow streets teeming with people of every nationality, where roving musicians vied with ragged child beggars for their attention, the two would head for some peaceful, airy spot far from the ceaseless tumult.

One of Maria's favorite retreats was the Battery. This park on the southern tip of Manhattan, with its graceful promenade lined with groves of young trees and its view of New York harbor, provided a welcome contrast to the dirt, noise, and disorder of the city's streets. She and John enjoyed it best at midnight when the moon was out and all was quiet except for the gentle splashing of the sea, and she could gaze at the great forest of masts which filled the harbor "in their dim and distant beauty." Occasionally the two would slip out of the house at dawn and walk down to the Battery to watch the sun rise and see the ships "stretch their sails to the coming breeze."[6]

New York was the busiest harbor on the Atlantic coast. Here ships of every size and nationality, under steam and sail, attested to the city's mercantile importance. By the 1840s its docks and warehouses were handling over half the nation's imports and nearly a third of her exports.[7] For Maria, as for many contemporary observers, New York was a city of contrasts. As she and John roamed the streets and parks she was alternately filled with hope and despair for the future of her native land. Standing in Battery Park in the stillness of early morning, watching the steamboats slipping past the graceful sailing vessels, all was beauty, harmony, and progress. Here it was possible to believe in the reality of human perfection. Yet only a few blocks away a visit to the Five Points slum threatened to shatter all such utopian dreams.

Maria saw Five Points for the first time one hot afternoon in late summer. The wretched inhabitants of the densely crowded tenements, many of whom were recent immigrants, had returned from their day's work and had not yet been driven indoors by police constables and the coming darkness. "There you will see nearly every form of human misery, every sign of human degradation. The leer of the licentious, the dull sensualism of the drunkard, the sly glance of the thief—oh, it made my heart ache for many a day. I regretted the errand of kindness that drew me there; for it stunned my senses with the amount of evil, and fell upon the strong hopefulness of my character, like a stroke of the palsy. What a place to ask one's self, 'Will the millennium ever come!' "[8]

The spread of poverty in New York in the early 1840s was caused in part by the recent economic downturn and in part by an expanding population. While this expansion included New Englanders and other Americans drawn to the metropolis by its commercial advantages, an increasing percentage of new arrivals came from abroad. As the decade progressed the number of foreign immigrants grew at what some considered an alarming rate. Many of these newcomers were illiterate, unskilled, and destitute. The problem of finding them jobs and decent housing, providing schooling and other services proved all but impossible for an inadequate and corrupt municipal government.

Occasionally Maria's rambles with John Hopper took her west and north to where the crowded, noisy streets of the older neighborhoods gave way to more genteel thoroughfares lined with the

comfortable houses of the well-to-do, or past the even grander
mansions of the new millionaires where, as Maria described it,
wealth dozed on "French couches, thrice piled, and canopied with
damask." Occasionally too, on a rare Sunday when the editor of
the *Standard* could afford to take a day off, the two would leave
the city and explore the surrounding countryside. Maria was delighted by the cheapness and ease of travel out of Manhattan. "For
six cents one can exchange the hot dusty city for Staten Island,
Jersey, or Hoboken." Only three cents would take you to Brooklyn.[9]

Hoboken, like the Battery, was best seen by moonlight when "the
dark, thickly shaded groves, . . . the high steep banks, wooded
down to the margin of the river; the deep loneliness, interrupted
only by the Katy-dids; all conspired to produce an impression of
solemn beauty." On a Sunday excursion to Hoboken, Maria met
the first Indians she had seen since her girlhood in Maine. But in
the full light of day, she was disappointed to discover that even this
romantic spot showed signs of spreading urban blight. Buried amid
the wooded groves stood a tavern with its bar and bowling alley,
"a place of resort for the idle and profligate."[10]

Maria's letters recounting these excursions with John Hopper
troubled her friends in Boston. Ellis and Louisa Loring took note
of the tender and affectionate language she used to describe her
youthful new admirer and wrote urging her to be careful. But Maria
insisted on the platonic nature of their friendship, claiming she
was much too old and plain to tempt a young man of twenty-six.
"My charms were *never* very formidable," she assured Ellis. "If there
is danger in being absolutely necessary to each other's happiness
for the time being, we are in great peril . . . I absolutely *could* not
stay in New York away from my husband, if I had not him to walk
with me, read to me, bring me pictures, and always greet me with
a welcoming smile. This ever-ready kindness is the *only* thing that
prevents my life here from being one 'demnition grind.' That I
can disturb his peace of mind seems to me scarcely possible; and
he will not *mine*, except the pain of parting from a friend sometimes
makes us regret that we ever formed the acquaintance."[11]

The Lorings, who perhaps knew Maria better than anyone,
would have been concerned less with John Hopper's peace of mind
than with the harm that could come to their friend from such an
attachment. Maria, they knew very well, was underestimating her
romantic appeal for a young man so "passionately fond of the
beautiful." At a time when few women ventured outside the accepted sphere of domesticity, the presence of a renowned woman

writer and reformer in his father's house was captivating enough for a young man of John's sensibilities. But when he discovered that this heroic and gifted woman combined a rich and lively mind with a warm-hearted gratitude for his friendly thoughtfulness, he was thoroughly smitten.

Ellis and Louisa's fears were hardly assuaged when Maria told them how much John Hopper's "thousand little deliberate attentions" reminded her of "Mr. Child," or when she insisted that such kindnesses were "insufficient for the cravings of a heart so fond of domestic life as mine." Maria liked to describe her relationship with John as that of mother and son. But John's devotion was more than filial. Once, after some trouble at the *Standard*, she returned home on the point of tears. John tried his best to console her but, having failed, he threw himself down on his bed and wept. Describing this scene to the Lorings, Maria declared ingenuously, "I think he lives for nothing else but to devise ways for my happiness. The best joke of all is, he calls me his *daughter* and says he feels bound to take fatherly care of me."[12]

The expeditions continued. During the warm summer months she and John promenaded on the Battery three or four nights a week, often not returning home until midnight. One August Sunday they took a picnic of cakes and oranges and the poems of Lamartine to some "rocky embowered nooks" at Fort Lee. With the coming of cooler weather in September, the evening walks came to an end, but the bittersweet air of romance lingered. Maria was now writing "sub rosa" for the *Liberty Bell*, an antislavery annual modeled on her *Oasis* and edited by Maria Chapman. In early December she sent Chapman her story "The Quadroons," which contains a good deal of romance. "It sounds more like a girl of sixteen than a woman of forty," she admitted in the letter accompanying the manuscript. A few weeks later she wrote to congratulate the poet James Russell Lowell, who had recently become engaged to her friend Maria White. She described her "earnest, loving sympathy with all mated ones," adding that on this subject she was as romantic as a young girl. For her fortieth birthday on February 11, 1842, John again produced cakes and oranges. The mild weather permitted an excursion to Staten Island, and "all along the road he gave sixpences, oranges, and coppers to every poor vagabond and child he met; because, he said he 'wanted everybody to be happy on his mother's birth-day.' "[13]

There could be little question by this time that Maria had fallen in love with John Hopper and he with her, and while she continued to refer to him as her "son," the emotions he had aroused in her could not be dismissed as maternal. Yet for all the implicit sexuality underlying their intimacy, there is no hint that the two ever became lovers, or that Maria, as far as her own conscience was concerned, ever betrayed her marriage vows to David. It was characteristic of her to adhere as firmly to principle in this matter as she did in all others. Not that she managed this without a struggle. In a letter to an old friend and fellow abolitionist, Frank Shaw, in the summer of 1846, she candidly admitted that " 'the strong necessity of loving' " had been "the great temptation and conflict" of her life," but she added her sincere belief "that few women are more pureminded than myself."[14]

A love scene from a story Maria published in the mid-1840s may well have been inspired by her moonlit walks with John Hopper. "The Legend of the Apostle John" concerns the forbidden and thwarted love of a young Greek named Antiorus for Miriam, the daughter of a wealthy and conservative orthodox Jew. Miriam's father, who opposes the match on religious grounds, forbids her to see Antiorus. But one night the two lovers escape the city of Ephesus for a moonlit rendezvous. Miriam warns Antiorus that this must be their only meeting, that she must obey her father and never see him again. He replies by insisting on a higher obedience than that due to parents.

> He took her hand and it trembled within his, while he spoke to her of flight, of secret marriage, and a hidden home of love in some far-off Grecian isle. He drew her gently toward him, and for the first time her lovely head rested on his bosom. As she looked up fondly and tearfully in his face, he stooped to kiss her beautiful lips, which trembling gave an almost imperceptible pressure in return. Faint and timid as was this first maiden kiss, it rushed through his system like a stream of fire. . . . He breathed with difficulty, his whole frame shook like a tree in a storm; but she lay on his bosom, as ignorant of the struggle as a sleeping babe. Rebuked by her unconscious innocence, he said inwardly to the tempting spirit, "Get thee behind me!"

In the end Antiorus succeeds in controlling "the earthly portion of love," and the two part, never to see one another again.[15]

Meanwhile these excursions in and around Manhattan were satisfying more than a craving for love and companionship. They also provided much of the material for Maria's weekly column in the *Standard* entitled "Letters from New York." Critics agree that these personal editorials contain some of Maria's best and most popular writing. The "Letters" began appearing in August 1841, a few months into her editorship, and from the first they functioned as a "safety valve" for Maria's "expanding spirit," which she described as "pent up like steam in a boiler."[16]

In common with other newcomers to the city, Maria could not resist seeing New York as a microcosm of the American nation. On the crowded docks and in the noisy bustling streets of this modern Babylon was hard evidence of the drive and energy of the American people. Their rootlessness and restlessness were echoed in the frenetic activity of Moving Day (May 1st), when leases traditionally expired and nearly every household in the city appeared to change its residence. There also, among the city's heterogeneous and mushrooming population, could be found nearly every vice known to modern society as well as nearly every evil suffered by it. Alcoholism and crime, poverty and disease existed there on a scale unmatched anywhere in the United States. Maria was not the first to note that compared to sober, respectable Boston, New York was rife with viciousness and turbulence.[17]

Nor is the subject of antislavery overlooked in these "Letters." In late summer the rising cry of the katydids reminds her that August was the month which "the persecuted abolitionists were wont to observe, brought out a multitude of snakes and southerners." She recalls that terrifying journey in the summer of 1836 when she and David had slipped George Thompson away from the angry Boston mobs, only to meet on board the steamboat an equally hostile group of Southerners. On recognizing Thompson, these "polished gentlemen" were transformed into "demons" who threatened the hated Englishman with swords and clenched fists. Maria notes that times have changed since then and that abolitionist sympathies have taken a firm hold on the people.[18]

Thus, the very "uproar of evil" which Maria sees everywhere around her in New York fails to daunt her romantic optimism or shake her faith in the ultimate triumph of human fellowship. If the coming of the age of commerce means that cunning has replaced force, this too she claims is "a step forward in the slow march of human improvement." Everywhere brave spirits are at work "for freedom, peace, temperance, and education. Everywhere the walls of caste and sect are melting before them; everywhere dawns the golden twilight of universal love!"[19]

But Maria's certainty that good will triumph over evil is not intended to breed complacency among her readers. Rather, it is to encourage greater reform efforts. Unlike many of her contemporaries, who viewed crime as the consequence of sin, Maria insists that if poverty were eliminated crime would disappear, and she blames society for perpetrating the very ills it seeks to remove. She is emphatic in pointing to some of the causes of the poverty and crime which she sees all around her in New York, blaming the greediness of the rich and the tendency of municipal authorities to punish rather than prevent crime. While she applauds New York's numerous benevolent societies for using the gentle art of persuasion to rehabilitate the fallen and perishing, she also recognizes the limitations of such private efforts in the face of large-scale destitution. But she can offer few practical solutions of her own beyond a vague endorsement of utopian socialism. A *"reconstruction of society is necessary,"* she announces in her letter of March 3, 1842. If great changes have already taken place in society, particularly in America, still greater changes, she predicts "lie imaged in the mirror of the future; and we are by no means certain that Charles Fourier has not seen them with a clearer vision than any other man."[20]

Maria enjoys gently prodding her readers to discard their conventional views and move into the modern age. One letter describes a sleepy old Dutch farming community in Tarrytown which has been invaded by that arch-symbol of change and progress, the railroad. Although several years have passed since the "fire king" first traversed this peaceful landscape, cutting through orchards and pastures, often dividing old homesteads, the Dutch inhabitants have not adjusted to its presence. Maria watches as trembling farmers muttering curses cautiously guide their horses and wagons over each railroad crossing, expecting at any moment to be ground to a fine powder. "Poor old men! what will they say when rail-roads are carried through all their old seed-fields of opinion, theological and political? As yet there are no twilight fore-shadowings of such possibilities; but assuredly, the day will come, when ideas, like potatoes, will not be allowed to sprout up peaceably in the same hillock where their venerable progenitors vegetated from time immemorial."[21]

In the winter of 1843 Maria made two important decisions. The first was to publish a collection of her "Letters from New York," and the second was to separate her financial affairs from David's so that she might have sole control over the money she earned.

Maria had not seen much of her husband since her move to New York. Back in November 1841 she had returned to their farm for a month's visit and found that David had let everything go in her absence. The little shanty she had worked so hard to fix up for him before she left was filthy, and David himself looked so thin and careworn after a summer of slogging in his beet fields that she hardly recognized him. The whole of her visit was spent putting the house and David back in order again; she returned to New York satisfied that she had left things comfortable and that her husband's health and spirits were restored.[22]

Nearly a year passed before the Childs saw one another again. Then in late October 1842 David arrived in New York with the predictably discouraging news that his beet sugar business had failed. More stones than beets had been harvested from his rocky acres. He was now nearly $30,000 in debt. To the unpaid notes dating back before his marriage were added the considerable sums borrowed for his sugar business. The future was not yet entirely bleak, however. In 1841, Congress enacted a bankruptcy law enabling thousands of debt-stricken Americans to claim insolvency. David decided to take advantage of this welcome piece of legislation, and on December 16, 1842, he filed for bankruptcy in the Northampton court. Maria's professed reaction to her husband's decision is conveyed in a letter to her friend Frank Shaw: "Mr. Child is now going through the bankrupt process. It will not make the slightest difference with him about paying his debts, as fast as he is able; but he will be more free; and to me, it will be an inexpressible relief to be relieved from his entanglements. If God spares my life the coming year, I intend to start afresh in the race and rebuild my literary reputation."[23]

Maria may have felt relief that she would at last be free of David's pecuniary entanglements, but she must also have bitterly resented the persistent legal fiction of marital unity which made a wife responsible for her husband's debts.

David was declared insolvent in February 1843, and all the Childs' personal property not already mortgaged to family members was sold at auction in June. Included in the sale were all the farm animals, tools, and other equipment. Maria lost most of her clothing and her small collection of jewelry, including the watch given to her by the Lynn and Salem Female Anti-Slavery Society. But the farm itself and the rights to all her books fortunately belonged to her father. Her losses could have been much worse.[24]

Still she realized that she could not continue living alone in New York while at the same time putting aside money for her and David's future. "I have come to be *afraid* to lean upon David in all matters connected with a *home* and *support*," she admitted to Ellis Loring on March 6, 1843. In New York, equity law permitted postnuptial agreements protecting a wife's property from her husband's creditors. It seems likely that Maria was referring to such an arrangement when she informed Ellis a few weeks later that David had agreed "to part partnership, so far as *pecuniary* matters are concerned." Since the approval of a man was needed before she could exercise any legal authority, she turned over to Ellis Loring the control of her earnings and the rights to some of her books.[25]

After fourteen years of uncertainty, of pumping water into a sieve, as she called it, Maria was ready to settle permanently in New York. "If I float about much longer, I feel that I shall become indifferent to everything, and lose my capacity for business," she wrote Ellis. The city was beginning to seem more and more like home. She had even grown attached to the street cries. Hand organs, she was finding, answered as well as cuckoos "for a wandering voice," and, with a little help from her imagination, she could admit how "picturesque" it was "to see the stars between openings in brick walls." Above all, Maria was glad to be in this city full of strangers, which, unlike Boston, had no old associations to give her pain.[26]

Free for the first time in her married life from David's legal and financial entanglements, and about to cut herself loose from the editorship of the *Standard*, Maria hadn't been as happy for years as she was that winter and spring of 1843. "The reason probably is," she told Ellis, "that after many fluctuations, and being influenced by a wish to please others, I have at last settled down upon a deliberate conviction of what course is best for my own soul." She was particularly happy with the prospect of resuming her literary career: "Such powers as I have, are in their maturity now; and I feel a resolution I never felt before—to cast from me all the fetters of sand which have so miserably bound me down to unprofitable drudgery." Her old ambition for literary glory had returned. "If my Pegasus can only get untied from the black ox," she wrote in April, "I think he may yet show what a glimpse of earth may be, as seen from the heights of heaven. I have at times, visions of exceeding glory."[27]

As long as Maria was editing the *Standard*, there was little time to spare for literary pursuits. But after receiving numerous requests from readers to publish a collection of her "Letters from New York," she asked Ellis in January 1843 if he would be willing to edit the volume and help underwrite the cost of publishing it. In April she signed a contract with Langley Brothers of New York to publish her "Letters." She told Ellis that she didn't dare imagine that the book might be a success, but she did hope it would serve as an "introduction to the literary world where I have so long been a stranger."[28]

During that winter and spring Maria and Ellis corresponded frequently about the letters to be included in the volume. Anxious to rebuild her literary reputation by appealing to a wider audience than that reached by the *Standard*, Maria showed far more caution in choosing the selections than Ellis. "I shall not print *all* the letters; only the best ones," she wrote in February. She then suggested eliminating the two about women's rights and another opposing capital punishment. Ellis evidently persuaded her to leave them in, but he had less luck convincing her to include the antislavery letters. The sketch of George Thompson, for example, was omitted. So was another about the religious experiences of a fugitive slave.[29]

Despite her own self-censorship, Maria's publishers felt she had not gone far enough. Langley Brothers informed her sometime in May that, while they didn't want to trammel her, it "would injure their business very much if any expression in a book they published should prove offensive to the south." In recounting this to the Lorings she could not help making a small dig at organized anti-slavery, by comparing "the *freedom*" the Langleys were offering her to the liberty she had enjoyed as editor of the *Standard*. From all directions, it seemed, her right of free speech was being threatened. In any event she refused to meet the Langley Brothers' conditions and decided to take the risk of underwriting the cost of the book herself.[30]

The risk paid off. *Letters from New York*, which a distant cousin in Boston, C. S. Francis, agreed to print, appeared in August 1843. If publishers were skittish about Maria Child's reputation as an abolitionist, the public no longer was. After barely two months the book was selling so well that several publishers offered to bring out a second edition. Meanwhile reviews were coming in from as far away as England, where, according to Maria's report, some of the papers were "cracking it up to the third heaven" while others were dismissing it as "ultra sentimental" and "mawkish." By December she had only forty copies left of an edition of fifteen hundred, and three months later C. S. Francis brought out the second edition. By the spring of 1844 Maria had enough offers from booksellers to keep her busy. These included a proposed series of children's books and a new edition of *Philothea*. She told Ellis that she much preferred earning a moderate income "in this quiet, independent way" to serving as a newspaper editor no matter how good the pay.[31]

Maria's *Letters from New York* did much to restore her literary reputation. One aspiring author, Thomas Wentworth Higginson, then a young man of twenty, had been so filled with "boyish admiration" for the book, he anonymously sent its author a bunch of flowers. He later claimed that quotes in the *Letters* from Swedenborg, Fourier, "and other authors who were thought to mean mischief" had helped to legitimize the growing interest in utopian socialism. To Higginson, Maria Child "seemed always to be talking radicalism in a greenhouse." At the end of the century her journalistic essays were still remembered among an older generation of newspaper editors as an ideal type of writing which had often been imitated but never equalled.[32]

13

Bohemia: 1843–1847

*I live henceforth for one undivided object; viz: to
build up my literary reputation, and make it the
vehicle of as much good to the world as I know
how.*
　　　　　—Lydia Maria Child to Louisa Loring,
　　　　　　　　　　　　　　　　　　　　　1845

In July 1843, a few weeks before the first volume of *Letters from
New York* came off the press, David journeyed down from
Northampton to take over the editorship of the *Standard*. The
newspaper had been without an official editor since Maria's resignation in May, but matters connected with his bankruptcy, including the auction, had kept David in Northampton longer than
expected. Now he joined his wife at the Hoppers'. A fire the previous August had forced Isaac and his family to vacate their house
on Eldridge Street. They then moved into a larger dwelling with
John's brother Joseph and his wife on the corner of Mulberry and
Grand Streets. Maria knew she should be pleased to have David
employed and by her side where she could care for him. But, given
her husband's penchant for courting disaster, she had little faith
that this period of domestic contentment would last.[1]

Until Maria's final acrimonious break with the AASS she had
planned to assist David with the editorship of the *Standard* without
using her name. She may even have felt obliged to help out with
the paper in the interim between her resignation and David's arrival. But once David took over she had nothing further to do with
the *Standard*. She even refused to give him any assistance with his
own writing for the paper. "I never inquire what his editorials are
to be, and never read them till the paper is issued," she announced
firmly to Ellis in September.[2]

Not everyone was happy that David was editing the *Standard*. Apart from Garrison and Ellis Loring, who both insisted he was the perfect choice for the job, most leaders of the AASS were lukewarm, and some outspokenly hostile, to the appointment. "Heaven avert such a catastrophe," wrote an indignant Abby Kelley Foster to Maria Chapman. "We shall all go over the dam if he takes it." She was particularly disturbed by David's political leanings, having read an article of his in the *New Hampshire Gazette* which she described as "a plain invitation to support the Whig party." Furthermore, she worried that David seemed to have "a killing influence" on everything he touched.[3]

If David threw himself into his new job with customary enthusiasm, his natural pugnacity brought him trouble almost from the start. Within weeks of his arrival in New York, Ellis Loring was warning that the editorial style which had served so well for the *Massachusetts Journal* was not suitable for a paper like the *Standard*. At first David seemed unperturbed by such criticism and went about his work with unfailing good cheer. With the coming of autumn, however, Maria was admitting to Louisa Loring that her husband was growing restless on the editorial treadmill and had expressed a longing to escape to a country tavern for a week and "kick up his heels." He paid no attention to Ellis' warnings to stay away from controversy. In October he was accused of using the paper to promote Henry Clay's Whig candidacy for the 1844 presidential election. David insisted that he wasn't urging Whig principles "*as such*" but was merely showing "the connection, where I see clearly that it exists, of any and every party with slavery." By the end of 1843, when even Garrison was charging him with lacking a good understanding of abolitionist principles, David was ready to resign. He stayed on, however, until early May 1844.[4]

Meanwhile, Maria did her best to keep things cheerful. On Christmas they shared the day with a homeless street urchin who had long been an object of her concern. The boy had recently been locked up in the Tombs, a notorious New York prison, because there was nowhere else to send him. At ten he was too old for an orphan asylum. So to cheer themselves up and give the boy a treat, on Christmas morning David went to the Tombs to fetch the child, who arrived at the Hoppers' in such a state of filth that Maria had to cut off his hair, scrub him from head to toe, and dress him in clean clothes, including a new pair of boots, before he was fit to have around. "You never saw any little fellow so changed, and so happy in the change!" Maria reported to Anna Loring. The boy was delighted with his boots and kept asking "Are them boots for *me?*" When Maria replied "yes," he beamed with pleasure and told her he would remember this Christmas for as long as he lived.[5]

Maria rarely entertained friends in her room at the Hoppers', but one February evening in 1843 an artist friend, William Page, was invited to meet Ralph Waldo Emerson, who was in town preparing to give a series of lectures. Emerson had surprised Maria by sending her tickets for his course and asking to come round and see her. Pleased and flattered by the great man's interest, she took John Hopper along to hear the lectures, which she found as "refreshing as a glass of soda-water; but, as usual, not *satisfactory.*"[6]

Maria's admiration of Emerson was qualified. While she considered him America's best poet and was invariably stimulated by what she read and heard of his, she always found an unfathomable quality in his talks, something "expansive and indefinite" about his theories. After conversing with him or any of the other Transcendentalists, she complained that her "spirit always has to bite its finger, to know whether it exists or not."[7]

Maria was far less enthusiastic about some of Emerson's disciples. Bronson Alcott, whose head was invariably in the clouds and whose language was the most indecipherable of all the Transcendentalists, came to New York in September 1843. One evening the Childs and John Hopper were invited to a "social 'palaver'" given by Alcott and two of his friends, Charles Lane and William Henry Channing. Repelled by the confused talk and stifling air of the small crowded room, Maria left early and later admitted to a friend that she was growing "less and less inclined to seek aid from any of these wandering prophets. Not a morsel of spiritual food did I ever gain from any of them."[8]

If Maria obtained little spiritual sustenance from Bronson Alcott and his ilk, she thoroughly enjoyed an evening in the company of yet another member of the Transcendentalist circle, Theodore Parker, who stopped by for a visit that September before sailing for Europe. Maria had known Parker since the early 1830s, when, as a young schoolteacher and aspiring divinity school student, he had been a frequent visitor at her brother's parsonage in Watertown. Convers had quickly taken a liking to this gifted young scholar who shared his own omnivorous love of learning, and he had helped prepare Parker for admission to Harvard Divinity School.

In recent years the Reverend Theodore Parker had acquired considerable notoriety in Boston Unitarian circles for his radical views; he claimed that neither Christ, nor the Bible, nor the Church was essential to religion. He had published a book entitled *A Discourse of Matters Pertaining to Religion* in 1842 which led to his ostracism from orthodox Unitarian circles. Even his old mentor, Convers Francis, who himself had proposed the idea of abandoning the Bible in favor of a system of universal morality, had cautioned Parker, after reading his book, that it would be best if they didn't see one another. While there is no record of what Maria Child and Theodore Parker discussed during their long evening together, Maria declared herself "extremely pleased" with this radical Unitarian minister.[9]

David, having resigned from the *Standard* in early May 1844, was still in New York later that month when the Hoppers moved into yet another house in a quieter part of the city on East Third Street. The Childs now had their own parlor. David, however, was not around very long to enjoy it. By June he had returned to Northampton and Maria was once again husbandless. She still had her "son" under the same roof, but John was now working hard trying to build up a new law practice. He was also seeing more women his own age and consequently had less time to escort her about the city.

Maria helped to dispel her loneliness with hard work. Capitalizing on the success of her *Letters from New York*, in December 1843 she began a second series of letters, which she mailed off not to the *Standard* but to the Boston *Courier*. The letters were widely reprinted in other newspapers, proving how quickly her literary reputation had been restored. Meanwhile, she was busy working on new editions of both *The Mother's Book* and *Philothea* and putting together a series of juvenile books entitled *Flowers for Children*. These last included old stories from the *Miscellany* as well as new compositions.[10]

By the summer of 1844, for the first time in years, Maria Child was earning enough to meet her modest personal needs and still have something left over to pay for an occasional concert or lecture. Maria wrote to Frank Shaw of her determination not to waste any more of her life agonizing over David's financial problems. In doing so, she claimed, she had neglected her true mission. "Now I intend to live for one individual object. Formed as my character now is, I cannot do otherwise than make literature the honest agent of my conscience and my heart."[11]

Maria tried to reassure friends like the Lorings and the Shaws that she had not renounced the holy calling of a reformer in favor of the bohemian life of a writer in New York. She was, she insisted, only returning to the work she felt particularly suited for. From now on she would help the slaves and other oppressed peoples in ways which made the best use of her talents and followed most closely the dictates of her conscience. "Men come into organizations with so many prejudices of sect and party," she told Shaw, "so many abominable traditions, and one-sided opinions, that it would be impossible for me ever to act with them, in any form or combination. But I think my writings indicate that I work to the same *end* as organized reformers; only I belong to the group of *sappers* and *miners*, instead of laying rails on the open direct road."[12]

The wide readership Maria had brought to the *Standard* and the popularity of her *Letters from New York* justified, in her own mind at least, her long-standing faith in the gentle art of persuasion, or, as she had put it earlier, promoting reform with "a troop of horse shod with felt." One's views need not be forced on others, she insisted. On the contrary, in order to be heard, it was only necessary to speak out quietly but firmly.[13] From now on she would rely on the method she had employed so effectively in the *Standard* and earlier in the *Juvenile Miscellany* and her *Ladies Family Library*, of making literature the principal vehicle of her reform efforts.

Maria later looked back on these years of independence in New York as her "Indian Summer," and in many respects it was a rewarding and productive time. City life agreed with her. So did boarding out. Relieved of the most burdensome household chores, she was free to spend as much time as she wished at her desk. "It is curious," she wrote in 1844, "but standing as I am on the verge of declin[ing] life, my senses are all growing more acute and clear. So acute that my sources of pain and pleasure are increased tenfold. I am a great deal more *alive* than I used to be." Convers Francis noted the visible change life in New York had made on his daughter when she visited him in the summer of 1846. "He really *complimented* me," Maria reported to Louisa, "a civility of which he was never before known to be guilty. After he had got over his first surprise, he held me at arms length, exclaiming, "Why you *sweet* creature! How *well* you look! What beautiful teeth you've got." The fact is, the last time the old gentleman saw me, I was gloomy, harassed, dirty and over-worked, at Northampton, a care-worn old woman, before my time; and no wonder my renovated N. York image should strike *him* agreeably."[14]

Maria far preferred New York to Boston. For one thing, her

books sold twice as well there. The atmosphere was also more congenial. Unlike Boston and Philadelphia, where cultural life was dominated by entrenched social elites, New York had a tradition of easy camaraderie between writers and artists. The openness and energy of its society, which welcomed new writers, painters, and musicians with a generosity and enthusiasm undreamt of by George Ticknor and his friends, delighted Maria.[15]

The cultural offerings were also more varied in New York than they had been in Boston. In the New England of Maria's youth, music and art had been largely scorned as corrupt luxuries. Concerts were few and opportunities to see good painting and sculpture even fewer. In New York, however, numerous galleries and frequent concerts provided Maria with a welcome opportunity to indulge her love of art and music. The relative leisure and financial security which she enjoyed after the publication of her *Letters from New York* allowed her to take advantage of these offerings. Early in 1845 she wrote her friend Maria White, now married to James Russell Lowell, that she decidedly preferred New York to any other city of her acquaintance. "One can lead a freer and more unmolested life, than is possible in more provincial towns. The democratic tendency of all things is likewise more to my liking, than the more starched social character of Boston."[16]

Within months of her arrival in New York, Maria had sat for the French silhouettist Auguste Edouart, who was touring the United States cutting profiles of the famous and not-so-famous wherever he went. Impressed by the vitality and delicacy of these "shadows," as she called them, Maria urged the Shaws and the Lorings to sit for Edouart when he came to Boston and to send her the results for a New Year's present.[17]

Another artist whom Maria befriended during her years in New York was William Page. When she first met this young painter of portraits and historical works, he was struggling to make ends meet for himself and several small children. During the winter of 1842 one of Page's few comforts was taking tea with Maria Child each Sunday afternoon.[18]

Always the champion of the underdog, and aware of the difficulties painters, sculptors, and musicians faced in a country where the climate was largely one of ignorance and indifference to the arts, Maria found herself besieged with requests for aid, comfort, and advice. One musician who sought her out was the Bohemian composer Anthony Philip Heinrich. "Papa Heinrich," as he was affectionately known, had enjoyed a brief success in New York in

1842 when a grand festival of his music had been held in the Broadway Tabernacle. Since then he had fallen on hard times, and when Maria met him in the spring of 1845 he was living in a room bare of all furniture except a piano with a leg missing and a single borrowed chair. He supported himself by giving piano lessons to little girls.[19]

But the musician who really captured Maria's heart and soul was Ole Bull. She first heard the widely acclaimed Norwegian violinist when he gave two concerts in New York in December 1843. The first evening she had entered the hall in a particularly depressed state of mind, only to be transfixed with joy and wonderment by the sound of Bull's rich harmonies. "I felt that my soul was for the first time, baptized in music," she wrote in one of her "Letters." Maria was smitten by Bull and his music. Not only was he an un-tutored genius whose gift came directly from heaven, even his appearance was godlike. Unusually tall and powerfully built, he looked as she imagined Adam in Paradise.[20]

"I seldom fall victim to hero-worship," she remarked ingen-uously to Ellis Loring in a letter describing the enchantment of Ole Bull's music, "but when I *do* I am an ultraist . . . I would stay in hell twice as long as Eurydice, if I could be brought out by this Norwegian Orpheus." When Ole Bull left on tour later that winter, he sent her his likeness and promised to visit her when he returned. On October 11, 1844, Maria was seated in the hall for the start of Bull's second round of New York concerts. Once again she was transported by the beauty of his playing, delighting particularly in a fantasia of Scottish music. Back home in bed she wept to think that the day would come when she would see and hear the violinist no more.[21]

Maria's infatuation for Ole Bull and his music did not replace her love for John Hopper, but it may have helped soften the pain she surely felt when her "son" announced his betrothal in December 1844 to an unidentified young woman. If the beauty of Ole Bull's music enabled Maria to steel herself against the certainty of one day losing John, her writing doubtless also helped. Take, for ex-ample, a story she published in the summer of 1845 entitled "Hilda Silfverling." The year is 1740. Hilda is a young Swedish woman living in Stockholm and earning her living as a domestic. Beautiful but friendless, Hilda meets and falls in love with a Danish sailor who gets her pregnant before being later lost at sea. A kindly old washerwoman, to whom Hilda confesses her disgrace, offers to slip the baby away with her when she returns to her native Norway.

Despite these careful arrangements, Hilda does not escape suspicion. She is accused of infanticide and condemned to die. Instead of being beheaded, however, Hilda becomes the subject of a scientific experiment. Placed in a frozen vault, she sleeps for a hundred years.

When Hilda wakes up it is 1840. There is not a familiar face in all of Stockholm but she is nonetheless besieged by curiosity-seekers who stare at her and annoy her with questions. Overcome with "an inexpressible longing to go where no one had ever heard of her, and among scenes she had never looked upon," Hilda is beckoned by a prophetic voice to Norway. There she takes a new name and settles in a beautiful but remote village on the edge of a fjord. She feels nothing can trouble her among these kindly, peace-loving people.

Soon after removing to this earthly paradise, two unsettling things happen. First, Hilda discovers a wooden trumpet which she recognizes as having belonged to the washerwoman who carried off her baby. Second, she learns about an extraordinary young man named Alerik, a native of the village then living abroad. By all accounts, Alerik is a charming, handsome, and fun-loving musician. Hilda dreams of this unknown paragon and wonders if he is really as remarkable as everyone says he is.

One day sounds of organ-playing drift over the waters from Alerik's house and everyone knows the youth has returned. Hilda first sees him at a wedding and is immediately struck by his resemblance to her sailor lover, the father of her baby. Alerik, charmed by Hilda's natural refinement, her spiritual beauty, and "simple, untutored modesty," falls in love with her. Their romance blossoms until Hilda learns that Alerik is her great-grandson. Afraid that once he discovers this he won't love her anymore, Hilda puts off telling him the truth. But when she finally does, he dismisses her worries, insisting that fairies have bewitched her into thinking she'd slept for a hundred years, when in fact she had simply died and her spirit had taken on a new form. He finally persuades her that there is nothing to prevent their union, and within a year the two are married.[22]

Maria, having consigned her alter ego, Hilda, to a Swedenborgian heaven with a lover who resembles Ole Bull and John Hopper rolled into one, was doubtless better able to cope with the many sorrows and difficulties which continued to plague her in the real world. For despite her efforts to separate her affairs from David's, her husband continued to trouble her heart and her conscience.

For a time after his resignation in the spring of 1844, David was caught up in the political fever surrounding the proposed annexation of Texas and the upcoming presidential election. In June he was back in Massachusetts vigorously campaigning for the Whig party and the election of Henry Clay. The Lowell *Courier* expressed delight to "find our old friend, Mr. Child taking the stump for Clay," claiming that he "understands the Texas question as well as any man in the United States." Back in New York, however, Maria was less sanguine about the outcome of all this excitement. Mr. Child is "carried away with the idea that Texas is *the* question on which the extension of American slavery depends," she wrote Frank Shaw in July, "and that Henry Clay is the only man that can save the country from annexation. I smile; for ever since I can remember men have been expending their energies in *saving the country;* and what comes of it?"[23]

In the end, Clay lost the election and David Child was once again without an occupation. In December he came down to New York just long enough for Maria to mend and wash his clothes and then set off for Washington, where he was briefly employed as a political reporter for the *Standard*. "I hate politics worse and worse," Maria complained after he'd left.[24]

A story Maria wrote in these years entitled "Home and Politics" reveals the depths of her frustration with David's shortcomings. The heroine of this sad tale, Alice White, is a plain, poetic schoolteacher who marries an ambitious young lawyer from New York. At first the union is a happy one and fits precisely Maria's own domestic ideal of a marriage based on mutual love, companionship, and respect. But after a year of domestic bliss George becomes ensnared by politics, "that pestilence which is forever racing through our land, seeking whom it may devour."[25] During the election campaign of William Henry Harrison in 1840, George is out nearly every evening at Whig gatherings, leaving poor Alice alone with her sewing. One night while he is away celebrating Harrison's victory, his little daughter dies of a fever. Filled with remorse for neglecting his wife and child, George might have left politics for good had he not been tempted by the offer of a government job. The next presidential campaign finds him more embroiled in politics than ever. Caught up in the excitement, he gambles all the couple's worldly possessions on the promise of a victory for Henry Clay.

But the Whigs lose the election of 1844 and Alice is forced to part with the cherished contents of the home she so loved. Everything, including the astral lamp—an oil lamp with a cylindrical wick—and the little round table where George and she used to read to each other when they were first married, is sold at auction. The hardship is too much for Alice. In the end she goes mad and has to be hospitalized and doesn't even recognize George when he comes to visit her.

Back in the early days of her married life, Maria would never have considered ending a story with such a despairing vision of domesticity. "Home and Politics" amounts to a public confession that the myth which she had been proclaiming all these years, that "married love is the only rose we have left of Paradise,"[26] has in the end proved false. Even the most promising marriages can fail when the husband doesn't provide for his family. Wouldn't it have been better if Alice White had remained a virginal schoolteacher, independent, self-supporting, and free to indulge her poetic dreams and fancies? Might it not have been better also had Maria Child remained true to her own youthful determination to be independent?

For a woman to dream of such independence was hardly more commonplace in the 1840s than it had been in the 1820s. In some respects society had hardened its views on woman's proper sphere, confining her more rigidly than ever to a life of domesticity. Yet a growing number of women were mustering the courage to ignore these strictures. Some were striking out on their own, hoping and sometimes managing to make a living by their pens. Catharine Sedgwick, of course, had continued to enjoy popularity as a novelist. She had been joined in the 1830s by Caroline Howard Gilman, Louisa Loring's sister-in-law. Another rising literary star was Maria McIntosh. The heyday for women novelists, however, wouldn't come for another decade, when writers like Harriet Beecher Stowe, Susan Warner, and E.D.E.N. Southworth achieved their first commercial successes.[27]

Women writers were rare creatures even in relatively bohemian New York circles, but late in 1844 Margaret Fuller moved down to New York to write for Horace Greeley's *Tribune*. Like Maria before her, Margaret had suffered the censure nineteenth-century society inflicted on ambitious and gifted women. Her critics of both sexes dismissed her as proud, self-centered, and disdainful. But those who knew her well saw behind the satirical mask she often wore to the sensitive, generous person underneath. Margaret had determined to make her mark in American letters. She had befriended Emerson and other members of his Transcendentalist

circle, and from 1840 to 1842 she had served as editor and chief
contributor for their magazine, the *Dial.*

Margaret, who had not lost her respect and admiration for Maria
Child, had hoped to renew their friendship. But Maria, somewhat
repelled by Margaret's aggressive intellectuality, was less eager for
intimacy and made no particular effort to see this old friend when
she arrived in New York. All aversion vanished, however, as soon
as Maria read Margaret's ecstatic review in the *Tribune* of one of
Ole Bull's concerts. We are now "sworn friends," she informed
Anna Loring a few days later.[28]

Margaret too enjoyed their renewed friendship. "I see Mrs. Child
often," she wrote on April 2, 1845, "and they are indeed pleasant
hours we pass together. She is so entertaining, and her generous
heart glows through all she says, and makes a friendly home around
her."[29] To begin with, Margaret boarded with Horace Greeley and
his wife, who lived outside the city on Turtle Bay. She did most of
her writing there at a desk in her room. One February day, Maria
endured the bumpy omnibus ride out to Turtle Bay to call on
Margaret, later describing the visit to Anna Loring:

> I went out in the Harlem omnibus to *forty ninth street*, where she told
> me she lived. But instead of a street, I found a winding zigzag cart
> track. It was as rural as you can imagine, with moss-covered ricks,
> scraggly bushes, and a brook that came tumbling over a little dam,
> and run [*sic*] under the lane. After passing through three great
> swinging gates, I came to the house, which stands all alone by itself,
> and is as inaccessible, as if *I* had chosen it, to keep people off. It is
> a very old house, with a very old porch, and very old vines, and a
> very old garden, and very old summer-houses dropping to pieces,
> and a very old piazza at the back. . . . Margaret's chamber looks out
> upon a little woody knoll that runs down into the water. . . . How
> anything so old and picturesque has been allowed to remain standing
> near New York so long, I cannot imagine. I spent three or four
> delightful hours with Margaret.[30]

What the two women discussed, besides Ole Bull, can only be
surmised, but they must quickly have discovered how many interests they had in common. Both were deeply committed to the progress of the human race, but both were also profoundly disturbed
by the degree of poverty, crime, and moral indifference which they
saw all around them in New York. Of particular concern to Fuller
and Child was the great number of prostitutes, many of whom were
young single girls attracted to New York by the prospect of employment and independence. On one of her visits to the prison on

Blackwell's Island, Maria had befriended an unfortunate Irish girl named Jane, lured down to New York from Montreal by the promise of employment as a milliner. Jane's travelling expenses had been paid and a high wage promised her, but upon reaching the city she had found not a milliner's shop but a brothel. There, as Maria described it in one of her "Letters from New York," Jane's "ruin was effected in spite of remonstrances and entreaties." Eventually, this young woman, like so many others before her, was charged with some petty crime and sent to jail.[31]

But Maria knew that money was not the only temptation responsible for the downfall of so many poor women. The need for love was also a powerful incentive, one which was grossly misunderstood and misrepresented in American society. "You *cannot* make men and women have a horror of each other; the impulses of nature are too strong," Maria declared in a letter to Frank Shaw, refuting the then commonly held belief that virtuous women were incapable of physical passion and that husbands had to look outside of marriage to satisfy their sexual drives. "I do not wonder that so many men are libertines," she told Frank, "I had *almost* said I do not *blame* them. Nature is so outrageously dammed up, her strongest instincts are so repressed, her plainest laws are so violated, in the present structure of society, that nature *will* revenge herself, in spite of all we can do." She admitted that while this was a subject she had thought long and hard about, it was not one on which she dared to speak openly.[32]

"The strong necessity of loving" was a passion Maria both shared and understood, and she had little trouble identifying with the temptations and sufferings of the prostitutes whom she found huddled in their dank cells. A prisoner whose story held particular poignancy for her was Amelia Norman. Unlike the Irish girl Jane, who was forced against her will into becoming a prostitute, Amelia had been seduced by false promises of love and fidelity. Upon learning of her betrayal she had assaulted her lover, a Mr. Ballard of Boston, in a fit of madness. When Ballard accused the unfortunate woman of attempted murder she was arrested and sent to jail to await trial. Public support for Amelia Norman was not lacking. According to Maria's recounting of the trial, "there were plenty of witnesses to prove that this was a case of deliberate seduction and base desertion," but without Maria's and John Hopper's effort to secure her an adequate defense the woman might never have gone free.[33]

Maria described the court case in detail in one of her "Letters from New York." Particularly galling to her were the arguments of the prosecutor, who claimed Eve was only the first seducer and spoke of the legions of "poor innocent men tempted, betrayed and persecuted by women." This, she told her readers, "was putting the saddle on the wrong horse, with a vengeance," adding that never before had she "felt so much intellectual respect, and so much moral aversion for the legal profession." She then gave her version of the situation in New York. "Seduction is going on by wholesale, with a systematic arrangement, and number and variety of agents, which would astonish those who have never looked beneath the hypocritical surface of things. In our cities almost every girl, in the humbler classes of life, walks among snares and pitfalls at every step, unconscious of their presence, until she finds herself fallen, and entangled in a frightful net-work, from which she sees no escape. Life and property are protected, but what protection is there for pure hearts, confiding souls and youthful innocence?"[34]

Nor was the poor working girl the only victim of such licentiousness. In 1843 Maria had published a story in the *Liberty Bell* entitled "Slavery's Pleasant Homes." This outspoken critique of plantation life had equated prostitution with the lot of female slaves.[35] More recently, in a "Letter from New York" on the subject of women's rights, Maria had made it clear that the evil of prostitution was simply one manifestation of a social outlook that regarded all women as subordinate. The gallantry men accorded women in polite society was equally odious. Such false esteem was "merely the flimsy veil which foppery throws over sensuality, to conceal its grossness." Women in the meantime had become so accustomed to regard themselves as "household conveniences or gilded toys" that they were unwilling to act in any way displeasing to the other sex. "There is no measuring the mischief," she told her readers, "done by the prevailing tendency to teach women to be virtuous as a duty to *man* rather than to *God*—for the sake of pleasing the creature, rather than the Creator. '*God* is thy law, *thou* mine,' said Eve to Adam. May Milton be forgiven for sending that thought 'out into everlasting time' in such a jeweled setting. What weakness, vanity, frivolity, infirmity of moral purpose, sinful flexibility of principle— in a word, what soul-stifling, has been the result of thus putting man in the place of God!"

True culture for women as well as men "consists in the full and free development of individual character, regulated by their *own* perceptions of what is true, and their *own* love of what is good." Maria was her old feisty, feminist self once again. No longer bedazzled by Milton's docile Eve, she was again eager to berate the English poet for his unwelcome assumption of masculine superiority.[36]

Women's rights was very much an issue in the 1840s. After the Grimké sisters stimulated a public debate on the question in 1837, the subject was kept alive by Garrisonian agents like Abby Kelley Foster, who regularly toured the country lecturing on the rights of women as well as slaves. "We have good cause to be grateful to the slave," Abby told her audiences. "In striving to strike his irons off, we found most surely, that we were manacled ourselves."[37]

Maria, long conscious of the parallel between the condition of women and that of slaves, was also keenly aware that women's scope had been widened by working for the antislavery movement and other benevolent organizations. Furthermore, as editor of the *Standard* she had admonished those who argued for an expanded role for women while at the same time denying them true freedom. In an article published in 1841 she compared such senseless reasoning to the predicament of the sorcerer's apprentice, who by certain incantations transformed an ordinary broom into a living creature. Upon discovering that his once-docile broom now had a mind of its own, the apprentice tried in vain to reverse the process. "Thus it is with those who urged women to become missionaries and join tract societies. They have changed the household utensil into a living energetic being; and they have no spell to turn it into a broom again."[38]

But while Maria wholeheartedly approved of women's emancipation in principle, she tended to look with disfavor on any public crusade in support of the issue. A "Letter from New York" on women's rights, published in her last months as editor of the *Standard*, grudgingly admitted that like other struggles "of the human soul for *freedom*," this call for reform was articulating a "perverted truth." But at that time she was weary of disputatiousness and ready to dismiss the style of feminist lecturers like Abby Kelley Foster as "offensive to taste, and unacceptable to reason."[39]

In contrast to Maria Child's reluctance to support the women's rights crusade, Margaret Fuller wholeheartedly approved the reform in a tract published early in 1845 entitled *Woman in the Nineteenth Century*. Fuller agreed with Child that every path should be as open to women as to men and insisted that women must take charge of their own lives and not rely on men to tell them what to think and do. But unlike her older friend, Fuller understood the need for sisterly solidarity. While Maria continued to believe that women could quietly gain men's esteem by working side by side with them, experience had taught Margaret that "women are the best helpers of one another." It had shown her how they must raise one another up before men will truly respect them.[40]

Maria read *Woman in the Nineteenth Century* shortly after it came out, and in a letter to Louisa Loring she commended Margaret for her courage. "I should not have dared to have written some things in it," she confessed, "though it would have been safer for me, being married. But they need to be said, and she is brave to do it. . . . She is a great woman, and no mistake."[41]

In the winter of 1845-1846 Margaret Fuller left the Greeleys' house on Turtle Bay and moved into lodgings in the city, where she was soon caught up in a more active social life. "She has got quite established in a literary set here," Maria informed Anna Loring in early December. "As for me, I grow more and more of a hermit." If Margaret had hoped Maria would accompany her to these social gatherings, she was disappointed. "Mrs. Child will not go out at all, either to evening party or morning call," Margaret complained to a friend. "She says she can't afford the time, the white gloves, the visiting cards, the carriage hire. But I think she lives at a disadvantage, by keeping so entirely apart from the common stream of things."[42]

Maria's sympathies readily responded to the plight of lonely widows, neglected orphans, and destitute artists. But she was becoming increasingly standoffish with her old friends, spurning efforts to make her more convivial and often returning the presents they sent her. When the Lorings invited her to accompany them to the seashore in the summer of 1843, she replied that she had neither the time nor the wardrobe for such occasions. She doubted they could imagine "how indifferent one becomes to society and amusements, after fourteen years of uninterrupted adverse fortune (with the constantly increasing conviction that the cause is incurable). The prosperous know not how pale life becomes under such circumstances, nor how the inclination for repose and seclusion strengthens with each discouraging year."[43]

If a friend was really in need, however, Maria was all care and attention. When Sarah Shaw came down from Massachusetts to be treated for threatened blindness, Maria visited her for two hours each day. "I do my utmost to amuse her weary twilight with my nonsense," she reported back to Frank, "often at the expense of that matronly dignity, which is considered respectable at my discreet age."[44]

Maria's change of mood was understandable. In the late winter of 1845 David was still unemployed, although rumors were circulating in Boston that he was in Arkansas proposing to build a railroad to the California gold mines. But a letter of Maria's written on February 6, which describes him sitting in the next room composing a letter, makes this unlikely. With the return of summer David was again back in Northampton, living in the shanty on their farm and hoping to make a profit by selling stones to the railroad. "He verily believes that he shall realize $2000 of the railroad, for stone that will cost an outlay of only $150," Maria wrote despairingly to Louisa. "I might try to convince him that the contractors must be crazy to make such a bargain; but it is of no use to argufy."[45]

Maria's growing disillusionment with the institution of marriage is stated even more explicitly in a letter to Louisa Loring in 1847. A married couple they both knew had separated, and Maria tried to persuade Louisa that the move had likely been a sensible one. "You may rely upon it," she assured her friend,

> that when people *are* incongruous and mutually *feel* that they are, it is the wisest and best thing to separate, let society say what it may. Nay *I* go so far as to consider it positively *wrong*, under such circumstances, to live together in the married relation. Look around you and see what fitty ricketty children, what miserable organizations, mind and body, are the consequences of widespread legalized prostitution! I know it is a dangerous subject to speculate upon; but experience and observation have *forced* upon me a close attention to it; and though I am bewildered when I try to harmonize the discordant elements of nature and law, thus far I *can* see clearly—that it is wrong to have children unless people love one another.[46]

Was Maria considering a permanent separation from David? Perhaps, but only if he could manage on his own without her, and as the months passed that appeared less and less likely. Nonetheless, the Childs saw very little of one another in the years following his resignation from the *Standard*. David's rare visits lasted just long enough for Maria to wash and mend his clothes, most of which were filthy rags by the time she got her hands on them. After one such reunion she sent him off with four new shirts she had made of particularly rugged material. Within weeks all four had either been lost or stolen. The futility of making even the smallest effort on David's behalf had taken its toll. Furthermore, as Maria noted in a letter to Frank Shaw, city life was making her more refined, while David was growing coarser. "Strongly as we love each other, our growth is more and more divergent."[47]

Thus, while Maria spoke dutifully of eventual retirement with David to some rural cottage, convincing even herself of the charms of such a life, in reality "the million lilliputian cords" of domesticity held little appeal for her. Although she was lonely, and increasingly felt the peculiarity of her position as a married woman pursuing a career apart from her husband, she still had her "son" John and her work.[48]

In February 1845 the new edition of *Philothea* was in press. Maria was compiling a collection of her second series of "Letters from New York" into a new volume, while continuing to write additional columns for the *Courier*, and several stories had been contracted for by the *Columbian Lady's and Gentleman's Magazine*. By the summer of 1845 Maria's popularity was assured. Her books were selling well and reviews were generally favorable. The *Broadway Journal* praised her second volume of *Letters from New York* for its success in appealing to a wide range of readers: "Mrs. Child instinctively seizes upon subjects which are of interest to all classes." The *Democratic Review* agreed that the pleasure of the *Letters* lay in their direct personal appeal to the reader's heart but criticized their author for "leaning toward Charity (so-called) too often at the cost of Justice."[49]

Edgar Allen Poe added his voice to the praises of Maria Child in an article on "The Literati of New York City," published in *Godey's Lady's Book* in 1846. Poe particularly commended her stories for displaying a "graceful and brilliant *imagination*—a quality rarely noticed in our countrywomen." In this same article he also provides a rare physical description of Maria in her mid-forties: "Mrs. Child, casually observed, has nothing particularly striking in her personal appearance. One would pass her in the street a dozen times without notice. She is low in stature and slightly framed. Her complexion is florid; eyes and hair are dark; features in general diminutive. The expression of her countenance, when animated, is highly intellectual. Her dress is plain, not even neat—anything but fashionable. Her bearing needs excitement to impress it with life and dignity. She is of that order of beings who are themselves only on 'great occasions.' "[50]

Poe is echoing here an impression of Maria Child hinted at by other observers. Friends in New York remarked that they never saw her, and yet she seemed to know more about the city than they did. Dressed in drab old-fashioned clothes, which she found both comfortable and concealing, Maria was easily lost in the crowd. She could walk down the sidewalk or slip into a hall or theater unobserved. Such anonymity gave her a freedom few women of her class enjoyed, the freedom to go about the city on her own.

Apart from Maria's writing, music and art were, as she put it, "her society." The walls of the little parlor in the Third Street house were so covered with paintings and prints that the room resembled a gallery. The added space had enabled her to acquire a piano, and she encouraged her musician friends to come and play it for her. Moreover, in her eagerness to learn as much as she could about music, she piled her table high with library books on the subject. She even entertained the fanciful dream of someday composing a piece of her own. She told Anthony Heinrich how music was such an absorbing passion with her that people "with natures less susceptible and earnest than my own may well deem it an insanity."[51] When news of his sister's musical obsession reached Convers Francis he dismissed it as an outgrowth of her Swedenborgianism.

Convers had a point. Transported to mystical heights by the sound of beautiful harmonies, Maria considered music the language of the soul, one of nature's voices through which deep mysteries were revealed. Great musicians, like great poets and great prophets, she believed, were in closer harmony with the spirit world than ordinary folk and became therefore the instruments through which certain higher truths were communicated to mankind.[52]

In one of her more fanciful stories written at this time, Maria explains the genius of Felix Mendelssohn by tracing the voyage of his spirit through the various forms it had inhabited on this earth, from agate rock and giant oak to nightingale, aspiring ever upward until at last it entered the soul of the infant Mendelssohn, whose music "repeats with puzzling vagueness all he has ever known, and troubles his spirit with prophecies of the infinite unknown." According to Maria, Mendelssohn's compositions are inspired by "powers above the circle of his being," and he will only understand them when he passes "through the gate which men call death . . . into more perfect life, where speech and tone dwell together forever in a golden marriage."[53]

For all the joy she received from listening to the violinist Ole Bull or the noted pianist Ernest Timm, both of whom played for her on her own piano, the feverish intensity of Maria's absorption in music was also symptomatic of a less happy frame of mind. As she admitted to Louisa Loring, her "intense devotion to music" sprang from a dread of "confirmed despondency." "I fly to it, as other weary and wounded spirits fly to fanaticism in religion. Such a cloud all the time hangs over my life, from David's incurable tendencies, and the changes in me produced thereby, that I have no choice between a listless and moping melancholy, or a *desperate* effort to keep young, and bright, and cheerful. In this state music came to me like an angel. I should have gone mad without it."[54]

When the first warm days announced the arrival of spring in April 1847, Maria had lived in New York for nearly six years and looked forward to remaining there for many more. Then came word that John Hopper had eloped with a young woman named Rosa DeWolf. The two had become engaged without the consent of her parents, who objected to their daughter marrying a propertyless young man, and the betrothal had promised to be a long one. "The news of their marriage came upon me like a thunderclap," Maria wrote Susan Lyman, the daughter of her old Northampton friend, Anne. Only a few weeks before she had told Susan that she was looking forward to a permanent home with John and Rosa after their marriage.[55] But since the young couple could not yet afford a home of their own, they had no place to live but the Hoppers'. She now realized that her parlor and bedroom would be needed and made preparations to move out. By early May she had packed up her books and other belongings and carried them out to New Rochelle, where she rented a room in Joseph Carpenter's farmhouse.

14

Sweeping Dead Leaves and Dusting Mirrors

*My soul is like a hungry raven, with its mouth
wide open for the food which no man offers.*
—*Lydia Maria Child to Lucy Osgood,
1846*

I am quite like a lady 'of property and standing,' with both country and city residences," Maria jokingly remarked to her brother Convers in a letter from New Rochelle. In reality her dream of a life of freedom and independence in New York had evaporated overnight. Although the Hoppers had kindly reserved an attic room for her to use whenever she wished, the cozy apartment which had come to seem like home was no longer hers. In any case, her presence in the household suddenly seemed superfluous. Like most newlyweds, John and Rosa had eyes only for each other, a clear signal to Maria that her "son" no longer needed her. Now everything she owned was crowded into a small room in a lonely country farmhouse. "I think there never was so still a place," she wrote in July. "From the beginning of the week to the end, I see nothing but a few Quakers solemnly pacing by to meeting with most weighty Christian gravity, and a set of meek hens meandering about without any apparent purpose."[1]

The Carpenter farm, situated in an old Quaker settlement in the village of New Rochelle just twenty-two miles from the city, was a familiar retreat. A decade earlier, when antislavery mobs in New York had threatened the Childs' safety, they had boarded there for more than six months. In recent years Maria had often escaped to the home of this Quaker farmer and his wife during anniversary week. On these occasions, when members of the AASS gathered for their annual meetings, she was hoping to avoid not antislavery mobs but her erstwhile colleagues.

But now the Carpenter farm was home, not just a convenient sanctuary. Maria's days were spent in her sunny, whitewashed room in the old farmhouse where the ceiling was so low it almost brushed the top of her head. Here were gathered her books and the little collection of art works she had acquired in New York. Here she wrote and read and slept, going downstairs only for meals or a walk.

In early June David came for one of his rare visits. As usual he was ill and careworn and his clothes were in tatters. Maria was happy for his company, however, and spent several weeks nursing him back to health, washing and mending his old clothes, and stitching up new ones. One Sunday, while observing the Quaker neighbors trudge by the farmhouse on their way to meeting, David remarked disrespectfully that it was a pity these pious Friends did not carry a few goose eggs in their pockets "that their long settings might be productive of *some* benefit." After four weeks, despite Maria's pleadings to remain, David returned to Northampton and the ill-fated farm. His departure left her lonely and depressed. She wrote Frank Shaw that she no longer felt *moved* to write anything. "I seem to have hopelessly lost my interest in the world and all it contains. . . . Of literary ambition, I am sorry to say I have not one particle. . . . As for money, it is of no use for me to make more than enough to feed and clothe myself decently. I cannot make a position for myself, as *men* can."[2]

As the weeks passed with no word from David, she worried that he was ill. An unpleasant dream filled with bad omens exacerbated these anxious thoughts, and she wrote Susan Lyman in late August for news of him. Pouring out her heart to this young friend, Maria complained further that she had not had a letter from the Lorings for over six months. First John Hopper, then her husband, and now even her dearest friends were abandoning her. "I feel as if I was all alone on a rock in the middle of the ocean," she told Susan.[3]

Occasional trips to New York relieved the overwhelming loneliness, at least for a time. In October Marianne Silsbee, an old acquaintance but a new friend, came down from Salem for a visit. Marianne, like so many of Maria's closest friends, was both wealthy and aristocratic. The two enjoyed discussing books, visiting museums, and going to the theatre and opera. As long as they avoided subjects like antislavery and politics their friendship flourished. "She is singularly frank and unaffected, for a woman who has always lived among the 'upper ten thousand,' " Maria remarked after Marianne returned home.[4]

In September 1847 came word that her sister, Mary Preston, had died, news which apparently inspired Maria to visit her father and long-neglected relatives and friends in Massachusetts. She paid a call on her brother Convers in Cambridge, where he and Abby had moved in 1842 following his appointment as Professor of Pulpit Eloquence and Pastoral Care at the Harvard Divinity School. In Medford she not only saw her old childhood friend, Lucy Osgood, but her niece Mary Preston Stearns, now married and living there with her husband. This revisiting of her childhood home, this renewal of severed bonds, was for Maria a "saddened pleasure. I met with extreme kindness and cordiality everywhere; but I could hardly tell whether pain or pleasure predominated in my mind during the five weeks I spent among early scenes."[5]

By January 1848 Maria was back in New Rochelle, dreading the long solitary winter and hoping that "some good spirit or other will put into my head something to write, that may do good to somebody." Joseph Carpenter and his wife made their literary tenant comfortable by keeping her well supplied with firewood. On clear days the sun poured in through the window of her white-washed room. Besides the Carpenters, her only acquaintances were two farmhands. She called them her "beaux." One was Jesse, a sixty-year-old colored man who sang Methodist hymns under her window when he was "drunk and spiritual minded;" the other was "Irish Michael," who touched his hat to her every morning and expressed "his regret that 'such a nice little woman should live all alone.' "[6]

Maria managed somehow to survive the winter. In a determinedly cheerful letter to her brother she spoke of eating well, sleeping well, and reading agreeable books, but made no mention of what, if anything, she was writing. Marianne Silsbee sent her the new novel *Jane Eyre*, which so carried her away that she stayed up all night to finish it.[7]

In April came the welcome news that David—whose scheme for hauling rocks for the railroad had long since evaporated—had been offered a steady job. His younger brother John, a successful engineer, had hired him to help build a railroad through Tennessee. Now that someone else was responsible for her husband's well-being, Maria felt freer to go her own way. For some time friends had been urging her to stop wasting her efforts on pieces for periodicals and suggesting that she undertake something more substantial. As long as David was out of work, she had not wanted to risk losing a guaranteed income. But now that David's future was out of her hands, at least temporarily, Maria embarked on the most ambitious literary undertaking of her career, a history of the world's religions.[8]

The diversity of religious experience had long been a compelling interest of hers. As a young woman Maria had been especially annoyed by certain Jewish and Christian writers who covered over the contradictions and absurdities of their own religious beliefs while dismissing all other creeds as "childish fables" or "filthy superstitions." Equally abhorrent were those who viewed all religions as impostures. The book's underlying theme—the revelation of religious truth through successive ages—had already been explored in her "Letters from New York," where she spoke of truth as immortal, claiming "no fragment of it ever dies."[9] Nor was Maria alone in holding these unorthodox views. Theodore Parker, the young Transcendentalist minister, concurred in viewing Christianity as simply one stage in the history of mankind's search for religious truth.

By April 17, 1848, Maria was occupying the small upper room reserved for her at the Hoppers and beginning the research for her new project. From the first she found the reading so dry and dull she feared the book itself would never "kindle anybody's mind." Later she would describe the whole experience as a "real pilgrimage of penance, with peas in my shoes, walking over rubblestones most of the way." But while she was often discouraged, she was as often deeply absorbed. "My aversion to theologicals is greatly diminished by the fact that they lived three or four thousand years ago. At *that* distance I find them rather endurable." Moreover, she admitted to falling in love with nearly every religion she studied.[10]

By thus immersing herself in the history of man's search for religious truth, Maria also found consolation for her own spiritual wanderings. She had assured her friend Lucy Osgood in 1846 that if she "could only *find* a church, most gladly would I worship there." Since moving to New York the religious services she attended had failed to gratify this craving. "My soul is like a hungry raven, with its mouth wide open for the food which no man offers," she complained.

The Unitarian meetings here chill me with their cold intellectual respectability. Mr. Barrett, the Swedenborgian, has only transferred the padlock of his chain from St. Paul to Swedenborg. . . . At the

Calvinistic meeting in the next street, the preacher, in his prayer, says, "We thank thee, O Lord, that there is a hell of despair!" I quote his very words. At the Episcopal churches, the minister, with perfumed handkerchief, addresses ladies in silks and satins, with prayer-books richly gilded, and exhorts them to contribute something toward building a chapel for the poor; it being *very* important that the poor should be taught sufficient religion to keep them from burning the houses and breaking open the stores of the rich. . . .

Now what can a poor sinner, like me, with an intense abhorrence of shams, do in such places?[11]

The best Maria could hope for was that at some future day "the spirit of extended, as well as narrow clanship" would end and Christianity itself would cease to be a sect. Meanwhile she would continue to search out an acceptable form of social worship while consoling herself with the reminder that "this which people call the real world, is not real to me; all its sights seem to me shadows, all its sounds echoes. I live at service in it, and sweep dead leaves out of paths, and dust mirrors, and do errands, as I am bid; but glad I am when work is done, to go *home* to rest."[12]

By the end of 1848, Maria was back in New Rochelle preparing for another lonely winter. This time she had a pile of religious histories to read, carried back from her last visit to the city. But perusing these dry, dusty tomes did little to lift her spirits. She was lonelier and more depressed than ever. Even David, it seemed, had abandoned her. Late in the fall he had returned briefly from Tennessee, going straight to Northampton. After spending several weeks there he passed through New York on his way south. But he never came out to New Rochelle. Instead he sent Maria a note through the Hoppers explaining that he was already late returning and if he delayed any longer he would lose his job on the railroad.[13]

A few months later came another blow. The Carpenters needed her little room for additional farmhands, and she would have to leave. Word of her banishment from yet another place she had come to regard as home made Maria lose heart. Dark thoughts chased through her mind, and a gloomy spirit began whispering persuasively into her ear: "Who will miss thee, if thou wert to die?" John didn't need her. David didn't need her. The Lorings had forgotten her and now even her good friend Joseph Carpenter was sending her away. Her wretchedness may well have been compounded by the realization that she was approaching fifty and that the end of her life might not be far off. Close to despair, Maria decided to set her financial affairs in order, and to this end she spent a week in early March rereading old correspondence.[14]

She expected to find this a melancholy exercise, and she burned over three hundred letters fearing they might give pain to others. She particularly dreaded opening a bundle marked "Ellis and Louisa," certain its perusal would reduce her to tears. Instead the contents made her smile. "It was well worth all the trouble of writing those letters," she reported to Louisa, "to have done my poor weary heart so much good. They let in a whole world of sunshine." Reading them helped Maria begin to realize that all was not lost. She was not alone in the world. There were many friends like the Lorings who loved her.

But with this understanding came an awareness of how badly she had behaved towards people like the Lorings whose generosity she had so often rebuffed. She asked Louisa to forgive her many faults and begged her to "believe that I am not in reality capricious, or ungrateful for the love you have bestowed on me. I have made strong resolutions to . . . be good and genial; and one favorable sign is that I feel a humble distrust of myself; I doubt whether I shall be *able* to do it. But I will *try*, and that earnestly."[15]

By late March Maria had left New Rochelle and was once again settled at the Hoppers', where she managed to crowd her belongings into her small attic room. John and Rosa graciously allowed her the use of her old parlor to entertain visitors, and she had a good many that spring as friends came down from Boston expressly to cheer her. No sooner had she settled in than the Lorings arrived, followed by Henrietta Sargent and later by Marianne Silsbee. It turned out to be a sociable and eventful return to urban life.

New York in 1849 was a very different city from the one Maria had known when she first came there eight years earlier. The economy had rebounded and a building boom was underway. On lower Broadway the private residences which had once lined this elegant promenade had either been converted into business establishments or torn down and replaced by new and bigger buildings. Here the first great American department store of Alexander T. Stewart had opened in 1846. Here also stood the new luxury hotels complete with gas lighting, interior plumbing, and steam heat. With the spreading commercialization of lower Manhattan, the well-to-do moved their homes farther and farther uptown; Fifth Avenue began to replace Broadway as the fashionable heart of the city.

While growth and expansion were clearly benefiting the rich in New York, the same could not be said for the poor, whose numbers were added to yearly by the thousands of immigrants who poured off the docks and into the city in search of housing and employment. Wages remained low while rents rose as the value of property increased. City residents became particularly alarmed during the winter of 1846–1847 when a flood of homeless, destitute foreigners sought charity from the already overcrowded almshouses and other public institutions. At midcentury, New York gave the appearance of two hostile cities—one rich, progressive, and Protestant, the other poor, foreign, and Catholic.

Less than two months after Maria returned, the latent hostility between these two classes erupted into open warfare. The occasion was the appearance of the famous English actor William Macready at the Astor Opera House on May 10, 1849. For some time a feud had been raging between Macready and Edwin Forrest, a popular, if crude American actor whose great public following did not include the rich and fashionable. Forrest was an ardent democrat and promoter of a national "American" theater. He scorned the aristocratic and European influence which Macready represented, and so, with the help of the Sixth Ward boss, Isaiah Rynders, Forrest deliberately goaded his supporters to form a mob outside the Opera House where Macready was appearing in *Macbeth*.

For three days the mob raged, setting fire to the Opera House and tearing up the pavement outside. Not until soldiers were brought in was order finally restored. Maria, no stranger to mob activity, found herself in the middle of this uproar when, on May 12th, accompanied by John and Rosa Hopper, she went to rescue her friend Marianne Silsbee, who was staying in the same hotel as Macready. While bullets flew over their heads the three pushed their way through the infuriated mob then blocking the entrance to the hotel. They found Mrs. Silsbee inside, brought her back out through the excited crowd and, depositing her safely in a friend's carriage, drove back to the Hoppers' by a circuitous route. When the terrified Mrs. Silsbee exclaimed, "Oh what a frightful city N. York is!" Maria could not resist reminding her friend that Boston had its own history of mob violence.[16]

Brave as she was under fire, and scornful as she might be of aristocratic squeamishness, Maria herself had little tolerance for mobs and even less for the "ruffianly" actor Edwin Forrest, whom she accused of making "coarse wicked appeals to bad, petty" national prejudices. Nor did she have any good words for Isaiah Rynders, whom she dismissed as "that Jacobin demon, who guides the destinies of Tammany Hall," and who was "doing his best to kindle a war between rich and poor by attacks on 'the white kid gentry who frequent the opera.' " In a letter to Louisa Loring she described her anger and frustration with the whole incident: "God knows my sympathies are with the ignorant million. There are *instants*, when the sight of rags and starvation make *me* almost ready to smash thro' the plate-glass of the rich, and seize their treasures of silver and gold. But alas for such outbreaks as these! They right no wrongs."[17]

Apart from this singular disturbance, Maria's time with Marianne Silsbee passed pleasantly enough. Avoiding the subject of politics altogether, the two women visited art galleries and went shopping. Maria, wearing a smart bonnet and shawl given her by Louisa Loring, was pleased to note that the salespeople treated her with respect. Marianne, however, thought her friend's dress not good enough for her elegant accessories and proceeded to buy Maria a new silk dress. "I am now caparisoned for the street for four years to come," she reported bemusedly to Louisa, adding that she was almost afraid to wear her shawl, "for fear The Empire Club will mob me as an aristocrat." Early in the summer the Shaws, who had recently moved to Staten Island, invited her to visit them. They held out the promise of some moonlight boating. When Maria hesitated, reminding them how much she hated sitting down to formal dinners in evening dress, Frank assured her she could wear a petticoat or a sack and sit or lounge on the straw carpet if she wished. In the end she went and enjoyed herself.[18]

By late July, however, Maria's misery had returned as the heat of midsummer made her attic room under the metal roof of the Hopper house stiflingly hot. She was finding it difficult to concentrate, and her progress on the history of religions was discouragingly slow. "The result of all this [reading]," she told her brother Convers, "is that I become more and more *rational*, and see more and more clearly that the Christian religion is only the pure blossom of a previous slowly progressive moral growth."[19] In September, David, having been temporarily laid off, joined her at the Hoppers' to await a summons from his brother to return to work. Maria was pleased to find him in good health and spirits. She wrote Louisa that they had had "quite a second honey-moon, a little flowery oasis in the desert of our domestic life." Meanwhile, news had reached her that her friend Margaret Fuller, then living in Rome, had secretly married an Italian nobleman, Giovanni Angelo, Marchese d'Ossoli, and had borne his child in September 1848. In fact the union hadn't been legalized until the summer of 1849, but Maria repudiated the malicious gossip surrounding the affair, declaring that she "approved of Margaret's taste in having a private marriage all to herself, and thus keeping a little of the *romance* of the tender sentiment." Unfortunately, this friend's life would be tragically cut short in the spring of 1850, when the ship bringing the three Ossolis to America was wrecked on a sandbar off Fire Island.[20]

In October the respected Swedish author Frederika Bremer visited New York. Bremer had read and enjoyed Maria Child's *Letters from New York* and was anxious to meet her. Maria, who disliked lionizing—she reported having declined several invitations to be introduced to Charles Dickens, when he came to New York in 1843—had no intention of calling on Miss Bremer. But one day a messenger arrived with a note proposing that, since Mrs. Child disliked making calls, Miss Bremer would come and see her instead. Within two hours of receiving the note Maria, dressed, according to her own description "like a woman of 'property and standing,' " had proceeded to the fashionable Astor House hotel on lower Broadway to call on the Swedish author. Maria later described Miss Bremer as "insignificant and rather unprepossessing" in appearance, but she was pleased by her simple and unaffected manner.[21]

A new friend who delighted Maria far more than Frederika Bremer was a pretty young Spanish woman known simply as Dolores. This penniless orphan had been reputedly rescued from a brutal husband by her uncle and brought to the United States. Maria, having met Dolores and learning of her plight, took her under her wing. The two were soon inseparable. Dolores showered Maria with fond words and compliments, calling her her "dear little sistita." Maria fussed over Dolores as if she were her own child. She persuaded rich friends to buy the clothes Dolores had stitched and searched the city for pupils to whom she could teach Spanish. Gently bred but destitute, Dolores struck a responsive chord in Maria's heart. Here was a cultivated woman overwhelmed by adverse circumstances, who, like herself, had suffered dreadfully. Moreover, as Maria informed Ellis, her little Spaniard was an "affectionate, pleasant little creature, and loves me to my heart's content; and you know I am avaricious of love."[22]

As David stayed on in New York the small attic room came to seem impossibly crowded. Maria dreaded the thought of another hot summer in the city and began to think of returning to Boston. She wanted to be near her old father and the Lorings. Meanwhile, the expected letter from David's brother calling him back to railroad work in Tennessee failed to arrive. David, who hated city life, talked of taking off for California with Josiah Hopper, a brother of John's. But that plan, like so many before it, fell through. Time passed, and still no word came from John Child. By March Maria was convinced that her brother-in-law never had intended to rehire David. While this act of betrayal infuriated her, it also confirmed her resolve to leave New York. She wrote Ellis Loring on March 24, asking if he might be willing to buy a "humble little place with three or four acres of land" which she and David could rent. She wanted the title to the property to be in Ellis' name, "to keep it safe from the fangs of Massachusetts laws, so much less liberal to women, than those of N.York." Ellis was happy to comply with Maria's request and immediately began looking for a suitable property. By mid-June 1850 the Childs and Dolores—Maria refused to be separated from her new friend—had left the city and were on their way to Boston.[23]

Years later Maria remembered how much she had hated to leave New York. Lonesome and forlorn as she had felt upon first arriving there in 1841, "after awhile, the noises of the great Babel ceased to confuse me, and the constantly recurring novelties and excitements became exceedingly agreeable to me. When forced to leave, because Mr. Child was without home or occupation, I found it a very bitter pill to go to the country again, and renew the old tiresome routine of cooking and sweeping."[24]

15

The Desert of Domesticity

*It is better never to be a butterfly, than to be obliged
to return from every short excursion among the
flowers, to fold up your wings, and crawl into your
grub case again.*
—Lydia Maria Child to Louisa Loring,
1852

B y mid-June 1850 the Childs, accompanied by Dolores, were
back in Massachusetts where they boarded with friends and
relatives until Ellis found them a place to live. Maria and
David joined the Lorings in July on a tour of resorts in New York
and Vermont. The travelers stopped briefly at Saratoga, then a
favorite wateringhole for rich New Yorkers. Maria found it "a curious place to examine human fossils" and wrote an amusing account of the "consumptive young beaux panting in tight stays, and
wrinkled old beaux with wigs, torturing their poor uncertain feet
with tight boots." A Mrs. Wetmore of New York had arrived at their
hotel with eighteen trunks, and Maria dubbed her and another
guest, a Mrs. Jones, the "Romeo and Capulet of Saratoga." One
day in the resort was enough. Both Lorings and Childs were glad
to say goodbye to the "human butterflies, their souls all boxed up
and directed 'this side up with care.' " By contrast Maria found the
unspoiled beauty of Lake George enchanting, "the very place to
dream of nymphs and fauns." After a few days there they returned
to Boston via Brattleboro, Vermont.[1]

In August the Childs and Dolores moved into what they hoped
would be a permanent home in West Newton. The house and its
few acres, which Ellis had found for them, was only ten miles from
Boston. Within a few days of their arrival a procession of friends
and relations came out to call. From the first, Maria expressed

guarded satisfaction with the place, complaining to Ellis on August 28 that the kitchen fireplace smoked, the house was too far from the Lorings, and the neighbor's cows were eating all their grass. While she was "slowly bringing order out of great confusion," she admitted to nearly breaking down twice from over-exertion. Since all David's farm equipment as well as their furniture and other household goods had been sold at auction back in 1843, they had to start from scratch. David as usual was penniless but Maria had $400 saved from her own earnings. Friends also went out of their way to help. One gave them an airtight stove to heat the sitting room, another a carpet for the stairs. Dolores made curtains. "My nest is getting very nicely lined," Maria wrote Louisa in September.[2]

By spring, whatever satisfaction Maria had felt in at last having a home of her own had vanished. Her letters complained of being perpetually driven by "coarse and vulgar cares." In addition to her other household chores she was making her own butter and her own bread. David, meanwhile, was struggling to farm their few acres. They had been assured the soil was good but, like the farm in Northampton, it turned out to be "remarkably full of rocks, stones, and stumps." Her husband was working hard, Maria assured Ellis, and he was being very careful not to spend a cent without consulting her.[3]

The next few years were hard. While David labored in vain to earn a living off the rocky soil, Maria kept house. Financial worries and bouts of ill-health took their toll. She told Ellis that she had "never before suffered so much from discouragement and pecuniary anxiety. I am no worse off in money matters than I was in Northampton; but I am older, and I have the remembrance of Northampton to terrify me perpetually."[4]

The West Newton house, which at first seemed so roomy and comfortable, turned out to be full of hidden flaws. The sink drain was constructed of rotten boards, the windows didn't latch properly. When the Lorings kindly installed a proper cooking stove to replace the smoking fireplace, Maria, ever the "frugal housewife," couldn't help chiding them for their extravagance by suggesting they'd have done better to get a secondhand one "instead of such a superior article." Much as she appreciated the Lorings' unfailing generosity, she could not stifle "the native inborn feeling that I ought to support myself, and have no right to live on the earnings of another." For the present, however, she had no choice but to submit to being a pensioner on their bounty.[5]

The new stove did save her a lot of time. Still, she complained to Louisa that "the treadmill *never* stops." If she and David had been able to earn a living from farming their few acres, she would willingly have borne the hard labor, but as usual Maria found herself "pumping into a sieve." The money went out faster than it came in. To add to their troubles both she and David suffered serious bouts of sickness. In their desperation the Childs were considering joining the North American Phalanx, a socialist community in Red Bank, New Jersey.[6]

Founded by the Transcendentalist Albert Brisbane in 1843, the North American Phalanx was the longest-lived of more than forty such utopian experiments established during these years. Its appeal for the Childs is not hard to understand. Here for a small salary David would be guaranteed employment on the farm or in the community school, and Maria, in return for a modest board fee, would be free to write. As Maria told Ellis, she despaired of being able to lead any sort of satisfactory existence as long as she was "involved in David's destiny."[7]

In the end the Childs never did join the Phalanx or any other community. By the fall of 1852 Maria was finding some time to write and had begun work on a biography of Isaac Hopper, who had died the previous spring. The book, published in 1853, sold well but it brought her no royalties. Maria, who felt deeply indebted to the family she had lived with for so many years, had promised Hopper before his death that the proceeds would go to his children.[8]

Maria's only other major literary undertaking from these years, *The Progress of Religious Ideas,* would not be a money-maker either. She was now sorry she had heeded advice to stop wasting her energies on magazine stories, and her publisher, C.S. Francis, was complaining that sales of her books were at a near standstill now that she was no longer in the public eye.[9]

In some respects the situation in which Maria found herself in the 1850s recalled that of the young Mrs. Child of the 1820s. As a new bride, Maria's love for David had persuaded her to forgo her independence and lofty ambitions and assume the role of devoted wife. While she remained the couple's chief breadwinner, her writings conformed more closely to the womanly standards of the day. Similarly, in 1850 Maria, having renounced all efforts to control her own destiny, once again linked her fortunes to those of her husband. This time, however, the charm of young love was not there to smooth the transition from a life of independence to one of domestic drudgery. Her restless spirit flailed helplessly in its confinement. Only a stern adherence to duty and a recognition that her need for love had overridden all other aspirations kept despair at bay.

Meanwhile, Maria continued to fend off attempts to make her more sociable. When friends, aware of her passion for music, tried to tempt her with invitations to concerts she turned them down, claiming that, far from cheering her up, such distractions only made her more miserable. "It is better never to be a butterfly, than to be obliged to return from every short excursion among the flowers, to fold up your wings, and crawl into your grub case again."[10]

To add to her despondency she learned in September 1853 that Dolores, unable to find work, had decided to return to New York. "I never felt the bitterness of poverty as I do in being compelled to part with her," Maria confessed to Ellis. "She *so* needs a sympathizing friend and protector, and I *so* need a loving daughter!" After Dolores left, Maria was wild with loneliness. "I feel as if I would rush *any*where for some exciting change," she wrote Louisa on September 12, adding that it was "a *new* experience for me to be seized with the universal mania of running away from one's self." In her despair, she slipped out of the house, writing David, who was absent, that she'd gone to Boston to spend a few days with an actress friend, Jeannie Barrett.[11]

In the end it was Maria's father, now an elderly man in his eighties, who rescued the Childs from the West Newton house. As he aged, Convers Francis had grown more dependent on his youngest daughter. During her last years in New York she had made several visits to Wayland, where her father had finally settled permanently in a small house not far from his eldest son, James. Maria had found these visits painful. While her heart told her that her father was a "kind, good old man," who took considerable comfort in her presence, she still found it "a stinging blister" to be with him, resenting as ever his endless faultfinding and lack of sympathy for her poetic nature. But when she went out to Wayland for a few weeks in March 1853 to nurse her father through a severe illness, the old bitterness had eased. He seemed determined to have her live with him. "My old father creates a bond between me and the place," she wrote Louisa. To entice her he had even planted some fruit trees. "Tis a humble little place, but it seems like home."[12]

In December, following Dolores' departure, Maria moved to Wayland to spend the winter with her father. Situated twenty miles west of Boston, this small agricultural community was even more remote than West Newton. Here no railroad disturbed the tranquility of the grass-bordered, elm-shaded streets. The chief excitement of the day was the arrival of the old stagecoach from Boston, which lumbered sedately into town each morning bringing the mail and the newspapers. Convers Francis' cottage was on the westerly side of the village a mile and a half from town. While the house itself was a modest low-roofed structure towered over by a large elm and a willow tree, the view from its windows was a grand one. It overlooked the broad sweep of meadows flanking the Sudbury River to the distant hills beyond. When David joined Maria there in early January the couple occupied a tiny room which was little more than a shed attached to the main house. Here they slept, ate, and worked and, though their quarters were cramped, they welcomed the privacy. Experience had shown that the less time David and his father-in-law spent together the better.

The next year was peaceful but productive. Convers Francis was now so dependent on his daughter that he hated her to be away even for a night. The time Maria didn't spend caring for her father and doing housework she was at her desk writing. If she was not precisely happy, she was at least contented. Her father was in good health. Their expenses were few, and David was actually bringing in a little money as a translator. Except for a rare trip to Boston, one day was exactly like another. Maria seldom ventured beyond the garden gate, even to call on her brother. Although James lived on a tidy farm less than half a mile down the road, he and his youngest sister apparently had little in common. Known in the neighborhood as an "old-line" Democrat, James Francis let it be known that Maria's attitude on the slavery question had caused him much grief.[13]

Even Wayland neighbors, anxious to catch a glimpse of Mr. Francis' illustrious daughter, rarely had their curiosity satisfied. The chief contact the townspeople had with Maria during her early years in Wayland was in the stagecoach. Once every few months the great yellow omnibus would stop in front of the Francis house and a small, cheerful looking woman in her fifties, attired in an old-fashioned bonnet and a simple dress and shawl, would clamber aboard for the two-hour journey to Boston.

Given Maria's reputation for reclusiveness, the eagerness with which she engaged her fellow passengers in conversation must have come as quite a surprise to them. Invariably they were struck by the contrast between her plain attire and matronly appearance and the "vivacity and elegance of her language and her ways." On one occasion a young woman recently returned from Europe boarded the stage. She seated herself next to Maria and soon noticed her neighbor stroking her dress while observing in a mockingly appreciative way, "true Parisienne I suppose?" Maria's favorite topic of conversation during these journeys was the current state of American society. She particularly enjoyed decrying the habits and mores of the new urban, moneyed aristocracy. This was a subject she had thought a lot about during her years in New York, and it was the idle existence led by the women of this growing class of Americans which particularly disturbed her. "The trouble with these fashionable, rich, aristocratic women," she informed the man seated next to her on one of her trips to town, "is they have nothing to do." She then proceeded to describe several of her acquaintances whose husbands had amassed tidy fortunes but were unwilling to have their wives work "or do anything." She assured her fellow passenger that these women, far from being content with their newly acquired leisure, were restless and unhappy.[14]

Maria usually came home by train via Concord where she transferred to a stagecoach for Wayland. One spring day in March 1853 an acquaintance named Richard Fuller seated himself next to her in the train and immediately began lecturing her on the importance of attending revival meetings. Mr. Fuller must not have known Maria Child very well, for, as she later reported to Louisa,

> You would have been amused, if not edified, if you had heard the anathemas I poured out upon Calvinism. He said it was particularly impressive and interesting to attend "the business-men's meetings, to hear men who had been so devoted to lucre singing and praying so devoutly." I told him I was afraid most of them were but taking out a new lease to cheat with impunity.
>
> He, very condescendingly, informed me that God did not make *me* to have *opinions*; that God made *me* for the *affections*; that he intended *me* to write about children and flowers; implying all the while, that it was for *him*, and such as *he*, to decide upon matters high [and] profound.

When the train arrived in Concord and she climbed into the stage, Maria was greatly relieved that Fuller had not followed her. Her happiness was short-lived, however, for she found herself seated next to another religious enthusiast, also fresh from the Boston revival meetings. The woman immediately pounced on her. "Her voice was as hard and sharp as her theology, and she had with her a very pert disagreeable little girl, whom she set to reciting verses about the "Lord Jesus," in a manner as mechanical as the Buddhist praying-machines. Alas for religion! What absurdities are everywhere enacted in its holy name!"[15]

Maria would have enjoyed observing the expressions on the faces of these pious folk had they been told their traveling companion was currently writing a history of world religions. The truth was that she herself was having her doubts about the value of this vast work. During the years in West Newton she had laid the book aside, but now she took it up again and was struck once more by the tediousness and difficulty of the endeavor. She wrote Ellis that there were many times when she had "almost broken down in utter despair" as she struggled to decipher the meaning of each religion and present it impartially. Furthermore, she was fully prepared for a torrent of criticism when the three volumes were finally published.[16]

But for all her complaints about its difficulties, Maria ultimately derived a deep satisfaction from the undertaking. The effort of studying and recounting humanity's spiritual history was for her a penitential pilgrimage; it enabled her to make her own personal peace with God by confirming what she had long suspected, that no single sect or church contained the whole of religious "truth." Rather, each successive faith down through the ages had served a particular function suited to the temperament and the social condition of the people for whom it was intended. The Jewish religion, for example, marked a great advance in man's spiritual progression by its worship of a single "Invisible Being," unrepresented by image or symbol.[17] Judaism in due course was followed by Christianity which, in its emphasis on the moral sentiment, its recognition of such humanitarian principles as antislavery and human equality, showed the world had progressed to a higher spiritual level.

The three volumes were finally completed in late 1854 and published under the title *The Progress of Religious Ideas through Successive Ages*. At first Maria was pleased with the critical response, much of which was gratifyingly positive. The clergy, however, had little good to say, calling it a "dangerous book" whose author had committed the ultimate sin of failing to cite her authorities. Maria later claimed that this clerical criticism had "injured her a good deal as a writer." The book never did have a wide readership and in the end barely paid for the printing costs. Thomas Wentworth Higginson perhaps provided the best explanation for the poor sales. He claimed that its dispassionate message went counter to the prevailing religious

views of the day, which demanded the taking of sides, and he
ventured further that it "was too learned for a popular book and
too popular for a learned one."[18]

Maria was doubtless anxious to learn what her brother Convers
thought of this religious history. It was he, after all, who had im-
planted in her young mind a knowledge of the historic roots of
Christianity and the other great world religions. Her evenhanded
approach owed much to his broad-mindedness. But, while Convers'
intellectual tastes were eclectic, he remained theologically conservative. Even as his personal religious sympathies reflected a touch
of Emersonian radicalism, he continued publicly to proclaim his
"faith in the miraculous message of Jesus."[19]

Shortly before the book was published Maria wrote Convers that
her chief purpose in writing it had been to clear away "the super-
stitious rubbish from the sublime morality of Christ!" No record
of Convers' response to *The Progress of Religious Ideas* has survived.
But a letter of Maria's answering one of his makes it clear that,
while he may have praised her fair-mindedness in giving all religions equal treatment, he was deeply disturbed by her insistence
that theology was not religion. Maria replied by declaring how much
she detested the word "theology." The term had been "so desecrated by the uses made of it, that I would prefer to call the embodiment of the religious sentiment in the *mind* a divine science."[20]

While Convers and a few close friends took issue with Maria's
rejection of theology, the more common criticism, as Higginson
had observed, was directed at her impartiality, particularly her
treatment of Christianity as simply one among many important
world religions. There was one reviewer, however, who rightly
questioned whether it was possible for someone brought up a Christian to be truly dispassionate.[21] And, as the following passage shows,
Maria left little doubt in her reader's mind as to her own religious
preferences: "The most powerful *external* testimony to the superior
excellence of Christ's teaching, seems to me to be found in the fact
that good men, and great men, and reflecting men, were irresistibly
attracted toward it, notwithstanding the corruptions that early gathered round it. . . . It contained within itself living and universal
principles, which no perversity of man could stifle."[22]

A constantly recurring theme in Maria's *Progress of Religious Ideas*
is her belief in the active agency of spirits in the religious history
of mankind. "Through all time," she wrote in the conclusion to the
second volume, "voices of invisible ones have been whispering to
listening souls that we are of celestial origin, and shall return to a

celestial home." Among such clairvoyants who served as transmitters of messages from the spiritual to the material world could be counted the ancient biblical prophets and the men and women who acted as Greek oracles.[23]

Spiritualism had long been a significant religious force in the United States, particularly for people like Maria, who, belonging to no church or sect, found systematic confirmation of their religious yearnings in such doctrines as Swedenborg's correspondences. But not until the Fox sisters of Hydesville, New York, began demonstrating their "toe rappings" before enthralled audiences in 1849 did the feverish interest in spirit communication sweep over the country.

Katherine and Margaret Fox claimed that spirits had established contact with them through mysterious rappings in their family's old farmhouse. Soon word of these rappings spread through the neighborhood and people came flocking to see this marvel for themselves. Meanwhile an older married sister, sensing financial possibilities, organized a series of public meetings where Katherine and Margaret could rap before audiences who paid for the privilege. The sisters claimed their rappings would reveal an important message to the world, and the popularity of these seances spread quickly. On June 4, 1850, Katherine and Margaret appeared for the first time in New York City, where their meetings were thronged. Editor Horace Greeley, who had hailed their arrival in the columns of the *Tribune* and even took them into his home, wrote that "it would be the basest cowardice not to say that we are convinced beyond a doubt of their perfect integrity and good faith."[24] Other newspaper editors were less convinced of the authenticity of the sisters' claims. But that did not prevent a host of other mediums from springing up in the city as hundreds of men and women, out of genuine interest or simple curiosity, flocked to seances to witness table rappings, mysterious appearances, and feats of clairvoyance.

No mention of the Fox sisters survives in Maria's correspondence, but numerous references to the spiritualist craze and her occasional attendance at seances indicate that she was interested in the phenomenon even if she distrusted many of its popular manifestations. In 1842, when Maria was editor of the *Standard*, the newspapers had been full of reports concerning the sensational murder in Weehawken of a young perfumery worker named Mary Rogers. Maria's attention was drawn to the story by the testimony of a blind girl who, while in a hypnotic trance, had witnessed a re-enactment of the crime and reported the identity of the murderer to the police. While such questionable testimony was dismissed at the time of the trial, it was later discovered to have been accurate, confirming for Maria, at least, her belief in the "soundness of animal magnetism."[25]

Maria had long welcomed efforts to break down the barriers between this world and the next, barriers which hid from the living the true path to righteousness. She would have agreed with the spiritualist Andrew Jackson Davis, who wrote in 1854 that "by spiritual intercourse we learn that all men shall ultimately be joined in one Brotherhood, their interests shall be pure and reciprocal; their customs shall be just and harmonious; they shall be as one Body, animated by Universal Love and governed by pure Wisdom." Maria did, however, seriously question some of the sensational methods employed by the Fox sisters and other mediums to tempt a gullible public into attending their seances. In the spring of 1855 she attended a seance in Medford where she received messages from both Swedenborg and William Ellery Channing. "I am altogether in a blue maze about it," she later wrote Ellis. "*Some* things said to me carry with them strong internal evidence of not originating in any mind contained in the visible bodies there in the room. But some *other* things excite distrust in my mind." While she believed that tables moved during these seances—she had seen this with her own eyes—and believed also that things were communicated which could not have been known by the people present, she dismissed the messages themselves as "the merest mess of old rags, saw-dust and clamshells."[26] In 1860 she summed up her assessment of the spiritualist craze by conceding that "its phenomena are not all impositions, or self-delusions; but they do not satisfy the wants of *my* soul. *I* do not need to be convinced that the spiritual world is all around us, and that our vision of it is obstructed only by the bodily senses. I believe most fully in a future, conscious state of individual existence. It seems to me that only a malignant Being could have placed us here, so walled in mysteries, with such an intense desire to penetrate beyond them . . . if there were no *reality* in our aspirations and hopes."[27]

16

Peace Principles
Shivering in the Wind

*I have such a fire burning in my soul, that it seems
to me I could pour forth a stream of lava, that
would bury all the* respectable *servilities, and all
the* mob *servilities, as deep as Pompeii.*
—Lydia Maria Child to Sarah Shaw,
1856

Maria Child had retreated to the sidelines of the antislavery
movement in 1843, and she remained there until the
mounting sectional crisis of the 1850s rekindled her interest. In the intervening years her efforts on behalf of the slave
had remained private and personal. While living with the Carpenters in New Rochelle she had opened the farmhouse door to more
than one frightened fugitive, providing them with warm food and
clothing before sending them on their way north to Canada and
freedom. When John Gorham Palfrey, a Unitarian minister in Boston and the son of a slaveholder in Louisiana, called on Maria in
New York in the early summer of 1844, she agreed to find places
for five of his family's slaves whom he was bringing north to freedom. Meanwhile, in her own writings she continued quietly to
preach the antislavery message.

During the years Maria had absented herself from the public
crusade, the majority of reformers—excepting the Garrisonians—
had turned to political action as the most effective way to rid the
nation of slavery. There were several reasons for this shift. First,
moral suasion had failed to convert more than a small percentage
of Americans to antislavery principles. Second, the locus of antislavery discussion had moved from the lecture room to the halls
of Congress, where by the mid-1840s a debate was raging over the
extension of slavery into newly acquired territories in the West.

Meanwhile, throughout the North the conviction was growing that a "slave power conspiracy" was at work, seeking to expand the "peculiar institution," and this had done more than all the persuasive arts of the Garrisonians to convert people to the cause.

In August 1846, three months after the start of a war with Mexico over the annexation of Texas, an obscure congressman from Pennsylvania, David Wilmot, introduced an amendment to an appropriations bill excluding slavery from all territories acquired from the Mexican Republic. While every Northern legislature but one endorsed Wilmot's Proviso, the South maintained its right to carry slaves into all newly organized territories. In the end the proviso itself was killed, but this apparent victory for the South masked the ominous division the free-soil issue had created in Congress. For the next three years the sound of increasingly bitter debates echoed in the chambers of the Senate and House, reaching a crescendo in 1849 when California asked to be admitted to the Union as a free state. Whichever way Congress voted on California, the balance of fifteen slave and fifteen free states would be upset, and Senator John C. Calhoun, the leader of the Southern rights movement, threatened to secede if slavery were banned.

In the end an uneasy peace between Northern and Southern lawmakers was restored by the passage of the Compromise of 1850, which patched together agreements on several issues in an effort to give something to both sides. California was admitted as a free state. The old Missouri Compromise line of 36° 30′, which had banned slavery in Louisiana Purchase Territory north of that line and permitted slavery south of it, was extended through the new land conquered from Mexico all the way to the California border. Below 36° 30′ in this region the concept of popular sovereignty was applied: the settlers themselves in these territories would decide whether to admit or deny slavery. Slavery was retained but the slave trade abolished in the District of Columbia. Texas relinquished large territorial claims beyond her present boundaries in exchange for federal assumption of most of her debts.

The most important concession to the South in the Compromise of 1850, as a sop for the admission of free California, was the stringent new Fugitive Slave Law. This measure, which made it easier for slaveholders to recapture their slaves in the North and more profitable for Northerners to help them do so, created an immediate and unexpected uproar in the North and added greatly to the list of converts to the antislavery cause.

In Boston there was widespread resistance to the new Fugitive

Slave Law, a development Maria would have applauded as she went about her chores. Following a public protest meeting in Boston in October 1850, a vigilance committee was formed, charged with organizing an effective opposition to enforcement of the new law. For a time the committee's efforts were successful. When agents of a Georgia slaveholder appeared in the city in December with warrants for the arrest of two fugitives, William and Ellen Craft, angry mobs managed to scare the kidnappers out of town. Two months later, a slave named Shadrach was seized by federal agents in Boston but later rescued by a group of black militants who sent him north on his way to freedom.

It happened, however, that one of those implicated in Shadrach's arrest was Marianne Silsbee's husband, Nathaniel. No sooner had Maria received word of Judge Silsbee's complicity in the case than she was seized by a violent and indignant rage and began pacing about the house proclaiming in angry tones that she never wished to lay eyes on the man again. When David gently reminded her of Marianne's unfailing kindness and warned of the deep hurt such hostile behavior would inflict on her friend, Maria burst into tears, crying out that of course he was right but "so help me God, I will bury every friendship on earth, rather than shake hands with a man that has assisted in restoring a fugitive slave."[1]

The intensity of this outburst exposed more than simple frustration with one Northerner's intransigence on the fugitive slave issue. It also showed how restless Maria had become in her domestic bondage and how ready she was, after ten years of distancing herself from the abolitionist movement, to reembrace it. While the mounting sectional crisis was an important factor in sparking this heightened interest, David's absorption in politics may have been another. He could think and talk of little else. In 1848 he had been one of the early supporters of the Free Soil Party, which had gathered into its fold a motley collection of antislavery sympathizers, including disaffected Whigs like himself. In such an atmosphere, Maria's own preoccupations quite naturally began shifting from the poetic to the political. Nor is it any wonder that, with little time to write and few satisfactory outlets for her abundant energies, the plight of the slave once more absorbed her. "What are we here for?" she poignantly inquired in a letter to Convers, "I wish I knew. 'For to be sold,' said the little slave girl. And some how or other, we *all* get fetters on us." Maria's own domestic slavery was once again reminding her of another more cruel bondage.[2]

As Maria Child chafed in her domestic isolation, another woman,

Harriet Beecher Stowe, tied down by a large family of children in Brunswick, Maine, had released her mounting indignation against the evil of slavery by writing a novel. Published in the spring of 1852, *Uncle Tom's Cabin* describes the trials and sufferings of a dignified old slave named Uncle Tom and includes a varied cast of characters, from the sadistic overseer, Simon Legree, to the angelic little Eva. In one stroke, Stowe—who credited God with writing the novel—had accomplished what Maria Child had been longing to do for years. She had produced a book of sufficient moral force and popularity to awaken great numbers of people to the evil of slavery. "The story is told with great pathos and power," Maria announced after finishing it in March 1852. In September, when word reached her that *Uncle Tom's Cabin* had sold over 100,000 copies, she expressed her delight with its success, calling it "a truly great work," one, she noted proudly, that had "done much to command respect for faculties of woman."[3]

The wide influence of Stowe's novel, far greater in the North than in the South, nevertheless failed to prevent further foot-dragging on the free-soil issue. Maria's own indignation was roused to new heights early in 1854. On January 30, Senator Stephen Douglas of Illinois, the best orator in the old Northwest (now the northern Midwest), stood up in Congress to introduce a bill organizing the Great Plains as the Territories of Kansas and Nebraska. Central to the measure was the concept of "popular sovereignty," which permitted new territories to come into the Union with or without slavery as a majority of their inhabitants might decide.

This concept had already been applied to what would eventually become the Arizona and New Mexico Territories by the Compromise of 1850. What Senator Douglas now sought to do was apply the idea to Kansas and Nebraska, but these territories lay north of the 36° 30′ line—and the old Missouri Compromise of 1820 had pronounced all territories north of that line to be "forever free." In other words, a question Northerners had regarded as settled once and for all in freedom's favor was now being reopened.

The threat of slavery expanding—the new Kansas territory lay directly west of Missouri, a slave state, and slaveholding Missourians were already planning to take their property there—touched off a firestorm of indignation across the North. For several months bitter debate raged in Congress, prompting Senator Seward of New York to predict a violent outcome if the Kansas-Nebraska Act became law. "We will engage in competition for the virgin soil of

Kansas, and God give the victory to the side that is stronger in numbers as it is in right."⁴ Seward's warning proved correct, for no sooner had the bill passed than a storm of protest erupted throughout the North as people gathered to denounce the "Nebraska outrage" and cooperated to finance free-soil settlements in Kansas. The first hint of trouble in the latter territory came in November 1854, when a large number of Missourians crossed the border into Kansas and helped elect a proslavery delegate to Congress. By the spring of 1856 Kansas had two governments—one proslavery, one antislavery, both illegal.

Then on May 19, 1856, Charles Sumner, the Whig senator from Massachusetts and a recognized antislavery spokesman, rose up on the floor of the Senate and delivered a speech that lasted the better part of two days. After denouncing President Pierce's policy in Kansas, which favored control by proslavery forces, and demanding that the territory be admitted as a free state, Sumner lashed out with harsh invective at Senators Mason of Virginia and Butler of South Carolina. Two days later, while sitting alone at his desk in the Senate Chamber, Sumner was caned to insensibility by a young South Carolina congressman, Preston Brooks, the nephew of Senator Butler.

The news of Sumner's beating produced a loud outcry among Northern abolitionists, but none reacted with greater dismay than Maria Child, for whom the junior senator from Massachusetts was a newfound hero. Early in 1853 she had written Sumner praising him for his comportment in the Senate chamber. He had returned her compliments by recalling the influence she had had on him as a young man. "Among all antislavery pens I found most sympathy with yours," Sumner declared in his reply. He then hinted that while he had always maintained cordial relations with Senators Butler and Mason, whose desks adjoined his in the Senate, he nevertheless would not hesitate to direct "harsh and personal criticism" against them if he felt it were called for.⁵

Maria's first impulse upon hearing of the attack on Charles Sumner had been to rush down to Washington and offer to nurse him. "If I had not been chained to my aged father," she told Anna Loring, "I verily believe I *should* have done it." As it was she didn't sleep for two nights: "if my eye-lids began to droop, I started up, shuddering with some vision of murdered men in Kansas, or of Charles Sumner, bleeding and dying. If I had only been supplied with any safety-valve of *action*, to let off the accumulating steam!"

She admitted to Anna that before the beating she had fallen into such a torpid state that she hadn't thought she could get excited about anything ever again.[6]

Maria released some of her pent-up energy by writing Sumner a lengthy letter telling him of her frustrated desire to come and comfort him, and praising him for what she termed his "last and greatest speech": "My heart has bled so freely for suffering Kansas! I have felt such burning indignation at the ever-increasing insults and outrages of the South, and the cold, selfish indifference of the North! I have so longed to seize a signal-torch, and rush all over the mountains, and through all the vallies [sic], summoning the friends of freedom to the rescue! . . . At times, my old heart swells almost to bursting, in view of all these things; for it is the heart of a man imprisoned within a woman's destiny." Maria then spoke of her disgust with those who denounced the offensiveness of Sumner's language and called his vitriolic attacks on individual Southerners unjustifiable. "Few persons have stronger aversion to harsh epithets and personal vituperation than I have;" she wrote, "but I confess I could find nothing in your Kansas Speech which offended either my taste or my judgment."[7]

The whole tone of Maria's letter to Sumner shows how far she had come in condoning violence, whether in word or deed, as an acceptable weapon to end slavery. But she continued to hope that ultimately moral suasion and not force would bring an end to slavery; she had written Sumner as late as 1855 that if only the North would stand firmly on the principles of freedom the South would surely "quail before her moral dignity."[8]

By the spring of 1856, however, Sumner's beating in the Senate Chamber, following on the heels of violence in Kansas, had led Maria and many other declared pacifists to condone and even support the use of force to end slavery. In her letter of commiseration to the wounded Sumner she admitted that her peace principles had been "sorely tried" and that nothing suited her mood so well as "Jeanne d'Arc's floating banner and consecrated sword. . . . I can never call those men murderers, who forsake home and kindred, and all that renders life agreeable, and with noble self-sacrifice go forth to suffer and die in the cause of freedom. Yet there is a higher standard than theirs, to which the human soul will gradually rise, until there remains no trace of the old ideas of overcoming evil by brute force." Still, Maria went on to argue, if the present imperfect condition of the human race condoned the use of force, it was nonetheless imperative that the higher standard of nonresistance continue to be upheld. For "they who *aim* at the stars will at least *hit higher*, than if they aimed at a pine tree."[9]

Maria summed up her feelings on the subject a few days later when she wrote Lucy and Mary Osgood that she had "always dreaded civil war and prayed that it might be averted; but if there is no *other* alternative than the endurance of such insults and outrages, I am resigned to its approach. In fact I have become accustomed to the thought that it is inevitable."[10] For Maria, freedom for the slave was always a priority, and if moral suasion failed and righteous violence succeeded then the less virtuous method must be resorted to. In a better world where brute force was no longer needed peace principles would reign.

In the months following the attack on Sumner both Childs were caught up in the excitement generated by the free-soil issue. David was now supporting a new party, the Republican, whose platform focused on antislavery resolutions and whose members had nominated John Fremont, the explorer/politician, as their candidate for president in the upcoming election. "We talk of little else but Kansas and Fremont," Maria wrote Sarah Shaw on August 3.

But talking was not enough. While David was free to leave home whenever he wished, Maria remained tied down by the care of her father. The old gentleman was in good health that summer, and had they lived in Boston Maria could easily have left him for an hour or two of antislavery work. But Wayland's isolation made this impossible. "I *never* was one of those who knew how to serve the Lord by standing and waiting," she told Sarah, venting her mounting frustration with the only weapon at her disposal, her pen. The lack of sympathy for Sumner on the part of certain public figures in Massachusetts further angered her. "God forgive me that I wanted to take Boston by the throat, and stop the sluggish blood that feeds its servile life." She had such a fire burning in her soul that she longed to "mount the rostrum" herself and "pour forth a stream of lava, that would bury all the *respectable* servilities, and all the *mob* servilities, as deep as Pompeii. . . . What a shame that *women* can't vote."[11]

Maria's spirit was "boiling over." Like the fictional heroes of her early children's stories who were "always better satisfied to plough the ocean and catch sharks" than they were "to dig fields for potatoes," Maria longed for a wider sphere of action. She wrote Ellis in February 1856 that she was "in a towering rage" because David had to sign her will. She was not angry with her husband, who "respects the freedom of women upon principle, and mine in particular by reason of affection superadded. But I was indignant for womankind made chattels personal from the beginning of time, perpetually insulted by literature, law, and custom. . . ."[12] In 1856 the only available release from the womanly bonds confining Maria to Wayland was through her pen. During that summer, while David was away canvassing for free soil and the new Republican party she spent the few free hours she had each day composing a long short story entitled "The Kansas Emigrants."

The heroes and heroines of this tale are law-abiding, peace-loving settlers from New England who suffer persecution at the hands of "fierce-looking" border ruffians from Missouri. The latter, in their determination to legalize slavery in the territory, think nothing of raping women and murdering innocent children. The story culminates with a description of the "Sack of Lawrence," which greatly exaggerates the horrors perpetrated by the Missourians and portrays the free-state settlers as the unsuspecting victims of an unprovoked, armed attack.[13]

The modern critic might easily dismiss "The Kansas Immigrants" as a piece of fictional propaganda intended to alert the American public to the horrifying events in Kansas. But the story is nonetheless a powerful one. As one Child scholar has pointed out, it articulates more compellingly than any other fictional work "the case for renouncing pacifism and resorting to armed struggle against slavery."[14] Maria was determined that her story should "serve as a signal torch," uniting antislavery friends in the cause of freedom.

Writing "The Kansas Immigrants" enabled Maria to give vent to the very real anger she nursed over the free soil issue. At the same time it allowed her to sweep aside the tedium of her domestic existence and get back on the track of her real life by doing brave deeds in behalf of a noble cause. The story's heroine, Kate Bradford, is the fearless, quick-witted wife of a free-soil settler. In her enthusiasm to serve the cause of freedom, Kate is ready to risk flying bullets and the rude taunts of border ruffians. One night when Missourians break into the Bradford cabin and threaten to shoot Kate's husband, she throws herself across him, exclaiming, "If you murder him, it shall be through my heart's blood." Later in the story, when volunteers are needed to carry a critical store of gunpowder safely past scouting parties of Missourians, Kate steps forward, arguing that the border ruffians will never suspect a woman of such an errand. Kate's righteous anger is roused to its fiercest pitch, however, when she learns that a woman settler has been raped by the ruffians. This flagrant disrespect for the modesty of women convinces Kate she must learn how to shoot. During the "Sack of Lawrence," she takes on the job of rescuing the free soilers' belongings from their burning houses. When the Missouri mob tries to drive her away with "oaths and ribald threats," she intimidates them by putting a hand on her pistol, prompting one admiring ruffian to exclaim, "What a hell of a woman!"[15]

By October "The Kansas Emigrants" was finished and mailed off to Horace Greeley in New York. The editor of the *Tribune* was so impressed with the piece that he interrupted Charles Dickens' *Little Dorrit* to run Child's story in its place. The timing was perfect. "The Kansas Immigrants," occupying the most prominent space in the newspaper, was serialized during the closing days of the fiercely contested presidential campaign between John Fremont and James Buchanan. The story was thus guaranteed an enormous readership. If its precise impact is impossible to measure, still, as Carolyn Karcher has pointed out, "John Fremont came closer to winning the election than any preceding Free Soil candidate, Northerners rallied to the support of Kansas, the free state settlers held their ground, and abolitionists closed ranks as they abandoned pacifism for armed struggle."[16]

A few months after its serialization in the *Tribune*, "The Kansas Immigrants" appeared in its entirety in a new collection of Maria Child's stories and poems, *Autumnal Leaves*. Most of the fiction in this new book had been written in the late 1840s and published either in the *Columbian Lady's and Gentleman's Magazine* or *Sartain's Union Magazine of Literature and Art*. There is no mention of Negro slavery in any of them. By contrast, two of the more recent pieces, including "The Kansas Immigrants" and "Jan and Zaida," reflect Maria's renewed preoccupation with the antislavery issue. "Jan and Zaida," first published in *Liberty Bell* in 1855, tells the story of a Javanese slave who eventually buys his own freedom.

Garrison, who doubtless hoped that Maria Child's renewed interest in the antislavery cause would bring her back into the fold, gave a warm reception to *Autumnal Leaves* in the pages of the *Liberator*. He took pains to remind his readers that its author had long ago sacrificed a promising literary career for the antislavery cause. "It cost her friends, reputation, pecuniary support, and subjected her to hostile influences such as few have been called to encounter," he told his readers, adding that "much is due to her by the reading public by way of atonement."[17]

But neither praise nor sympathy would persuade Maria to devote herself exclusively to antislavery work. In the first place, she lived too far from Boston. And in the second, she had long ago lost patience with societies as instruments of reform and found many of the old abolitionists much too narrow and bigoted. For instance, when Maria Chapman dismissed Charles Sumner's antislavery efforts in the Senate as "ephemera" because of his failure to subscribe to the creed of the AASS, Maria was incensed. While she never questioned the nobility and truth of the Garrisonian message she was afraid that it didn't carry very far.[18] In a letter to Sarah Shaw she recalled that

> in the early days of the Anti-Slavery enterprise, it was a common thing for our speakers to say that *eventually* the work must be completed by *politicians*. How we should have *then* rejoiced over any man that would have stood up on the floor of Congress, with even *half* the courage of Giddings, Sumner and Wilson! But *we*, in the meantime, have been marching ahead; and the van of the long army has the folly to despise the rear! As if there could be a van *without* a rear! As if *all* the forces were not *needed*, to attack the enemy at *all* his weak points! . . . for my own part, I am willing to ride about here and there, "promiscuous like," as I see occasion.[19]

Meanwhile, David shared his wife's unfulfilled dreams of going west to fight for the free-soil cause. But advancing age and physical infirmities forced him to acknowledge his unfitness for the rigors and dangers of frontier living. He would have to content himself with "scouring the Commonwealth for Kansas" as a member of the New England Emigrant Aid Committee.[20] The purpose of the Committee was to encourage those opposed to the extension of slavery to settle the new territory. During October David traveled from one town to another in Berkshire County recruiting settlers and raising funds for supplies and guns needed by the free-soilers.

At home in Wayland, Maria started her own relief program. She and a group of local churchwomen began collecting clothes to send to the free-soil emigrants. The auxiliaries of the Congregational and Unitarian churches contributed $60 worth of clothing. Meanwhile, she and a neighbor spent eight days cutting and sewing sixty yards of cloth which had been donated to the cause by an abolitionist dry-goods merchant. Maria wrote David on October 27 that for the last eight days she had been staying up until eleven o'clock each night "stitching as fast as my fingers could go." As she sat bent over her sewing, her thoughts carried her to Kansas and the brave women for whom the clothes were intended. So aroused were her sympathies for these women that she imagined she could hear the sound of drums beating and "rifle-shots whizzing at dead of night."[21]

Maria's letters reveal a renewed ambivalence that fall, as election day neared, about the effectiveness of political action as an anti-slavery tactic. While she had come to accept its function in the crusade, she also saw its dangers and feared that the whole pre-election frenzy was a dangerous safety valve, "letting off the steam which is needed to propel the car of freedom in its onward track." While she longed for the whole North "to rise and rise *now*," she shared the fears of many abolitionists that the new Republican party was only halfhearted in its commitment to the abolishment of slavery and the granting of equality to the blacks. By September her initial enthusiasm for Fremont as the party's choice for president began to wane. She wrote Sarah Shaw that she did not like the man's face and held him responsible for stirring up "that most unjust war with Mexico." Still, she did hope the "Pathfinder" would win. He was, after all, the only candidate opposed to the extension of slavery.[22]

By the time election day arrived in early November, the clothes for the Kansas immigrants had been shipped off and Maria's attention once again turned to her father, whose health had taken a sudden turn for the worse. Greatly enfeebled by an attack of palsy, he yet refused to sit still and had to be watched continually. David, meanwhile, was still away on Kansas business and, as Maria wrote Sarah Shaw, "the absence of cheering influences, either public or private," was weighing her down. Early in November David returned briefly to vote and helped carry his father-in-law to the polls. The old man had enjoyed boasting that he had cast his first ballot for George Washington and wanted to cast his last for John Fremont.[23]

In the days immediately following the election Convers Francis' health improved somewhat, leading both Childs to think he might live through the winter. So David returned to the Berkshires to resume his work for the Kansas Committee, having taken care to leave Maria enough firewood to last until his return. Her father's spell of good health did not last long, however. By November 23 he was so feeble that Maria was afraid he might not last the night. Four days later, on November 27, Thanksgiving Day, he was dead, and Maria was filled with a sad peacefulness. She was glad for her father's sake that he need no longer suffer. Yet, after all these months of caring for him, she would miss him sorely. "I shall be more free to come and go, as I will," she told Ellis, "but there will be no one looking out at the window for the stage to stop; no moaning voice saying 'Why *don't* my *darter* come? I'm afraid she is going to stay all night.'" Above all there would be no father to welcome her when she finally did come in the door.[24]

The sense of sad relief soon gave way to depression. David remained away for most of December and Maria found it hard to settle down to work in the silent, empty house. Early in the month she went to Boston for a change of scene, and the sight of old friends eased the dreariness somewhat. But when, after four days, she returned to the house and found everything dark and quiet, with no accustomed fire burning in the grate and no familiar greeting "You're welcome back, Maria," she almost cried herself blind.[25]

In mid-December came a season of bitter cold when Maria moved a cot into the small parlor which contained the only stove in the house. She wrote David that she was glad she had done so, as one morning she woke up to find so much ice in the glass of water by her bedside that she couldn't even break it with her hand. When she went to light the stove the chimney caught fire, but fortunately not enough to cause any damage. Later in the month she went to Boston to attend the antislavery fair and enjoyed a long visit with her wounded hero, Charles Sumner. "He seemed to me absolutely *holy*," she wrote her old abolitionist colleague John Greenleaf Whittier, "so gentle is he in his manner of speaking of Brooks, and of others, who have injured and insulted him." The fact that Sumner might have done some insulting of his own never seems to have crossed her mind. After returning to Wayland she wrote the senator asking for a lock of his hair, assuring him that her request was no "childish whim," that he could "form no adequate idea of the affectionate reverence with which I regard everything connected with you."[26]

With the coming of spring and warmer weather Maria went to work cleaning up her father's house, a job which she claimed had not been done properly during his sixteen years there. In letters to friends she spoke of selling the place, preferring to live nearer Boston. "Oh, what *would* I not do, if I could only be within walking distance of even one or two, who loved me, and sympathized with some of my views and tastes!" she wrote Sarah Shaw in early 1857. But Maria decided, against her own best interests perhaps, that financial considerations and David's happiness would have to come first. Meanwhile she went to work beating carpets, changing bedticks, washing feathers, and piecing fragments of old cloth together to make curtains, as if she knew the little cottage would continue to be home.[27]

With no elderly father to care for and David away most of the time on Kansas business, Maria was freer to leave home during the spring and summer of 1857. In March she stayed with the Lorings and went to see Fanny Kemble in a performance of "A Midsummer Night's Dream." In June she paid a visit to Medford and later went to Beverly to spend a week with the Lorings in their summer house. This interlude of relative freedom came to an end in September when David suffered such a severe attack of rheumatism she feared he might die. After more than two months spent nursing her husband, during which she packed him daily in wet sheets and blankets, declaring that cold water cured everything except original sin, she too came down with some undisclosed illness. The couple spent a lonely Thanksgiving, their first since Maria's father's death, but by this time their health had finally improved and Maria was able to make one trip to Boston for the antislavery bazaar before winter set in. "For the first time in my life, *I* am seized with a mania for change of air and scenery," she disingenuously informed Louisa that December.[28]

Maria spent the following spring painting and repapering several rooms in the Wayland house and was preparing to invite the Lorings to come for a visit when news came of Ellis' sudden death on May 24. The cause of his death is not known, but he was fifty-five, a year younger than Maria. The news almost killed her. For thirty years, he had been her dearest and staunchest friend. She had gone to him when she was troubled. Her small property was in his hands, and she had counted on him to see her through her old age. Now he was gone and she couldn't imagine how she would do without him. "My poor heart has been crushed by so many repeated disappointments and bereavements, that I think they will find it in my coffin thin and flat as an autumn leaf," she told Sarah Shaw.[29]

After Ellis' death there was no further talk about selling the Wayland house. Without this trusted friend around to advise them, the Childs probably decided it was prudent to remain where they were. There may also have been no market for houses in remote rural villages in 1858 when the nation was gripped by a severe, if brief, financial panic. In any case Maria and David accustomed themselves to the idea of the little cottage as home. That summer David went on a tour of New England and Canada with his sister Lydia to visit relatives and recoup his health. Maria stayed home.

Several friends came to visit while David was absent, including Marianne Silsbee and Sarah Shaw. Maria enjoyed their company, but lacking a servant she was forced to rise at four o'clock each day to cook and clean. She told David she didn't want either of them to suspect "how much greasing the wheels need in such a humble establishment." On June 20 she spent a day in Boston seeing old abolitionist friends and acquaintances. She ran into Whittier on the street. Although the two had corresponded, they had not seen one another for nearly twenty years. In the interim, Maria had grown to love the man through his poetry. He in turn greatly admired her. That day several hours of good talk cemented a friendship that would last the rest of their lives. "How it brought back those early anti-slavery days!" she wrote Whittier after she returned home. "Those noble self-forgetting days! When love to our fellowmen was the basis of all our ethics, and willing obedience to the God of love was the broad basis of our creed!"[30]

Despite her nostalgia for the early days of the antislavery movement, Maria continued to resist efforts to make her rejoin the abolitionist ranks. When Maria Chapman wrote asking her to attend an antislavery meeting, she declined. At such gatherings she felt "like a ghost on its own grave. So *many* have passed away since the days when I enjoyed the Anti-slavery meetings; and so few remain, in whom I take interest, or who seem to take interest in me."[31]

The winter of 1858–1859 was a difficult one. David suffered a renewed attack of rheumatism and Maria was almost continually depressed. She complained that the only intellectual effort she had made was to read Henry Thomas Buckle's popular *History of Civilization in England,* which took a scientific approach to the study of history. She was disturbed, however, by its rationalist and determinist slant. "His theories make me uncomfortable," she wrote Sarah Shaw, "the more so because I have, for the last ten years, been struggling hard against a tendency to believe in Fate. When I look back upon my own experience, when I set to thinking how I can extricate myself from a situation extremely uncongenial to me, and which I feel is killing my soul, I find that I have been, and am, so overborne and trampled upon by external circumstances, that I really feel as if I had no volition."[32] Only a sudden call to action would jolt Maria alive once again; it came in late October 1859 following John Brown's Raid on Harper's Ferry.

17

Strong as an Eagle

I must be true to the principles of freedom, *as
well as of* peace.
— *Lydia Maria Child to Sarah Shaw,
December 1859*

I n the quiet darkness of Sunday evening, October 16, 1859,
twenty-one armed men and their white-bearded leader, Captain John Brown, slipped out of a secluded farmhouse in the
mountains of western Maryland and made their way down a country road toward the Potomac River. Their destination was seven
miles away in Harper's Ferry, Virginia. Brown's plan was to storm
the federal arsenal, armory, and rifle works, and seize control of
the town. From there, having armed the thousands of black fugitives whom he expected to join him, he would lead a raiding party
first into the Virginia mountains and then on south, inciting slave
insurrections as he went. Brown had assured his recruits that both
the Virginia and the Maryland countryside were filled with antislavery supporters who would willingly join their ranks.

Only a man convinced he was God's instrument would have
embraced such a foolhardy scheme. While Brown and his men did
manage to capture and hold the Harper's Ferry armory for two
days, the expected mobilization of slaves and white farmers sympathetic to their cause never materialized. Meanwhile, as news of
the attack spread through the countryside, local militia companies
rushed to defend the town and its federal installations, driving
Brown and those of his men who had neither been killed nor
wounded out of the armory into the firehouse. There on Tuesday
morning, less than forty-eight hours after the raiders had stormed

the town, a detachment of Marines led by Colonel Robert E. Lee seized Captain Brown and his four remaining recruits.

John Brown's raid on Harper's Ferry sent shockwaves of alarm through the nation. Southern leaders damned the raid as "an act of war," and Southern newspapers cried out for the blood of Brown and his men. In the North the first reaction of the press was to dismiss the old man as a lunatic, but Brown's composed and dignified behavior following his capture brought many editors and their readers around to admiring him for his extraordinary faith, courage, and idealism.

Brown had always known his raid might fail, but he also realized that even an aborted attack could provoke a crisis over the slavery issue. From the moment of his capture he began playing the part of a martyr for the antislavery cause. In the initial questioning following his arrest, Brown lay wounded on a pile of old bedding in a room crowded with people, including his captors and several newsmen. He responded gravely but eloquently to his interrogators. When asked upon what principle he justified his acts, Brown replied, "Upon the Golden Rule. I pity the poor in bondage that have none to help them: that is why I am here; not to gratify any personal animosity, revenge or vindictive spirit. It is my sympathy with the oppressed and the wronged, that are as good as you and as precious in the sight of God."[1]

These words, together with news of the attack itself, were read by thousands of Northerners, who trembled with horror and awe as they learned of the courageous behavior of this madman who fomented slave uprisings and then defended his actions with the eloquence and dignity of an Old Testament prophet. The myth of John Brown, the hero of Harper's Ferry, was being fashioned with matchless skill by the old warrior himself. Even his Virginia captors were taken by their prisoner's superb behavior. Governor Henry Wise of Virginia described Brown at the time of his arrest as a "man of clear head, of courage, fortitude, and simple ingenuousness."[2]

Maria Child had never met John Brown, but she had certainly heard of him. During the Kansas troubles of 1856 and 1857 the abolitionist newspapers printed glowing reports of his antislavery activities in that territory, glossing over his penchant for lawless violence. When Brown came to Boston in the winter of 1857 on a fund-raising expedition for the free-soil cause, he met with David and other members of the Kansas Emigrant Aid Committee, including George Luther Stearns, the husband of Maria's niece Mary Preston Stearns. A wealthy Medford industrialist, Stearns was one of Brown's most generous benefactors, and the Kansas warrior was a welcome visitor in the Stearns' parlor. Brown's fanaticism and flawed judgment were kept hidden from his admirers, who saw only a deeply purposeful man who seemed devoid of human frailties.[3]

In the spring of 1858, following one of Brown's visits to Boston, George Stearns was appointed chairman of the Secret Committee of Six to raise funds for what Brown had described as a violent attack on slavery. Theodore Parker was one of the six. So was Thomas Wentworth Higginson. Other members were Samuel Gridley Howe, the renowned director of the Perkins Institute for the Blind; Gerrit Smith, a wealthy New York abolitionist; and, finally, a young schoolteacher fresh out of Harvard, Franklin Sanborn.

Had Maria Child known of this plan to support Brown with money and guns she would certainly have condemned it. When she first heard of Brown's raid on Harper's Ferry she denounced it as very ill-timed.[4] Events in Kansas had grown quiet by the end of 1859 and the state's free-soil future seemed assured. Why provoke further violence? Then there was the future of the Republican party to consider. With a presidential election only a year away, an armed attack on the South threatened to drive away much-needed support.

But whatever reservations Maria may have voiced about the means Brown employed in his attack on Harper's Ferry, she was nonetheless deeply stirred by the man's gallantry in braving such risks and incurring such peril on behalf of the slave. She understood his courage; it matched her own. Furthermore, she had always had a weakness for fearless champions fighting in the name of a holy cause.

Maria had been staying in Medford with Lucy Osgood when news came of the raid on Harper's Ferry. Despite her underlying disapproval of the affair, her sympathies were instantly roused when she read of Brown's wounds and learned of his dignified behavior as a prisoner. Her niece Mary Stearns, who happened to be a neighbor of Lucy's, was equally moved by the old warrior's plight and spoke to Maria of her desire to go to Virginia and nurse him. Meanwhile, reports implicating George Stearns and other members of the Secret Six in Brown's attack began appearing in the Boston newspapers. Panicked by the prospect of being appre-

hended and imprisoned, Stearns was persuaded by the old hero
of the Greek Revolution, Dr. Samuel Gridley Howe, to flee with
him to Canada.[5]

Whatever poor Mary Stearns thought of her husband's unmanly
behavior, she wisely dropped all plans for going to Virginia. Whereupon her Aunt Maria, offered to go in her place. On October 26,
just one week after his arrest, she wrote Brown the following letter:

> Dear Capt Brown,
>
> Though personally unknown to you, you will recognize in
> my name an earnest friend of Kansas. . . .
>
> Believing in peace principles, I cannot sympathize with the
> method you chose to advance the cause of freedom. But I
> honor your generous intentions, I admire your courage,
> moral and physical, I reverence you for the humanity which
> tempered your zeal. I sympathize with your cruel bereave-
> ments, your suffering, and your wrongs. [Two of Brown's
> sons died in the raid.] In brief, I love you and bless you.
>
> Thousands of hearts are throbbing with sympathy as warm
> as mine. I think of you night and day, bleeding in prison,
> surrounded by hostile faces, sustained only by trust in God
> and your own strong heart. I long to nurse you, to speak to
> you sisterly words of sympathy and consolation. I have asked
> permission of Gov. Wise to do so. If the request is not granted,
> I cherish the hope that these few words may, at least, reach
> your hands, and afford you some little solace. May you be
> strengthened by the conviction that no honest man ever sheds
> his blood for freedom in vain, however much he may be
> mistaken in his efforts. May God sustain you, and carry you
> through whatsoever may be in store for you!
>
> Yours with heartfelt respect, sympathy, and affection.
>
> L. Maria Child[6]

Maria enclosed the above in a letter addressed to Governor Wise
of Virginia, asking him to read hers to Brown before delivering it.
She then repeated to the governor her request to be allowed to go
and nurse the prisoner. She took pains to assure Wise that, as a
believer in peace principles, she deeply regretted Brown's actions.
But at the same time she felt a "natural impulse of sympathy for
the brave and suffering man" and declared that if any people were

justified in fighting for their freedom, slaves above all were entitled to that right.[7]

With her letters in the mail, Maria turned her attention to packing a trunk for the journey and collecting a quantity of old lint suitable for bandages. She then waited for word to come that she might start for Charlestown. On November 3 a polite but chilly reply arrived from Governor Wise. Although he promised Maria Child that he would deliver her letter to Brown and could not prevent her from coming to nurse the prisoner, he urged her to stay away lest her presence incite further violence. Wise then proceeded to put all the blame for Harper's Ferry squarely on Maria and her fellow abolitionists.

A few days later Maria received a more appreciative letter from Brown. He thanked her for her kind offer to come to Charlestown but insisted that he was adequately cared for and, having mostly recovered from his wounds, no longer needed nursing. Since he did not see how her coming could possibly do any good, he suggested she show her sympathy for him by helping his family. Back home in North Elba, New York, he had a wife and three young daughters. He also had two daughters-in-law whose husbands had died at Harper's Ferry. The families of the other men who had fought with him needed care as well. "Now dear friend would you not as soon contribute fifty cents now; & a like sum *yearly* for the relief of those very poor & deeply afflicted persons to enable them to supply themselves and Children with Bread; & very plain clothing; & to enable the children to receive a common English education: & also to devote your energies to induce others to join you in giving a like or other amount to constitute a little fund for the purpose named?" Brown concluded this poignant letter by assuring Maria that despite his "afflicting circumstances and prospects," he felt quite cheerful and had the "peace of God which passeth all understanding" to rule in his heart.[8]

While Brown was careful to sound pleased and grateful in his reply to Maria Child, he firmly told his lawyer to keep all women, including his wife, away. Fearing their presence in his cell might "unman his heroic determination to maintain a firm and consistent composure," he was further concerned that if such a notorious abolitionist as Mrs. Child were ever seen in Charlestown, he and his associates would all be lynched.[9] Maria took old Brown's advice and turned her abundant energies to helping his family.

Meanwhile, Maria's role as a publicist for the antislavery cause was being widened in ways she had not anticipated. She had barely replied to Governor Wise in a letter vilifying the slavocracy and praising disunionism when word reached her that it, together with the rest of her correspondence with him and with Brown, had been published in the New York *Tribune*. Wise himself had apparently released the letters, and they were soon reprinted widely in the antislavery press. In the weeks that followed, mail addressed to Mrs. L. Maria Child began pouring into the Wayland post office from all over the United States and Canada.

Many of these letters praised her generous sympathy on behalf of the wounded prisoner and contained offers of money for Brown's family. Emerson wrote that he cherished "to the last, hope for his [Brown's] brave life. He is one of those on whom miracles wait." An old friend and fellow abolitionist, Eliza Follen, reported that discussions of Maria's letters to Governor Wise could be heard everywhere and that they were awakening many a soul to the subject of slavery. Other friends, however, were less enthusiastic. John Greenleaf Whittier, for one, was a steadfast nonresistant. In a letter to Maria he extolled her generosity, but insisted that Brown had been sadly misguided. "As friends of peace as well as freedom, as believers in the Sermon on the Mount, we dare not lend *any* countenance to such attempts as that at Harper's Ferry. . . . I quite agree with thee that we must judge of Brown by *his* standards, but at the same time we must be true to our own settled convictions, and to the duty we owe to humanity."[10]

A good number of Maria's correspondents, however, were openly critical. Convinced unionists, "old fogies" as she called them, were dismayed by her outspoken advocacy of Southern secession. They urged her to remember " 'the sacredness of our constitutional obligations' and the danger of dissolving the 'blessed Union.' " Others were far less polite, particularly writers from Virginia, where newspaper reports of threatened slave insurrections led by armies of abolitionists kept the populace in a continual state of excitement. The violence and obscenity of letters arriving from that tension-filled state surprised Maria. She had not supposed "that even Slavery could produce anything so foul." So blinded was she by the righteousness of her own cause that she failed to see how sharply the raid on Harper's Ferry had divided the nation. If, in her eyes, John Brown was the hero of a holy crusade, Southerners, and those in the North sympathetic to slavery, branded him as a "notorious old thief and murderer" who had now added treason to his list of sins. "The Harper's Ferry invasion," announced the Richmond *En-*

quirer, "has advanced the cause of Disunion more than any other event that has happened since the formation of the Government."[11]

One outraged Virginian was Margaretta Mason, the wife of James Mason, the congressman who had questioned Brown following his capture at Harper's Ferry and who was known in the North as the author of the Fugitive Slave Act. "Do you read your Bible Mrs. Child?" Mason boldly inquired in her letter to John Brown's benefactor. "If you do," Mason continued, "read there, 'Woe unto you, hypocrites,' and take to yourself with twofold damnation that terrible sentence." She condemned Maria first for offering aid and comfort to a slave insurrectionist. In doing so she had consigned her Southern white sisters to the torment—one she would never inflict on her fellow women in the North—of watching their husbands and children butchered in a servile war. Second, Maria was guilty of minding other people's business while neglecting her own; she had offered to nurse John Brown in Virginia while ignoring the sufferings of the poor in Massachusetts. " 'Take first the beam out of thine own eye,' " Mason charged, " 'then shalt thou see clearly to pull the mote out of they neighbor's.' "[12]

Maria was not used to being challenged on her knowledge of Scripture or for her lack of benevolence to the poor and needy. She therefore took her time replying to Margaretta Mason, carefully marshaling her arguments and strengthening them with biblical quotations and other illustrations. Meanwhile, Brown's trial had opened in Charlestown, Virginia, on October 27. Lying on a cot in a courtroom crowded with reporters, the old veteran, with a skill lacking in his military exploits, made full use of this forum to rally Northern support to the antislavery cause. During the weeks of his trial Brown uttered some of the most stirring rhetoric ever to emerge from an American courtroom. Over and over again he insisted that God had been present in his cell and was inspiring him to speak noble words on behalf of the slave. In his final address he reminded his listeners that Christ in the New Testament had taught him "that all things whatsoever I would that men should do to me, I should do to them. It teaches me further to remember them that are in bonds, as bound with them."[13]

As they read Brown's words, most abolitionists were forced to agree that here was the most effective propagandist their movement had ever produced. "How I rejoice in you," Maria wrote Brown on November 16, "because you remain so calm and steadfast in the midst of your great tribulations!" She assured him that his sufferings were not in vain. "From your prison a mighty influence is going forth, throughout the length and breadth of the land." The whole affair had given Maria new life. Before Brown's raid she had complained of feeling "old and drowsy," but now she felt "strong as an eagle." Even at night she lay awake thinking of the prisoners and imagining herself in their place. She told one friend she was so "full of electricity" that "one word of apology for slavery makes the sparks fly." She could think of nothing, talk of nothing, and write of nothing but John Brown.[14]

On December 2, six weeks after his capture, Brown was executed for treason. Southerners felt that justice had been done, and this sentiment was echoed by Republican leaders and other conservative Northerners. But antislavery sympathizers gathered by the hundreds in communities all over the Northeast to honor the hero of Harper's Ferry. In Boston's Fanueil Hall, a large meeting was held on the evening of December 2, which Maria had helped plan. But she derived far more satisfaction from attending a service in a Negro church. She told Susan Lesley she preferred to be with people who "had no doubts at the old hero's sanity, no question about his claim to reverence. They knew, and asked to know no more than that he was the friend of their oppressed race and proved it by dying for them."[15]

In the weeks following Brown's execution Maria went to work soliciting help on behalf of his family and those of his accomplices. It was not a difficult job. "I have no need to ask," she told Lucy Osgood; "everybody who takes any interest in free principles, hastens to *offer*." She thought of writing a biography of the antislavery martyr. But when she learned that James Redpath, a friend of Brown's, had already embarked on one, she turned instead to answering the growing pile of letters from critics and admirers, including Margaretta Mason.[16]

Since a copy of Mason's letter to Maria Child had been sent to the Virginia papers, Maria mailed a copy of her reply to Horace Greeley, asking him to run it in the *Tribune*. "I am extremely anxious for the success of the Republican party," she explained in her accompanying note. Maria was convinced that all the publicity surrounding Harper's Ferry was swaying the South, particularly Virginia, against slavery. Therefore, the time had arrived for her to rise up like some brave warrior and destroy the institution of slavery with an arsenal of her choicest verbal weapons.[17]

Maria opened her letter to Mrs. Mason with the announcement that John Brown and his reputation were of "small consequence in comparison with principles" and that the real issue between them was slavery. In response to Mason's biblical vindication of slave-holding, she fired off eighteen of the abolitionists' favorite texts. "I have given her such a dose of Scripture," Maria later boasted to Lucy Osgood, "that I think she will repent having asked me whether I read my Bible. It's a grand old armoury [sic] when one wants weapons to fight the Devil withal."[18] In case Mrs. Mason remained unconvinced, Maria followed the texts with a lengthy description of Southern slavery, substantiated by quotes from slave laws and advertisements for runaways, by the testimony of fugitive slaves and emancipated slaveholders, and finally by quotes from Southerners themselves. She urged Mrs. Mason and her other readers to examine the matter dispassionately.

> For thirty years, abolitionists have been trying to reason with slave-holders, through the press, and in the halls of Congress. Their efforts, though directed to the *masters only,* have been met with violence and abuse almost equal to that poured on the head of John Brown. Yet surely we, as a portion of the Union, involved in the expense, the degeneracy, the danger, and the disgrace, of this iniquitous and fatal system, have a *right* to speak about it, and a right to be *heard* also. At the North, we willingly publish pro-slavery arguments, and ask only a fair field and no favor for the other side. But you will not even allow your own citizens a chance to examine this important subject. . . . The despotic measures you take to silence investigation, and shut out the light from your own white population, prove how little reliance you have on the strength of your cause. In this enlightened age all despotisms *ought* to come to an end by the agency of moral and rational means. But if they resist such agencies, it is in the order of Providence that they *must* come to an end by violence. History is full of such lessons.[19]

Before ending her letter, Maria addressed the issue of women's public responsibility. She refuted Mrs. Mason's charge that Northern women, while speaking out publicly against slavery, ignored their own poor. On the contrary, she assured her Southern correspondent, "It would be extremely difficult to find any woman in our villages who does *not* sew for the poor, and watch with the sick, whenever occasion requires." Servants in the North are well paid and well cared for, she insisted. Even in cases of childbirth, "I have never known an instance where 'the pangs of maternity' did not meet with the required assistance." In this connection she could not resist pointing out that "here at the North, after we have helped the mothers, *we do not sell the babies.*"[20]

Thus while Maria willingly conceded that Virginia matrons were often kind mistresses, she found their assertions of true sympathy with the slave hypocritical. "Kind masters and mistresses among you are merely lucky accidents," she reminded Mrs. Mason. "If anyone *chooses* to be a brutal despot, your laws and customs give him complete power to do so." Moreover, even under the best conditions the lot of the slave is precarious. "In case of death, or pecuniary difficulties, or marriages in the family, they may at any time be suddenly transferred from protection and indulgence to personal degradation, or extreme severity. . . ." The fact is, Maria said in conclusion, "the whole civilized world proclaims slavery an outlaw, and the best intellect of the age is active in hunting it down."[21]

Early in 1860 the American Anti-Slavery Society published the whole *Correspondence between Lydia Maria Child and Gov. Wise and Mrs. Mason of Virginia* in pamphlet form. Maria would later look back on this as the most notable of her antislavery efforts. Three hundred thousand copies of the pamphlet were distributed all over the free states, an enormous circulation for those days. If she was disappointed that more copies hadn't found their way into the slave states, she had at least had plenty of exposure in the Southern press where, as she described it, her pamphlet was "blazoned by all manner of anathemas."[22]

Some Northern papers were equally scathing. An editorial published in a Worcester paper, not long after a terrible industrial fire in Lawrence had killed and wounded hundreds of textile workers, echoed Mrs. Mason, and accused Maria of neglecting her own. *"Why is it, then, that we do not hear of the presence of Lydia Maria Child at this scene of woe?"* the writer queried. "Can she not for once forget her partialities, and bear with the afflicted, whose only fault to her is their white complexions?" Meanwhile the Southern press was spreading rumors that Mrs. Child had an unmarried daughter living in Mississippi to whom she had refused any form of assistance. Maria, of course, denied that she had borne any children, and it later turned out that while the woman in question was a native of Massachusetts, her name was Childs not Child.[23]

The raid on Harper's Ferry and its aftermath had revived Maria's wholehearted commitment to the antislavery cause. "Others may spend their time in debating whether John Brown did wrong or not; whether he was sane or not," she wrote Maria Chapman after Brown's execution. "All I know or care to know is that his example has stirred me up to consecrate myself with renewed earnestness to the righteous cause for which he died so bravely." God Himself was urging her on, of this she was certain. He had put it into her heart to write John Brown that she might "command a large audience" and thereby spread the antislavery message, and He was now speaking to her very plainly, telling her to "Stand by the slave, come what will!"[24]

But, while Maria would later credit John Brown's example with having inspired her to rededicate her life to antislavery, she remained ambivalent about the whole Harper's Ferry episode. "I *can't* explain it," she admitted to Maria Chapman in January 1860. "The more I cogitate upon it, the more unaccountable it seems to me that any man in his senses could have undertaken such an enterprise." At the same time Maria refused to censure Brown for what he had done. No one "who believes it good to fight under *any* circumstances" can blame him for more than want of *judgment.* She admitted that peace-loving abolitionists like herself had been driven "into a perplexing corner. We cannot help reverencing the *man* while we disapprove of his *measures.* . . . I must be true to the principles of *Freedom,* as well as of *peace.*" Maria at least had the satisfaction of knowing that if in the end war could not be averted she at least had used only "spiritual weapons" in the campaign against slavery.[25]

18

Secession Winter

*When there is anti-slavery work to be done, I feel
as young as twenty.*
—Lydia Maria Child to Lucretia Mott,
1861

In the last weeks of 1859, as Maria Child and others united in
extolling John Brown's martyrdom, Boston's men of business
joined their voices in denouncing the Yankee madman whose
attack on Harper's Ferry had rekindled Southern fears of a Northern plot to overthrow slavery. For more than thirty years Boston's
manufacturing and shipping interests had been allied to the fortunes of the Cotton Kingdom, as New England mills spun and wove
the cotton picked by slaves and New England ships carried the
finished goods to market. Meanwhile, a good number of Boston
bankers had grown rich supplying credit to Southern planters,
further strengthening the ties between the powerful cotton growers
and the Yankee commercial magnates.

By the 1850s, as the free-soil issue increasingly divided the two
sections of the country, these same New England business interests,
or "Cotton Whigs" as they were familiarly known, struggled against
increasing odds to maintain their political and economic ties with
the South. Thus, when news reached Boston of John Brown's raid,
they were understandably outraged. On December 8, 1859, less
than a week after Brown's execution, the Cotton Whigs gathered
in Faneuil Hall to form their own political organization, the Constitutional Union Party. But the new party had little following outside of Boston and other New England cities. Nor did it succeed
in convincing the South that its views were at all representative of

Northern opinion. Southerners continued to regard the North as a land of Brown-loving abolitionists, and the "Great Fear" which swept over the region after Brown's raid deepened with each passing month as rumors of invasions by "Black Republicans" multiplied.[1]

As sectional divisiveness intensified, politicians were preparing for another presidential election. In the North public support rallied around the Republican party, which at its Chicago convention in May 1860 nominated the dark horse, Abraham Lincoln. Maria was familiar with the rail-splitter from Illinois. In 1858, when he had run against the Democrat Stephen Douglas for the United States Senate, she had paid close attention to Lincoln's speeches, applauding when he claimed the Negro as his equal, "as good as I am." Now she was pleased with his nomination, and, despite her distrust of all political parties, she was ready to claim him as "an honest, independent man, and sincerely a friend to freedom."[2]

If Lincoln's campaign speeches in 1858 had shown a commitment to racial justice, there was little evidence of this in the Republican platform of 1860. Determined to appeal to a wide spectrum of Northern opinion, Lincoln and other party leaders knew they would have to take a moderate stand on slavery and Negro rights if they hoped to win the election. Thus in their platform the Republicans pledged themselves to checking the advance of slavery but made it clear that they had no intention of extending social and political equality to blacks.

The failure of the Republican leadership to take a firm stand on the issue of slavery and Negro rights left many abolitionists ambivalent about supporting the party. On the one hand they welcomed the prospect of even a halfhearted antislavery administration in Washington. At the same time the willingness of both Lincoln and other Republican politicians to equivocate on slavery vexed them. If Maria did not go so far as her friend Wendell Phillips, who dismissed Lincoln as "The Slave-hound of Illinois," she thought most of the party leaders had done "more than was *necessary* to prove they were not abolitionists." When Henry Wilson, the Republican congressman from Massachusetts, spent an hour trying to convince her that the people were "not *ready* for the truth on the subject of slavery," Maria retorted that even if this were so, "the question arises how are they ever to *become* ready, if the leaders of public opinion systematically keep back the truth from them."[3]

One outspoken Republican on the slavery issue was Charles Sumner. Within weeks of Lincoln's nomination, he delivered his first speech in the Senate chamber since his caning by Preston Brooks in May 1856. Sumner's recovery had been slow and painful; psychic injuries lingered long after his physical wounds had healed. Not until December 1859 did he fully resume his senatorial duties. Even then he was slow to take an active part in debate. With Lincoln's nomination, however, and the triumph of what Sumner viewed as moderate Republicanism, he felt the time had come to reassert radical abolitionist principles. At precisely noon on June 4, Sumner entered the Senate Chamber and launched into a four-hour oration on "The Barbarism of Slavery." Maria was delighted with Sumner's speech and wrote him that she particularly liked his "exposé of the *meanness* of Slave-holding. It has always excited my indignation to have those dissipated despots boast of their *chivalry.*" As always, she admired the senator's forthrightness and disagreed with those who criticized his coarse language. "Honest utterance generally frightens, or offends the wise and prudent; but it gains the *popular heart.*"[4]

By summer, when the campaign was in full swing, there were two contests underway: one in the North between Lincoln and the Northern Democratic candidate, Stephen Douglas; the other in the South between the Constitutional Union candidate, John Bell, and the Southern Democrat, John C. Breckinridge. When election day arrived on November 6, it was clear that Abraham Lincoln had convinced a majority of Northerners to vote for him. Warnings that the South would never submit to the humiliation and degradation of an administration presided over by an antislavery president went unheeded. Voters across the North chose Lincoln. Meanwhile, not one slave state gave him a single electoral vote.

Shortly after news of the Republican victory reached Boston, Wendell Phillips stood before a packed house in Tremont Temple and announced that for the first time in American history "the *slave* has chosen a President of the United States." The election, Phillips claimed, was less a triumph for Abraham Lincoln than it was a victory for free labor and the American Anti-Slavery Society. If the abolitionist audience in Tremont Temple applauded Phillips' words, the address confirmed the Southerners' worst fears. Talk of secession mounted, and one member of the South Carolina legislature later credited Phillips' speech with influencing his state's decision to leave the Union.[5]

Meanwhile, Massachusetts industrialists grew further alarmed as rumors of secession began hurting trade with South. In the weeks following Lincoln's election, word of factory closings and business failures multiplied. On December 3 a Boston newspaper reported that the city streets were full of discharged workmen. A rising mood of hysteria led many in the North to put the blame for their troubles on the abolitionists' uncompromising stand on slavery. In Boston, industrialists organized Union meetings, circulated petitions favoring compromise, and begged Washington to avoid civil war. They also tried to silence antislavery extremists by encouraging outraged mobs of workingmen to attend abolitionist meetings and shout down the speakers. Their prime target was Wendell Phillips, who went out of his way to add fuel to the fire by denouncing his opponents as Union-loving "cotton aristocrats."[6] For two months, beginning in early December, Bostonians witnessed an outbreak of mob warfare reminiscent of the 1830s.

Maria was in the thick of things that winter. Before Thanksgiving she and David had closed the house in Wayland and moved to Medford for six months. There they boarded with Lucy Osgood, who had lost her sister the year before and welcomed their company. For the first time in nearly a decade Maria was free of domestic responsibilities, free to devote her days to writing for the antislavery cause, and free to attend abolitionist meetings in Boston whenever she wished. All complaints about the dreariness and loneliness of life vanished. "When there is anti-slavery work to be done," she wrote Lucretia Mott, "I feel as young as twenty."[7]

Maria was in the audience at Tremont Temple on December 3, 1860, for a ceremony honoring the anniversary of John Brown's death. As the meeting was called to order a group of rowdies, including Beacon Street lawyers and merchants, invaded the hall. They ousted the chairman, James Redpath, from the platform and took over the meeting. The ensuing commotion was broken up by police, who, since their sympathies were with the mob, closed the hall. But the meeting resumed that evening in a Negro Church on Joy Street. There Phillips lashed out at the Boston authorities for failing to protect free speech, causing one young businessman to cry out "Damn him! He has depreciated stocks $3,000,000 by his slang." Maria, however, was delighted with Phillips' harangue and applauded him so enthusiastically that, according to one account, she broke her wedding ring.[8]

Maria's own courage was put to the test later that winter after another of Wendell Phillips' lectures. On this particular evening a large crowd had gathered outside the closed doors of the Music Hall uttering ugly threats against the speaker. Samuel Gridley Howe, who was in the audience, later told his wife that when the doors finally opened "Phillips came forth, walking calmly between

Mrs. Chapman and Lydia Maria Child. Not a hand was raised, not a threat was uttered. The crowd gave way in silence, and the two brave women parted from Phillips at the door of his own house."[9]

There is no mention of this incident in Maria's own writings. Nor does she describe another occasion that winter when she herself was the object of mob violence. One Sunday in mid-December, Wendell Phillips had just completed the second of a series of lectures in the Music Hall. Maria was making her way out of the building and through the boisterous crowd which had gathered there when she was observed being "tumbled up and down" by "one burly rioter." After first grabbing the man himself by the collar, Maria turned her attention to a well-dressed mobster standing nearby. First, she lectured him on his unruly behavior, and then wrung from him a promise to reform his ways.[10]

The violence of those months reached a climax on January 24, 1861, the day set aside for the annual meeting of the MASS. Merchants and shopkeepers had given their employees the day off and encouraged them to attend the meeting and shout down the abolitionists. The night before, Maria had lain awake consumed with anxiety for Wendell Phillips' safety. As she listened to the clock strike hour after hour, visions passed through her mind "of that noble head assailed by murderous hands, and I obliged to stand by, without power to save him." Early the next morning she slipped unnoticed into Tremont Temple by a back door. A group of armed bodyguards had already preceded her, and one by one other women entered the hall by the same rear entrance. Maria joined the dignitaries on the platform, seating herself near the organ. If she was nervous or anxious, no one noticed it. With cheeks aglow and eyes flashing, she waved enthusiastically to all present.[11] "It was a solemn gathering, I assure you," Maria wrote Sarah Shaw the following day. While the meeting opened without incident,

soon the mob began to yell from the galleries. They came tumbling in by hundreds. . . . Such yelling, schreeching [sic], stamping, and bellowing, I never heard. . . . I should think there were four or five hundred of them. At one time, they all rose up, many clattered down stairs, and there was a surging forward toward the platform. My heart beat so, that I could hear it; for I did not *then* know how Mr. Phillips' armed friends were posted at every door, and in the middle of every aisle. They formed a firm wall, which the mob could not pass. At last it was announced that the police were coming. I saw and heard nothing of them; but there was a lull. Mr. Phillips tried to speak, but his voice was again drowned. Then by a clever stroke of management, he stooped forward and addressed his speech to the reporters stationed immediately below him. This tantalized the mob, and they began to call out, "Speak louder! We want to hear what you're saying!" Whereupon he raised his voice, and for half an hour seemed to hold them in the hollow of his hand. But as soon as he sat down, they began to yell and sing again, to prevent any more speaking.[12]

In the end the police cleared the galleries, but when the abolitionists assembled for the evening meeting they found that the new Democratic mayor, Joseph Wightman, had ordered the doors of the hall closed against them.[13]

By February tempers had cooled. While the abolitionists expressed official dismay at the violence directed towards them and decried the spirit of compromise which inspired it, the uproar in fact had done more to help than hinder their cause. As Wendell Phillips told the reporters sitting in the front rows of Tremont Temple on January 24, "We have got the press of the country in our hands. Whether they like us or not, they know that our speeches sell their papers. With five newspapers we may defy five hundred boys."[14]

Maria shared a similar confidence in the ultimate triumph of the printed word over the mob. The wide circulation of her *Correspondence* with Governor Wise and Mrs. Mason had convinced her anew of the potential effectiveness of such verbal weapons, and she had published three additional pamphlets since then, each for a particular audience. The first, entitled *The Right Way, The Safe Way*, was intended for Southern readers. Written in the aftermath of John Brown's raid, this short treatise was a sincere effort to let cooler heads prevail in the escalating public debate over slavery. Maria realized that Southerners, particularly Virginians, remained terror-stricken by the prospect of future abolitionist attempts to foment slave uprisings. Her intention was to show how misplaced these fears were. What should incite terror was not freedom for the Negroes but their continued bondage, she argued. The institution of slavery, far from serving as the foundation of Southern security, was its greatest threat. Only by emancipating the blacks could the South enjoy certain peace and prosperity. In support of her argument, Maria pointed to the successful example of the British West Indies, where the slaves had been freed for over twenty years and where none of the dire consequences so dreaded by her countrymen had occurred.[15]

The Right Way, The Safe Way offered an array of evidence proving not only that emancipation was safe but that it brought with it a much greater sense of security than was possible under slavery. "It is an undeniable fact," Maria assured her readers, after marshaling the overwhelmingly positive testimony of governors and magistrates, slaveholders and freedmen in favor of emancipation, "that not one white person has ever been killed or wounded, or had life or property endangered by any violence attendant upon immediate emancipation." Furthermore, she declared that West Indian planters, by freeing their slaves, have shown economic good sense. Claiming that the outcry over economic ruin on the islands erupted long before either slavery or the slave trade were abolished, Maria insisted that free labor guarantees greater prosperity in the long run than slavery ever did.[16]

When the tract was published in early April 1860, Maria immediately went to work distributing copies to any Southerner whose name and address she could find. She sent them to all the members of Congress as well as to all the governors and judges listed in the *American Almanac*. She gathered the names of Southern students attending Northern colleges and mailed tracts to them. A Republican lawyer living in Virginia sent her two hundred names and told her that "the cause of freedom is now making astonishing progress" in that state and that her tract exactly met the wants of the time. By October, Maria had mailed off a thousand copies of *The Right Way, the Safe Way*. But it was not always easy to obtain the necessary information. When she wrote for a list of North Carolinians to whom her pamphlet could be sent, she was told firmly that Negroes were too numerous in that state for the tract to be acceptable there.[17]

The Right Way, The Safe Way was deliberately mild and courteous in its tone and relied on simply stated facts to convey its message. Another of Maria's tracts—this one intended as a Republican campaign document—was very different. Aimed at the Northern voter, *The Patriarchal Institution* provided a darkly humorous glimpse of the "peculiar institution." A section entitled "Southern Proof that Slaves are Happy and Contented" contained an assortment of newspaper advertisements for runaways. Under "Southern Proofs of the 'Chivalrous and High-Minded Character' Produced by Slavery," she recounted a conversation overheard in a St. Louis slave market in 1856: "Girl is sound, I suppose?" a potential purchaser carelessly inquires. "Wind and limb," the trader assures him, "but strip her naked and examine every inch of her, if you wish; I never have any disguises with my customers."[18]

The most eloquent and powerful of Maria's antislavery writings from this time, however, was a small pamphlet directed at the state lawmakers of Massachusetts, *The Duty of Disobedience to the Fugitive Slave Act*, which censured the legislators for their indifference to the plight of escaped slaves. It opens with the pronouncement that women are as qualified as men to address the government on such matters: "In view of all that women have done and are doing, intellectually and morally for the advancement of the world, I presume no enlightened legislator will be disposed to deny that the 'truth of heaven' *is* often committed to them, and that they sometimes utter it with a degree of power that greatly influences the age in which they live."[19]

This appeal to the Massachusetts legislators aimed its fire specifically at strengthening a recently enacted bill which secured trial by jury for individuals claimed as slaves. "It is *something* gained to require legal proof that a man is a slave, before he is given up to arbitrary torture and unrecompensed toil," Maria announced in the preface to this third pamphlet. "But is *that* the measure of justice becoming the character of a free Commonwealth? '*Prove* that the man is property, according to *your* laws, and I will drive him into your cattle pen with sword and bayonet,' is what Massachusetts practically says to Southern tyrants. 'Show me a Bill of Sale from the Almighty!' is what she ought to say. No other proof should be considered valid in a Christian country. Shame on my native state! Everlasting shame!"[20]

The pamphlet then recounted several affecting stories of fugitive slaves who struggled in vain to maintain their freedom. Maria concluded with a plea for true justice on behalf of the slave and a hearing for herself:

Law was established to maintain justice between man and man; and this Act clearly maintains injustice. Law was instituted to protect the weak from the strong; this Act delivers the weak completely into the arbitrary power of the strong. "Law is a rule of conduct prescribed by the supreme power, commanding what is right and forbidding what is wrong." . . . The tears of a secluded woman, who has no vote to give, may appear to you of little consequence. But assuredly it is not well with any Commonwealth, when her daughters weep over her degeneracy and disgrace.[21]

Maria's deep concern for the plight of the fugitive slaves had been heightened in recent months. She'd spent a good part of the previous summer editing the memoirs of a fugitive from North

Carolina, Harriet A. Jacobs. *Incidents in the Life of a Slave Girl* was published early in 1861. Privately printed with an introduction by Child, it describes the sexual oppression Jacobs suffered as a slave, the years she spent in hiding in her grandmother's attic, and her successful struggle to free herself and her children. Although *Incidents* is now regarded as a major antebellum autobiography of a black woman, the timing of its publication in the months just prior to the outbreak of civil war brought it little public notice.[22]

On April 4, 1861, Maria wrote Whittier that the nation, like some victim of a raging fever, would either succumb to the evil that was strangling it or would rise triumphant, a free republic at last. At times she was hopeful. The fact that an antislavery political party was in power in Washington led her to anticipate the peaceful departure of the slave states from the Union. "My *own* soul utters but *one* prayer," she told Whittier, "and that is that we may be effectually separated from *all* the Slave States. . . . In no *other* way [can we] present to the world a fair experiment of a free Republic."[23] At other times, as various compromise measures were introduced in Congress requiring the North to make all the concessions, Maria began to have "more hope in Southern arrogance and rashness, than . . . in Northern courage and conscientiousness." "The crisis *must* come," she wrote Frank Shaw on January 8, 1861,

> and it seems to me there can never be a time more favorable than the present. Certainly, I shudder at the *possible* consequences; but if we seek to avoid them at the expense of principle, we shall only prepare a worse crisis for our posterity. The demands of despotism are insatiable and can never be satisfied, short of the entire annihilation of our free institutions. My own belief is, that if the North would only show a bold, united front *now*, despotism would quail before it, and be compelled to become subordinate to freedom; and if once subordinated, it must ere long cease to be.[24]

Maria recognized the difficult challenge facing the Republican leadership, but she refused to condone the slightest sacrifice of principle. When Charles Sumner sent her a pamphlet written by William H. Seward, Lincoln's designated secretary of state and the chief author of the compromise measures, she asked the Massachusetts senator never again to send her anything bearing Seward's name. "It is an immeasurable crime for a public man to chill the moral enthusiasm of his countrymen, to lower the standard of the public conscience, to make it impossible for honest minds to trust in political leaders."[25]

In any case neither the "audacious" slaveholders nor "the miserable, wriggling, sinuous" statesmen in Washington would let Maria rest. As she wrote Lucretia Mott two months before the outbreak of war, "when Charles Sumner was stricken down in the Senate, I swore a solemn oath, in the depths of my soul, that, so long as God spared my life, I would hunt the Demon Slavery with all the energy and all the activity I possessed."[26]

Since 1856 Maria's spirit had boiled in anger and frustration against "the million Lilliputian cords" which bound her to David and domesticity and prevented her from participating fully in the growing national crisis. For the six months of that secession winter the cords had loosened. Once again housewifely responsibilities could be laid aside. She could write as much as she pleased, go into the city as much as she pleased, attend lectures and concerts as much as she pleased. She could even help repel mobs. For another brief period her man's heart, "imprisoned within a woman's destiny," was set free.[27]

19

"God Is Ruling the Whirlwind": War Years, 1861–1865

If we rightly exert the power which God has put into our hands, this may prove the last great battle, in open field, between the forces of Despotism and the forces of Freedom.
—Lydia Maria Child to Jesse Freemont,
1861

E arly on the morning of April 16, 1861, only hours after President Lincoln had issued a call for seventy-five thousand troops to defend the Union, the first company of volunteers arrived in Boston. There, despite the driving sleet, throngs of shouting spectators gathered near the State House steps to help Governor Andrew cheer the new recruits on to war. Barely forty-eight hours earlier, the Union garrison defending Fort Sumter in South Carolina had surrendered to the Confederacy. The bloodiest war in American history had begun.[1]

While the North erupted in a frenzy of patriotism, with bands playing and cheering crowds waving regiments off to war, the Childs bade farewell to Lucy Osgood and all their Boston friends and slipped quietly back home to Wayland. There in the peaceful countryside, the sight of a carthorse passing by on the road with a small Union flag clipped to its ears was the only reminder of the national crisis.[2]

The winter in Medford had not agreed with David. Plagued by chronic dyspepsia, he had suffered repeated attacks of diarrhea, nausea, and faintness. By the time the Childs reached home he was so weak that Maria began to fear for his life.[3] For most of the summer he continued poorly, but with the arrival of cooler weather his health returned. David was happiest in the country, working out of doors in his garden or making improvements to the Wayland house.

Not so Maria. After six months of stimulating company and freedom from domestic chores, the sight of the damp, cold cottage under a leaden April sky drained away all her energy. Instead of vigorously attacking the usual round of spring chores, she sat hunched in front of the fire feeling listless and dispirited.[4]

Maria's mood lightened with the coming of warmer weather, but the war years were generally quiet ones for them. One warm, still Sunday in June 1861, Maria sat at her desk near the window in the sittingroom writing letters. As she watched the cloud shadows drifting peacefully across the broad green meadows she found it hard to imagine the fierce passions which were raging only a few hundred miles away. But even "drowsy Wayland" produced its own war fever in the weeks following the firing on Fort Sumter. At a town meeting called to raise supplies for the Union Army, David had the temerity to speak of the government's duty toward the slaves. This prompted one zealous citizen to declare that the war had "nothing to do with the damned niggers," a contention supported by menacing threats from other zealous citizens. Fortunately, David escaped unharmed. But as word got around that the Childs favored both freeing and arming the slaves, another enraged neighbor, Captain Wade of the United States Navy, called for mob action against them.[5]

Such incidents confirmed the Childs' doubts that the Union cause was allied with the crusade to end slavery. While other abolitionists optimistically announced that a victory for the Union spelled liberty for the blacks, Maria disagreed. "I do not think there is much of either right principle, or good feeling, at the foundation of this unanimous Union sentiment," she wrote Lucy Osgood in late April.

> Our merchants are alarmed about dangers to commerce; our national vanity is piqued by insults to the U.S. flag. . . . Great numbers of people think there is an imperious necessity of defending the government *now*, lest there should *be* no government to protect us from utter anarchy; and still greater numbers are ready to rush into whatever is the fashion. Two thirds would be as ready to throw *away* sop to Cerberus, if he would only be content to spare the passengers in *our* boat, and eat everybody else. But thank God, Cerberus is ferocious to eat up *every*thing. May he continue so, till the work of complete separation is accomplished![6]

Shortly after her return to Wayland Maria read with horror of rumors that slaves seeking protection from the Union had been chained and returned to their masters. She also learned that General Benjamin Butler, a commander of Massachusetts troops, had ordered a rumored slave insurrection in Maryland to be put down. Nor was she comforted when the solidly Republican Boston *Advertiser* announced it didn't want to hear another word about "niggers," that the war was being fought for one reason only: to put down treason. "God knows I *want* to love and honor the flag of my country," Maria exclaimed to Lucy Osgood, "but how *can* I when it is used for *such* purposes?" For the duration of the war she hung a white flag at the garden gate, a gesture which scandalized her more patriotic neighbors.[7]

During the spring and summer of 1861 more than a dozen men left the little town of Wayland to fight in the war. A Soldier's Aid Society was formed in May by the village women, who met monthly to sew blankets and quilts, shirts and sheets for the Union Army. Had the women asked Maria to join them, she would have refused, at least at first. Not until the government expressed concern for the welfare of the slaves did she begin knitting socks for the army. Meanwhile, as word reached her that fugitives were pouring into Union camps and being allowed to remain there, she went to work sewing for them rather than for the soldiers.

Ironically, the same General Butler who had ordered the suppression of a threatened slave insurrection in Maryland in late April refused a month later to return three fugitives who had crossed the Union lines near Fortress Monroe in Virginia. After labeling them "contraband of war," Butler put the men to work constructing a new bakehouse. By July, nine hundred "contrabands" were employed in one fashion or another at Fortress Monroe, and the term, which normally referred to captured military goods, became universally applied to fugitive slaves present within Union lines.[8]

As winter approached and Maria read of the contrabands' lack of warm clothing and bedding, she went to work to supply them, making her house a receiving station for donations of money and supplies. Early in November she sent off a big box to Fortress Monroe containing secondhand clothing and books, as well as sewing materials. She packed lengths of cloth, thread, tape, buttons, and needles so the black women could make garments for themselves and their menfolk. Included among the books were biographies of runaway slaves and six copies of *The Right Way, the Safe Way*. "If the poor creatures have *half* as much satisfaction in receiving the contents, as I had in buying, making and repairing, I shall be glad," she wrote. Maria's work for the freedmen had begun.[9]

Scattered efforts on the part of individual soldiers and commanders to make some provision for the safety and welfare of fugitive slaves coming into their camps continued. At the same time the Union's official policy of honoring the right of the Southern states to maintain slavery within their borders remained unchanged. Maria was briefly elated when news reached her on August 31, 1861, that John C. Fremont, now a Union general, had declared martial law in Missouri and freed the rebels' slaves. A day later, however, Lincoln revoked the order. This came as no surprise, since most Americans accepted without question the constitutional inviolability of slavery in the Southern states. Maria and her fellow abolitionists were forced to acknowledge that some constitutional sanction in support of emancipation would have to be found before the people would consent to the idea. She therefore refrained from openly censuring the president.[10]

Maria worried that many of the escaped slaves were being mistreated. She was incensed to learn that, while Mary Lincoln spent taxpayers' money decking herself out with "foreign frippery," the contrabands at Fortress Monroe who lacked proper clothing were forbidden to wear uniforms. She also feared that the Negroes were neither being paid for their work nor prepared for life in a free society. She herself longed to go South and teach the blacks but David's health prevented her. The help she tendered the freedmen, both during and after the war, would be carried out at home.[11]

Maria may have been removed from the sights and sounds of war, but she could think of little else. Her vivid imagination conjured up battlefields strewn with wounded and dying men, and she had visions of bondsmen being turned away from the protection of Union camps. "Every instance of sending back poor fugitive slaves has cut into my heart like the stab of a bowie-knife," she told Henrietta Sargent. Yet even as she agonized over the tales of suffering which reached her from the front, Maria had no wish for the war to end quickly. "My belief is that order is to be brought out of all this chaos," she wrote shortly after the first Union defeat at Bull Run in July 1861. But such order could not be accomplished unless the slaves were free. Her greatest fear was of a hollow victory, that the government in Washington would make peace with the slaveholders and leave everything unchanged. She consoled herself with the conviction that the nation was in God's hands and that He was "ruling the whirlwind."[12]

Every moment she could spare from housework and caring for David, Maria devoted to the war effort. By November 1861 she marked her satisfaction with the Union Army's improved treatment of fugitive slaves by starting to knit socks and mittens for the Union soldiers. That winter, in addition to her work for the contrabands, she made lint, bandages, and clothes for the army. In order to have more to give away, she saved money by patching her old clothes and wearing her old bonnets.[13]

"A hurra goes up from my heart, when the army rises to carry out God's laws," Maria wrote the Republican congressman George Julian in the spring of 1862. But she continued to believe that moral, not military, means would most effectively subdue the South. Nearly everything she wrote bore some relation to the conflict. When a new edition of the *The Right Way, The Safe Way* was published in early 1862, Maria directed as many copies as she could to legislators in the border states, hoping the book would convert them to emancipation. Newspapers in Wilmington, Delaware, published extracts from it, while others in Virginia and Missouri accepted articles she sent them supporting emancipation. It pleased her that, thanks to the war, light on the slavery question was reaching into dark places. "I am all the time sending paragraphs and collections of facts to the newspapers, to help public opinion on in the right direction," she wrote Sarah Shaw. "I *want* to do other things, but *always* there is kneeling before me that everlasting slave, with his hands clasped in supplication."[14]

The degree to which Maria's writings helped turn the tide of public opinion in favor of emancipation is, of course, impossible to gauge. But the fiction she wrote in these years was carefully designed both to calm public fears on the emancipation question and to gently prepare her Northern readership for the Negro's eventual acceptance as a full-fledged member of a free republic. Her chief worry was that the contrabands would continue to be regarded as property instead of persons, that the widely held view that blacks belonged to a separate and inferior species would prevail. The most explosive issue for most Northern whites was racial intermarriage. Maria set out to allay fears on this question with her story "Willie Wharton," published in the *Atlantic Monthly* in March

1863, just two months after Lincoln's Emancipation Proclamation became law.[15]

This story of a friendship between a white boy and an Indian girl, which ripens into love and eventual marriage, appears at first glance to have little connection with the Civil War. But a closer examination of "Willie Wharton" reveals that Maria is using this tale to raise questions on the whole issue of interracial marriage. The children, Willie and A-Lee-lah, meet when they are very small and are therefore unconscious of the taboos against their friendship. Maria even describes them sharing the same bed, where they lie "with their arms about each other's necks, the dark brow nestled close to the rosy cheek, and the mass of brown hair mingled with the light brown locks. The little white boy of six summers and the Indian maid of four slept there as cozily as two kittens with different fur." Sometime after A-lee-lah and Willie meet, Willie is lost on a hunting expedition and is taken in by an Indian tribe who care for him for many years. When he finally does return home, his appearance and behavior have so altered that he has a hard time readjusting to white people's ways. An uncle, who understands the young man's dilemma, urges other family members to be patient with him: "We shall win him if we manage right," he tells them. "We mustn't try to constrain him. The greatest mistake we make in our human relations is interfering too much with each other's freedom. We are too apt to think *our* way is the *only* way." After a time Willie goes to fetch A-lee-lah and brings her back home with him as his wife. She too then undergoes a period of adjustment to white customs and beliefs. But while she is guided into "increasing conformity with civilized habits," A-lee-lah also retains something of her Indian identity.[16]

Through the story of Willie and A-lee-lah, Maria is gently suggesting that the freed slaves, given time, encouragement, and education, will learn to adopt white ways, and in time too the white race will become less fearful of social equality and intermarriage. Her views on this question were put most succinctly and directly in a letter she wrote to the Ohio congressman, William P. Cutler.

> If there is an "instinctive antipathy" [between the races] as many assert, surely that antipathy may be trusted to prevent amalgamation. If there is *no* instinctive antipathy, what reason is there for the horror? If the colored people are *really* an "inferior race," what danger is there of their attaining to an "equality" with us? If they are *not* inferior, what reason is there for excluding them from equality? *My* belief is, that when generations of colored people have had a fair

chance for education and the acquisition of wealth, the prejudice
against them, originating in their degraded position, will pass away,
and our moral and intellectual estimate of a man will be no more
affected by the color of his skin, than it now is by the color of his
hair.[17]

The spring and summer of 1863 were the hardest months of
the war for Maria. As bloody battles raged in the South and West,
she dreaded reading the list of dead and wounded published each
day in the newspapers for fear of finding the name of someone
she knew. But the first and greatest loss occurred closer to home.
Early in March her brother Convers was taken suddenly ill. For
the next month Maria traveled frequently to Cambridge to be with
him, and she was at his bedside when he died. The serenity of
Convers' last hours did little to cheer her. "The decease of my
brother adds greatly to my loneliness," she wrote Sarah Shaw. "In
my isolated position, he was almost my only medium with the world
of intellect." She had loved Convers deeply; the suddenness of his
departure left her stunned and miserable.[18]

The next blow came in June when a kitchen chimney fire nearly
destroyed the Wayland house. A few weeks earlier Maria had finished the long and laborious job of painting and repapering some
of the rooms. A back wing once occupied by tenants had been
refurbished the previous spring, and the Childs were as comfortably situated as they ever had been. There was now plenty of room
for guests, and Sarah Shaw was their first overnight visitor. The
day after she left, Maria was upstairs taking a nap when she heard
David's terrified screams. The kitchen by then was in flames, but
she managed to escape down the front stairs and out the front
door. By the time the neighbors had put the fire out, the whole
back wing had been destroyed.[19]

"My dear blessed Maria!" Sarah Shaw wrote when she heard the
news. "I can hardly credit it! I try to think of that neat, perfect,
shiny little home changed to what you describe!" The main part
of the dwelling had been saved, but much of it was charred and
the kitchen was in ruins. Fortunately, before he died Ellis Loring
had seen to it that the house was insured. But Maria, understandably, was in despair. What disheartened her most was the immense
amount of labor it would take to put things to right again. "I am
getting old now," she confessed to a friend; "such hard jobs fatigue
me more than they did." But most discouraging was the prospect
of losing the hours she had hoped to be able to spend on more
congenial tasks, such as reading and writing.[20]

When she had recovered from the initial shock and exhaustion brought on by the fire, Maria went to work cleaning up the mess of blackened walls and furnishings. She consoled herself by thinking how mild her suffering was compared to that of the Union soldiers and the contrabands. Meanwhile schemes ran through her head of moving to Boston for the winter or going south to help teach the freedmen. Port Royal, an island off the coast of South Carolina then in the hands of Union troops, particularly tempted her. Eight thousand Negroes had been abandoned there by their owners when the island was captured, and Maria had learned that these ex-slaves were among the most ignorant and backward in the entire South. The challenge of educating them to live happy and productive lives in freedom proved irresistible to abolitionists anxious to counter anti-emancipation arguments.[21]

Despite Maria's interest in the Port Royal experiment and her longing to get away from Wayland, in the end she never left home. As she explained to the Shaws, if she went alone to Port Royal, David would be sure to have a recurrence of his illness. If he went with her, he would probably also get sick, and there might be other difficulties for him as well. "They say it is necessary to practice a great deal of prudence, and some diplomacy, in all situations connected with our camps," she told Sarah, adding that this might prove difficult for David who was "always under the *necessity* of trying to right all the wrongs that come under his notice." As for escaping to Boston for the winter months, that plan had to be abandoned as well. Wartime inflation had pushed up rents prohibitively high.[22]

The final heartache came in late July when Maria read in the papers that the Shaws' only son, Robert, had been killed in battle. The young man's ardent abolitionism, his frank and easy manner, had made him a favorite of Maria's, and she had followed his wartime career closely.[23] When Governor Andrew chose Shaw to command a regiment of colored soldiers, she was as proud of him as if he were her own son. "Colonel Shaw of the Mass'ts 54th is a friend of mine," she boasted to a soldier nephew of David's, Willie Haskins. She described Shaw as "a noble-hearted young gentleman, who left wealth and luxury, and a most happy home, to serve his country in her hour of need." What pleased Maria most, however, was the success Robert was having with his black volunteers. "His mother writes me that he is delighted with his regiment," she told Willie, "he finds so many of them more intelligent than he expected, and all of them orderly, full of pluck, and quick at acquiring military skill. From the very outset of this war, I said we could never effectually put down the rebellion till we emancipated the slaves, treated them in a manner to gain their confidence, and made the fullest use of their knowledge of the rebel country, and of their natural antipathy to their masters."[24]

Maria would have liked to join the crowd lining the streets of Boston on that bright spring day in late May when Robert led his regiment off to war. But she had to make do with a description of the occasion from her Quaker friend Whittier, who wrote that Colonel Shaw, "the flower of grace and chivalry," had seemed to him both "beautiful and awful, as an angel of God come down to lead the host of freedom to victory." Robert's sister Ellen was with her parents on a second floor balcony as her brother led his regiment down Beacon Street. She too saw on him "the face of an angel," and as he kissed his sword she "felt perfectly sure he would never come back."[25]

"Oh, darling! darling! . . . what I have so long dreaded has come upon you," Maria exclaimed in a letter to Sarah Shaw, having just read that Robert had been shot on July 16 while leading his regiment in an attack on Fort Wagner in South Carolina. But mingled with Maria's sorrow was the very real consolation that this "beautiful and brave boy" had "died nobly in the defense of great principles."[26] The courage Robert Shaw and his men had shown at Fort Wagner would erase all doubts about using black troops to crush the rebellion.

Throughout the summer and fall of 1863 Maria was harried and overworked. Cleaning up after the fire took much longer than she had expected. David, whether because of ill-health or incompetence or both, was apparently of little use, and she was forced to hire outside help to make most of the repairs. For months the house was surrounded by piles of lumber and rubbish and everything was out of place. Thanks to the wartime shortage of manpower, carpenters and other workmen came only sporadically. On the days they did appear, Maria occupied the forenoon cooking their lunch and the afternoon cleaning it up. The evening was spent sewing and mending winter clothes while David read aloud the war news. It was, she admitted, "not an enlivening mode of existence."[27]

But while Maria complained of feeling more tired than she had ever been in her life, David seemed to flourish. He enjoyed planning improvements to the house and busied himself making small repairs. In September he went away from home for three weeks, leaving Maria with all the outside, as well as the inside, work. While visiting his sister Lydia in West Boylston he bought a secondhand cookstove for the new kitchen. This arrived home broken, "as I expected it would," Maria reported to Lydia, observing that there were plenty of good used cookstoves to be obtained closer to home.[28]

To add to Maria's despondency, she learned in December that a book of readings she had compiled expressly for the elderly would, thanks to a printers' strike, not be published for another year. Advertisements for *Looking Toward Sunset* had already appeared in the papers, and Maria was very upset by the delay. Writing, collecting, and editing the stories, essays, and poems to be included in the book had cheered many lonely hours. Furthermore, she had planned to use the proceeds for the benefit of the freed slaves. The prospect of the volume's appearance had been the one ray of sunshine in an otherwise dreary year.

Maria's complaints of loneliness and fatigue worried her friends, who did their best to tempt her away for visits. The bereaved Shaws invited the Childs to come to Staten Island for a month, but Maria declined, citing the confusion of her household and her dread of leaving the place unoccupied. A neighbor, Mrs. Wyman, was more successful. She managed to lure the Childs to an evening party attended by several other notables, including Charles Sumner, Wendell Phillips, Julia Ward Howe, and the renowned naturalist Louis Agassiz. Nor could Maria and David very well refuse an invitation to Anna Loring's marriage to the musician Otto Dresel in early November. At the time, Maria was more than out of sorts with domesticity, and while she liked Otto well enough she couldn't help brooding over the "irrevocableness of the step" Anna was taking and the uncertainty of its success.[29]

With the arrival of the New Year, however, the picture brightened up a bit. Freezing temperatures brought repairs on the house to a halt, and, while confusion still reigned, at least they had the place to themselves. David stayed cheerful and healthy, occupying himself with "stopping up chinks and finishing unfinished jobs," all the time singing "The Star-Spangled Banner." Maria, for her part, was devoting every spare moment to making needlebooks for the Missouri freedwomen. In late January she emerged from her rural seclusion long enough to attend the annual antislavery reception in Boston. She did so reluctantly, complaining of the noisy, greedy crowds who attended these affairs. "To *me*, it is one of the

most unpleasant scenes I ever mingled in," she bluntly informed
Garrison, who had written for permission to add her name to the
list of patrons. She even questioned whether, at a time when pecuniary demands were "so incessant, and so immense," there was
any money left for "*old fashioned* anti-slavery."[30]

In the end, friends and colleagues coaxed Maria into attending
the reception, and she quite enjoyed herself. During the train ride
to Boston she sat with Emerson's Transcendentalist friends, Bronson Alcott and Elizabeth Peabody. Alcott's appearance and behavior
struck her as wonderfully out of step with the times; he occupied
the whole journey musing aloud serenely on the difference between
'personality' and 'individuality.'[31]

At the reception Maria saw many old friends of antislavery,
including the poet Whittier. In an account of the occasion published
in the *Liberator* she said she could generally recognize those who
had early consecrated themselves to antislavery work. "I know them
by their honest, thoughtful countenances, by their cordial grasp of
the hand, by their bold straightforward utterance." New antislavery
friends, she wryly observed, were "becoming as plenty as roses in
June." A woman from Tennessee who spoke to Maria at the reception admitted she had once considered her "a most misguided
and mischievous woman." Now, she claimed, her views had entirely
changed: "I detest the system of slavery as sincerely as you do."[32]

But of all those she met at the reception, the person who interested Maria the most was Edmonia Lewis, a young artist of black
and Indian heritage who had recently come to Boston to study
sculpture. This small, bright, exotic-looking woman combined the
Native American's straight black hair with distinctly African features. But Maria was above all impressed by Lewis' simple directness
of manner and "frank, intelligent countenance." After the two
women had conversed for a time, Lewis invited Maria to come to
her rooms and see her first effort at sculpture, a bust copied from
a head of Voltaire. Maria was pleased to find the piece held "a great
deal of life and expression." While it was too early, she told the
readers of *Liberator*, to know if Edmonia Lewis was a creative genius,
"she seems to possess a native talent which is capable of being
developed fairly by industry and perseverance." Maria, for the time
being at least, was impressed enough with what she had seen to
take Lewis under her wing.[33]

Back in Wayland, Maria settled once again into the routine of
domestic life. One March afternoon, she took up pen and paper
and described her surroundings to Lucy Osgood. "I am sitting here

all alone, as I do day after day. The little river, not yet dried by summer heat, is sparkling in the western sunlight. In my little sitting-room, books, pictures, chairs, even the ashes on the hearth are glowing with touches of airy splendor, from prisms, which I am childish enough to suspend in the windows." For all the coziness of her surroundings, Maria admitted to feeling lonely and apprehensive about the future. She wished Lucy lived next door so she would have someone to talk to. She also felt guilty to be sitting quietly writing letters while the nation was in such turmoil. "I have never dreaded the battles as I do this spring," she confessed. At the same time it seemed pointless to agonize over events she could not control. "What a fool I am to be breaking my brains over the destinies of the world! It is a great steam-engine that is whirling along, and I am only a fly on the roof." But such thoughts failed to still her anxieties. "I am not comfortable in *that* conclusion, either," she admitted. "I cannot get rid of the consciousness that I was not sent here merely to have a ride on the cars. I wish I knew what I *was* sent here for. If I could see it plainly, I'd go and do it."[34]

If Maria yearned for the wheels of fate to carry her away from Wayland, she also knew such longings were fruitless. Early in May, she made one of her brief trips to Boston. The night she returned, David was taken ill with another of his intestinal attacks. As she explained to Lucy, after a year free of such problems she had begun "to build castles in the air" that they could again spend the winter in Medford. But that dream had once again evaporated and her burdens were now heavier than ever. "Oh, for some willing and intelligent working-woman to take the *weight* of work and care from my shoulders!" she complained to another friend, Eliza Scudder. "But that is an article not to be had; so there is no use in groaning." She could not, however, resist comparing her lot to that of the slave, telling Eliza, "if I could *only* get my freedom, I'd buy myself at any price."[35]

Early the next year, Maria listed on paper her "Employments" for 1864. These included writing six articles for newspapers and correcting proofs for her book *Looking Toward Sunset*, together with a daunting inventory of household chores, from cooking and cleaning to sewing David's clothes. While the list mentioned twenty-five needlebooks she had made for the freedwomen, it failed to include her most enduring contribution to the welfare of the newly freed slaves, her *Freedmen's Book*, for which she had begun collecting material in the spring of 1864.[36]

During the last year of the war, as the numbers of dead and wounded continued to mount, Maria's thoughts dwelt increasingly on the period of reconstruction that would follow a hoped-for Union victory. Ever since Lincoln's Emancipation Proclamation of 1 January 1863, she had pondered the vast problem of educating the freed slaves. Among other things, Maria was concerned by the lack of suitable reading material available to them. It occurred to her that she could help meet this need by compiling a book of readings. She would include biographies of colored people, stories about slaves, a few good hymns, and finally a selection of Negro verse. Her object was to give the freedmen "good moral instruction in a simple attractive form; to encourage them by presenting honorable examples of what *has* been done by people of color; and to infuse kindly feelings toward their former masters." Above all, she wished to promote self-respect and self-reliance among them.[37]

Collecting materials for her *Freedmen's Book* was a welcome distraction from household cares, but the problem of publishing the book was another matter. Maria was determined that it sell for the lowest possible price, and that all earnings from sales be invested in other books for the freedmen's schools. While she knew no publisher would accept a manuscript on these terms, she was unable to raise the $1000 it would cost to print the book. So in July she decided to postpone the project indefinitely.[38]

In the dog days of August 1864, as the New England landscape lay parched by a long drought, Northern morale plunged to a new low. After a spring of raised hopes on the battlefields, the Union armies were accomplishing little but more bloodshed. In Georgia, General Sherman was inching his way towards Atlanta. Meanwhile, farther north in Petersburg, Virginia, General Grant's troops were prosecuting a long siege of trench warfare.

But the crisis in Northern morale that summer had as much to do with politics as warfare. Defeatism and a longing for the bloodshed to end were playing into the hands of the Democrats. Lincoln, up for re-election that fall, found himself caught in the middle. On one side stood the Radical Republicans, men like Senator Sumner, who were pushing for the total destruction of the slavocracy and demanding full rights for the freed slaves. On the other were the Copperheads, or peace Democrats, who urged an end to hostilities through negotiations rather than victory. Of the two, Lincoln felt he had the most to fear from the antiwar faction, which threatened to undermine his commitment to emancipation and unconditional surrender.

Since the announcement of the Emancipation Proclamation in September 1862, Democrats had been exploiting the race issue, playing on northern fears of black equality. That year's elections saw the party score significant gains. Meanwhile, each military setback strengthened the peace wing. In March 1863, the enactment of a conscription law further stimulated antiwar sentiment as party newspapers warned the white workingman that while he was off fighting for black freedom the Negroes would come north and take away his job. That summer draft riots broke out in several northern cities. In New York, mobs terrorized the metropolis for four days, leaving at least 105 people dead.[39]

As the election of 1864 neared, Confederates hoped that northern war weariness would persuade voters to choose a president willing to make peace with the South on terms guaranteeing its independence from the Union. George B. McClellan, erstwhile commander of the Union forces in Northern Virginia, was the Democratic candidate. Although McClellan repudiated his party's peace plank, he did his best during the campaign to capitalize on Northern defeatism.

"The worst that can befall us is to have McClellan made President, and a false peace patched up, by bringing the whole country under the dominion of slavery," Maria declared in mid-September. While she strongly favored Lincoln's re-election, she feared that his sympathy for the wrongs and sufferings of the Negro was secondary to his fear of the Democrats. She failed to understand that it was precisely the Democratic threat to end the war with slavery intact which had forced Lincoln to play a cautious game. As election day approached her anxiety mounted. On November 8 she wrote Whittier that for the first time in her life she wished she could vote. "To think that a drunken Irishman may decide the destiny of this great nation, while, I, who have so long and carefully watched all the springs in the machinery of State, would be contemptuously thrust from the polls! What a burlesque on human institutions!"[40]

Lincoln's victory cheered Maria's flagging spirits and gave her renewed confidence "that our republican form of government rests on secure foundations." But the event that made these last months of the war particularly happy for her was the long-awaited publication of *Looking Toward Sunset*. This anthology of prose and poetry for the elderly was intended to give them "words of consolation and cheer." Only nine of the pieces were hers. The rest came from sources old and new: poems by Bryant, Holmes, Wordsworth, and Whittier; essays by Theodore Parker and Frederika Bremer; stories by Dickens and Harriet Beecher Stowe. There were less well-known writers as well. Maria persuaded Lucy Osgood to write something cheerful about single women. "No class *deserves* to be canonized so much as these 'Aunt Mary's' of the community," she assured her old Medford friend.[41]

To Maria's delight, *Looking Toward Sunset* was a great success. By the end of the year the whole first edition of four thousand copies had been sold and she had earned $450 for the freedmen. Never in her life had she had so much money to give away. For her it was a moment of supreme, long-awaited satisfaction. "No prince or nobleman can discover or invent, any mode of enjoyment equal to *earning* with one hand and *giving* with the other," she exulted to Anna Loring Dresel. Meanwhile letters praising the volume poured in to the Wayland post office. Whittier wrote that "It was an exceedingly happy thought of thee to send out these words of cheer." Louisa Loring told her it was the best present she'd received since Ellis' death. "I'm sure he thanks you for giving me such sweet comfort." A favorable notice in the *Atlantic Monthly* equated *Looking Toward Sunset* with Maria Child's best writings: "Every one of her chief works has been a separate venture in some new field, always daring, always successful, always valuable."[42]

"When the war is over, I intend to purchase a new bonnet," Maria announced with uncharacteristic frivolity in February 1865, "I have not had one for five years." She only had two months to wait. But when the news reached her that Lee had surrendered to Grant on April 9, all the giddiness had vanished. While she was glad the bloodshed was over, she rejoiced "with trembling. I am *so* afraid," she told Lucy Osgood," that, in our zeal to get the rebel states back into the Union, we shall reconstruct on a basis that will make future trouble. . . . If we can use success with magnanimity, and at the same time be strict and uncompromising in all that regards the future welfare of the country, the war will prove a prodigious blessing!"[43] It was a big IF.

20

We Are All Brethren

It is my *mission to help in the breaking down of classes, and to make* all *men feel as if they were brethren of the same family, sharing the same rights, the same capabilities, and the same responsibilities. While my hand can hold a pen, I will use it to this end; and while my brain can earn a dollar, I will devote it to this end.*
—Lydia Maria Child to Lucy Osgood,
1878

Maria turned sixty-three in February 1865; David turned seventy-one that July. While his health remained precarious, hers was generally good. "We live like a real old Darby and Joan, waiting upon ourselves, and serving each other," Maria announced brightly to her friend Henrietta Sargent in 1870. She continued determined to make the best of her secluded and monotonous existence. As always the beauties of nature helped to lift her spirits. In spring and summer her flower garden was a particular pleasure. In winter she relished those rare mornings after an ice storm when the tree branches glistened in the bright sunlight. Otherwise she occupied her few spare hours each week reading novels or looking over her mounting collection of photographs and engravings. In 1869, Harriet Sewall, the second wife of David's old Harvard classmate Samuel Sewall, sealed her friendship with Maria by sending her a stereoscope for her birthday. No other present ever provided so many happy hours as this popular optical instrument, which imparted a three-dimensional effect to two pictures of the same object taken from slightly different angles. Friends, previously at a loss for something to send Maria for Christmas or her birthday, now flooded her with stereoscopic pictures.

She particularly loved scenes of distant places. When Anna Loring Dresel moved to Germany with her husband and children, she sent back views of picturesque German villages. Maria could now travel to all those foreign lands she'd written about but never visited.[1]

Now her greatest personal satisfaction came from helping the freed slaves. In September 1865 she wrote Sarah Shaw an exuberant letter, announcing that Ticknor and Fields had agreed to publish her *Freedmen's Book* on condition that she pay $600 toward the cost of printing it. She wanted the volume to be as inexpensive as possible so the freedmen themselves could afford to buy it. Thanks to the success of *Looking Toward Sunset* and her household economies, she had the money put aside. Word had circulated among the abolitionists that spring that Maria Child, by denying herself tea, sugar, butter, servants, and new clothes, had saved $200 to be used for the freedmen. After years of struggling with David's pecuniary liabilities, she explained to Sarah Shaw, "the process of saving with one hand, and giving with the other" was particularly satisfying.[2]

One economy which concerned some of Maria's more fashion-conscious friends was her preference for dowdy headgear. "When the war is over, I will buy a new bonnet," she had promised in February 1865, but two years later this purchase had yet to be made. As she explained to Marianne Silsbee, she was waiting until all the freedmen had homes and spellingbooks. She also knew, she said, that "if I ever should get one, within hailing distance of the fashion, I shall find myself in a *dilemma*, for I have promised several people that I will *call* upon them when I get a fashionable bonnet. Wouldn't *that* be a scrape to get into?"[3]

Maria's *Freedmen's Book*, a volume of prose and poetry filled with words of cheer and encouragement for the newly freed slaves, was in print by the end of the year. Biographies of two great black leaders, Toussaint L'Ouverture, the revolutionary ruler of Santo Domingo, and Frederick Douglass, the most prominent of the black abolitionists, show that even ex-slaves could rise to positions of great power and influence. On a less ambitious level there is a sketch of the eighteenth-century black poet and Northern slave, Phillis Wheatley, who never allowed her talents or her thirst for knowledge to interfere with her womanly duty. A lively account of two renowned fugitive slaves, William and Ellen Craft, reveals Maria Child at her storytelling best. This fast-paced tale of disguise and escape is filled with little ironies. William had a dark complexion, but his handsome wife, Ellen, could pass for a white. When preparing for their escape to the free states, Ellen dressed herself as a rich young Southern gentleman, while William played the part of her slave. How it must have delighted Maria to describe the attentive behavior of the Virginia aristocrat traveling north to Baltimore with his eligible daughters in the same car as Ellen. "At parting the Virginian gave him [Ellen disguised as Mr. Johnson] his card and said: 'I hope you will call upon me when you return. I should be much pleased to see you, and so would my daughters.' He gave ten cents to William, and charged him to be attentive to his master. This he promised to do, and he very faithfully kept his word."[4]

But *The Freedmen's Book* also displays a cautionary tone. Maria is careful to warn the ex-slaves that their continued freedom depends upon their judicious behavior. In her sketch of Toussaint L'Ouverture, she emphasizes his generous treatment of the whites who had once ruled the island. "He knew that the freedom of his race depended upon their good behavior after they were emancipated, and that insurrections would furnish the French government with a pretext for reducing them to Slavery again."[5]

If Maria is urging the freedmen to display patience towards their old masters and to prove by their sober, honest, and industrious behavior their worthiness for freedom, she has words of caution for their white employers as well. In her description of the violent and cruel behavior of the freed blacks of Santo Domingo towards their one-time masters who were attempting to restore slavery to the island, she is warning her readers that similar dangers threaten ex-slaveholders in the South. She describes how the blacks in Santo Domingo, "driven to desperation, became as cruel as their oppressors. They visited upon white men, women, and children all the barbarities they had seen and suffered." Maria is suggesting that unless southern whites take care to treat their black employees justly, they can expect a similar reprisal.[6]

Maria also has words for the Northerners she hoped would read *The Freedmen's Book*. First, with her accounts of industrious, talented, and distinguished blacks, she is seeking to prove that the black race is as worthy as the white race of citizenship in a free republic. Second, she is sending a warning to American voters and their representatives in Washington not to be too lenient toward the ex-rebels, lest tyranny and even slavery be restored and everything the Union fought for be lost. One essay in the book, drawn from her pamphlet *The Right Way, The Safe Way*, describes the British abolition of slavery in the West Indies in the 1830s. Here she chides the English for not having trusted the blacks to make a smooth transition to freedom. Instead, the home government had heeded the fears of the white planters and postponed real freedom by instituting an apprentice system which bound the ex-slaves to their old masters for six years without pay. On the island of Antigua, however, the planters had had more confidence in their freed slaves. Eschewing the apprentice system, they had paid their black laborers from the start. These employers, Maria observed, had "judged wisely for their own interest, as well as for the comfort and encouragement of their laborers. When the negroes found that they were paid for every day's work, they put their whole hearts into it. So zealous were they to earn wages, that they sometimes worked by moonlight, or by the light of fires kindled among the dry cane-stalks. In all respects, the change from the old order of things to the new went on more smoothly in Antigua than it did anywhere else."[7]

The Freedmen's Book became a valuable contribution to the educational efforts of Reconstruction. Historian Eric Foner has observed that in an era when "few Northerners involved in black education could rise above the conviction that slavery had produced a 'degraded' people, in dire need of instruction in frugality, temperance, honesty, and dignity of labor," a volume like *The Freedmen's Book* was a rare phenomenon. Unlike other primers it imparted a sense of racial pride in its Negro readers.[8]

Maria herself was generally pleased with the reception of the book. She had hoped the freed slaves would buy copies, but their wages proved too low. By 1870 she had spent $1200 getting the volume distributed through the Freedmen's Aid Societies. Letters from teachers in the South described their pupils' deep interest in the book. The most literate apparently took pleasure in reading it aloud to others as yet unable to read.[9]

Maria's interest in public affairs continued unabated during these first years of Reconstruction. When she learned of President Lincoln's assassination on April 14, 1865, she was shocked and distressed but consoled herself that this act of violence, like the war itself, was God's doing. "Dreadful as this is perhaps it is only another of the wonderful manifestations of Providence. The kind-hearted Abraham, was certainly in danger of making too easy terms with the rebels. Perhaps he has been removed, that he might not defeat his own work, and that another, better calculated to carry it to a safe and *sure end,* might come into his place."[10]

Abolitionists generally had great confidence in the new president, Andrew Johnson. Charles Sumner and other Radical Republicans concurred in believing his views on reconstruction were sounder than Lincoln's. In 1864, as wartime governor of Tennessee, Johnson had announced that "treason must be made odious, and traitors must be punished and impoverished." He had also promised the blacks he would be their "Moses" and lead them out of bondage. In the weeks following the assassination Maria shared this faith in the new president. "He *seems* to have honesty, and sincerity," she told Sarah Shaw. "His being Southern born is a favorable circumstance, and the fact that he belongs to the class of 'poor whites' will, I think, have quite an important influence in bringing over that class." In a letter published in the *Independent*, she spoke of her delight "in having such a plain man of the people to rule over us. I fully sympathize with his hearty aversion to aristocracy."[11]

Those who expected Johnson to overturn the old regime in the South were soon disappointed. In reality, the president, while he despised the planter class, had no intention of using federal power to bring justice to the freed slaves. Nor did he envision any role for the blacks in a reconstructed South. Once Johnson assumed the presidency he realized that to achieve his goal of restoring white rule to the South, he would have to forget his hatred of the planter class. He also realized he would need the planters' support if he was to gain a second term in the White House.

In May 1865, just as the abolitionists were launching a propaganda campaign in support of Negro suffrage, Johnson announced his reconstruction policy for North Carolina. He would confer amnesty and pardon, including the restoration of property rights, on all but the wealthiest and most powerful rebels as long as they were willing to renounce slavery and take an oath of allegiance. This was only the beginning. By fall it was evident to many in the North that Johnson had allied himself with the planter aristocracy, was ready to be extraordinarily lenient towards the erstwhile rebels, and was determined to return the Southern states to the Union on the basis of white suffrage.

It took a while, however, for Maria to lose her faith in Johnson. "The poor freedmen!" she wrote on August 11. "I feel so anxious about them! I don't know what to make of Andy Johnson's course; and yet my confidence in him is too strong to be easily shaken." With the coming of the new year that confidence had evaporated. On January 22, 1866, in a letter to Congressman George Julian, she acknowledged that Johnson's actions since assuming the presidency revealed him to be "one of that very common class of spurious democrats, who hate the aristocracy merely because they are not born into it. *Such* democrats are always ready to kiss the feet of aristocrats as soon as they doff their hats to them."[12]

For Maria there were three essential components to a successful reconstruction program in the South, and they amounted to political and economic revolution. She wished to keep power out of the hands of the rebels, particularly the planter class, while at the same time granting both land and suffrage to the freedmen. On the land question, she felt Congress should have confiscated the plantations of the rich rebels and allowed the freedmen to purchase small lots at low prices. But she opposed outright grants of property to the blacks, believing it to be "more salutary to all classes of people to *earn* a home than to have it *given* to them." The idea that the freedmen, after years of unpaid labor, might already have earned the right to a house and a few acres apparently did not occur to her.[13]

On the suffrage question she declared it a "very imperious necessity" that Southern blacks be given the vote, "not only for their own protection, but also for the safety of the small minority of whites who are true to the Government." Although she agreed in principle with those who favored an educated electorate, she disapproved of a literacy requirement for new black voters. In an article published in the *Independent* early in January 1867, she pointed out that if such a condition were included in a proposed constitutional amendment, it would bar freed slaves from voting while giving the ballot to thousands of recent immigrants, "who cannot write their own names, or read their own votes." Meanwhile, "numerous native citizens, who are ignorant because our own laws have hitherto prevented them from obtaining the rudiments of learning, would be excluded from the polls. . . . Either *all* voters should be required to have some degree of education," she declared, "or *none* should be subject to such limitations."[14]

The guarantee of the rights of black citizenship and suffrage would eventually be embodied in the Fourteenth and Fifteenth Amendments to the federal Constitution. But when congressional friends of the freedmen were seeking the most politically palatable wording for these amendments they collided with the crusaders for another disfranchised group, American women. The prewar women's rights movement had drawn much of its strength from abolitionist ranks. Elizabeth Cady Stanton, Susan B. Anthony, and other feminists now hoped that women as well as blacks could benefit from the current drive to enlarge political rights. Their optimism was further buoyed by the presence in Congress of old abolitionist colleagues who had risen to become powerful Radical Republican voices in the House and Senate.

But if Stanton and Anthony had presumed that men like Senator Sumner would be willing to champion votes for women as well as black men, they were soon disappointed. Beginning in the late summer of 1865, as debate mounted over a proposed Fourteenth Amendment granting citizenship to the freed slaves, feminists grew alarmed by talk of restricting political rights to males. Abolitionists and congressional Radicals generally agreed that if the Union victory in the South was to be preserved, the blacks must have the vote. While many abolitionists agreed in principle that suffrage was a right of all citizens, they feared that introducing the woman suffrage issue might jeopardize suffrage for black men.

At first Maria Child supported the women's rights advocates in their drive to join the two causes. Late in 1866, in a letter to Elizabeth Cady Stanton, she expressed full sympathy with her views on the woman question.

> I believe it to be right and just that women should vote, for many of them are taxed to support the Government, and 'taxation without representation' is contrary to the principles on which our republic was founded. Women are imprisoned and hung by the laws, and therefore they have a right to a voice in *making* the laws. As for our capacity to vote as intelligently as the mass of men, *that* is a point I would scarcely condescend to argue. It is absurd, on the very face of it, that an illiterate foreigner, ignorant of our institutions, and with nothing at stake in the welfare of the country should be allowed to vote, while a woman like Mrs. [Harriet Beecher] Stowe is excluded from the privilege of thus influencing the public affairs which she understands so well. Grant that many women would but echo the opinions of husbands, fathers, or brothers; how is it with the crowds of ignorant foreign voters? Do they not notoriously vote according to the dictation of others? The number of women capable of forming opinions for themselves, and sufficiently independent to do so, is by no means small, and the sense of responsibility involved in voting would rapidly increase the number. I believe the effect would be to enlarge and strengthen the character of women, and all will admit that the dignity and safety of a state depends greatly on the character of its women.[15]

Later, in her *History of Woman Suffrage*, Stanton would claim that Maria Child's name had headed one of the many petitions sent to Congress opposing the use of the word "male" in the Fourteenth Amendment, but no record survives supporting this claim. For all

her sympathy with feminist goals, Maria evinced her usual reluctance to play a public role in the women's rights crusade. As she
admitted to Stanton, she had "little energy for enlisting in a new
war."[16]

If Maria in principle supported the idea of enfranchising both
women and blacks, when it came down to which should come first
she unhesitatingly favored the Negro. "The suffrage of woman can
better afford to wait than that of the colored people," she declared
in her letter to the *Independent* published in January 1867, just a
month after she had assured Stanton of her support. Like other
abolitionists she felt the urgency of giving blacks the vote. How else
could the erstwhile slaveholding rebels be prevented from once
again controlling the federal government?[17]

Maria's insistence that the needs of the freedmen should come
first was bolstered by events in the South. No sooner had the war
ended than white Southerners began searching for a legal means
to subordinate the black population and coerce it to produce plantation staples. By the summer of 1865 a number of states had
established apprenticeship systems for Negro workers which were
supported by statutes known as Black Codes. These laws, besides
restricting employment opportunities for Negroes, limited their
freedom of movement and their right to buy or rent property.
Maria Child's dream that each black family would be free to tend
its own plot of land would, in the end, be realized by very few.

Maria's devotion to the plight of the freedmen kept her pen busy
writing articles and letters on their behalf. With the war's end,
pressure was again put on her to attend conventions in support of
the freedmen and women's rights. But she had little interest in the
machinery of reform and used Wayland's isolation and David's
health as excuses to remain detached. She was also thinking of
writing another novel.

The nucleus of a plot with the theme of interracial marriage had
been in her mind for some time. In 1841 she had written a piece
of short fiction called "The Quadroons," a tragic love story in which
two light-skinned mulattos, a mother and daughter, die of grief
when their white lovers abandon them. This time her purpose was
more positive and prophetic. She intended to present an idealized
vision of postemancipation America in which blacks would be truly
integrated into white society. In the fall of 1865, Maria told her
publisher, James T. Fields, that she had an idea for a novel but did
not say what it was. She found it hard to begin writing, complaining
in October 1866 that her muse, which she called Pegasus, was

"somewhat stiff in the joints" and that her "imaginations" did not always come when called for. Once begun, however, the writing went quickly. By the spring of 1867 the book was finished. It was in the bookstores later that summer. Fields seemed unperturbed by the story's controversial subject matter and liked it well enough to offer Maria $1000 outright. But she declined his offer, preferring to take her ten percent share of the royalties.[18]

A Romance of the Republic traces the lives of two mulatto sisters from their kindly and sheltered upbringing as slaves in New Orleans, through the trials and sorrows of their early adult life, to their eventual acceptance as respectable Boston matrons. When we first meet them, Flora and Rosabella are living with their French father, Mr. Royal, a once-wealthy New Orleans merchant. Their mother, a slave of Spanish extraction, is long dead. The two girls, both graceful and accomplished young women, have been raised by their father in complete isolation from society and never question their free status. Except for a deep, rosy blush suffusing their complexions, they could easily pass as whites. Unfortunately, Mr. Royal, who had every intention of manumitting his daughters, dies before he can do so, leaving behind a great many debts. Flora and Rosa soon learn that in the eyes of the law they are nothing more than pieces of property to be used in reconciling their father's estate.

The sisters are saved from the auction block, however, by a dashing white admirer of Rosa's, Gerald Fitzgerald. Fitzgerald, a Georgia slaveholder, smuggles them out of New Orleans, pretends to marry Rosa in a mock ceremony, and then hides the two away in a secluded cottage on his sea island plantation. Rosa is soon carrying his child, but Fitzgerald's fidelity to her is short-lived. After trying unsuccessfully to seduce Flora, he marries a rich northern wife by whom he has a second child. Having learned of her supposed husband's treachery, Rosa, in a fit of despair, manages to guarantee her own child's freedom by switching him with the freeborn legitimate baby who is of identical age, sex, and appearance.

Eventually the two sisters escape Fitzgerald's clutches. Rosa is carried by old family friends to safety in Italy, where she becomes a great opera singer. Flora is rescued by a kindly Boston matron who takes the girl home and adopts her without exposing her slave origins. In the end both sisters marry respectable white husbands and settle permanently in Boston. Meanwhile, the two babies Rosa switched have grown up. They meet and befriend one another on a Civil War battlefield and later discover their true identities. Rosa's son, who had been brought up in freedom and is every inch a cultured gentleman, must now learn to accept his black ancestry. He falls in love with his cousin, Flora's daughter Eulalia, and later dies at the Battle of Bull Run. His half-brother, who has been raised in slavery and is married to a mulatto, must leave behind his rough, uncouth ways and allow himself and his wife to be educated for life in a refined white world where he will eventually inherit a great fortune.

Maria Child's intention when she wrote *A Romance of the Republic* was to bring her white readers one step closer to accepting the idea of a truly egalitarian society, one in which blacks and whites in all walks of life could mingle freely and easily. But as critics have pointed out, instead of breaking down contemporary racial stereotypes, Maria may in actuality have helped to reinforce them. Carolyn Karcher in her analysis of the novel has suggested that the conventions of nineteenth-century antislavery fiction, a genre largely shaped by middle-class white women, severely restricted Child's exploration of both slavery and alternative social orders. "By dictating a romance plot involving refined heroines, by proscribing frank treatment of sexuality and violence, and by imposing a white middle-class code of values as the ideal toward which all were to aspire, antislavery fiction reproduces and may well have reinforced the ideological assumptions that marginalized the masses of American blacks and circumscribed the freedom of white women."[19]

A Romance of the Republic succeeds in highlighting America's social ills: the racism, sexism, and class antagonisms plaguing the nation. But the novel ultimately fails in its effort to portray a future egalitarian social order. While this failure can be traced to the limits imposed by the genre of romantic fiction, it also stems from Maria's apparent inability to really imagine what such a society would be like. Despite the fact that there are three interracial marriages in the book, the old stereotypes of subservient women, docile blacks, and dominant white males persist. Even in appearance, the American multiracial family as portrayed in *A Romance of the Republic* has hardly altered, its members ranging in complexion from white to beige instead of white to black.[20]

When the novel was ready for distribution, Maria expressly asked for no advance publicity. She wanted no public mention of what the story was about. "Let it speak for itself, as it comes out," she urged Fields. Once out, however, sales of the book proved disappointing and notices brief or nonexistent. Particularly galling was the response of Maria's friends. Most said nothing. Joseph Carpenter and Frank Shaw were among the few who took the trouble to speak in the book's favor. Lucy Osgood announced quite frankly that she had not liked the subject. In January 1868, after the novel had been out more than a year, Maria confessed to Louisa Loring that *A Romance of the Republic* had brought her "a great deal of disappointment and humiliation" and that the lukewarm response was having a very depressing effect on her. "When I completed the book, I felt as if I could write another and better novel, and was full of earnestness to set about it; but the apathy of my friends took all the life out of me, and has made me feel as if I never wanted to put pen to paper again."[21]

Critics of *A Romance of the Republic* have various explanations for the novel's poor reception. William Osborne suggests that its sentimental, suspenseful, and contrived plot was more suited to the 1830s than the 1860s, that postwar readers wanted more realistic fiction. But this does not explain the strangely chilly response of Maria's closest friends. Perhaps a clue lies in Lucy Osgood's claim that she did not like the subject. Interracial marriage was no less distasteful to many Northerners in 1867 than it had been in 1824 when Maria published *Hobomok*. The idea may actually have seemed more threatening following the emancipation of the slaves. The belief in Anglo-Saxon superiority flourished at mid-century, and only a radical few among the abolitionists openly encouraged a mingling of the races.[22] Was Maria, loyal as ever to her youthful vision of a better world in which race no longer mattered, simply trying to make interracial mariage more acceptable to the tastes of the day?

The cool response to *A Romance of the Republic* left Maria deeply hurt. She had put her whole self into the novel, which combines better than anything else she wrote the idealistic and reformist strains in her thinking. Writing the book had also brought some color and passion back into her drab life. It had allowed her imagination to escape the harsh New England winters for balmier climes, to transform the spare surroundings of her own bleak homestead into a lush, tropical world adorned with flowers and filled with music.

By the late 1860s, Maria's need for cheer and warmth heightened as David's health deteriorated. For most of 1866 he had been sick with chronic diarrhea and Maria was almost at her wit's end trying to keep him quiet and out of trouble. A terrible attack the night before Thanksgiving kept them home eating boiled rice for lunch, but the following day David insisted on driving his wagon into Boston to do some errands. As he was crossing the Mill Dam a carriage hit him and threw him violently onto the curbstone. Fortunately some people came to his rescue. After dressing his wounds, which were minor, and repairing the broken carriage, they sent him home. He reached Wayland by ten that evening, grateful that his neck was not broken, and calling himself "the most lucky, unlucky man that ever lived."[23]

David recovered quickly from his bruises, but his chronic ills continued. Time after time invitations from friends to visit or dine had to be turned down. "Clearly, I was not sent into the world to be entertained," Maria told Louisa in early December; "or if I was, *that* part of the universe is a decided failure." David's health was better in the summer of 1867 but by the autumn several bad falls had left him lame and stiff with rheumatism. "He *will* undertake so *many* things, and work *so* hard!" Maria complained to Lydia Child. "Just now he is making cider, and making sugar, and pointing a stone wall, and repairing a shed, and building an arch over a rain-water cistern, and plastering his bath-house. He had 9 teeth out lately, preparatory to having a new set, and after they were drawn, he walked nine miles from the dentist's home; having missed the cars. I wonder he is alive, he does so many imprudent things; but thanks to the Heavenly Father, he comes safely out of all his perils."[24]

Meanwhile, Maria's friends, knowing how much she fretted over her isolation in Wayland, continued to urge her to move closer to the city where she would have more distractions and stimulations. Her reply was invariably the same: she is tired of "being knocked about 'from post to pillar' "; she can't earn enough to afford a home in or near Boston; David's precarious health would suffer from any change of routine; and, finally, their present situation limits David to harmless pursuits. As she explained to Sarah Shaw, "If his energies had not these safe and healthy occupations, he would inevitably spend them on projects at once unprofitable and expensive."[25]

In the spring of 1868 the Childs made plans for an extended visit with friends in and around Boston. But this long-awaited excursion was doomed from the start. An invitation to stay with Anna Loring Dresel's family fell through when her children came down with scarlet fever. Then David had a relapse of his own illness. The couple finally left Wayland on April 27. Upon reaching Boston, they stopped first at the Sewalls, where all was in confusion "with the great housecleaning which mars every Spring for housekeepers." Meanwhile, Lucy Osgood sent word that she would not be able to receive them, having been called unexpectedly to Philadelphia. Most discouraging of all, they found Louisa Loring alarmingly ill. "I had an uncomfortable feeling of being in everyone's way," Maria wrote Eliza Scudder after an early return to Wayland. When an invitation came from Marianne Silsbee to visit her in Salem, Maria politely but firmly declined. "I think my attempt to make a visit to Boston has used up all my enterprise in that way for a long time to come."[26]

After the rush and confusion of the city, Wayland for once seemed a welcome refuge. Now that warmer weather had returned Maria had the pleasure of her flower garden. She also enjoyed visits from her younger neighbors. The Cutting children, who spent the summers on an adjoining farm, often stopped by in the morning to ask Mr. Child about the weather and to talk with Mrs. Child about her flowers. Alfred Cutting was a particular favorite. "My next door neighbor's little boy has me completely under his thumb, merely by virtue of his beautiful eyes and sweet voice," Maria told a friend. She composed verses for the boy and exchanged letters with him each winter after he and his family had returned to Boston. By this time, her longing for children of her own had deepened, as one by one her links with the past were broken. Anna Loring Dresel's little daughter was another favorite. "A visible little fairy. I should get foolishly fond of her, if I saw her much," Maria confessed to Sarah Shaw, "for my old heart will not unlearn its trick of loving. I feel latterly, more than I ever did, what a misfortune it is not to have had children. I should dote on grandchildren."[27]

Meanwhile, a host of public issues competed for her attention. Following the overwhelming Republican victory in the elections of 1866, Andrew Johnson's reconstruction program had been successfully overpowered by the Radicals. They were now seeking to impeach him. A vote in the House on February 24, 1868, had upheld the impeachment charges, and Johnson was put on trial in the Senate on March 4. "I am glad Andy Johnson is impeached at last," Maria declared shortly after the trial got underway. But she wished "the terms of indictment had expressed something about the slaughter of loyal whites and blacks, and the sufferings and discouragements of the freed people, caused by his nefarious 'policy.' " In the end the President failed by one vote to be convicted in the Senate, and attention soon turned to the election of his successor.[28]

"Taking all things into consideration, the nation *might* fare worse than it would be likely to in the hands of General Grant," Maria had written in March of the Union general's proposed candidacy for the Republican nomination. As she wrote to Samuel Sewall, she would have preferred a good Radical like Sumner. In the same letter she spoke much more disparagingly of the recent alliance between Elizabeth Cady Stanton and George Francis Train. Flamboyant, wealthy, but unreliable, Train was an ambitious Democrat who hoped to further his career by promoting a woman suffrage amendment in Kansas. "I am sorry Mrs. Stanton carries such a *Train* with her," Maria quipped. "I think it is an error of judgment. The question of Woman's Right to Suffrage requires more than any *other* reform, great care to avoid making it ridiculous." Such eccentric alliances as that between Train and Stanton did little to endear Maria to the radical wing of the woman suffrage movement.[29]

In the winter and spring of 1868 Maria's attention was diverted to an old cause, the plight of the American Indian. While the Civil War had raged in the eastern half of the nation the western half had been marked by persistent conflict between the Plains Indians and advancing white settlers. Open warfare had erupted in November 1864 following the bloody and unprovoked massacre of the Cheyennes at Sand Creek in eastern Colorado. This, along with mounting evidence of fraud and corruption, alerted the federal government to the need for a new Indian policy. To this end, an Indian Peace Commission was established. Early in 1868 it published a lengthy report. After lashing out against the evils of the existing system, the commissioners defended "the savage ferocity" of the Indians as a natural response to centuries of ill-treatment. Had these tribes not been driven back from civilization, their "passions might have been subjected to the influences of education and softened by the lessons of Christian charity." The commissioners' solution to the Indian crisis included kindlier treatment and the eventual absorption of the Native Americans into white civilization.[30]

Maria came close to shedding tears of joy when she read the Indian Peace Commissioners' report. "We have, at last, an Official Document which manifests something like a right spirit toward the poor Indians!" she exclaimed in a letter published in the *Standard* and later reprinted in pamphlet form. Here she found ground for hope that Anglo-Saxons as well as Indians were capable of civilization. But despite her enthusiasm over the tone of the report, Maria disagreed with the commissioners in a number of particulars. She strongly objected, for example, to their charge that the Indians' "barbarous language should be blotted out" and only English taught in their schools. This, she said, "partakes too much of haughty Anglo-Saxon ideas of force." Instead, she suggested that schoolbooks be printed at first in Indian with English translations. Drawing on the example of her own *Freedmen's Book*, she suggested that these primers include Indian folk tales as well as edifying accounts of Indian warriors.[31]

While Maria's criticism of the federal report revealed her greater sensitivity to the Native Americans' predicament, and questioned some of the means the commissioners favored for improving the Indians' lot, she had no quarrel with their ends. In common with other humanitarians, Maria could imagine no other alternative but to civilize these "peoples less advanced than ourselves." If she abhorred all evidence of pride and contempt in their treatment, she nonetheless insisted that the Indians be "protected, instructed and encouraged, till they are capable of appreciating and sharing all our advantages."[32]

Maria concluded her plea on behalf of the Indians by decrying the tendency of government officials to justify even their worst policies with biblical quotes. Indian removal, she claimed, was now vindicated, much as slavery once was, with verses from the Old Testament. How must such a religion appear to the Indians, "who have always believed in One Great Spirit, the Father of the whole human race? No wonder there has been so little success in attempts to convert them to Christianity. Their ideas of politeness prevent them from ever ridiculing or contradicting the theological opinions of other people; but when missionaries told them of a hell, where sinners were punished to all eternity, perhaps there was some latent sarcasm in their reply, 'If there be such a place, it must be for white men only.' "[33]

After a lifetime of observing Scripture employed as a weapon of subjugation, Maria was readier than ever to dispute those who claimed too much for Christianity. "My sense of justice is roused when I see the tendency to assume that all the wisdom of the world originated in Jesus," she wrote Lucy Osgood in 1870. She had been delighted, therefore, when a group of radical Unitarians had drawn up plans for an independent religious body unfettered by Christian creeds. Called the Free Religious Association, its members held their first convention in Boston in 1867. Among those attending were Emerson and Bronson Alcott. The intention of these religious radicals was to promote free religion as an idea, not as an institution, and to adapt their thinking to modern forms of culture and science, such as the emerging theory of evolution, rather than to an outmoded theology. Maria couldn't help observing that the Free Religious Association, by refusing to admit the truth or falsity of any creed, was based on precisely the same principles as her *Progress of Religious Ideas*. "It has been a great hindrance to genuine progress," she announced in a letter to the *Standard* in the summer of 1868, "that religion has not been free, and freedom has not been religious." People cannot have faith prescribed for them. "They may outwardly conform, but belief grows out of the individual soul which no man can arrange for another."[34]

But if Maria was ready to replace an outmoded Christianity with a liberal, dynamic, and all-inclusive world faith, she was not ready to give up the Protestant ethic. Christianity was still in her view the best teacher of morals, because it was "heir to the antecedent growth of the world, added some of its own, and has been ever since receiving contributions from progressive thought." And she was firm in insisting that Protestantism alone could coexist comfortably with republican institutions. The continuing fraternization between American Catholics and the Democratic Party alarmed her. By the early seventies she was labeling the Roman Catholic Church freedom's worst enemy and blaming it for the difficulties European nations were having in establishing republican governments.[35]

As ever, Maria's dream for humanity was to do away with all false distinctions. She was certain that the division of people into classes according to sex, sect, color, or employment had greatly retarded the progress of society. And, while she rejoiced to see the advances made by reformers like herself who had worked to free the slave, enlarge women's rights, and promote free religion, she was nonetheless aware that other signs pointed to widening divisions in postwar America. The competitive, monopolistic, and exploitative tendencies of modern industry, for example, had succeeded in widening, not diminishing, the gap between rich and poor. Even as the fortunes of successful entrepreneurs reached new heights, the income of workers had declined. Wage-earning factory operatives, now the majority of laborers in America, were expected to work longer hours under deteriorating conditions. As all prospects for future advancement and independence dimmed, workers aligned themselves against their employers to protest this wage slavery.[36]

From her outpost in Wayland, Maria observed with mounting unease this schism between employer and employee. She had little trouble deciding where to put the blame: "It began with the rich setting themselves above labor," she announced in 1871, which in turn had encouraged a "universal tendency to consider labor a degradation, and excited a general scramble after gentility." Maria made it plain that while she had the workers' best interests at heart, she had little sympathy with the coercive methods used to forward those interests. For example, although she was ready to admit that strikes called public attention to injustices, she feared that the fierce antagonisms they generated would prove injurious to both sides. She had a similar objection to the eight-hour law, which men like Wendell Phillips were promoting. "I believe money and labor ought to be left to regulate themselves, without any interference of government." Human beings, she maintained, could not be made equal by legislation. For her, as for others of her generation, equality meant giving every man and woman an equal chance to use his or her own powers. It did not mean guaranteeing them a certain wage or standard of living. Maria's solution to the growing antagonism between capital and labor was not coercion but cooperation. "We need a system by which all shall become workers, and thereby all shall become capitalists," she wrote in May 1871. But she had no practical suggestions for achieving this beyond emulating the Shakers and other small-scale cooperative efforts. How such systems could be adapted to the cutthroat American business world of the 1870s she did not say.[37]

In January 1870, unusually mild weather and a promised reunion with old friends persuaded the Childs to make a rare winter visit to Boston. The occasion was the last official gathering of New England abolitionists. Now that the Fifteenth Amendment appeared certain of ratification, many crusaders, including William Lloyd Garrison, considered their "pledge to the Negro race" fulfilled. The Childs, however, shared Wendell Phillips' view that neither the government nor the churches could be trusted to do the work of reformers—to make the cause of the colored people their own. "We must not consider ourselves dismissed from service," they told the friends of antislavery. At the same time, like other aging abolitionists, Maria and David were eager to rest from their long labors and ready to celebrate the great work they had accomplished.[38]

At the Subscription Festival, held as usual the evening before the annual meeting, friends had convened to honor veteran crusaders like the Childs. "There were many interesting people there, and everybody seemed disposed to make much of us," Maria later reported to Lucy Osgood. But she found the whole affair confusing and fatiguing: "so many introductions, that there was no chance for five minutes chat with any one." Her own ambivalence about the dissolution of the organized antislavery movement also made it hard for her to rejoice over a job well done. As she told Lucy, "The colored people and the loyal white people of the South, write us too many letters describing their persecutions and their dangers, and imploring us to stand by them, and say *for* them that which they dare not say for themselves."[39]

A greater cause for celebration was the birth of the Massachusetts Woman Suffrage Association. The Childs had been among the signers of a published invitation to attend the founding meeting on January 28, and at 10 A.M. that day Maria was among the friends of the crusade who gathered in Horticultural Hall to launch the new society. Several prominent suffragists addressed the gathering, including Julia Ward Howe and Mary Livermore. "Mrs. Howe talks sensibly and philosophically," Maria reported to Eliza Scudder, "and her manner is lady-like and dignified; but the strait jacket of propriety, with which 'elegant society' invested her in her youth, fetters the freedom of her soul." By contrast, Maria found Mary Livermore an "electrifying" speaker. This "product of the untramelled West" displayed "a good deal of argumentative power." "She introduces many little humorous anecdotes and illustrations, which contrast well with touches of genuine pathos, and even of sublimity."[40]

Following her return to Wayland, Maria spent every free moment collecting books and other articles for a colony of freedmen in Georgia. She feared that the Ku Klux Klan, a growing menace, might cut off her supply lines. Meanwhile, her interest in national affairs continued. In 1871 she wrote an introduction for a published collection of George Julian's speeches as a Radical Republican congressman.[41]

A year later, as campaigning got underway for the 1872 presidential election, Maria found herself caught in the crossfire between her idol Charles Sumner and his declared enemy President Grant. Sumner had never forgiven Grant for his effort to annex the Dominican Republic. This was an admittedly ill-advised scheme, but the senator's opposition had cost him the chairmanship of the prestigious Foreign Relations Committee. For this and other reasons he refused to back the president in his bid for reelection, choosing instead to campaign for the Democratic candidate, Horace Greeley.

Maria, who despised the Democrats and had long distrusted Greeley for his conciliatory attitude toward the rebellious South, was backing Grant. Thus Sumner's vitriolic attacks on the president put her in a cruel position. When she defended the Massachusetts senator in print against the "calumnies of the Grantites," she was immediately assumed to be supporting Greeley. Difficult as it was to publicly air any disagreement with Sumner, she felt she had no choice but to declare Greeley's candidacy "an incalculable calamity to the country." When Sumner personally reproached her for failing to understand his motives, she was deeply hurt but determined to stand her ground. "Painful as it is to have him feel so, I will endure it, rather than utter a syllable that can be twisted into an expression of toleration of the Democratic Party." This rupture in their friendship was never healed, and when news of Sumner's death reached her in March 1874, Maria was filled with sadness and remorse. "He was my ideal of a hero, more than any of the great men in our national history," she wrote Sarah Shaw. "I almost worshipped him."[42]

In February 1872 Maria celebrated her seventieth birthday. Her own health was good, but she watched with sadness as one by one old friends and relatives sickened and died. Louisa Loring's death four years before in May 1868 had been followed by Henrietta Sargent's in 1869, the same year in which Maria nursed her older brother James through his last illness. In June 1873 she said farewell to her old childhood friend Lucy Osgood. That September she also learned of the death of Edmund Benson, one of many friends from her New York years. To her great surprise, Benson, who had amassed a considerable fortune, left her a legacy of $7800. She was overwhelmed, but also grateful. Once invested, the interest from this sum would add $400 to the Childs' annual income, bringing it to $1200.[43]

The Childs were hardly rich even by the day's standard, but they now had enough for their own simple needs. For the first time in her married life, Maria was relieved of all financial anxiety about the future. Most important perhaps, Benson's bequest enabled her to hire some badly needed help. By the spring of 1874 David, weakened by illness, could no longer work out of doors. What with nursing and caring for the house, Maria had more than enough to keep her busy. Characteristically, she employed a reformed drunkard to run errands and take over David's chores. By summer she also had efficient indoor help. Lucy Ann Pickering, a genteel widow who had once worked for the Lorings, arrived sometime in June and relieved Maria of much of the cooking, cleaning, and washing. Maria now spent most of her time by her husband's bedside, sorting old papers and writing occasional letters and articles for the newspapers. She marveled at David's patience. Despite severe pain, he was never irritable.[44]

By early August, repeated attacks of dyspepsia had left David so weak that Maria feared to leave his bedside for more than an hour. His last attack came in mid-September. For three days he was wracked by continual sharp pain. Then, near midnight on September 17, the pain suddenly ceased. David fell asleep "gently and peacefully as a tired babe," his head resting on Maria's shoulder.[45]

21

Free to the Last

Not for brief days thy generous sympathies
Thy scorn of selfish ease;
Not for the poor prize of an earthly goal
Thy strong uplift of soul.
—J. G. Whittier, "Within the Gate"

Kind words poured in from friends in the days following David's death, but nothing eased Maria's loneliness and desolation. Her husband, her child, the chief companion of her old age, was gone. In many respects their last years together had been happy ones. The deep gulf that had opened between them in the 1840s had closed. Money problems had eased, cooling Maria's anger and frustration. The urgent ambitions and desires of her youth and middle age no longer troubled her. Each had depended on the other, but Maria's principal fear had been that her husband would outlive her, that there would be no one to care for him when she was gone.

David's departure reduced the Wayland house to a lifeless, empty shell, and Maria's one thought was to move out as soon as possible. She would spend the winter visiting friends and then look for another place to live, preferably two rooms in a house where she could be cared for. In a frenzy of activity she and Lucy Ann Pickering went through the house sorting its contents. Old clothes of David's were mailed off to nephews. Presents which friends had sent her over the years were returned. In the end she kept enough furniture to fill two rooms. These pieces, along with her remaining possessions, were placed in storage to await her return in the spring.

It was mid-November before Maria finally left the empty Wayland house. After a week of staying with friends and relatives in

291

and around Boston she headed south to Staten Island to spend the winter with the Shaws. "I have a pretty, sunshiny room all to my-self," she wrote her niece Abby Francis, after settling into the house overlooking the Hudson River. The view from her window was "alive with sea-gulls, sloops and steam-boats." The room's furnish-ings had been used by Colonel Robert Shaw. But after the simplicity of her life with David, the unaccustomed luxury of her new sur-roundings made her feel bewildered and confused and perhaps a bit guilty about fleeing the reminders of David so fast.[1]

While living with the Shaws, Maria spent most of the time in her room, sewing and knitting for asylums and hospitals, making and mending for herself. She came down for meals or for a walk, but if guests arrived she retreated back upstairs. When all the Shaw relatives gathered for Christmas, Maria escaped into New York City and spent the day with Rosa Hopper, who was now a widow. On Christmas Eve she went to a party for poor children where an old abolitionist colleague, Oliver Johnson, impersonated Santa Claus. Back in Staten Island all she could think of was the empty Wayland house. "My heart yearns more and more toward my humble little nest," she wrote an old neighbor. "I know it can never again be what it *was*; but I think it will seem *more* home-like than any other place can."[2]

Maria returned to Wayland in early April 1875, where snow-drifts and impassable roads prevented her from moving back into her own house. She spent a month with kindly neighbors. But, "like a hungry child lost in a dark wood," she could not "banish the desolate feeling that I belong to nobody and nobody belongs to me." A month later she was home with Lucy Ann Pickering for company and felt comforted by the familiar surroundings.[3]

Maria's friends were appalled that even without David she in-sisted on maintaining her reclusive ways. But in the end, except during the coldest months, the old Wayland house remained home. Although the Shaws tried to persuade her to return to Staten Island the following winter, she stubbornly insisted on boarding with neighbors—an experience which left her utterly forlorn. Once back in her own house that spring, her spirits revived. In May 1876, feeling more like her old frisky self, she went into Boston for a visit. On her way back home she stopped in Concord to pay a promised call on the Alcotts. The household delighted her. She had a long, cozy chat with her girlhood friend Abba, "talking over the dear old eventful times." She was pleased to discover that Louisa Alcott, the author of *Little Women*, was unspoiled by fame. She even had words of praise for old Bronson, whose philosophic musings had once bored and bewildered her. He "has an architectural taste more intelligible than his Orphic Sayings," she reported to Sarah Shaw, describing with delight the old house with its "queer nooks and corners, and all manner of juttings in and out." Perhaps this feckless breadwinner, with his unsung mechanical gifts, reminded her of David. But what pleased her most about the whole Alcott family was their straightforwardness and sincerity. As she told Sarah,

> They have a Christian hatred of lionizing; and the Leo Hunters are a very numerous and impertinent family. Moreover, they don't like conventional *fetters* any better than I do. There have been many attempts to saddle and bridle me, and teach me to keep in respectable processions; but they have never got the lasso over my neck *yet*; and "old hoss" as I am now, if I see the lasso in the air, I snort and gallop off, determined to be a free horse to the last, and put up with the consequent lack of grooming and stabling.[4]

Maria and Lucy Ann Pickering spent the winter of 1876-1877 in rented rooms at 7 Groton Street in Boston's South End. They ate all their meals out—breakfast in a bakery and dinner in a restaurant. Maria much preferred this bohemian existence to sharing a dining room with other boarders. A Boston writer named Elizabeth Ward later remembered being taken to call on this legendary figure in her drab surroundings. "I felt a certain awe upon me, as if I were visiting a martyr in prison," Ward admitted. After climbing the steep stairs of the boardinghouse, she and her companion entered a little sittingroom as colorless as a monk's cell. Ward couldn't help noting how sadly the poverty of that interior "contrasted with the rich nature of its occupant." Maria, who was alone at the time, greeted her visitors warmly, regaling them with stories of old antislavery days. As she talked, a sudden shaft of pale sunlight lightened the somber interior. Interrupting her story, Maria rose quickly, and, taking a little prism, hung it in the window. Instantly, the room filled with rainbows and she, standing in the midst of them, smiled at her guests as if to say, "You see I have not much to offer; but I give you of my best."[5]

Despite a steadily increasing procession of callers, Maria's days in the city were spent quietly. She wrote letters and occasional articles. But mostly she read. In these years nothing pleased her more than a new book by George Eliot. "Oh dear! what *shall* I do, now that 'Daniel Deronda' is finished," she wrote Sarah Shaw. "It has been the one solitary excitement in my life since 1876 came in." Maria considered Eliot by far the best living novelist, "an empress among women," who combined "masculine power with feminine grace." On Sundays Maria was a regular attendant at the meetings of the Free Religious Association. February 11, her birthday, was filled with little pleasures. In the morning she heard a lecture on revivals, followed by dinner with the Sewalls at their home on Park Street. The day ended with a lecture on Swedenborg at Horticultural Hall. By the time Maria returned home that evening she had climbed seven sets of stairs and her back was tired. But, as she wrote a Wayland neighbor, "I had improved my mind, and refreshed my heart, and the flowers and kindness of my friends rested me."[6]

Maria even made a new friend that winter. Anne Whitney, a neoclassical sculptor then in her fifties, wrote asking if she could make a bust of her. Maria warmly but firmly declined. While she felt greatly honored by the proposal, she told Whitney she had "too much reverence for the high mission of Art to consent to its being desecrated by the portraiture of my old visage." She would, however, be happy to become better acquainted. The Yankee artist was just Maria's sort. A small, energetic woman, Whitney was known for her acerbic wit. She fervently supported abolitionism and women's rights but sidestepped organized reform, preferring to crusade through her art. Over the course of her long life she produced portrait busts of many eminent nineteenth-century figures, including Garrison, Sumner, Stowe, and Mary Livermore. Anne Whitney was the last of Maria Child's many artistic protegées. When James Redpath, the biographer of John Brown, was looking for someone to sculpt a bust of the old warrior, Maria recommended Anne Whitney as having "more than talent; she has decided *genius* for sculpture."[7]

Whitney also took Maria under *her* wing. She even tried to tempt her into moving into her house on Mount Vernon Street. But Maria characteristically resisted such well-meant efforts. "I am an irreclaimable Bohemian, eschewing above all things, both the fetters and expenses of gentility," she explained in a letter to this new friend, adding with questionable candor that she was "most at home among plain farmers and mechanics."[8] In these last years Maria was determined to live her life as she wished. Putting aside all efforts to please others, she preferred to reside in small, unfashionable rented rooms, eat out when and where she wished, and hang up her prism to catch the light.

Once back in Wayland the following summer, however, Maria complained of having no real friends in whom she could confide. The anguish following David's death had subsided but she missed his companionship. "We sympathized so much in our opinions and pursuits," she told her niece Sarah Parsons, "that I let every thought bubble forth as it would, sure of a hearty response." She couldn't do the same with her companion, Lucy Ann Pickering. Mrs. P., as she called her, was all kindness and conscientiousness, but her genteel pride and conservatism inhibited spontaneous confidences.[9]

Among the subjects Mrs. P. disdained was spiritualism. Since David's death, Maria in her loneliness had made several unsuccessful attempts to communicate with him through professional mediums. Then Mrs. P., in an effort to demonstrate that the whole business of receiving messages from the dead was a sham, had experimented with a planchette (ouija board) herself. To her mortification she displayed her own mediumistic gifts by tapping out in the dark the name of a deceased friend. Other messages followed, convincing Maria that through Mrs. P. she was really communicating with David and others in the spirit world.[10]

While these tapped messages buoyed Maria's sagging faith in the existence of an afterlife, they hardly reconciled her to the more fraudulent aspects of the spiritualist movement. "In common with most thoughtful minds," she wrote Thomas Wentworth Higginson in 1879, "I have been repelled by the low communications, and the disgusting trickery of many of the professional mediums." But, as she explained to Higginson, if the years had made her more skeptical of spiritual fads, they had magnified her interest in religious questions.[11]

In the summer of 1877 Maria began gathering materials for what she called her "eclectic Bible," a collection of religious writings reflecting the liberal spirit of the Free Religious Association but designed for the general reader. As she described her anthology to James T. Fields, "I have put Oriental and Grecian ideas into a plain English dress." *Aspirations of the World*, Maria's last book, was in print by May 1878. She assured Fields that she didn't expect to make any money from it. Nor did she expect it to enhance her literary reputation. Before she died, however, she did want "to do something more towards loosening the fetters with which old superstitions shackle the minds of men."[12] *Aspirations of the World* contained edited extracts of holy writings from various ages and nations. Maria wished to show the ordinary reader how much there is "in which all mankind agree," and tried her best to be impartial.

"I do not assume that any one religion is right in its theology, or that any others are wrong. I merely attempt to show that the primeval impulses of the human soul have been essentially the same everywhere; and my impelling motive is to do all I can to enlarge and strengthen the bond of human brotherhood."[13]

Friends responded warmly to *Aspirations of the World* but sales were slow.[14] Despite the author's avowed impartiality, critics had little trouble identifying her personal religious prejudices. In her eagerness to avoid theology, for example, Maria had omitted the great Protestant divines in favor of such freethinkers as Emerson and Octavius B. Frothingham. But if the book's reception disappointed her, she was philosophical about it. At the age of seventy-six there was little to be gained or lost by espousing even an outmoded radicalism.

Maria published little more in these last years, but her interest in a wide range of political, social, and cultural issues did not lessen. Like other veteran reformers she had wearied of trying to do good. But how could she remain silent amidst the mounting corruption of the postwar Gilded Age? The continued harsh and oppressive treatment of southern blacks concerned her deeply. Nor could she ignore widening divisions in American society. There were times, such as during the great railroad strike of 1877, when she was certain such confrontations between capital and labor would destroy the republic.[15] Still, the old optimism refused to die. How else could she justify her own lifelong struggle to bring about the millennium?

On October 8, 1879, Maria was sitting in her rented parlor in Dover Street, Boston, watching the crowd of strangers hurrying past her window. "Like ants in an ant-hill," she observed in a letter to Frank Shaw. She admitted she found the comparison mortifying, since, like humans, ants "make war upon each other, and one tribe carries off another tribe as prisoners, and makes slaves of them." But there was a reassuring difference between the two species: "ants don't produce abolitionists. Let us comfort ourselves with that reflection. . . . The world *does* slowly become wiser and better, as the centuries roll on," she assured him. "You and I have tried to help onward the process; and if we have accomplished ever so little, it is something to be thankful for."[16]

Maria returned home to Wayland for the last time in the spring of 1880. That June she suffered an acute attack of rheumatism and spent most of the summer confined to her bed. Increasing frailty convinced her to remain in Wayland that winter. Anne Whitney, who knew how much Maria profited from her months in the city, was dismayed by the news. "There is a little leaven of offishness in you, that will not allow of the best things possible falling to you," Whitney crossly but shrewdly observed in a letter chastising Maria for deciding not to come to Boston.[17]

On September 23 Maria wrote cheerfully to Sarah Shaw that she had all kinds of plans for the good deeds she would do when she felt better. Rheumatism, however, continued to trouble her. A friend who visited the house in mid-October found her lame but comfortable and full of interest in the coming election. On the morning of October 20 she awoke feeling remarkably well. Then, just as she was getting ready to leave her bedroom, she complained to Mrs. P. of a severe pain in her chest. Within an hour Maria Child was dead of heart failure.[18]

Three days later, on a blustery fall day, friends and neighbors gathered at the house for a private funeral service. Wendell Phillips gave the eulogy, bidding farewell to his old friend and colleague with characteristic eloquence. He began by claiming her as a true New Englander, the finest fruit of the region's theology, traditions, and habits. As Maria herself a few years earlier had praised George Eliot for blending "masculine vigor with feminine grace," so Wendell Phillips in a characteristic Victorian way spoke of Maria Child as combining in her person "all the charms and graceful elements which we call feminine . . . with a masculine grasp and vigor." Her life, he said, had been governed by the divine rule "Bear ye one another's burdens," yet its pains and sorrows had never conquered her. Despite her advanced years, she "had still the freshness of girlhood, the spirits nothing could dull or quench; the ready wit, quick retort, mirthful jest." Phillips spoke too of her remarkable courage. "We felt that neither fame, nor gain, nor danger, nor calumny had any weight with her." She "was ready to die for a principle and starve for an idea. . . ."[19]

After the brief service, as the plain wooden coffin was being removed from the house on its way to the cemetery, a flock of blackbirds perching on a nearby tree broke into song, a fitting tribute, one neighbor observed, to one who had loved nature so well.[20] Many years earlier Maria had spoken of her wish to be buried in a Negro cemetery, but instead her coffin was placed next to David's in the old Wayland burial ground. Claiming that a spirit hand had traced her epitaph she had asked that the following words be placed on her tombstone: "You think us dead. We are not dead. We are truly living now."

Epilogue

Aﬁ fter her death Lydia Maria Child's estate was valued at more than $36,000. For a woman whose married life had been burdened with financial worries she died remarkably well off. The previous summer she had signed a will bestowing handsome bequests on needy friends and relatives and a variety of worthy causes. Eight thousand dollars was designated for Lucy Ann Pickering. Hampton College in Virginia would get $2,000. So would the Homeopathic Hospital in Concord. One thousand dollars was earmarked for the Home for Old Colored Women in Boston, and another $1,000 was to be used for "the elevation of the character of women, and the enlargement of their sphere." The list was a lengthy one, and the pleasure Maria derived from such largess can only be imagined.[1]

The size of Maria Child's estate is clear evidence of her ability to prosper on her own. And it raises the tempting, if speculative, question of what her life would have been like if she had never married David, what accomplishments could have been hers had she not spent so much time "pumping water into a sieve." But such speculations detract from what this remarkable woman accomplished despite her many trials. If Edgar Allen Poe was correct in describing Maria Child as someone who needed great occasions to be fully herself, perhaps it is more accurate to view the difficulties and disappointments she faced in her union with David as necessary somehow to her vigor and creativity as a writer and reformer. To see Maria Child as a tragic character, merely as the victim of gender oppression, is to obscure her ability to overcome the obstacles that lay in her path. Like the heroines of some of her early stories, she is admirable precisely because she did muster the strength to triumph over adversity.

Marriage to David not only provided Maria with the challenge she required to be fully herself, it also freed her in ways to lead the kind of life she preferred. His very fecklessness, for example, often supplied the excuse she needed to defy convention and be a working woman. What if David had made a success of his sugar beet business in Northampton? Maria might then have spent the rest of her life as a dutiful but frustrated farm wife, expending her few leisure moments in mystical musings on music or on the swallows. Instead, financial necessity freed her from "the million Lilliputian cords" and carried her to New York, where she passed some of the happiest and most productive years of her life. In this light even her childlessness can be seen as a boon.

The founders of the women's movement assumed that a woman on her own in a man's world was powerless. Maria Child set out to prove single-handedly that this was not true. As a woman who could boast for her sex no tradition of power or sense of achievement in the realm of politics, art, or culture, she found strength and support in the creative life of the spirit. Moreover, she proved by her own example that a woman could be as effective as a man in shaping and defining the issues of her day. She didn't see herself as weak or lacking in influence, and she was deeply frustrated by the presumption of men like Charles Sumner that women took no interest in public affairs.

In the end there was much for Maria to be grateful for. David had lived to a good old age; their debts had been paid and she had money to give away. If these were not the fulfilled dreams of her girlhood they were satisfactory enough. She had long believed that "in toiling for the freedom of others we shall find our own." And her life was a testimonial to that belief.

Abbreviations

AS-BPL	Antislavery Collection, Department of Rare Books and Manuscripts, Boston Public Library
C-BPL	Child Papers, Department of Rare Books and Manuscripts, Boston Public Library
C-LC	Child Papers, Manuscript Division, Library of Congress
C-MR	Child Family Papers, Milton Ross Collection, Corona del Mar, California
C-SLib	Child Papers, Schlesinger Library, Radcliffe College
C-UM	Child Papers, Clements Library, University of Michigan
C-WHS	Child Papers, Wayland Historical Society
HL	Houghton Library, Harvard University
JM	*Juvenile Miscellany*
L-APSL	J. Peter Lesley Collection, American Philosophical Society Library
L-SLib	Loring Family Papers, Schlesinger Library, Radcliffe College
LMC-AAS	Lydia Maria Child Letters, American Antiquarian Society, Worcester, Massachusetts

LMC-C	Lydia Maria Child Papers, Department of Rare Books, Cornell University Library
LMC-*L*	*Letters of Lydia Maria Child* (1882)
LMC-*LFL*	Lydia Maria Child, *Ladies Family Library*
LMC-*LNY*	Lydia Maria Child, *Letters from New York*
LMC-*SL*	*Lydia Maria Child: Selected Letters, 1817–1880* (1982)
LMC-SLib	Lydia Maria Child Papers, Schlesinger Library, Radcliffe College
MDJ	*Massachusetts Daily Journal*
MHR	*Medford Historical Register*
MHS	Medford Historical Society
Micro	Microfiche of *Collected Correspondence of Lydia Maria Child*, 1980. (Card and letter numbers are given.)
MJ	*Massachusetts Journal*
MJ&T	*Massachusetts Journal and Tribune*
MWJ	*Massachusetts Weekly Journal*
NAR	*North American Review*
NYPL	Manuscript Division, New York Public Library
Standard	*Standard* is the abbreviation of *American Anti-Slavery Standard*
W-BPL	Weston Family Papers, Department of Rare Books and Manuscripts, Boston Public Library
WHS	Wayland Historical Society
WJ	*Woman's Journal*

Notes

Please note that except for those letters which are published in whole or in part in *Lydia Maria Child: Selected Letters, 1817–1880* (1982), the sources for published letters found in the microfiche of the *Collected Correspondence of Lydia Maria Child* are not listed in the notes. These are referred to solely as "micro."

Introduction

1. John Greenleaf Whittier, "Introduction," LMC-*L*, x.
2. L. M. Child to William Lloyd Garrison, 2 September 1839, LMC-*SL*, 123, micro 8/186.
3. L. M. Child to Maria White, 20 July 1842, HL, micro 12/294.
4. L. M. Child to Lucy Osgood, 28 June 1846, LMC-*SL*, 227, micro 23/660.
5. L. M. Child to Sarah Shaw, 20 February 1857, HL, micro 36/992.

1. The Baker's Daughter

1. L. M. Child to Lucy Osgood, 26 March 1847, LMC-C, micro 25/705.
2. Anna D. Hallowell, "Lydia Maria Child," MHR (July 1900), 96.
3. L. M. Child, "Boys of Olden Times," in *A New Flower for Children* (New York: C. S. Francis & Co., 1856), 202–11; Hallowell, "Lydia Maria Child," 96; John Weiss, *Discourse Occasioned by the Death of Convers Francis* (Cambridge, 1863), 6.

4. L. M. Child to Lucy Osgood, 17 December 1870, LMC-C, micro 74/1966; Weiss, *Discourse*, 62.

5. William Newell, "Memoir of the Rev. Convers Francis," *Proceedings of the Massachusetts Historical Society*, March 1865: 236. According to one account, Convers Francis retired from business in 1816 with a fortune of $50,000. See Hallowell, "Lydia Maria Child," 96.

6. Quoted in Newell, *Memoir*, 235.

7. Margaret Kellow, "Must the Baby Go Out with the Bathwater? Psycho-history, Biography and Lydia Maria Child." Paper given at the 1988 American Studies Association Meeting.

8. Kellow, "Must the Baby," 7–9.

9. L. M. Child to John Weiss, 15 April 1863, LMC-*SL*, 425–6.

10. Ibid.

11. Walter H. Cushing, "Slavery in Medford," *MHR* (July 1900), 118–19.

12. James O. Horton and Lois E. Horton, *Black Bostonians* (New York: Holmes & Meier, 1979), vii; Jeremy Belknap, quoted in Leon F. Litwack, *North of Slavery* (Chicago: The University of Chicago Press, 1961), 8.

13. Charles Brooks, *History of the Town of Medford* (Boston: James M. Usher, 1855), 438.

14. Nothing is known of the education received by the three oldest surviving children of Convers and Susannah Francis.

15. Brooks, *History*, 283; Weiss, *Discourse*, 9; Newell, *Memoirs*, 236–37.

16. Higginson, "Lydia Maria Child," 112.

17. L. M. Child, "The New-England Boy's Song about Thanksgiving Day," in *Flowers for Children*, 2d ser. (New York: C.S. Francis & Co., 1844), 25–28; L. M. Child, "Thanksgiving Day," *JM*, 2d ser., 1 (January 1829): 261.

18. Quoted in Nancy Cott, *The Bonds of Womanhood* (New Haven: Yale University Press, 1977), 106.

19. Newell, *Memoir*, 238.

20. L. M. Child to John Weiss, 15 April 1863, LMC-*SL*, 425–26, micro 55/1476.

21. Newell, *Memoir*, 238–39.

22. L. M. Child, "Valentine Duval," *JM*, 3d ser., 1 (Nov./Dec. 1831): 201.

23. L. M. Child to Louisa Loring, 19 July 1840, L-SLib, micro 8/209; L. M. Child, "Charles Wager," *JM*, 1st ser., 3 (Nov. 1827): 164–74; L. M. Child, *The Mother's Book* (Boston: Carter, Hendee & Babcock, 1831), 129.

24. Clifford K. Shipton, "David Osgood," *Sibley's Harvard Graduates* (Boston: Massachusetts Historical Society, 1979), vol. 17, 570–83.

25. Henry C. Delong, "Some Letters of Miss Lucy Osgood," *MHR* 10 (Oct. 1907): 82; L. M. Child to Lucy Osgood, 13 April 1870, LMC-C, micro 73/1939.

26. Shipton, "David Osgood," 574.

27. Brooks, *History*, 240.

28. Ibid., 243–46; Shipton, "David Osgood," 579; Sidney A. Ahlstrom,

A Religious History of the American People (New Haven: Yale University Press, 1972), 391–92.

29. L. M. Child, *Emily Parker, or Impulse, not Principle* (Boston: Bowles & Dearborn, 1827), 9.

30. L. M. Child, "My Mother's Grave," *JM* 3 (Jan./Feb. 1833): 311–12.

31. L. M. Francis, "Maria and Frances and the Birthday Present," *JM*, 1st ser., 1 (Nov. 1826): 3–34.

32. L. M. Child, *The Mother's Book*, 75–76. In this same passage she noted that her own response to this gloomy attitude to death was a strong prejudice against wearing mourning. See also L. M. Child, "Honours Paid to the Dead," *JM*, 1st ser., 3 (Sept. 1827): 75–86. In a story Child wrote when she was in her forties she describes the awful impression made on a young girl by the sight of her dead mother with large coins placed over her eyelids: "the image followed her everywhere, even in her dreams." L. M. Child, "Elizabeth Wilson," in *Fact and Fiction* (New York: C.S. Francis & Co., 1846), 128.

33. Hallowell, "Lydia Maria Child," 96–97.

2. On the Banks of the Kennebec

1. L. M. Child, *Mother's Book*, 129.

2. L. M. Child, *Emily Parker*, 9–10. Another fictional father in a story Lydia wrote in the 1840s is described in much the same way. "Of clothing for the mind, or food for the heart, he knew nothing; for his own had never been clothed and fed. He came home weary from daily toil, ate his supper, dozed in his chair awhile, and then sent the children to bed." L. M. Child, "Elizabeth Wilson," 128.

3. See, for example, L. M. Child, "The Unlucky Day," *JM*, 1st ser., 2 (Nov. 1826): 58.

4. L. M. Child, *Emily Parker*, 19.

5. Hallowell, "Lydia Maria Child," 97; Brooks, *History*, 293. The only reference Child ever made to her year at Miss Swan's school was in a letter written in 1859. See L. M. Child to Lucy Osgood, 1 January 1859, LMC-C, micro 40/1099.

6. Cott, *Bonds of Womanhood*, 26; L. M. Child, *The American Frugal Housewife* (Boston: Carter, Hendee & Co., 1833), 93. *The Frugal Housewife*, first published in 1829, was renamed *The American Frugal Housewife* in the 1833 edition because of an English work of the same name.

7. See Whittier, "Introduction," vi.

8. Charles Henry Preston, *Descendants of Roger Preston* (Salem, MA, 1931), 176–77.

9. Elizabeth Miller, interview with author, 11 May 1987; Henrietta Danforth Wood, *Early Days of Norridgewock* (Freeport, ME: Freeport Press, 1933), 76.

10. Preston, *Descendants*, 177; Wood, *Early Days*, 75; Miller, interview with author, 11 May 1987; Miller to author, 28 May 1987.

11. Cott, *Bonds of Womanhood*, 49.

12. L. M. Child, *Emily Parker*, 14.

13. The christening dress stitched by Lydia Francis is in the collections of the Medford Historical Society; L. M. Child, *Frugal Housewife*, 16, 78.

14. L. M. Child to Marianne Silsbee, 5 February [1867], LMC-AAS, micro 66/1761a; William Allen, *The History of Norridgewock* (Norridgewock, 1849), 111.

15. Wood, *Early Days*, 76; Ronald F. Banks, *Maine Becomes a State* (Middletown, CT: Wesleyan University Press, 1970), 149.

16. J. W. Hanson, *History of the Old Towns of Norridgewock & Canaan* (Boston, 1849), 221.

17. Preston was appointed probate judge shortly after King's election as the first governor of the new state of Maine. See Allen, *History*, 105; Banks, *Maine*, 149; Hanson, *History of the Old Towns*, 251.

18. Banks, *Maine*, 183–202.

19. Miller, interview with author, 11 May 1987.

20. *General Catalogue of Middlebury College* (Middlebury, VT, 1950), 10; Allen, *History*, 196, 209–10; Hanson, *History of the Old Towns*, 245–51.

21. Mary Mackie Burgess, "Recollections," unpublished manuscript, Norridgewock Library, Norridgewock, ME; Allen, *History*, 252.

22. LMC-*LNY*, 1st ser. (New York: C. S. Francis & Co., 1845), 29.

23. John Milton, *Paradise Lost*, bk 4, lines 634–37.

24. L. Francis to C. Francis, 5 June 1817, micro 1/1.

25. A discussion of Unitarianism at Harvard can be found in Ahlstrom, *Religious History*, 394.

26. L. Francis to C. Francis, 5 June 1817, micro 1/1.

27. Whittier, "Introduction," LMC-*L*, vi.

28. L. Francis to C. Francis, 3 February 1819, micro 1/3.

29. Ibid; L. Francis to C. Francis, 21 November 1819, micro 1/4.

30. L. Francis to C. Francis, n.d., September 1817, LMC-*SL*, 2, micro 1/2 and 26 December 1819, micro 1/5.

31. L. Francis to C. Francis, 10 April 1820, micro 1/8 and 12 March 1820, LMC-*SL*, 2, micro 1/7.

32. L. M. Child, "Charles Wager," *JM*, 1st ser., 3 (Nov. 1827): 171–72.

33. Lee Chambers-Schiller, *Liberty, A Better Husband: Single Women in America: The Generation of 1780–1840* (New Haven: Yale University Press, 1984), 1.

34. *Gardiner Home Journal*, 10 August 1892, clipping in scrapbook on schools and churches, Gardiner Public Library.

35. L. M. Child, "Letter from New York," *Standard*, 19 January 1843, micro 16/444; L. Francis to ?, n.d., quoted in J.W. Hanson, *History of Gardiner, Pittston and West Gardiner* (Gardiner, ME, 1852), 216–17.

36. L. Francis to C. Francis, 10 April 1820, micro 1/8 and 31 May 1820, LMC-*SL*, 2, micro 1/9.

37. Weiss, *Discourse*, 15.

38. Perry Miller, "From Edwards to Emerson," *Errand into the Wilderness* (New York: Harper Torchbooks, Harper & Row, 1964), 184–203.
39. Whittier, "Introduction," LMC-*L*, xvii.

3. A Writer's Beginnings

1. Lydia was settled in Watertown by 1 September 1821, as on that date she was elected treasurer of the Watertown Female Society for the Relief of the Sick. See Records of First Church, Watertown Public Library, Watertown, MA.; L. M. Francis to [Mary (Francis) Preston], 26 May 1822, Walter G. Perry Collection, Westfield, NJ, micro 1/10.
2. Vital Records, Medford, MA. No record exists giving the date of the baptism, but she gave Lydia Maria as her name when she joined the Swedenborgian Church in November 1821, so it would have been before that date. See "Creed, Records, &c. relative to the Spiritual Affairs of the Boston Society of the New Jerusalem, Sept. 25: 1821 to 1841," no. 2, courtesy of Louise Woofenden; L. M. Child to Theodore Tilton, 27 May 1866, LMC-*SL*, 460, micro 65/1722.
3. Solon F. Whitney, *Historical Sketches of Watertown Massachusetts* (Watertown, 1893), 332–34.
4. Newell, "Memoir," 250; L. M. Child to C. Francis, 8 August 1858, micro 39/1073.
5. L. M. Child to Lucy Osgood, December 1862, micro 54/1447.
6. Many years later Maria wrote that her hatred of Calvinism had been nurtured by her father's fear of going to hell. See L. M. Child to [Lucy Osgood?], 17 December 1870, LMC-C, micro 74/1966.
7. Lisa Johnson Ponder, "The Making of an Abolitionist: The Early Life Jurisprudential Development of L. Maria Child, 1802 to 1833," Master's Thesis, University of Oregon, 1987; L. M. Francis to C. Francis, 31 May 1820, LMC-*SL*, 2, micro 1/9.
8. Philip F. Gura, *The Wisdom of Words: Language, Theology and Literature in the New England Renaissance* (Middletown, CT: Wesleyan University Press, 1981), 18–19.
9. An abbreviated version of Sampson Reed's "Oration on Genius" can be found in Perry Miller, *The Transcendentalists: An Anthology* (Cambridge, MA: Harvard University Press, 1950), 49–53; "Creed, Records, &c."
10. Miller, *Transcendentalists*, 49–50; "Creed, Records, &c."
11. Ahlstrom, *Religious History*, 483–86.
12. LMC-*LNY*, 2d ser., 113–14; L. M. Child to Louisa Loring, 20 June 1858, L-SLib, micro 38/1064; L. M. Child to Parke Godwin, 20 January 1856, LMC-*SL*, 275, micro 32/899.
13. L. M. Child, *The Rebels; or, Boston before the Revolution* (Boston: Cummings, Hilliard & Co., 1825), 79; L. M. Child, *Emily Parker*, 26.
14. L. M. Francis to Mary Preston, 26 May 1822, Walter G. Perry Collection, Westfield, NJ, micro 1/10. The parsonage still stands and is now a funeral home.

15. [John Gorham Palfrey], review of *Yamoyden*, *NAR* 12 (1821): 466–88.

16. Robert F. Berkhofer, *The White Man's Indian* (New York: Vintage Books, 1979), 86. In 1846 Maria told Rufus Griswold, the New York journalist, that when she wrote *Hobomok* she had "never dreamed of such a thing as turning author," but Whittier in his introduction to her *Letters* quotes her as saying that she was first inspired to write a novel after reading Scott's *Waverley*. L. M. Child to Griswold [October? 1846?], LMC-*SL*, 232, micro 23/646; Whittier, "Introduction," LMC-*L*, vi.

17. L. M. Child to Griswold [October? 1846?], LMC-*SL*, 232, micro 23/646.

18. L. M. Child, *Hobomok, A Tale of Early Times* (1824), 133. Citations used here refer to a modern edition of Lydia Maria Child's writings on Indians, Carolyn L. Karcher, ed., *Hobomok & Other Writings on Indians* (New Brunswick, NJ: Rutgers University Press, 1986).

19. I am indebted for this and other insights to Karcher's introduction to *Hobomok & Other Writings*, xxiii.

20. L. M. Child, *Hobomok*, 69.

21. Higginson, "Lydia Maria Child," 114.

22. L. M. Child, *Hobomok*, 47, 78.

23. Ibid., 35.

24. Ibid., 35, 116; Karcher, "Introduction," *Hobomok*, xxxi.

25. Quoted in Jean Fagan Yellin, *Women & Sisters: The Antislavery Feminists in American Culture* (New Haven: Yale University Press, 1990), 71.

26. Mary Kelley, *Private Woman, Public Stage* (New York: Oxford University Press, 1984), 180–83.

27. Patricia G. Holland, "Lydia Maria Child as a Nineteenth-Century Professional Author," *Studies in the American Renaissance* (1981):157–67.

28. L. M. Francis to George Ticknor, 29 March 1825, LMC-*SL*, 3–4, micro 1/11; Holland, "Lydia Maria Child," 159; review of *Hobomok*, *NAR* 19 (July 1824): 262–63.

29. David B. Tyack, *George Ticknor and the Boston Brahmins* (Cambridge, MA: Harvard University Press, 1967), 160.

30. Guy R. Woodall, ed., "The Journals of Convers Francis," pt. 1, *Studies in the American Renaissance* (1981): 324; Tyack, *Ticknor*, 160; L. M. Francis to George Ticknor, 29 March 1825, LMC-*SL*, 4, micro 1/11.

31. [Jared Sparks], "Recent American Novels," *NAR* 21 (1825): 86–95.

32. L. M. Child to Rufus Wilmot Griswold, n.d. [1845?], Frank H. Stewart Collection, Glassboro State College, Glassboro, NJ, micro 23/646.

4. A Wee Bit of a Lion

1. Walter Muir Whitehill, *Boston: A Topographical History* (Cambridge, MA: Harvard University Press, 1963); Oscar Handlin, *Boston's Immigrants: A Study in Acculturation* (New York: Athenaeum Press, 1968), 18–19.

2. Handlin, *Boston's Immigrants*, 1–24; Frederic Cople Jaher, "Nine-

teenth Century Elites in Boston and New York," *Journal of Social History* (Fall 1972): 34–63; E. Digby Baltzell, *Puritan Boston and Quaker Philadelphia* (New York: The Free Press, 1979), 200.

3. Edward Everett Hale, *A New England Boyhood* (Boston: Little, Brown, 1964), 164–65.

4. Ronald Story, *The Forging of An Aristocracy: Harvard and the Boston Upper Class, 1800–1870* (Middletown, CT: Wesleyan University Press, 1980), 7–13; Martin Green, *The Problem of Boston: Some Readings in Cultural History* (New York: Norton, 1966), 22–27.

5. Baltzell, *Puritan Boston,* 198–200; Louise Hall Tharp, *The Appletons of Beacon Hill* (Boston: Little, Brown, 1973), 104; Hallowell, "Lydia Maria Child," 100.

6. [Samuel Lorenzo Knapp], *Extracts from a Journal of Travels in North America* (Boston, 1818), 26–32.

7. Tyack, *Ticknor,* 89; Van Wyck Brooks, *The Flowering of New England* (New York: E.P. Dutton & Co., 1936), 99; Caroline Dall, "Lydia Maria Child and Mary Russell Mitford," *Unitarian Review* 19 (June 1883): 520.

8. Hannah Adams, *A Memoir of Miss Hannah Adams* (1832), 56; LMC-LNY, 2d ser., 132–33.

9. For Maria Child's recollection of prejudice against literary women, see letter to *Independent,* before 10 January 1867, micro 66/1759; L. M. Child to C. Francis, 12 July 1838, micro 6/138.

10. Matthew J. Bruccoli, ed., *The Profession of Authorship in America: The Papers of William Charvat* (Athens, OH: Ohio State University Press, 1968), 29–34; Higginson, "Lydia Maria Child," 116.

11. L. M. Child, "The First and Last Book," first published in *MJ,* 13 November 1830: 1, later in *The Coronal; A Collection of Miscellaneous Pieces, Written at Various Times* (Boston: Carter & Hendee, 1832), 282; L. M. Child, *The Rebels,* 46; L. M. Child, "The Importance of Resources within Ourselves," in "Booklet of Quotations and Poems," unpublished manuscript, LMC-C.

12. Mary Caroline Crawford, *Romantic Days in Old Boston* (Boston: Little, Brown, 1910), 10–11; Whitehill, *Boston,* 73; Hallowell, "Lydia Maria Child," 100.

13. See advertisement in *MJ,* 13 September 1827:2; L. M. Francis to M. Preston, 11 June 1826, LMC-*SL,* 7, micro 1/18.

14. Virginia Tatnall Peacock, *Famous American Belles of the Nineteenth Century* (Philadelphia: J.B. Lippincott, 1901), 91–97; Samuel Eliot Morison, *Harrison Gray Otis* (Boston: Houghton Mifflin Co., 1969), 492–96; Josiah Quincy, *Municipal History of the Town and City of Boston* (1852), 281; L. M. Child to A. Loring, 14 February 1858, L-SLib, micro 38/1046.

15. L. M. Francis to M. Preston, 11 June 1826, LMC-*SL,* 7, micro 1/18.

16. L. M. Child to M. Silsbee, 5 February 1867, LMC-AAS, micro 66/1761a.

310

17. L. M. Child, *Rebels*, 183.

18. L. M. Child, "Harriet Bruce," first published in *MJ*, 23 May 1829, later in *The Coronal*, 125–42; L. M. Child, "Happiness," *JM*, 1st ser., 2 (July 1827): 92.

19. L. M. Child, "Happiness," 92; L. M. Child to *Standard*, 27 June 1868, micro 69/1840.

20. L. M. Francis to M. Preston, 11 June 1826, LMC-*SL*, 6–8, Walter G. Perry Collection, Westfield, NJ, micro 1/18.

21. L. M. Child to Rufus Wilmot Griswold, n.d. [? October 1846?], LMC-*SL*, 232, micro 23/646.

22. L. M. Child, "George and Georgiana," *The Juvenile Souvenir* (Boston: Marsh & Capen, and John Putnam, 1828), 173; L. M. Child to L. Osgood, 15 July 1867, LMC-C, micro 65/1730; L. M. Child to S. Shaw, 11 February 1859, HL, micro 40/1102.

23. L. M. Child, *Evenings in New England* (Boston: Cummings, Hilliard & Co., 1824), iii.

24. Ibid., 10–11.

25. Ibid., 11.

26. Anne Scott Macleod, *A Moral Tale, Children's Fiction and American Culture, 1820–1860* (Hamden, CT: Shoe String Press, 1975), 25; L. M. Child to Lucy Larcom, 12 March 1873, LMC-*SL*, 511.

27. L. M. Child, *Evenings*, 138.

28. Ibid., 146.

29. Review of *Rebels*, *NAR* 22 (April 1826): 402.

30. L. M. Child, *Rebels*, 197.

31. Ibid., 78, 283.

32. Holland, "Lydia Maria Child as Author," 157; Bruccoli, *Profession of Authorship*, 34–48.

33. Maud de Leigh Hodges, *Crossroads on the Charles: A History of Watertown, Massachusetts* (Watertown, MA, 1980), 90; L. M. Francis to M. Preston, 11 June 1826, LMC-*SL*, 7, micro 1/18.

34. L. M. Francis to M. Preston, 28 August 1826, micro 1/19; L. M. Francis to Mary Preston, 6 January 1827, LMC-*SL*, 8, micro 1/23.

35. Dall, "Lydia Maria Child," 526.

36. Patricia G. Holland and Milton Meltzer, "Biography of Lydia Maria Child," in *Guide and Index* to *The Collected Correspondence of Lydia Maria Child*, 24; L. M. Child, *JM*, 1st ser., 1 (Sept. 1826): iii-iv.

37. Macleod, *Moral Tale*, 25.

38. L. M. Francis to M. Preston, 6 January 1827, LMC-*SL*, 8, micro 1/23.

39. Paula Blanchard, *Margaret Fuller: From Transcendentalism to Revolution* (New York: Delacorte Press, 1978), 61; Robert Hudspeth, ed., *The Letters of Margaret Fuller* (Ithaca: Cornell University Press, 1987), 1:56.

40. L. Osgood to L. M. Child, 8 May 1843, LMC-C, micro 17/493.

5. Maria's "Knight of Chivalry"

1. L. M. Child, "Autobiography," LMC-C.
2. Ibid.
3. Fragment of D. L. Child's diary in L. M. Child, "Autobiography," LMC-C.
4. George Ticknor Curtis, "Reminiscences of N.P. Willis and Lydia Maria Child," *Harper's New Monthly Magazine* 81 (October 1890): 719.
5. L. M. Child, "Concerning Women," newspaper clipping in "Scrapbook," LMC-C.
6. L. M. Child to F. Shaw, 2 August 1846, LMC-*SL*, 229, micro 23/664.
7. D. L. Child, *An Address Delivered at Watertown March* 4, 1825 (Boston, 1825).
8. Caleb Cushing to Daniel Webster, 17 August 1825, in Charles M. Wiltse, ed., *Papers of Daniel Webster: Correspondence, vol.* 2 (Hanover, NH: University Press of New England, 1976), 70.
9. John Mayfield, *The New Nation*, 1800–1845 (New York: Hill & Wang, 1982), 96–97; Arthur M. Schlesinger, Jr., *The Age of Jackson* (Boston: Little, Brown, 1945), 36–37.
10. *MJ*, 19 October 1826:2.
11. Daniel Webster to John C. Wright, 30 April 1827, in *Papers of Daniel Webster: Correspondence*, vol. 2; 195, 243; William Lloyd Garrison to editor of *Newburyport Herald*, 21 April 1837, in *Letters of William Lloyd Garrison*, ed. Walter M. Merrill, vol. 1, *I Will Be Heard* (Cambridge, MA: Harvard University Press, 1971), 38.
12. Fragment of D. L. Child's diary, 19 October 1827, LMC-C; Curtis, "Reminiscences," 719.
13. L. M. Child to M. Preston, 28 October 1827, LMC-*SL*, 9, micro 1/25.
14. D. L. Child to Lydia [B.] Child, 20 October 1827, C-MR.
15. Baer, *Heart is Like Heaven*, 49; Lydia Merrill, interview with author, Boston, October 1986; D. L. Child to L. [B.] Child, 7 September 1822, C-MR.
16. D. L. Child to L. [B.] Child, 2 July 1819, C-MR.
17. D. L. Child to Zachariah Child, 14 November 1824, C-MR.
18. For sample reviews of Maria's books and notice of prize, see *MJ*, 23 September 1826:3; 4 November 1826:3; 5 April 1827:4.
19. *MJ*, 20 March 1828:2; 29 March 1828:2; 15 April 1828:2.
20. Letter from subscribers to *MJ*, 20 May 1828:3; D. L. Child, Bankruptcy Petition, filed 16 December 1842, Federal Archives, Waltham, MA #2369.
21. L. M. Child to Lydia Bigelow Child, 11 July 1828, LMC-SLib, micro 1/28; L. M. Child to Lydia Bigelow Child, 26 July 1828, LMC-SLib, micro 1/29.
22. L. M. Child to M. Preston, n.d. [before October 19, 1828], micro 1/32; Curtis, "Reminiscences," 719–20.

6. "Le Paradis des Pauvres"

1. L. M. Child to Lydia [B.] Child, 14 November 1828, C-SLib, micro 1/34; L. M. Child, *Mother's Book,* 19; Mary Beth Norton, *Liberty's Daughters* (Boston: Little, Brown, 1980), 22.

2. L. M. Child to Lydia [B.] Child, 14 November 1828: C-SLib, micro 1/34; *MJ,* 18 November 1828: 2.

3. L. M. Child to Lydia B. Child, 14 January [1829], LMC-*SL,* 13, micro 1/35.

4. L. M. Child to Lydia B. Child, 11 February 1875, LMC-*SL,* 530, micro 84/2217. Maria did not sign any of her contributions to the *Journal,* but many stories and articles later published elsewhere can be found in its columns, and on 30 January 1830 David acknowledged her "constant assistance" to him on the paper. Since David's interests were historical and political, I have presumed that articles of social or literary interest, published after their marriage, are by her.

5. *Trial of the Case of the Commonwealth versus David Lee Child* (Boston, 1829), 3; Schlesinger, *Age of Jackson,* 170–71.

6. *Trial of David Child,* 10–15.

7. Ibid., 3, 82.

8. Ibid., 88–103; Ponder, "Making of an Abolitionist," 219.

9. *MJ,* 28 January 1829:4.

10. Horace Mann to Mary Peabody Mann, 2 September 1850, Mann Papers, Massachusetts Historical Society; quoted in *Review of the Report of the Case of the Commonwealth versus David Lee Child* (Boston, 1829), 11–12.

11. Ibid., 16.

12. *The Boston Annual Advertiser,* 1826; Baer, *Heart is Like Heaven,* 47.

13. D. L. Child to Webster, 3 January 1829, *Papers of Daniel Webster: Correspondence,* vol. 2, 386. Webster marked on the letter "An[swered]— declining."

14. L. M. Child to Henry A. S. Dearborn [May 1829], Massachusetts Historical Society, micro 1/37.

15. L. M. Child to George Ticknor, n.d. [1829?], LMC-*SL,* 15–16, micro 2/41.

16. *MJ,* 16 December 1828: 3; *MDJ,* 12 December 1829:3.

17. L. M. Child, *Frugal Housewife,* 95–96.

18. Ibid., 91–96; L. M. Child, "Adelaide de Montreuil," *JM,* 2d ser., 6 (May/June 1831): 196.

19. L. M. Child, *Frugal Housewife,* 6, 99.

20. L. M. Child, *Mother's Book,* 130.

21. Ibid., 168.

22. Ibid., 86, 95.

23. Ibid., 90.

24. Kelley, *Private Woman, Public Stage,* 130.

25. Sedgwick to L. M. Child, 12 June 1830, AS-BPL, micro 2/43.

26. Quoted in Kelley, *Private Woman, Public Stage,* 15.

27. L. M. Child, "The First and Last Book," *The Coronal,* 282–84.
28. L. M. Child, *Frugal Housewife,* 91; *MJ,* 12 March 1829:1; 24 January 1828:2.
29. Holland, "Lydia Maria Child as Professional Author," 159; L. M. Child to Lydia B. Child, n.d. [February? 1830], LMC-*SL,* 16–17, micro 2/42.
30. L. M. Child and D. L. Child to Lucretia Child, 27 September 1829, C-SLib, micro 1/39.
31. L. M. Child to L. Loring, June-August 1831, L-SLib, micro 2/51.
32. Caroline Wells Dall, *Alongside* (Boston, 1900), 7.
33. *American Traveller,* 19 March 1830:2.
34. Ibid., 21 May 1830:3.
35. L. M. Child to D. L. Child, 8 August [1830], LMC-*SL,* 18–19, micro 2/44.
36. D. L. Child to L. M. Child, 29 September–3 October 1830, LMC-C, micro 2/45.
37. L. M. Child to Lydia [B.] Child, 23 June 1831, C-SLib, micro 2/48.
38. L. M. Child to D. L. Child, [2 October 1831], LMC-*SL,* 20, micro 2/52.
39. L. M. Child to Lydia B. Child, 14 October 1832, C-SLib, micro 2/55.
40. L. M. Child, *Good Wives,* LMC-*LFL,* vol 3, 89, 117–120.
41. Ibid., 164–67.
42. L. M. Child, *The Biographies of Madame de Staël and Madame Roland* (1832), LMC-*LFL,* vol. 1, 203.
43. Ibid, 108. In a letter to George Ticknor, Child admits that de Staël "might have wished a more able biographer; but she could not have had a more partial one." L. M. Child to George Ticknor, n.d. [1831–32?], LMC-*SL,* 22, micro 2/56.
44. L. M. Child, *Biographies of de Staël and Roland,* 58.
45. Renée Winegarten, *The Double Life of George Sand* (New York: Basic Books, 1978).
46. L. M. Child to L. and M. Osgood, 12 June 1857, LMC-*SL,* 315–16, micro 38/1062.
47. L. M. Child, "William Burton," *JM,* 3d ser., 1 (Sept. 1831): 1–45.
48. *MDJ,* 14 August 1829:2.
49. L. M. Child, "Autobiography" and "Scrapbook," LMC-C.

7. "Exciting Warfare"

1. Walter M. Merrill, *Against Wind and Tide: A Biography of William Lloyd Garrison* (Cambridge: Harvard University Press, 1963), 29–30.
2. Ibid., 21.
3. Ibid., 31.
4. L. M. Child to *Independent,* before 28 December 1865, micro 64/1698.

5. Merrill, *Against Wind and Tide*, 45.

6. Ibid., 51–52.

7. Ibid., 53; *MJ&T*, 21 October 1831:1. Beginning in August 1830 the paper was published by Carter & Hendee in conjunction with the *Tribune*.

8. Ibid., 15 September 1827:3; Litwack, *North of Slavery*, 25; *MJ&T*, 26 November 1831:1–2.

9. L. M. Child, *Evenings in New England*, 138; L. M. Child, "Jumbo and Zairee," *JM*, 2d ser., 5 (Jan./Feb. 1831): 285–99; L. M. Child, *An Appeal in Favor of That Class of Americans Called Africans* (1833; reprint, New York: Arno Press, 1968), 84.

10. L. M. Child, *The First Settlers of New-England; or, Conquest of the Pequods, Narragansets and Pokanokets* (Boston: Munroe and Francis, 1828), 30.

11. Ibid., 65–66.

12. Merrill, *Against Wind and Tide*, 57–58.

13. *Liberator*, 18 February 1832:25; *MJ&T*, 7 January 1832:3; *MJ&T*, 4 February 1832:1.

14. L. M. Child to Anne Whitney, 25 May 1879, LMC-*SL*, 558, micro 92/2451. In a letter to Samuel J. May, Child later claimed that this conversation with Garrison had occurred shortly before she was given free use of the Athenaeum Library and that she first used the Athenaeum for research on slavery. The list of books Child began taking from the library in January 1832, however, contains only a few related to the slavery question and thus leaves up in the air the exact time when she joined the Garrisonians. L. M. Child to Samuel J. May, 29 September 1867, LMC-*SL*, 474, micro 67/1749; Athenaeum Reader's Ledger, 18 (1827–1834), 66.

15. John L. Thomas, *The Liberator: William Lloyd Garrison* (Boston: Little, Brown, 1963), 130; Merrill, *Against Wind and Tide*, 12; L. M. Child, "Stand from Under," *Liberator*, 28 January 1832: 16. This story was also published in *Coronal*, 184–89. In her *Appeal*, Child states she once had "a very strong prejudice against anti-slavery." But a "candid examination" had convinced her she was in error. She undoubtedly meant here a prejudice against abolitionism, not antislavery per se. L. M. Child, *Appeal*, 142; L. M. Child to W. E. Channing, 2 April 1836, micro 4/91; Lawrence J. Friedman, *Gregarious Saints: Self and Community in American Abolitionism, 1830–1870* (New York: Cambridge University Press, 1982), 49.

16. L. M. Child to Gerrit Smith, 4 April 1864, LMC-*SL*, 441, micro 58/1555.

17. L. M. Child to Weld, 10 July 1880, LMC-*SL*, 563, micro 94/2509.

18. Blanche Glassman Hersh, *The Slavery of Sex: Feminist-Abolitionists in America* (Urbana: University of Illinois Press, 1978), 10–11; Jane H. Pease and William H. Pease, *Bound With Them in Chains: A Biographical History of the Antislavery Movement* (Westport, CT: Greenwood Press, 1972), 29.

19. *Liberator*, 18 January 1833:14; D. L. Child, *The Despotism of Freedom* (Boston, 1833).

20. Athenaeum Reader's Ledger, 18 (1827–1834), 66.

21. Carolyn L. Karcher, "Censorship American Style: The Case of Lydia Maria Child," *Studies in the American Renaissance* (1985), 285–87.

22. L. M. Child, *Appeal*, iii.

23. Ibid., 23.

24. Ibid., 134–35.

25. Ibid., 139–40.

26. Ibid., 121. According to Edward P. Crapol, Child's *Appeal* was the first systematic exposition of the slave power thesis in the United States. The issue of the nonrecognition of Haiti is used to point up "the basic contradictions inherent in prevailing American ideology, whereby a republic based on the principle of human liberty, defended and promoted racial equality and sanctioned chattel slavery for millions of human beings." Edward P. Crapol, "Lydia Maria Child: Abolitionist Critic of American Foreign Policy," in Edward P. Crapol, ed., *Women and American Foreign Policy: Lobbyists, Critics, and Insiders* (Westport, CT: Greenwood Press, 1987), 4.

27. L. M. Child, *Appeal*, 169.

28. Ibid., 195; Alexis de Toqueville, *Democracy in America*, vol. 1 (New York: Knopf, 1953), 359.

29. L. M. Child, *Appeal*, 198, 200.

30. Ibid., 216.

31. *Liberator*, 10 August 1833:127.

32. Samuel May, *Some Recollections of Our Antislavery Days* (1833; reprint, New York: Arno Press, 1968), 97.

33. Crapol, "Lydia Maria Child," 2; Oliver Johnson, *William Lloyd Garrison and His Times* (Boston: Houghton Mifflin & Co., 1881), 140; *Liberator*, 5 November 1836: 178; James Forten to James McCune Smith, 8 September 1835, AS-BPL; L. M. Child to Charles Sumner, 7 July 1856, LMC-*SL*, 286, micro 33/925; L. M. Child, "Reminiscence of William Ellery Channing," LMC-*L*, 48–50.

34. *NAR 37* (July 1833): 138–64.

35. May, *Recollections*, 99. Whittier later wrote, "It is quite impossible for any one of the present generation to imagine the popular surprise and indignation which the book called forth, or how entirely its author cut herself off from the favor and sympathy of a large number of those who had previously delighted to do her honor." LMC-*L*, ix.

36. Baer, *Heart is Like Heaven*, 68; Mary B. Claflin, *Personal Recollections of John G. Whittier* (New York: Thomas Y. Crowell & Co., 1893), 80.

37. *NAR* 88 (July 1835): 170.

38. Quoted in Leonard L. Richards, *"Gentlemen of Property and Standing": Anti-Abolition Mobs in Jacksonian America* (New York: Oxford University Press, 1979), 21.

39. Quoted in George M. Fredrickson, ed., *William Lloyd Garrison* (Englewood Cliffs, NJ: Prentice-Hall, 1968), 32.

40. L. M. Child to S. J. May, 29 September 1867, LMC-*SL*, 473–74, micro 67/1794; L. M. Child to Whittier, 20 June 1858, LMC-C, micro 39/1065.

41. *Liberator*, 19 October 1833:168.

42. L. M. Child to S. J. May, 29 September 1867, LMC-*SL*, 474, micro 67/1794. Child checked her last book out of the Athenaeum on 2 February 1835. See Athenaeum Readers Ledger, 18 (1827–1834), 66. Presumably the note from the trustees was sent to her sometime after that date. That spring Maria Chapman apparently succeeded in raising sufficient funds to buy her friend an Athenaeum ticket, but there is no evidence that the trustees allowed Child even to pay for the privilege of taking out books. See D. Weston to A. B. Weston, 18 May 1835, W-BPL.

43. Quoted in Robert Rich, "A Wilderness of Whigs," *Journal of Social History* (Spring 1971): 263–76. See also Mitchell Snay, "A World in Themselves and Each Other: Leadership in the New England Anti-Slavery Society," seminar paper, Brandeis University, 1976; L. M. Child to Lucy Searle, 18 November 1860, LMC-C, micro 47/1268.

44. L. M. Child to Boston Female Anti-Slavery Society, n.d. [before 19 November 1835], micro 3/84.

8. Mob Year

1. Quoted in James Brewer Stewart, *Holy Warriors: The Abolitionists and American Slavery* (New York: Hill and Wang, 1976), 54–55.

2. Quoted in Keith Melder, *The Beginnings of Sisterhood: The American Woman's Rights Movement, 1800–1850* (New York: Schocken Books, 1977), 57.

3. L. M. Child to Charlotte Phelps [2 January 1834], LMC-*SL*, 28, micro 2/63.

4. Sarah H. Southwick, *Reminiscences of Early Anti-Slavery Days* (Boston, 1893), 8.

5. Ibid., 7–8.

6. L. M. Child to Jonathan Phillips, 10 December 1835, William Phillips, Jr. Collection, Salisbury, CT, micro 96/2531.

7. May *Recollections*, 100.

8. Friedman, *Gregarious Saints*, 55.

9. See Edward S. Adby, *Journal of a Residence and Tour in the United States of North America*, vol. 1 (London, 1835), 153; Holland, "Child as Professional Author," 160.

10. L. M. Child, ed., *The Oasis* (Boston: Allen and Ticknor, 1834), vii.

11. Ibid., vi; L. M. Child to S. Shaw, n.d. [1833], micro 2/62.

12. L. M. Child, *Oasis*, vii. Historian Eric Foner makes the valid point that antebellum reformers distinguished sharply between natural, civil, political, and social rights: "social relations—the choice of business and

personal associates—most Americans deemed a personal matter. . . ." Eric Foner, *Reconstruction: America's Unfinished Revolution* (New York: Harper & Row, 1988), 231.

13. John L. Thomas, *The Liberator: William Lloyd Garrison* (Boston: Little, Brown, 1963), 183; Litwack, *North of Slavery*, 217. In her *Appeal*, 135, Maria mentioned that she had only once seen a white person walking arm in arm with a person of color. In her *Anti-Slavery Catechism* (Newburyport, MA: Charles Whipple, 1836), 32, she asserts that she "would not select an ignorant man as her companion," but if she was asked "if that man's children shall have as fair a chance as my own, to obtain an education and rise in the world, I should be ashamed of myself as a Christian and a republican if I did not say, Yes, with all my heart."

14. L. M. Child, "Mary French and Susan Easton, *JM*, 3d ser., 6 (May/ June 1834): 186–201. I am indebted for some of my insights on this story to Carolyn Karcher's paper, "The Woman of Letters as Political Activist: A Literary Approach to the Biography of Lydia Maria Child," and Shirley Samuels' paper, "The Identity of Slavery," given at the American Studies Association meeting in October 1988.

15. L. M. Child, *Appeal*, 196, 207–208.

16. Harriet Martineau, *The Martyr Age of the United States* (Boston: Weeks, Jordan & Co., 1839), 5; S. Davenport to C. Weston, n.d. [1834], W-BPL.

17. Baer, *Heart is Like Heaven*, 77–81.

18. L. M. Child to Benjamin [Franklin] Butler, 25 February 1835, Simon Gratz Collection, Historical Society of Pennsylvania, micro 3/70 & 71.

19. Baer, *Heart is Like Heaven*, 81–82.

20. *Letters and Addresses by George Thompson During his Mission in the United States* (Boston: Isaac Knapp, 1837).

21. *Liberator*, 6 December 1834:194.

22. L. M. Child, "Letters from New York," *Standard*, 18 August 1842:43, micro 15/399; L. M. Child to *Standard*, 27 February 1864, micro 58/1544.

23. Howard Temperly, *British Antislavery, 1833–1870* (London: Longman, 1972), 28. For the selection of the Childs as agents in Great Britain, see C. Weston to L. G. R. Hammett, 8 May 1835, W-BPL.

24. L. M. Child to Maria Chapman & Other Ladies, 1 June 1834 [1835?], LMC-*SL*, 29, micro 2/64; L. M. Child to Ellis Gray Loring, 20 January 1836, LMC-*SL*, 43, micro 4/90. A notice in the *Liberator*, 1 August 1835:123, signed by D. L. Child, announced that "House Furniture" would be "sold at public vendue" on Thursday, August 6 at 9 o'clock A.M.

25. L. M. Child to L. Loring, 15 August [1835], LMC-*SL*, 31–32, micro 3/80.

26. David wrote his mother that, as they were about to embark for Liverpool, G.H. Snelling, "my former partner and professed friend caused me to be arrested on a pretended claim for money which he as a partner, put into the establishment of the Massachusetts Journal. I think that this

was the result of a conspiracy in Boston to prevent our proceeding to England as agents." D. L. Child to Lydia [B.] Child, 30 December 1835, C-MR. Harriet Martineau also described David's arrest as "malicious," Martineau, *Martyr Age*, 5. David was not the only abolitionist lawyer whose career was hurt by his abolitionist sympathies. Ellis Loring also lost most of his clients, as well as the friendship of such leading intellectuals as George Ticknor. The Lorings, however, unlike the Childs, had enough private income to live comfortably. See Snay, "A World in Themselves and Each Other," 29.

27. L. M. Child, "Letter from New York," *Standard*, 18 August 1842, micro 15/399.

28. L. M. Child to the BFASS, n.d. [before 19 November 1835], LMC-*SL*, 40, micro 3/84.

29. L. M. Child to E. Loring, 30 January 1836, LMC-*SL*, 45, micro 4/90.

30. Ibid.

31. In the preface to the first edition of *Philothea*, her third novel, which she worked on during these months in New Rochelle, Maria spoke of times when she felt "restless in this bondage" and wanted to "bid adieu to the substantial fields of utility, to float on the clouds of romance." L. M. Child, *Philothea: A Romance* (Boston: Otis Broaders & Co., 1836), vi.

9. A Reluctant Reformer

1. Jane H. Pease and William H. Pease, *Bound with Them in Chains* (Westport, CT: Greenwood Press, 1972), 90.

2. Garrison called the venture a "hazardous project." Garrison, *Letters*, vol. 2, *A House Divided Against Itself*, 78. At one stage in their planning Lundy had proposed that he and David Child proceed in disguise to Matamoros via New Orleans ahead of the other settlers. Maria was terrified that David would go along with this suggestion. See L. M. Child to Benjamin Lundy, 14 March [1836], in William Clinton Armstrong, *The Lundy Family and their Descendants* (New Brunswick, NJ, 1902), 391–92. In late December 1835 David wrote the Charge d'Affaires of Mexico, Señor Castillo, offering to provide the Mexican government with a regiment consisting largely of colored persons. D. L. Child to Señor Castillo, 26 December 1835, C-BPL.

3. L. M. Child to E. and L. Loring, 30 January 1836, LMC-*SL*, 43, micro 4/90. In a letter to David's mother, Maria put it this way: "Somewhere we must go, if we ever hope to get out of debt." L. M. Child to Lydia [B.] Child, 10 March 1836, LMC-*SL*, 48, micro 4/93.

4. L. M. Child to E. Loring, 30 January 1836, LMC-*SL*, 43, micro 4/90.

5. L. M. Child, *Philothea*, vii. Unless otherwise noted, subsequent citations refer to the reprint of the second edition of the novel published

in 1848 by C. S. Francis & Co. of New York, *Philothea: A Romance* (Freeport, NY: Books for Libraries Press, 1969).

6. Ibid., 2, 185, 223.

7. Ibid., 19–21, 114.

8. Ibid., 72.

9. L. M. Child, *Philothea* (Boston: Otis Brothers & Co., 1836), vi.

10. Ralph Waldo Emerson, *Nature* (1836; reprint, Boston: Beacon Press, 1989), 5–6, 79–80.

11. Joel Myerson, "Convers Francis and Emerson," *American Literature* (March 18, 1978): 18.

12. Caroline Weston to Anne Weston, n.d. [July 1836], W-BPL; Cornelius C. Felton, review of *Philothea; NAR* 44 (Jan. 1837): 85; Boston *Atlas*, 12 August 1836:2; Edgar Allen Poe review, *Southern Literary Messenger* 2 (Sept. 1836): 659–62; Kenneth W. Cameron, *Philothea, or Plato against Epicurus* (Hartford, CT, 1975), 3.

13. L. M. Child to Thomas Carlyle, 7 April 1838, National Library of Scotland, micro 5/134; Sarah Josepha Hale, review of *Philothea, American Ladies Magazine* 9 (August 1836): 480–84.

14. L. M. Child to L. Loring, 3 May [1836], LMC-*SL*, 49, micro 4/95. In these months David was being considered as a possible editor for the *Emancipator*. Garrison promised to support him if the current editor, Phelps, stepped down. See Garrison to D. L. Child, 6 August 1836, Garrison, *Letters*, vol. 2, 152–54; D. Weston to A. Weston, 6 June 1836, W-BPL.

15. L. M. Child to D. L. Child, 28 July 1836, LMC-*SL*, 51, micro 4/102.

16. L. M. Child to D. L. Child, 31 July [1836], LMC-C, micro 4/103.

17. LMC-*SL*, 53; *Liberator*, 3 September 1836:143, and 24 September 1836:153; L. M. Child to Esther Carpenter, 4 September 1836, LMC-*SL*, 53, micro 4/106. Shaw's decision in this case was eventually incorporated into the law of almost every free state. See Paul Finkelman, *Slavery in the Courtroom* (Washington, D.C: Library of Congress, 1985), 25–26.

18. L. M. Child to Maria Marshall, 28 July 1836, Maurice Family Papers, Southern Historical Collection, University of North Carolina, micro 4/105.

19. L. M. Child to Lydia [B.] Child, 19 October 1836, LMC-*SL*, 54, micro 4/108. Maria herself sent out appeals for funds to support David's beet sugar enterprise. See L. M. Child to Gerrit Smith, 17 September 1836, Gerrit Smith Collection, Syracuse University, George Arents Research Library for Special Collections, micro 4/107.

20. L. M. Child to Lydia [B.] Child, 19 October 1836, LMC-*SL*, 55, micro 4/108.

21. L. M. Child to L. Loring, 27 November 1836, LMC-*SL*, 58–59, micro 4/111.

22. L. M. Child to L. Loring, 30 April 1837, L-SLib, micro 5/123; L. M. Child to Lydia B. Child, 2 April 1837, LMC-*SL*, 65, micro 5/120.

23. L. M. Child, *The Family Nurse; or, Companion of the Frugal Housewife* (Boston: Charles J. Hendee, 1837); *Authentic Anecdotes of American Slavery*

(Newburyport, MA: Charles Whipple, 1838). "The Fountain of Beauty" was first published as "The Palace of Beauty," *MJ&T*, 25 December 1830:3.

24. L. M. Child to Lydia B. Child, 17 January 1837, LMC-*SL*, 60, micro 5/115; 2 April 1837, LMC-*SL*, 65, micro 5/120.

25. L. M. Child to Henrietta Sargent, 13 November 1836, LMC-*SL*, 56–57, micro 4/110; L. M. Child to L. Loring, 27 November 1836, LMC-*SL*, 59, micro 4/111.

26. Miller, *Transcendentalists*, 21; L. M. Child, "Reminiscence of William Ellery Channing," LMC-*L*, 48–50.

27. William Ellery Channing, *Slavery* (Boston: James Munroe & Co., 1835), 135, 138; Arthur W. Brown, *Always Young for Liberty: Biography of William Ellery Channing* (Syracuse, NY: Syracuse University Press, 1956), 48; L. M. Child to Channing [Jan.? 1836], *Liberator*, 2 April 1836, micro 4/91. Channing admitted in his pamphlet that he was personally acquainted with very few of the movement's supporters. Channing, *Slavery*, 164.

28. L. M. Child to L. Loring, 19 July 1836, L-SLib, micro 4/100; L. M. Child to H. Sargent, 13 November 1836, LMC-*SL*, 56–57, micro 4/110.

29. Ibid.

30. L. M. Child to L. Loring, 27 November 1836, LMC-*SL*, 58–59, micro 4/111; H. Sargent to A. Grimké, 21 January 1837, in Gilbert H. Barnes and Dwight L. Dumond, eds., *Letters of Theodore Dwight Weld, Angelina Grimké Weld and Sarah Grimké, 1822–1844*, vol. 1 (New York, 1934), 357; L. M. Child, "The Ladies Fair," *Liberator*, 2 January 1837:3.

31. L. M. Child to Samuel May Jr., n.d. [after January 25, 1862], Alma Lutz Collection, Schlesinger Library, Radcliffe College, micro 51/1371.

32. L. M. Child, *History of the Condition of Women in Various Ages and Nations* (1835), LMC-*LFL*, vol. 5:210. In their history of the suffrage movement, Elizabeth Cady Stanton and Susan B. Anthony, eds., *History of Woman Suffrage*, vol. 1 (1882; reprint, Salem, NH: Ayer Co. Publishers, 1985), 38, note that Child's *History of the Condition of Women* stimulated agitation on the suffrage issue.

33. Ibid., 210–11; L. M. Child, "William Lloyd Garrison," *Atlantic Monthly* 44 (August 1879): 237.

34. A. Weston to D. Weston, 18 April 1837, W-BPL; L. M. Child to H. Sargent, 17 April [1837?], LMC-*SL*, 67–68, micro 5/122; L. M. Child to L. Loring, 31 April 1837, L-SLib, micro 5/123.

35. *Liberator*, 2 June 1837:90; Lerner, *Grimké Sisters*, 161.

36. *Proceedings of the Anti-Slavery Convention of American Women* (New York: William S. Dorr, 1837).

37. Ibid, 10; quoted in Blanch Glassman Hersh, *The Slavery of Sex: Feminist-Abolitionists in America* (Urbana: University of Illinois Press, 1978), 16.

38. *Proceedings of Anti-Slavery Convention*, 10–11.

39. Lerner, *Grimké Sisters*, 166.

40. Quoted in Keith Melder, *The Beginnings of Sisterhood: The American*

Woman's Rights Movement, 1800–1850 (New York: Schocken Books, 1977), 83.

41. Lerner, *Grimké Sisters*, 192.

42. L. M. Child to Jonathan Phillips, 26 February 1838, William Phillips, Jr. Collection, Salisbury, CT, micro 96/2533.

43. D. L. Child to A. Grimké, 12 February 1838, in Barnes and Dumond, eds., *Letters of Weld and Grimké*, 544. Gerda Lerner claims Francis Jackson was the only male abolitionist who supported Angelina, *Grimké Sisters*, 218.

44. L. M. Child to New York *Tribune*, published in *Standard*, 5 April 1862, micro 52/1400.

45. L. M. Child to Lydia Bigelow Child, 6 April 1838, LMC-*SL*, 73, micro 5/133. The Northampton Sugar Beet Company had been formed in March 1837.

10. The "Iron-bound Valley of the Connecticut"

1. L. M. Child to Lorings, 10 July 1838, LMC-*SL*, 76, micro 5/137. On 30 May 1838 the *Gazette* announced David's arrival and commencement of sugar beet cultivation.

2. L. M. Child to L. Loring 3 June 1838, L-SLib, micro 5/135.

3. L. M. Child to Lorings, 10 July 1838, LMC-*SL*, 77, micro 5/137. The *Courier* on 1 August 1838 published a complimentary article on L. M. Child and her writings. "We are glad to find the intellectual efforts of this lady, (who has become an acceptable resident of Northampton) suitably appreciated and rewarded."

4. L. M. Child to Lorings, 10 July 1838, LMC-*SL*, 77–78, micro 5/137.

5. L. M. Child to S. Lesley, 3 August 1874, L-ASPL, micro 83/2167.

6. L. M. Child to C. Weston, 27 July 1838, LMC-*SL*, 80, micro 6/141; L. M. Child to Lydia B. Child, 7 August 1838, C-SLib, micro 6/142. Unfortunately, Maria doesn't say who these two real abolitionists are. In a letter to C. Weston, 7 March 1839, LMC-*SL*, 108, micro 7/172, she claims not to know a single Garrison abolitionist in Northampton.

7. Many of Northampton's summer visitors were from aristocratic families, whose sons had once attended the progressive Round Hill School. See *Hampshire County Journal*, centennial ed. (Northampton, MA, 1887), 10; *Northampton Book* (Northampton, MA: Tercentenary Committee, 1954), 358. Years later, in her novel, *A Romance of the Republic*, Maria would recreate Napier in the character Deacon Stillham.

8. L. M. Child to C. Weston, 27 July 1838, LMC-*SL*, 80–81, micro 6/141.

9. L. M. Child to Lorings, 10 July 1838, LMC-*SL*, 77, micro 5/137.

10. L. M. Child to Francis and Sarah Shaw, 17 August 1838, LMC-*SL*, 85–86, micro 6/146.

11. L. M. Child to C. Weston, 27 July 1838, LMC-*SL*, 81–82, micro 6/141; L. M. Child to Angelina Grimké Weld, 2 October 1838, LMC-*SL*, 92. In *A Romance of the Republic*, published in 1867, Maria gives a fictional account of this incident in which the slave stays in the North because enough money is raised to buy her and her children. L. M. Child, *A Romance of the Republic* (Boston: Ticknor and Fields, 1867), 368.

12. L. M. Child to Theodore Dwight Weld, 18 December 1837, LMC-*SL*, 101, micro 6/156; L. M. Child to L. Loring, 30 April 1839, LMC-*SL*, 112, micro 7/179.

13. L. M. Child to C. Weston, 27 July 1838, LMC-*SL*, 81, micro 6/141.

14. In a letter to Angelina Grimké, Maria wrote that she was regularly attending antislavery prayer meetings, known as "Monthly Concerts." L. M. Child to A. Grimké Weld, 18 December 1838, micro 6/155; L. M. Child to *Liberator*, before 6 March 1840, micro 8/198.

15. L. M. Child to H. Sargent, 18 November 1838, LMC-*SL*, 93–94, micro 6/152.

16. L. M. Child to A. Grimké Weld, 2 October 1838, LMC-*SL*, 91–92, micro 6/150.

17. L. M. Child to A. Kelley, 1 October 1838, LMC-*SL*, 89, micro 6/149; L. M. Child to L. Loring, 30 April 1839, LMC-*SL*, 113, micro 7/179.

18. L. M. Child to L. Loring, 12 January 1839, L-SLib, micro 7/162.

19. L. M. Child to E. Loring, 24 March [1839], NYPL, micro 7/176.

20. L. M. Child to Lydia B. Child, 9 June 1839, C-SLib, micro 7/181; L. M. Child to L. Loring, 30 April 1839, LMC-*SL*, 112–113, micro 7/179.

21. L. M. Child to Lydia B. Child, 18 November 1839, C-SLib, micro 8/190.

22. L. M. Child to A. Loring, 9 February 1840, L-SLib, micro 8/197.

23. L. M. Child and D.L. Child to MASS, 15 January 1839, *Liberator*, 8 February, 1839, micro 7/165; James Brewer Stewart, *Holy Warriors* (New York: Hill & Wang, 1976), 90.

24. L. M. Child to *Liberator*, 6 March 1840, LMC-*SL*, 127, micro 8/198; L. M. Child to C. Weston, 7 March 1839, LMC-*SL*, 108, micro 7/172; L. M. Child and D.L. Child to MASS, 15 January 1839, *Liberator*, 8 February 1839, micro 7/165; L. M. Child to *Liberator*, 2 September 1839, LMC-*SL*, 123.

25. Merton L. Dillon, *The Abolitionists: The Growth of a Dissenting Minority* (New York: Norton, 1974), 121–23.

26. L. M. Child to E. Loring, 30 April 1839, LMC-*SL*, 114, micro 7/179: L. M. Child to *Liberator*, 2 September 1839, LMC-*SL*, 120–22, micro 8/186.

27. Ibid, 122–23; L. M. Child to *Liberator*, 6 March 1840, LMC-*SL*, 127–28, micro 8/198.

28. On 29 May 1839, a public meeting was held in support of the *Liberator*. Both Childs were listed on the roll of the convention. Maria Child was listed as a member of the business committee. *Liberator*, 31 May 1839:87 and 7 June 1839:90.

29. *Liberator*, 19 April 1839:63; Melder, *The Beginnings of Sisterhood*, 95–96, 103–104.

30. L. M. Child to Lydia B. Child, 12 December 1839, LMC-*SL*, 125, micro 8/190; L. M. Child to Mott, 5 March 1839, LMC-*SL*, 106–107, micro 7/171. Although Maria did not attend the 1838 Women's Anti-Slavery Convention in Philadelphia, she agreed to write the convention's address to be distributed to all northern members of Congress, *Address to the Senators and Representatives of the Free States, in the Congress of the United States, by the Anti-Slavery Convention of American Women* (Philadelphia, 1838).

31. L. M. Child to Lydia B. Child, 12 December 1839, LMC-*SL*, 125, micro 8/190; L. M. Child to BFASS, *Liberator*, before 3 April 1840, micro 8/201.

32. L. M. Child to Lydia B. Child, 9 June 1839, C-SLib, micro 7/181.

33. C. A. Browne, "The Centenary of the Beet Sugar Industry in America," unpublished paper in Forbes Library, Northampton, MA, (1937), 11; L. M. Child to Lydia B. Child, 12 December 1839, LMC-*SL*, 125, micro 8/190. Convers Francis bought 134 acres from Edward Storrs. See deed dated 3 June 1840, Hampshire County Land records. L. M. Child mentions this farm in a letter to Lydia Bigelow Child, 7 June 1840, LMC-*SL*, 132, micro 8/205.

34. L. M. Child to Lydia [B.] Child, 7 June 1840, LMC-*SL*, 131–32, micro 8/205.

35. L. M. Child to C. Francis, 20 October 1840, LMC-*SL*, 134, micro 9/215; L. M. Child to L. Loring, 19 July 1840, L-SLib, micro 8/209.

36. Alice Eaton McBee, *From Utopia to Florence* (Northampton, MA: Smith College Studies in History, 1947), 10–12.

37. L. M. Child to C. Francis, 20 October 1840, LMC-C, micro 9/215.

38. Ibid. See also LMC-*SL*, 132–34; L. M. Child to A. Loring, 21 June 1840, C-UM, micro 8/206 and 16 August 1840, C-UM, micro 8/211.

39. Barbara M. Cross, "Maria White Lowell," *Notable American Women* (Cambridge MA: Belknap Press, Harvard University, 1971), 439–40; Beth Gale Chevigny, *The Woman and the Myth: Margaret Fuller's Life and Writings* (Westbury, NY: The Feminist Press, 1976), 210–14; L. M. Child to [Maria White], 30 March 1840, HL, micro 8/200.

40. Miller, *Transcendentalists*, 410; Brooks, *Flowering of New England*, 244; L. M. Child to L. Loring, 20 December 1840, L-SLib, micro 9/221.

41. L. M. Child to C. Francis, 8 January 1841, LMC-C, micro 9/222; L. M. Child to F. Shaw, 24 October 1840, micro 9/217.

42. A. Weston to D. Weston, 29 March 1841, W-BPL; L. M. Child to M. Chapman, 23 August 1840, AS-BPL, micro 8/212; L. M. Child to L. Loring, 12 December 1840, L-SLib, micro 9/219.

43. L. M. Child to L. Loring, 17 February 1841, LMC-SLib, micro 9/226; L. M. Child to E. Loring, 9 February 1841, LMC-*SL*, 136, micro 9/225.

44. L. M. Child to F. Shaw, 27 May 1841, LMC-*SL*, 140–41, micro 10/233.

45. L. M. Child to E. Loring, 9 February 1841, LMC-*SL*, 136, micro 9/225; L. M. Child to F. Shaw, 27 May 1841, LMC-*SL*, 141, micro 10/233.

46. L. M. Child to Gerrit Smith, 28 September [1841], Gerrit Smith Collection, George Arents Research Library for Special Collections, Syracuse University, micro 11/266; E. Loring to L. M. Child, 29 April 1841, Loring Letterbook, HL, micro 9/227.

11. Editor in Harness

1. Edmund Quincy to Maria W. Chapman, 18 May 1840 [1841], AS-BPL.

2. Minutes of the Executive Committee of the AASS, December 7, 1841– May 8, 1843, unpublished manuscript, AS-BPL.

3. L. M. Child to E. Loring, 27 May 1841, L-SLib, micro 9/231.

4. L. M. Child to E. Loring, 17 May 1841, C-UM, micro 9/229.

5. L. M. Child, "To the Readers of the Standard," *Standard,* 20 May 1841:198.

6. L. M. Child, "Moral Influence," *Standard,* 2 December 1841:102; "Charles Stuart," *Standard,* 22 July 1841:27.

7. Garrison to Elizabeth Pease, 1 June 1841, AS-BPL; Mott to A. Weston, 8 July 1841, W-BPL; O. Johnson to M. Chapman, 3 September 1841 W-BPL.

8. L. M. Child to E. Loring, 31 August 1841, NYPL, micro 10/253.

9. L. M. Child to E. Loring, 28 September [1841], LMC-*SL*, 146–47, micro 11/265.

10. L. M. Child to E. Loring, 24 November 1841, LMC-*SL*, 153, micro 11/286; L. M. Child to James Miller McKim and Philadelphia Friends, 24[&25] November 1841, LMC-*SL*, 153–55, micro 12/290.

11. L. M. Child to E. Loring, 11 May 1842, LMC-*SL*, 173, micro 14/372.

12. L. M. Child to AASS Board, 21 February 1843, LMC-*SL*, 190–92, micro 16/456.

13. L. M. Child to E. Loring, n.d. [29? October 1842], NYPL, micro 15/419, and 6 December 1842, NYPL, micro 15/429.

14. For a discussion of the treatment of foreign policy issues in the *Standard* under Child's editorship, see Crapol, "Lydia Maria Child," 9. Child described her article on Transcendentalism, *Standard,* 25 November 1841:99, as "the beginning of a series of merely *popular* explanations of subject[s] much talked of and little understood." L. M. Child to E. Loring, 24 November 1841, LMC-*SL*, 152, micro 11/286.

15. L. M. Child to Caroline Weston, 7 March 1839, LMC-*SL*, 109, micro 7/172.

16. L. M. Child, "Talk about Political Party," *Standard*, 7 July 1842:18.

17. *Liberator*, 2 September 1842:139.

18. Alma Lutz, *Crusade for Freedom: Women of the Antislavery Movement* (Boston: Beacon Press, 1968), 184; O. to *Standard*, 26 May 1842, micro 14/380; Kelley to *Standard*, 27 April 1843, micro 17/480; Gibbons to C. Weston, 4 April 1842, W-BPL. Gibbons wrote Kelley after Maria resigned that "the forcing of Mrs. Child from the editorship was the most fatal calamity that every befell the antislavery cause." Quoted in Lutz, *Crusade for Freedom*, 187. Historians have also had high praise for the *Standard* under Maria Child's editorship. Gilbert Barnes considered her efforts "brilliant," noting that if the *Standard*'s editorial troubles ceased after she and David left the paper, "its distinction ceased also." Gilbert H. Barnes, *The Antislavery Impulse, 1830–1844* (New York: D. Appleton-Century Co., 1933), 174.

19. For a more detailed discussion of the complaints she received from various quarters see L. M. Child, "Farewell," *Standard*, 4 May 1843:190.

20. L. M. Child to E. Loring, 16 May 1844, LMC-*SL*, 207, micro 19/555.

21. L. M. Child to E. Loring, 9 March 1842, LMC-*SL*, 164, micro 13/345; L. M. Child, "Sects and Sectarianism," *Standard*, 16 February 1843:136.

22. L. M. Child, "The Course of the Standard," *Standard*, 3 November 1842:88.

23. [Unsigned], "The Union," *Standard*, 24 February 1842:151.

24. L. M. Child, "The Union," *Standard*, 31 March 1842:170.

25. Aileen S. Kraditor, *Means and Ends in American Abolitionism* (New York: Pantheon Books, 1969), 198.

26. *New York Herald*, 27 April 1842:2; 6 May 1842:2; 10 May 1842:2; Kraditor, *Means and Ends*, 199. Anne Weston described Child as having been so frightened by the mob that she had hidden all her valuables. A. Weston to D. Weston, 11 May 1842, W-BPL; *Liberator*, 13 May 1842:75. In a letter to Wendell Phillips written in early May, Maria admitted that Garrison's editorial had presented her with a "line of policy which we had no time to examine." She claimed that she and others of the executive committee were no longer worried about the prospect of violence at the meeting but she was certain such violence would have occurred had she not published the circular in the papers. L. M. Child to Phillips, 3 May 1842, LMC-*SL*, 171–73, micro 96/2535.

27. Kraditor, *Means and Ends*, 198–99.

28. L. M. Child, "The Anniversary," *Standard*, 19 May 1842:196.

29. L. M. Child, "Prospects of the Anti-Slavery Cause," *Standard*, 9 June 1842:2; L. M. Child, "Prospectus of the Standard," *Standard*, 9 June 1842:3. At the time of her death in 1880 an article in the Springfield *Republican* described Maria Child as a respected figure in the history of journalism. As editor of the *Standard*, "she had that independence of character

and that general cultivation of mind which are now recognized, though they were not then, as the indispensable and distinguishing traits of a good journalist." Reprinted in the *Woman's Journal*, 6 November 1880: 354–55.

30. Gibbons to [Chapman], 21 February 1843, W-BPL; Chapman to D. L. Child, 14 April 1843, W-BPL.

31. L. M. Child to M. Chapman, 11 May [1842], LMC-*SL*, 174–76, micro 14/373; M. Chapman to A. Weston [Fall 1842], W-BPL; L. M. Child, "The Course of the Standard," *Standard*, 3 November 1842:87; L. M. Child to E. Loring, 12 October 1842, NYPL, micro 15/413.

32. J. Gibbons to C. Weston, 4 April 1842, W-BPL.

33. L. M. Child to E. Loring, 24 January 1843, LMC-*SL*, 187, micro 16/447; L. M. Child, "Farewell," *Standard*, 4 May 1843:190.

34. Garrison, "The Anti-Slavery Standard," *Liberator*, 19 May 1843:79.

35. L. M. Child to M. Chapman, 19 May [1843], LMC-*SL*, 197, micro 17/494.

12. Letters from New York

1. L. M. Child, *Isaac T. Hopper: A True Life* (1854, reprint, New York: Negro Universities Press, 1969), 363, 377–79.

2. Ibid., 392–93. Margaret Hope Bacon, *Lamb's Warrior: The Life of Isaac T. Hopper* (New York: Thomas Y. Crowell Co., 1970), 128–41.

3. L. M. Child, *Hopper*, 339.

4. L. M. Child to L. Loring, 16 May 1841, LMC-SLib, micro 9/228.

5. Bacon, *Lamb's Warrior*, 147.

6. LMC-*LNY*, 1st ser., 15–16.

7. Edward K. Spann, *The New Metropolis: New York City, 1840–1857* (New York: Columbia University Press, 1981), 1–2.

8. LMC-*LNY*, 1st ser., 26.

9. Ibid., 13, 27–28.

10. Ibid., 27–30.

11. L. M. Child to E. Loring, 17 July 1841, NYPL, micro 10/244.

12. L. M. Child to E. Loring, 11 August 1841, NYPL, micro 10/246; 21 September 1841, NYPL, micro 11/262; and 28 September 1841, LMC-*SL*, 147, micro 11/265.

13. L. M. Child to E. Loring, 17 June 1841, LMC-*SL*, 145, micro 10/235 and 11 August 1841, NYPL, micro 10/246; Henry. G. Chapman to D. Weston, 26 November 1841, W-BPL; L. M. Child to M. Chapman, 1 December 1841, AS-BPL, micro 12/292. L. M. Child to M. Lowell, 13 December 1841, HL, micro 12/300; L. M. Child to A. Loring, 14 February 1842, C-UM, micro 13/332. "The Quadroons" was later republished in *Fact and Fiction* (New York: C.S. Francis & Co., 1846).

14. L. M. Child to F. Shaw, 2 August 1846, HL, micro 23/664. In 1855 Maria wrote a friend, Peter Lesley, that the passion of love was altogether respectable in her eyes. She blamed theology for "trailing the slime of the

Serpent over the rose of life." L. M. Child to P. Lesley, 1 January 1855, L-APSL, micro 31/877.

15. L. M. Child, "The Legend of the Apostle John," *Fact and Fiction*, 100. In another story from this time, "She Waits in the Spirit Land," Maria applauds the natural eroticism among the Indians, whom she describes as innocent and free from the degradation of Victorian mores. See Karcher, ed., *Hobomok*, 191.

16. LMC-*LNY*, 1st ser., 270. Previous biographers of Child have thought that the first series of her "Letters from New York," those published between August 1841 and May 1843, first appeared in the Boston *Courier*, but an examination of that paper shows no evidence that the "Letters" were published there. The second series of "Letters," however, did appear in the *Courier*, beginning on 23 December 1843.

17. Spann, *New Metropolis*, 43.

18. L. M. Child, "Letters from New York," *Standard*, 18 August 1842, micro 15/399.

19. LMC-*LNY*, 1st ser., 53, 129.

20. LMC-*LNY*, 1st ser., 204, 19; "Letters from New York," *Standard*, 3 March 1842, micro 13/343.

21. LMC-*LNY*, 1st ser., 174–76.

22. D. L. Child to Lydia B. Child, 1 August 1841, C-MR; L. M. Child to E. Loring, 24 November 1841, LMC-*SL*, 151, micro 11/286.

23. L. M. Child to F. Shaw, 15 January 1843, LMC-*SL*, 185, micro 16/441.

24. L. M. Child to E. Loring, 26 December 1844, NYPL, micro 21–595.

25. For a list of David's debts, see Bankruptcy File # 2369 in Federal Archives, Waltham, MA. For a list of the goods sold at auction, see *Hampshire Gazette*, 6 June 1843. Even those goods mortgaged to Convers Francis and John Childe are listed in the advertisement, although they were not actually for sale. For example in 1850 Convers Francis deeds the farm to Ellis Loring for one dollar in trust for Maria.

26. L. M. Child to E. Loring, 6 March 1843, NYPL, micro 16/463; Norma Basch, *In the Eyes of the Law* (Ithaca: Cornell University Press, 1982), 89; L. M. Child to E. Loring, 21 March 1843, NYPL, micro 17/470.

27. L. M. Child to E. Loring, 16 June 1843, NYPL, micro 17/499; L. M. Child to L. Loring, 14 August 1843, C-UM, micro 17/505.

28. L. M. Child to E. Loring, 15 January 1843, LMC-*SL*, 185, micro 16/441 and 18 April 1843, NYPL, micro 17/484.

29. L. M. Child to E. Loring, 21 February 1843, LMC-*SL*, 188, micro 16/445. The issue of self-censorship in Child's *Letters from New York* is discussed in Karcher, "Censorship, American Style," 288–98.

30. L. M. Child to L. Loring, 29 May 1843, C-UM, micro 17/496; Karcher, "Censorship, American Style," 293–94.

31. Ibid., 294; L. M. Child to E. Loring, 18 October 1843, C-UM, micro 18/517 and 25 October 1843, NYPL, micro 18/518; L. M. Child to James

Munroe, 20 December 1843, LMC-*SL*, 205, micro 18/524; L. M. Child to E. Loring, 3 June 1844, NYPL, micro 19/560.

32. Thomas Wentworth Higginson, "Lydia Maria Child," *WJ*, 27 November 1880:377. Higginson's first published work was a review of *Letters from New York* in *The Present;* Higginson, "Lydia Maria Child," 128; Edward Everett Hale, *James Russell Lowell and His Friends* (Boston: Houghton Mifflin, 1899), 97.

13. Bohemia

1. L. M. Child to L. Loring, 14 August 1843, C-UM, micro 17/505.

2. L. M. Child to E. Loring, 26 June 1843, NYPL, micro 17/500 and 26 September 1843, LMC-*SL*, 204, micro 18/515. Before he arrived in New York, David was hoping that Maria would at least help him with the selection of materials to be included in each issue. D. L. Child to Maria Chapman, 18 June 1843, C-BPL.

3. Abby Kelley Foster to M. Chapman, 3 May 1843, W-BPL. Anne Weston thought she could vote for David Child as editor but worried about some "misty sentences" in his letters to the MASS Board. A. Weston to C. and D. Weston, 22 May 1843, W-BPL.

4. E. Loring to D. L. Child, 14 September 1843, C-BPL; L. M. Child to L. Loring, 18 October 1843, C-UM, micro 18/517; Charles C. Burleigh to D. L. Child, 26 October 1843, C-BPL; D. L. Child to M. Chapman, 14 November 1843, C-BPL and 28 December 1843, C-BPL.

5. L. M. Child to A. Loring, 26 December 1843, LMC-*SL*, 206, micro 18/527. Maria eventually found a home for the boy. See [L. M. Child] to [A. Loring], [August] 1845, C-UM, micro 22/629.

6. L. M. Child to E. Loring, 21 February 1843, LMC-*SL*, 188–89, micro 16/455.

7. LMC-*LNY*, 2d ser., 127–28.

8. L. M. Child to Augusta King, 19 September 1843, LMC-*SL*, 202–203, micro 18/511.

9. Henry Steele Commager, *Theodore Parker, Yankee Crusader* (Boston: Beacon Press, 1960), 77; L. M. Child to A. King, 19 September 1843, LMC-*SL*, 202, micro 18/511.

10. L. M. Child to F. Shaw, 18 July 1844, LMC-*SL*, 209–10, micro 20/565. The first volume of *Flowers for Children* was ready for the press in early July 1844, L. M. Child to Charles S. Francis, 3 July 1844, LMC-SLib, micro 19/564.

11. L. M. Child to F. Shaw, 18 July 1844, LMC-*SL*, 210, micro 20/565.

12. L. M. Child to F. Shaw [October 1846], LMC-*SL*, 230, micro 24/676.

13. L. M. Child to S. Shaw, 12 November 1844, HL, micro 20/585; LMC-*LNY*, 1st ser., 198–99.

14. L. M. Child to A. King, 30 October 1844, LMC-*SL*, 216, micro 20/584; L. M. Child to L. Loring, 2 August 1845, LMC-SLib, micro 23/663.

15. L. M. Child to James Miller McKim, 25 September 1843, LMC-C, micro 18/514; Neil Harris, *The Artist in American Society* (New York: George Braziller, 1966), 262–82.

16. L. M. Child to M. Lowell, 18 February 1845, HL, micro 21/606. In a letter to the composer Anthony Heinrich, Child mentioned that she had not had the opportunity to hear good music when she was young. L. M. Child to Heinrich, 29 April 1845, LMC-*SL*, 220, micro 22/613.

17. L. M. Child to F. Shaw, 12 October 1841, LMC-*SL*, 149, micro 11/273; LMC to E. Loring, 12 October 1841, LMC-SLib, micro 11/272.

18. L. M. Child to E. Loring, 18 September 1842, NYPL, micro 15/407.

19. LMC-*SL*, 219.

20. LMC-*LNY*, 2d ser., 23–24. Ole Bull gave two concerts that month in New York, on December 13 and 18. See New York *Evening Post*, 16 December 1843:2.

21. L. M. Child to E. Loring, 22 May 1844, NYPL, micro 19/557; L. M. Child to A. Loring, 13 October 1844, C-UM, micro 20/578.

22. L. M. Child, "Hilda Selfverling," *Fact and Fiction*, 205–40. This story was first published in the *Columbian Ladies and Gentleman's Magazine* in October 1845.

23. Quoted in the *Standard*, 4 July 1844:19; L. M. Child to F. Shaw, 18 July 1844, LMC-*SL*, 210, micro 20/565.

24. L. M. Child to E. Loring, 26 December 1844, NYPL, micro 21/595.

25. L. M. Child, "Home and Politics," *Autumnal Leaves* (New York: C. S. Francis & Co., 1857), 109. The story was first published in 1848 in *Sartain's Union Magazine of Literature and Arts*.

26. L. M. Child, *Good Wives*, 55.

27. Kelley, *Private Woman*, 12–17.

28. Ibid; L. M. Child to A. Loring, 28 December 1844, C-UM, micro 21/597.

29. M. Fuller to A. Loring, 2 May 1845, in Robert Hudspeth ed., *The Letters of Margaret Fuller*, vol. 4 (Ithaca: Cornell University Press, 1987), 66.

30. L. M. Child to A. Loring, 6 February 1844, LMC-*SL*, 217–18, micro 21/604.

31. L. M. Child, "Letters from New York," *Courier*, 19 April 1844, micro 19/548. Maria did her best to find employment for ex-prostitutes. L. M. Child to Jonathan Phillips, 7 March 1843, William Phillips, Jr. Collection, Salisbury, CT, micro 96/2536.

32. L. M. Child to F. Shaw, 2 August 1846, LMC-*SL*, 229, micro 23/664.

33. L. M. Child, "Letter from New York," *Courier*, 6 February 1844, micro 19/536.

34. Ibid.

35. L. M. Child, "Slavery's Pleasant Homes," *Liberty Bell* 4 (1843), 147–60.

36. LMC-*LNY*, 1st ser., 249–50.

37. Quoted in Nancy Woloch, *Women and the American Experience* (New York: Knopf, 1984), 185.

38. L. M. Child, "Speaking in Church," *Standard*, 15 July 1841: 22.

39. This grudging admission that the movement for women's rights had a worthwhile goal was left out of the version of the letter included in the book. See "Letter from New York," *Standard*, 23 February 1843, micro 16/547; LMC-*LNY*, 1st ser., 245.

40. Margaret Fuller, *Woman in the Nineteenth Century* (1855: reprint, New York: Norton, 1971), 172–74.

41. L. M. Child to L. Loring, 8 February 1845, LMC-*SL*, 219, micro 21/605.

42. L. M. Child to A. Loring, 8 December 1845, C-UM, micro 23/641. Fuller to Mary Rotch, 9 January 1846, in Hudspeth, ed., *Letters of Margaret Fuller*, vol. 4: 166.

43. L. M. Child to L. Loring, 14 August 1843, C-UM, micro 17/505.

44. L. M. Child to F. Shaw, 18 February 1847, HL, micro 26/696.

45. Henrietta Sargent to [?], 16 February 1845, AS-BPL; L. M. Child to A. Loring, 6 February 1845, LMC-*SL*, 218, micro 21/604; L. M. Child to L. Loring, 22 June 1845, LMC-*SL*, 224, micro 22/623.

46. L. M. Child to L. Loring, 15 January 1847, LMC-*SL*, 235, micro 24/691.

47. L. M. Child to L. Loring, 2 August 1846, HL, micro 23/664. In a letter Maria wrote to Convers after David had been with her for a visit she spoke disparagingly of country people as "drowsy animals . . . stalled and yoked." L. M. Child to C. Francis, n.d. [23 May 1844?], Massachusetts Historical Society, micro 23/658.

48. L. M. Child to S. Lyman, 28 March 1847, L-APSL, micro 25/706.

49. *Broadway Journal* 1 (10 May 1845): 295–96; *United States Democratic Review* 16 (June 1845): 573.

50. Edgar A. Poe, "The Literati of New York City," *Godey's Lady's Book* (September 1846): 129–30.

51. L. M. Child to John Jay, 2 April [1844?], Jay Family Papers, Special Collections, Columbia University, micro 19/546; L. M. Child to Anthony P. Heinrich, 29 April 1845, LMC-*SL*, 220, micro 22/613.

52. L. M. Child, "Letter from New York," *Courier*, 30 January 1846, micro 23/648.

53. L. M. Child, "The Poet's Dream of the Soul," *Fact and Fiction*, 189.

54. L. M. Child to L. Loring, 31 May 1846, LMC-SLib, micro 23/659.

55. L. M. Child to S. Lyman, 9 April 1847, L-ASPL, micro 25/707 and 28 March 1847, L-ASPL, micro 25/706.

14. Sweeping Dead Leaves and Dusting Mirrors

1. L. M. Child to C. Francis, 20 January 1848, micro 26/725. Maria's letter to Susan Lyman describes John and Rosa as "too excessively taken up with one another to notice who came, or went. Love is a very blissful dream." L. M. Child to Lyman, 4 July 1847, L-APSL, micro 25/710. In the spring of 1846 Maria described John as the "only bond strong enough to bind me to N. York for a single month." L. M. Child to L. Loring, 31 May 1846, LMC-SLib, micro 23/659.

2. L. M. Child to S. Lyman, 4 July 1847, L-APSL, micro 25/710 and 8 August 1847, L-ASPL, micro 25/712. In this letter Maria writes, "David's visit was right pleasant to me, and seemed like a faint gleam of the good old times, when we had a home, though a very humble one"; L. M. Child to F. Shaw, 11 July 1847, HL, micro 25/711.

3. L. M. Child to S. Lyman, 8 August 1847, L-APSL, micro 25/712. She implies in another letter that this or a similar dream included a premonition of death. See L. M. Child to E. Loring, 24 March 1850, LMC-SL, 253, micro 28/778. For her conviction that the Lorings had laid her on the shelf and didn't care about her anymore, see L. M. Child to E. Loring, 7 March 1850, C-UM, micro 28/777.

4. L. M. Child to S. Lyman, 4 November 1847, L-APSL, micro 25/717.

5. In a letter to Susan Lyman written in early 1848, Maria describes "flying about from one town to another, to visit relatives and friends." L. M. Child to S. Lyman, 12 January 1848, L-APSL, micro 26/724.

6. Ibid.; L. M. Child to M. Silsbee, 6 February 1848, LMC-AAS, micro 26/726; L. M. Child to Relief Loring, 12 February 1848, L-SLib, micro 26/727; L. M. Child to Parke Godwin, 22 August 1848, NYPL, micro 26/737.

7. L. M. Child to C. Francis, 20 January 1848, micro 26/725; L. M. Child to M. Silsbee, 17 April 1848, LMC-SL, 238, micro 26/729.

8. L. M. Child to Lucretia Haskins, 26 April 1848, Simison Papers, Beinecke Rare Book and Manuscript Library, Yale University, micro 26/730; L. M. Child to E. Loring, 27 October 1851, LMC-SL, 261, micro 29/815.

9. L. M. Child, *The Progress of Religious Ideas through Successive Ages*, vol. 1 (New York: C.S. Francis & Co., 1855), vii, 84; LMC-LNY, 1st ser., 840.

10. L. M. Child to S. Lyman, 28 January 1849, L-APSL, micro 26/745; L. M. Child to L. Osgood, 9–11 February 1856, LMC-SL, 276, micro 32/906; L. M. Child to L. Loring, [24? 26?] June 1849, L-APSL, micro 26/754 and 30 July 1849, C-UM, micro 27/757.

11. L. M. Child to L. Osgood, 28 June 1846, LMC-SL, 226, micro 23/260.

12. LMC-LNY, 1st ser., 35, 183.

13. L. M. Child to Lydia [B.] Child, 16 February 1849, LMC-SL, 241, micro 26/747.

14. L. M. Child to L. Loring, 8 March 1849, LMC-*SL*, 242–44, micro 26/750; L. M. Child to E. and L. Loring, 14 May 1849, C-UM, micro 27/751.

15. L. M. Child to L. Loring, 8 March 1849, LMC-*SL*, 243–44, micro 26/750.

16. L. M. Child to E. and L. Loring, 14 May 1849, LMC-*SL*, 246–47, micro 26/251.

17. Ibid.

18. Ibid; L. M. Child to L. Loring, 24 June 1849, C-UM, micro 27/753.

19. L. M. Child to C. Francis, 18 September 1849, LMC-C, micro 27/760.

20. L. M. Child to L. Loring, 21 October 1849, LMC-*SL*, 250, micro 27/761.

21. Bremer to L. M. Child, 25 March 1847, L-APSL, micro 25/704; L. M. Child to L. Loring, 21 October 1849, LMC-*SL*, 249–51, micro 27/761.

22. L. M. Child to D. L. Child, 31 August 1849, LMC-*SL*, 249, micro 27/758; L. M. Child to E. Loring, 7 November 1849, LMC-SLib, micro 27/763; L. M. Child to M. Silsbee, 24 January 1850, LMC-AAS, micro 27/775.

23. L. M. Child to E. Loring, 24 March 1850, LMC-*SL*, 253–54, micro 28/778; L. M. Child to L. Loring, 12 November 1849, C-UM, micro 27/764. John had changed the spelling of his name from Child to Childe.

24. L. M. Child to Eliza Scudder, 10 July 1870, LMC-C, micro 73/1952.

15. The Desert of Domesticity

1. L. M. Child to L. Searle, 18 July 1850, LMC-C, micro 28/786.

2. L. M. Child to E. Loring, 28 August 1850, LMC-SLib, micro 28/787; L. M. Child to L. Loring, 24 September 1850, C-UM, micro 28/792.

3. L. M. Child to M. Silsbee, n.d. [1850], LMC-AAS, micro 28/800; L. M. Child to E. Loring, 13 April 1851, LMC-*SL*, 258–59, micro 28/804.

4. L. M. Child to E. Loring, 31 August 1851, LMC-SLib, micro 29/811.

5. L. M. Child to E. Loring, 27 October 1851, LMC-*SL*, 261, micro 29/815 and 31 August 1851, LMC-SLib, micro 29/811.

6. L. M. Child to L. Loring, 8 August 1852, LMC-SLib, micro 29/827; L. Loring to Anna Loring, 15 March 1852, L-SLib.

7. L. M. Child to E. Loring, 6 February 1852, LMC-*SL*, 263, micro 29/820.

8. L. M. Child to E. Loring [1852?], LMC-SLib, micro 29/836.

9. L. M. Child to E. Loring, 27 October 1851, LMC-*SL*, 261, micro 29/815.

10. L. M. Child to L. Loring, 17 October 1852, L-SLib, micro 29/831.

11. L. M. Child to E. Loring, 1 September 185[3], LMC-SLib, micro 30/849; L. M. Child to L. Loring, 12 September 1853, L-SLib, micro 30/

851; L. M. Child to D. L. Child, n.d. [after 12 September 1853?], AS-BPL, micro 30/852.

12. L. M. Child to L. Loring, 12 November 1849, C-UM, micro 27/764; L. M. Child to L. Loring, 16 March 1853, L-SLib, micro 30/840.

13. David was at work on a lengthy translation for the Mexican minister to the United States for which he was paid over $400. L. M. Child to E. Loring, 18 November 1854, L-SLib, micro 31/875; Alfred Sereno Hudson, "The Home of Lydia Maria Child," *New England Magazine*, new series, 2 (1890): 407.

14. Hudson, "Home of Lydia Maria Child," 405; Beatrice Herford, unpublished paper on Lydia Maria Child, WHS, 4; John Langdon Sibley, private journal, no. 1, Harvard University Archives, 368–69.

15. L. M. Child to L. Loring, 16 March 1853, LMC-*SL*, 267–68, micro 30/840.

16. L. M. Child to E. Loring, 5 March 1854, LMC-SLib, micro 30/862; L. M. Child to L. and Mary Osgood, 11 May 1856, LMC-C, micro 33/915.

17. L. M. Child, *Progress of Religious Ideas*, vol. 1:401.

18. L. M. Child to G. Smith, 27 November 1861, Gerrit Smith Collection, George Arents Research Library for Special Collections, Syracuse University, micro 50/1351; Higginson, "Lydia Maria Child," 131–32.

19. Octavius Brooks Frothingham, *Boston Unitarianism* (New York: G. P. Putnam's Sons, 1840), 189.

20. L. M. Child to C. Francis, 13 November 1854, LMC-C, micro 31/874; L. M. Child to C. Francis, 21 November 1855, LMC-C, micro 32/892.

21. Osborne, *Lydia Maria Child*, 133.

22. L. M. Child, *Progress of Religious Ideas*, vol. 3:424.

23. Ibid., vol. 2:175–77.

24. Alice Felt Tyler, *Freedom's Ferment* (New York: Harper & Row, 1962), 83.

25. L. M. Child to E. Loring, 23 November 1842, LMC-*SL*, 181–82, micro 15/425.

26. Quoted in Tyler, *Freedom's Ferment*, 79. Later in life Maria claimed that her long-held belief in clairvoyance dated back to the 1820s and was based on evidence examined and published by French scientists. L. M. Child to *Independent*, before 25 March 1869, micro 71/1891; L. M. Child to E. Loring, 9 May 1855, C-UM, micro 3/883; L. M. Child to Parke Godwin, 20 January 1856, LMC-*SL*, 275, micro 32/899.

27. L. M. Child to L. Searle, 15 May 1860, LMC-*SL*, 350, micro 45/1219.

16. Peace Principles Shivering in the Wind

1. L. M. Child to M. Silsbee, 27 March 1852, LMC-*SL*, 257, micro 28/803.

2. D. L. Child to Robert Haskins, 9 August 1848, C-MR; L. M. Child to C. Francis, n.d. [1853], Beinecke Rare Book and Manuscript Library,

Yale University, micro 30/855. In 1868 Maria described David as "a man of *facts*, and I am always alone in the *mystical* and *poetical* chambers of my soul." She thought such a difference was very common between men and women. L. M. Child to Harriet Sewall, 30 July 1868, Robie-Sewall Papers, Massachusetts Historical Society, micro 69/1843.

3. L. M.Child to Susan (Lyman) Lesley, 29 March [1852], LMC-*SL*, 264, micro 29/822; L. M. Child to F. Shaw, 5 September 1852, LMC-*SL*, 265, micro 29/828.

4. Quoted in James M. McPherson, *Battle Cry of Freedom* (New York: Oxford University Press, 1988), 145.

5. Charles Sumner to L. M. Child, 14 January 1853, micro 29/837.

6. L. M. Child to A. Loring, 8 June 1856, L-SLib, micro 33/918.

7. L. M. Child to C. Sumner, 7 July 1856, LMC-*SL*, 283–84, micro 33/925.

8. L. M. Child to C. Sumner, 12 February 1855, HL, micro 31/879.

9. L. M. Child to C. Sumner, 7 July 1856, LMC-*SL*, 285, micro 33/925.

10. L. M. Child to L. and M. Osgood, 9 July 1856, LMC-*SL*, 287, micro 33/928.

11. L. M. Child to S. Shaw, 3 August 1856, LMC-*SL*, 289–91, micro 33/933.

12. L. M. Child, "Charles Wager," 176; L. M. Child to E. Loring, 24 February 1856, LMC-*SL*, 279, micro 32/908.

13. L. M. Child, "The Kansas Immigrants," *Autumnal Leaves: Tales and Sketches in Prose and Rhyme* (New York: C. S. Francis & Co., 1856), 317–44.

14. Carolyn L. Karcher, "From Pacifism to Armed Struggle: L. M. Child's 'The Kansas Immigrants,' *Emerson Society Quarterly* 34 (1988), 141–42.

15. L. M. Child, "Kansas Immigrants," 339–40, 348, 355, 361.

16. LMC-*SL*, 294; Karcher, "From Pacifism to Armed Struggle," 154.

17. Quoted in *Standard*, 27 December 1856, 3.

18. L. M. Child to A. Loring, 7 August 1856, LMC-SLib, micro 33/934; L. M. Child to S. Shaw, 20 February 1857, HL, micro 36/992.

19. L. M. Child to S. Shaw, 20 March 1857, HL, micro 36/998.

20. L. M. Child to L. Loring, 26 October 1856, C-UM, micro 34/949; Frank Preston Stearns, *The Life and Public Services of George Luther Stearns* (Philadelphia, 1907), 125.

21. L. M. Child to D. L. Child, 27 October 1856, LMC-C, micro 34/951; Lloyd C. Taylor, "To Make Men Free: An Interpretive Study of Lydia Maria Child." Dissertation, Lehigh University, 1956, 259–60; L. M. Child, "To the Women of Kansas," 28 October 1856, *Standard*, 2 January 1857, micro 34/954.

22. L. M. Child to Peter Lesley and Susan [Lyman] Lesley, 9 August 1856, L-APSL, micro 33/935; L. M. Child to S. Shaw, 14 September 1856, LMC-*SL*, 292, micro 34/941.

23. L. M. Child to Sarah Shaw, 9 November 1856, LMC-*SL*, 300, HL, micro 34/956.
24. L. M. Child to E. Loring, 27 November 1856, C-UM, micro 34/961.
25. L. M. Child to S. Shaw, 8 December 1856, LMC-*SL*, 300–301, micro 34/964.
26. L. M. Child to D. L. Child, 21 December 1856, LMC-C, micro 35/971; L. M. Child to Whittier, 2 January 1857, LMC-*SL*, 302, micro 35/975; L. M. Child to C. Sumner, 3 January 1857, HL, micro 35/978.
27. L. M. Child to S. Shaw, 20 February 1857, HL, micro 36/992 and 3 May 1857, HL, micro 36/1001. In December 1856 Maria wrote: "I have a very clear idea of what I *want* to do; but I must make that wait upon what I *can* do." L. M. Child to S. Shaw, 20 December 1856, HL, micro 35/969.
28. L. M. Child to L. Loring, December 1857, C-UM, micro 37/1038.
29. L. M. Child to S. Shaw, 29 May 1858, HL, micro 38/1058 and 6 June 1858, HL, micro 38/1060; L. M. Child to L. and M. Osgood, LMC-*SL*, 314–15, micro 38/1062.
30. L. M. Child to D. L. Child, 20 June 1858, LMC-C, micro 38/1063; L. M. Child to Whittier, 20 June 1858, C-LC, micro 39/1065.
31. L. M. Child to A. Loring, 20 January 1859, C-UM, micro 40/1097.
32. L. M. Child to S. Shaw, 12 January 1859, LMC-*SL*, 319, micro 40/1092.

17. "Strong as an Eagle"

1. Quoted in Stephen B. Oates, *To Purge this Land With Blood: A Biography of John Brown* (Amherst: University of Massachusetts Press, 1984), 305.
2. Quoted in David M. Potter, *The Impending Crisis* (New York: Harper & Row, 1976), 375–76.
3. Potter, *Impending Crisis*, 357–58.
4. L. M. Child to S. Shaw, 4 November 1859, HL, micro 41/1131.
5. L. M. Child to *Tribune*, 10 November 1859, micro 42/1133.
6. L. M. Child to Brown, 26 October 1859, LMC-*SL*, 324–25, micro 41/1123.
7. Child's letter to Wise, 26 October 1859 was first published in the *Tribune*, 12 November 1859, and then in the *Correspondence between Lydia Maria Child and Gov. Wise and Mrs. Mason, of Virginia* (Boston: American Anti-Slavery Society, 1860); see also micros 42/1125, 1127–28, 1134, 1148.
8. Brown to L. M. Child, 4 November 1859, micro 42/1132.
9. Quoted in Oswald Garrison Villard, *John Brown* (New York: Knopf, 1943), 478–79.
10. Emerson to L. M. Child, 23 November 1859, Berg Collection, NYPL, micro 42/1139; Eliza Follen to L. M. Child, 7 December 1859, Miscellaneous Bound, Massachusetts Historical Society, micro 42/1144; Whittier to L. M. Child, 21 October 1859, micro 41/1122.

11. L. M. Child to Daniel Ricketson, 22 December 1859, micro 43/ 1156; Oates, *To Purge this Land*, 322; Craig M. Simpson, *A Good Southerner: The Life of Henry A. Wise of Virginia* (Chapel Hill: University of North Carolina Press, 1985), 211; L. M. Child to M. Chapman, 28 November 1859, AS-BPL, micro 42/1141; quoted in Oates, *To Purge this Land*, 320, 323.

12. Mason to L. M. Child, 11 November 1859, micro 42/1134.

13. Quoted in Oates, *To Purge this Land*, 327.

14. L. M. Child to Brown, 16 November 1959, LMC-*SL*, 328, micro 42/1135; L. M. Child to Parke Godwin, 27 November 1859, LMC-*SL*, 330, micro 42/1138; L. M. Child to S. Lesley, 25 December 1859, L-APSL, micro 43/1163; L. M. Child to L. Osgood, 25 December 1859, LMC-C, micro 43/ 1164.

15. L. M. Child to S. Lesley, 25 December 1859, L-APSL, micro 43/ 1163.

16. L. M. Child to P. and S. Lesley, 20 November 1859, LMC-*SL*, 330, micro 42/1138.

17. L. M. Child to Greeley, 18 December 1859, LMC-*SL*, 333, micro 42/1149. According to Wise's biographer, Brown chose to assault a portion of Virginia where slavery was in retreat. Simpson, *A Good Southerner*, 205.

18. L. M. Child to L. Osgood, 25 December 1859, LMC-C, micro 43/ 1164.

19. L. M. Child to Mason, 17 December 1859, micro 42/1148.

20. Ibid. Jean Fagan Yellin calls Child's letter to Margaretta Mason "a major contribution to the ongoing debate over the definitions of true womanhood. . . . It is northern women like herself, Child writes, who act as true women by acknowledging that, regardless of condition and color, all women are sisters." Yellin, *Women and Sisters*, 62, 64.

21. L. M. Child to Mason, 17 December 1859, micro 42/1148.

22. L. M. Child to S. J. May, 29 September 1867, LMC-*SL*, 474, micro 66/1794. The revolution in communication and printing of the 1840s and 1850s meant that a pamphlet like Maria's *Correspondence* was capable of reaching huge audiences. See James Brewer Stewart, *Wendell Phillips: Liberty's Hero* (Baton Rouge: Louisiana State University Press, 1986), 180.

23. Article from Worcester *Bay State* reprinted in *Liberator*, 27 January 1860:13; *Liberator*, 30 March 1860:49; L. M. Child to New York *Bee*, reprinted in *Liberator*, 29 June 1860, micro 45/1221; *Liberator*, 28 September 1860:153.

24. L. M. Child to Chapman, 22 December 1859, AS-BPL, micro 42/ 1155 and 11 January 1860, AS-BPL, micro 42/1181; L. M. Child to L. Osgood, n.d. [January 1860], LMC-C, 42/1182.

25. L. M. Child to Chapman, 15 January 1860, AS-BPL, micro 44/ 1189; L. M. Child to S. Shaw, 28 December 1859, HL, micro 42/1169; L. M. Child to S. Johnson, 3 February 1860, Samuel Johnson Collection, James Duncan Phillips Library, Essex Institute, Salem, MA, micro 44/1197.

18. Secession Winter

1. Oates, *To Purge this Land,* 360.
2. L. M. Child to H. Sargent, 27 May 1860, LMC-*SL,* 352–53, micro 45/122.
3. Stewart, *Wendell Phillips,* 210; L. M. Child to Sumner, 4 April 1860, HL, micro 45/1211 and 17 June 1860, LMC-*SL,* 354, micro 45/1227.
4. David Donald, *Charles Sumner and the Coming of the Civil War* (New York: Knopf, 1961), 336–56; L. M. Child to Sumner, 17 June 1860, LMC-*SL,* 354, micro 45/1227.
5. Stewart, *Wendell Phillips,* 211; James M. McPherson, *The Struggle for Equality* (Princeton: Princeton University Press, 1964), 28.
6. Thomas H. O'Connor, *Lords of the Loom: The Cotton Whigs and the Coming of the Civil War* (New York: Charles Scribner's Sons, 1968), 144–45; Stewart, *Wendell Phillips,* 212–13.
7. L. M. Child to L. Mott, 26 February 1861, LMC-*SL,* 376–77, micro 47/1290.
8. Quoted in McPherson, *Struggle for Equality,* 42–43; Baer, *Heart is Like Heaven,* 261–62.
9. Julia Ward Howe, *Reminiscences* (Boston: Houghton Mifflin, 1899), 157.
10. E. Heywood to S. May, 19 December 1860, AS-BPL.
11. McPherson, *Struggle for Equality,* 43; L. M. Child to S. Shaw, 25 January 1861, LMC-*SL,* 370, micro 47/1280; Lutz, *Crusade for Freedom,* 277.
12. L. M. Child to S. Shaw, 25 January 1861, LMC-*SL,* 370–71, micro 47/280.
13. McPherson, *Struggle for Equality,* 44.
14. Quoted in McPherson, *Struggle for Equality,* 43.
15. L. M. Child, *The Right Way, The Safe Way, Proved by Emancipation in the British West Indies* (New York: 5 Beekman Street, 1860).
16. Ibid., 93, 94. It is unlikely that many copies of the earlier pamphlet, *The Evils of Slavery, and the Cure of Slavery* (Newburyport, MA: Charles Whipple, 1836), found their way south.
17. L. M. Child to John Curtis Underwood, 15 November 1860, LMC-*SL,* 364–65, micro 46/1266; L. M. Child to L. Osgood, 10 April 1860, LMC-C, micro 45/1213; L. M. Child to Robert Folger Wolcutt, 15 November 1860 and 5 December 1860, Special Manuscript Collection, Columbia University, micros 47/1267 and 47/1272; L. M. Child to Underwood, 26 October 1860, LMC-*SL,* 362–63, micro 46/1263.
18. L. M. Child, ed., *The Patriarchal Institution, as Described by Members of its Own Family* (New York: AASS, 1860), 22.
19. L. M. Child, *The Duty of Disobedience to the Fugitive Slave Act* (Boston: AASS, 1860), 3.
20. Ibid.
21. Ibid., 21–23.

22. Harriet A. Jacobs, *Incidents in the Life of a Slave Girl, Written by Herself* (1861; reprint Cambridge: Harvard University Press, 1987). This reprint is edited with a valuable introduction by Jean Fagan Yellin.
23. L. M. Child to Whittier, 4 April 1861, LMC-*SL*, 379, micro 48/1300.
24. L. M. Child to F. Shaw, 8 January 1861, LMC-*SL*, 369, micro 47/1278.
25. L. M. Child to Sumner, 28 January 1861, LMC-*SL*, 372–73, micro 47/1281.
26. L. M. Child to L. Mott, 26 February 1861, LMC-*SL*, 376–77, micro 47/1290.
27. L. M. Child to Sumner, 7 July 1856, LMC-*SL*, 283, micro 33/925.

19. "God Is Ruling the Whirlwind"

1. *Commonwealth History of Massachusetts*, vol. 4 (New York: The States History Company, 1927–1930), 507.
2. L. M. Child to L. Osgood, 26 April 1861, LMC-*SL*, 380, micro 48/1302.
3. L. M. Child to L. Osgood, 5 November 1861, C-SLib, micro 50/1343.
4. L. M. Child to L. Osgood, 15 April 1861, LMC-*SL*, 380, micro 48/1302.
5. L. M. Child to L. Searle, 9 June 1861, LMC-*SL*, 384, micro 48/1312; L. M. Child to L. Osgood, 7 May 1861, LMC-*SL*, 381, micro 48/1306; L. M. Child to Eliza Scudder, 22 April 1864, LMC-*SL*, 444, micro 58/1561; Mary Trageser, "Wayland in the Civil War," unpublished paper, Wayland Historical Society.
6. L. M. Child to L. Osgood, 26 April 1861, LMC-*SL*, 380, micro 48/1302. Maria was far less sanguine than men like Wendell Phillips, who in July 1861 described a prevailing sentiment "at the North, that the Union either does or shall mean liberty in the end." Quoted in McPherson, *Struggle for Equality*, 59.
7. L. M. Child to L. Osgood, 26 April 1861, LMC-*SL*, 380, micro 48/1302. L. M. Child to *Independent*, before 23 July 1865, micro 63/1672.
8. McPherson, *Struggle for Equality*, 69–70.
9. L. M. Child to Helen Frances Garrison, 5 November 1861, LMC-*SL*, 397–98, micro 50/1344.
10. L. M. Child to L. Osgood, 1 September 1861, LMC-*SL*, 393, micro 49/1330; L. M. Child to Whittier, 22 September 1861, C-LC, micro 49/1337; McPherson, *Struggle for Equality*, 66–67. Late in the summer of 1861 the AASS published a pamphlet of David's entitled *The Rights and Duties of the United States Relative to Slavery Under the Laws of War*.
11. L. M. Child to L. Searle, 11 October 1861, LMC-*SL*, 396, micro 49/1340; L. M. Child to G. Smith, 7 January 1862, Gerrit Smith Collection, George Arents Research Library for Special Collections, Syracuse Uni-

versity, micro 50/1364; L. M. Child to S. Shaw [March ?] 1862, LMC-C, micro 51/1398.

12. L. M. Child to H. Sargent, 26 July 1861, LMC-C, micro 49/1321; L. M. Child to S. Shaw, 9 June 1862, NYPL, micro 52/1413 and n.d., LMC-C, micro 48/1304.

13. L. M. Child to L. Searle, 19 November 1861, General Manuscripts, Princeton University, micro 50/1349; L. M. Child to W. Haskins, 28 December 1862, LMC-*SL*, 423–24, micro 54/1446.

14. L. M. Child to G. Julian, 16 June 1862, micro 52/1414; L. M. Child to L. Tappan, 23 March 1862, Lewis Tappan Papers, Manuscript Division, Library of Congress, micro 51/1396; L. M. Child to Roger Wallcut, 20 April 1862, AS-BPL, micro 52/1405; L. M. Child to Mattie Griffith, 21 December 1862, LMC-*SL*, 421, micro 96/2554; L. M. Child to S. Shaw [1862, after January 18?], LMC-C, micro 50/1368.

15. This proclamation, which declared that all slaves in areas still under rebellion were free, actually freed none. It applied only to areas over which the federal government as yet had no control.

16. L. M. Child, "Willie Wharton," *Atlantic Monthly* (March 1863): 324–45.

17. L. M. Child to William P. Cutler, 12 July 1862, LMC-*SL*, 414, micro 52/1417.

18. L. M. Child to S. Shaw, n.d. [1863], 172–73, micro 55/1478.

19. L. M. Child to S. Shaw, 16 June 1863, LMC-*SL*, 432–33, micro 55/1483.

20. Sarah Shaw to L. M. Child, n.d. [June 1863], AS-BPL, micro 55/1485; L. M. Child to Samuel Sewall, 21 June 1863, Robie-Sewall Papers, Massachusetts Historical Society, micro 55/1484.

21. McPherson, *Struggle for Equality*, 158–60. In March 1862 the Childs had sent a cash contribution to the newly formed Massachusetts Educational Commission for the contrabands, which proposed sending supplies, teachers, and other workers to places like Port Royal. L. M. Child to William Endicott, 2 March 1862, E. Atkinson Papers, Massachusetts Historical Society, micro 51/1392.

22. L. M. Child to S. and F. Shaw, 17 July 1863, C-WHS, micro 56/1490.

23. In August 1862 Child wrote that she was "constantly worried that Sarah Shaw's son will be killed in battle." L. M. Child to H. Sargent, 21 August 1862, LMC-C, micro 53/1424.

24. L. M. Child to W. Haskins, 30 April 1863, LMC-*SL*, 427, micro 55/1477.

25. Quoted in Peter Burchard, *One Gallant Rush: Robert Gould Shaw and His Brave Black Regiment* (New York: St. Martin's Press, 1965), 93–94.

26. L. M. Child to S. Shaw, 25 July 1863, LMC-*SL*, 433, micro 56/1491.

27. L. M. Child to E. Scudder, 13 December 1863, LMC-C, micro 57/1520.

28. L. M. Child to Lydia B. Child, 23 November 1863, C-SLib, micro 57/1517.

29. L. M. Child to S. Shaw, 29 November 1863, HL, micro 57/1518; L. M. Child to E. Scudder, 6 November 1863, LMC-C, micro 56/1510.

30. L. M. Child to L. Loring, n.d. [January 1864], L-SLib, micro 57/1528; L. M. Child to Garrison, 27 December 1863, AS-BPL, micro 57/1525.

31. L. M. Child to L. Osgood, 21 March 1864, LMC-C, micro 58/1551.

32. Ibid.; L. M. Child to *Liberator*, 19 February 1864, micro 58/1538.

33. Ibid.

34. L. M. Child to L. Osgood, 21 March 1864, LMC-C, micro 58/1551.

35. L. M. Child to L. Osgood, 8 May 1864, LMC-C, micro 59/1563; L. M. Child to E. Scudder, 8 May 1864, LMC-C, micro 59/1564.

36. L. M. Child, "Employments in 1864," LMC-C.

37. L. M. Child to G. Smith, 4 April 1864, LMC-SL, 441, micro 58/1555; L. M. Child to Whittier, 19 June 1864, micro 59/1569.

38. L. M. Child to G. Smith, 4 April 1864, LMC-SL, 441, micro 58/1555; L. M. Child to Whittier, 3 July 1864, C-LC, micro 59/1573.

39. McPherson, *Battle Cry of Freedom*, 609–10.

40. L. M. Child to Lydia B. Child, 18 September 1864, C-SLib, micro 59/1583; L. M. Child to Whittier, 8 November 1864, C-LC, micro 60/1588.

41. L. M. Child to E. Scudder, 14 November 1864, LMC-C, micro 60/1593; L. M. Child, *Looking Toward Sunset* (Boston: Ticknor and Fields, 1865), v; L. M. Child to L. Osgood, 11 January 1862, LMC-C, micro 54/1452.

42. L. M. Child to H. Sargent, 8 January 1865, LMC-C, micro 61/1614; L. M. Child to Anna Loring Dresel, 18 January 1865, C-SLib, micro 61/1619; Whittier to L. M. Child, 15 November 1864, Berg Collection, NYPL, micro 60/1594; L. Loring to L. M. Child, 10 February 1865, L-SLib, micro 61/1632; *Atlantic Monthly* 15 (February 1865), 255.

43. L. M. Child to Annie Fields, 9 February, James Thomas Fields Collection, Huntington Library, Pasadena, CA, micro 61/1631; L. M. Child to L. Osgood, 13 April 1865, LMC-SL, 451–52, micro 62/1653.

20. We Are All Brethren

1. L. M. Child to H. Sargent, 24 July 1870, LMC-C, micro 74/1953; L. M. Child to H. Sewall, 12 February 1869, Robie-Sewall Papers, Massachusetts Historical Society, micro 70/1882.

2. L. M. Child to S. Shaw, 3 September 1865, HL, micro 63/1680; Ellen Wright to Martha Wright, April 1865, quoted in Mary E. Massey, *Bonnet Brigades* (New York: Knopf, 1966), 27.

3. L. M. Child to M. Silsbee, 5 February 1865, LMC-C, micro 66/1761a and 24 February 1865, LMC-AAS, micro 66/1765.

4. L. M. Child, *The Freedmen's Book* (Boston: Ticknor & Fields, 1865), 188.

5. Ibid., 55.
6. Ibid., 81.
7. Ibid., 138.
8. Foner, *Reconstruction*, 146.
9. L. M. Child to L. Osgood, 14 February 1870, LMC-*SL*, 490, micro 72/1928; L. M. Child to L. Tappan, 1 January 1869, Lewis Tappan Papers, Manuscript Division, Library of Congress, micro 70/1867.
10. L. M. Child to S. Shaw, n.d. [1865], LMC-*SL*, 453, micro 62/1657.
11. Quoted in Foner, *Reconstruction*, 177; L. M. Child to S. Shaw, n.d. [1865], LMC-*SL*, 454, micro 62/1657; L. M. Child to Theodore Tilton, 6 May 1865, micro 62/1659.
12. L. M. Child to S. Shaw, 11 August 1865, LMC-*SL*, 457, micro 63/1676; L. M. Child to Julian, 22 January 1866, micro 64/1704.
13. L. M. Child to S. Shaw, 7 September 1866, LMC-*SL*, 463, micro 65/1738; L. M. Child to A. (Kelley) Foster, 28 March 1869, LMC-*SL*, 486, micro 71/1892.
14. L. M. Child to *Independent*, 17 January 1867, LMC-*SL*, 468–69, micro 66/1760.
15. L. M. Child to E. C. Stanton, n.d., LMC-*SL*, 467–68, micro 66/1750.
16. Elizabeth Cady Stanton et al., *History of Woman Suffrage*, vol. 2 (New York, 1881), 96; L. M. Child to E. C. Stanton, n.d., LMC-*SL*, 467, micro 66/1750. Meltzer and Holland claim that a search of the National Archives petition collection produced none signed by her, LMC-*SL*, 467.
17. L. M. Child to *Independent*, before 17 January 1866, LMC-*SL*, 469, micro 66/1760.
18. L. M. Child to J. T. Fields, 19 October 1866, James Thomas Fields Collection, Huntington Library, Pasadena, CA, micro 63/1686 and 3 November 1867, HL, micro 67/1799.
19. Carolyn L. Karcher, "Lydia Maria Child's *A Romance of the Republic:* An Abolitionist Vision of America's Racial Destiny," in Arnold Rampersad and Deborah E. McDowell, eds., *Slavery and the Literary Imagination* (Baltimore: Johns Hopkins University Press, 1988), 81.
20. Karcher, *"A Romance of the Republic"*; Jean Fagan Yellin, *Women & Sisters*, 74–76.
21. L. M. Child to J. T. Fields, 30 March 1867, James Thomas Fields Collection, Huntington Library, Pasadena, CA, micro 66/1768; L. M. Child to F. Shaw, 28 July 1867, HL, micro 67/1789; L. M. Child to L. Loring, 1 January 1868, L-SLib, micro 68/1806.
22. Osborne, *Lydia Maria Child*, 145; Karcher suggested to me that the miscegenation theme may have been in part responsible for Maria's friends' cool response to the book.
23. L. M. Child to A. Loring, 3 December 1866, L-SLib, micro 66/1749.
24. L. M. Child to L. Loring, 10 December 1866, L-SLib, micro 66/1752; L. M. Child to Lydia B. Child, 18 October 1868, C-SLib, micro 67/1795.

25. L. M. Child to S. Shaw, LMC-*SL*, 475–76, micro 68/1811.

26. L. M. Child to E. Scudder, 10 May 1868, LMC-C, micro 69/1828; L. M. Child to M. Silsbee, 10 May 1868, LMC-AAS, 69/1830.

27. Alfred W. Cutting, "Childhood Memories," unpublished manuscript, WHS, 12; L. M. Child to S. Shaw, 17 June 1866, LMC-*SL*, 462, micro 65/1724. Child's letters to Alfred Cutting are in the collection of the Society for the Preservation of New England Antiquities in Boston.

28. L. M. Child to S. Sewall, 21 March 1868, LMC-*SL*, 478, micro 68/1819.

29. Ibid.

30. Francis Paul Prucha, *The Great Father: The United States Government and the American Indians*, vol. 1 (Lincoln, NE: University of Nebraska Press, 1984), 479–92.

31. L. M. Child, *An Appeal for the Indians* (1868) reprinted in Karcher, *Hobomok & Other Writings*, 216, 219.

32. Ibid., 220.

33. Ibid., 231–32.

34. L. M. Child to L. Osgood, 18 March 1870, LMC-C, micro 73/1936; Ahlstrom, *A Religious History*, 764–66; David Robinson, *The Unitarians and Universalists* (Westport, CT: Greenwood Press, 1985), 107–13; L. M. Child to *Standard*, before 25 July 1868, micro 69/1842.

35. L. M. Child to L. Osgood, 18 March 1870, LMC-C, micro 73/1936; L. M. Child to *Standard*, 1 October 1870, micro 74/1959c.

36. L. M. Child to L. Osgood, 4 February 1869, LMC-*SL*, 484, micro 70/1878; Foner, *Reconstruction*, 460–88.

37. L. M. Child to Lucy Larcom, 15 May 1871, Larcom Collection, Essex Institute, Salem, MA, micro 75/1994; L. M. Child, to *Standard*, 17 September 1870, micro 74/1959a.

38. For the Childs' views on the disbanding of the antislavery societies see D. L. Child and L. M. Child to Anti-Slavery Friends, *Standard*, 16 April 1870, micro 73/1942.

39. L. M. Child to L. Osgood, 14 February 1870, LMC-*SL*, 489–90, LMC-C, micro 72/1928.

40. L. M. Child to E. Scudder, 6 February 1870, LMC-*SL*, 488–89, micro 72/1926. Maria was elected a vice-president of the Massachusetts Woman Suffrage Association and later of the New England Woman Suffrage Association. See *WJ*, 5 February 1870:40; 3 June 1871:22.

41. George W. Julian, *Speeches on Political Questions* (New York: Hurd and Houghton, 1871).

42. L. M. Child to G. W. Curtis, 22 July 1872, Special Manuscript Collection, Columbia University, micro 78/2056; L. M. Child to S. Shaw, n.d., LMC-*SL*, 519, micro 82/2142. Child's initial defense of Sumner was published in the *Boston Journal*, 2 July 1872, micro 78/2052.

43. L. M. Child to H. Sewall, 16 December 1873, LMC-*SL*, 517, micro 81/2123. In 1868, the Childs had an annual income of a little under $800; see L. M. Child to S. Shaw, 2 February 1868, LMC-*SL*, 475, micro 68/1811.

44. L. M. Child to H. Sewall, 4 July 1874, Robie-Sewall Papers, Massachusetts Historical Society, micro 82/2160.
45. L. M. Child to Lydia B. Child, 18 September 1874, Alma Lutz Collection, Schlesinger Library, Radcliffe College, micro 79/2176.

21. Free to the Last

1. L. M. Child to A. Francis, 23 November 1874, micro 84/2201; L. M. Child to John Wight, 13 December 1874, C-WHS, micro 84/2204.
2. L. M. Child to Susan Damon, 11 February 1875, C-WHS, micro 84/2218.
3. L. M. Child to S. Shaw, 11 April 1875, HL, micro 85/2227.
4. L. M. Child to S. Shaw, 18 June 1876, LMC-*SL*, 534–35, micro 87/2276.
5. Elizabeth Stuart Phelps Ward, *Chapters from a Life* (Boston: Houghton Mifflin, 1897), 182–84.
6. L. M. Child to S. Shaw, n.d. [1876], LMC-*SL*, 536, micro 87/2284; L. M. Child to A. [Loring] Dresel, 12 August 1868, LMC-*SL*, 482, micro 69/1844; L. M. Child to H. Sewall, 10 July 1868, LMC-*SL*, 481, micro 69/1841; L. M. Child to E. Damon, 13 February 1877, C-WHS, micro 87/2305.
7. L. M. Child to Whitney, 8 April 1877, LMC-*SL*, 540–41, micro 88/2317; L. M. Child to James Redpath, LMC-*SL*, 547, micro 89/2360.
8. L. M. Child to Whitney, 14 August 1878, Anne Whitney Papers, Wellesley College, micro 91/2406.
9. L. M. Child to Parsons, 8 July 1877, LMC-C, micro 2332; L. M. Child to S. Shaw, 22 July 1877, HL, micro 88/2334.
10. L. M. Child to S. Shaw, 13 July 1877, HL, micro 88/2333.
11. L. M. Child to T. W. Higginson, 20 June 1877, AS-BPL, micro 88/2325 and 9 September 1877, HL, micro 88/2340.
12. L. M. Child to J. T. Fields, 28 October 1877, LMC-*SL*, 545, micro 89/2343.
13. L. M. Child, *Aspirations of the World: A Chain of Opals* (Boston: Roberts Brothers, 1878), 1–2.
14. L. M. Child to J. T. Fields, 9 June 1878, James T. Fields Collection, Huntington Library, Pasadena, CA, micro 90/2395.
15. L. M. Child to S. Shaw, 31 July 1877, LMC-*SL*, 542–43, micro 88/2335.
16. L. M. Child to F. Shaw, 26 October 1879, LMC-*SL*, 559, micro 93/2475.
17. Whitney to L. M. Child, 22 September 1880, Anne Whitney Papers, Wellesley College, micro 95/2521.
18. L. M. Child to S. Shaw, 23 September 1880, micro 95/2522. Sources describing Maria Child's last days include: "Graveside Memorial Service for Lydia Maria Child, October 18, 1880," a manuscript in the Wayland

Public Library, and Marcia Cutting's journal entry for 23 October 1880, Society for the Preservation of New England Antiquities.

19. "Remarks of Wendell Phillips at the Funeral of Lydia Maria Child, October 23, 1880," in LMC-L, 263–68.

20. Hudson, "Home of Lydia Maria Child," 410.

Epilogue

1. A copy of the will from the Probate Court in Cambridge, Massachusetts is in Baer, *Heart is Like Heaven*, 311–16.

Selected Bibliography

Works of Lydia Maria Child

An Appeal in Favor of That Class of Americans Called Africans. Boston: Allen & Ticknor, 1833.

Anti-Slavery Catechism. Newburyport, MA: Charles Whipple, 1836.

Aspirations of the World: A Chain of Opals. Collected, with an introduction, by Child. Boston: Roberts Brothers, 1878.

Authentic Anecdotes of American Slavery. Nos. 1, 2, and 3, anonymous, attributed to Child. Newburyport, MA: Charles Whipple, 1835, 1835, 1838.

Autumnal Leaves. New York: C. S. Francis & Co., 1857.

The Collected Correspondence of Lydia Maria Child. Edited by Patricia G. Holland, Milton Meltzer, and Francine Krasno. Millwood, NY: Kraus Microform, 1980. Microfiche.

The Coronal; A Collection of Miscellaneous Pieces, Written at Various Times. Boston: Carter & Hendee, 1832.

Correspondence between Lydia Maria Child and Gov. Wise and Mrs. Mason of Virginia. Boston: American Anti-Slavery Society, 1860.

The Duty of Disobedience to the Fugitive Slave Act. Boston: American Anti-Slavery Society, 1860.

Emily Parker, or Impulse, not Principle. Boston: Bowles and Dearborn, 1827.

Evenings in New England. Boston: Cummings, Hilliard & Co., 1824.

The Evils of Slavery, and the Cure of Slavery. Newburyport, MA: Charles Whipple, 1836.

345

Fact and Fiction: A Collection of Stories. New York: C. S. Francis/ Boston: J.H. Francis, 1846.

The Family Nurse; or Companion of The Frugal Housewife. Boston: Charles J. Hendee, 1837.

The First Settlers of New-England; or, Conquest of the Pequods, Narragansets and Pokanokets. Boston: Munroe & Francis, 1828/ New York: C. S. Francis, 1829.

Flowers for Children, 3 vols. New York: C. S. Francis/ Boston: J. H. Francis, 1844, 1845, 1847.

The Freedmen's Book. Edited with contributions by Child. Boston: Ticknor and Fields, 1865.

The Frugal Housewife. Boston: Marsh & Capen, and Carter & Hendee, 1829. Republished as *The American Frugal Housewife.* Boston: Carter & Hendee, 1832.

Hobomok: A Tale of Early Times. 1824. Reprinted in *Hobomok & Other Writings on Indians by Lydia Maria Child.* Edited by Carolyn L. Karcher. New Brunswick, NJ: Rutgers University Press, 1986.

Incidents in the Life of a Slave Girl, by Harriet A. Jacobs. Edited with a preface by Child. Boston, 1861.

Isaac T. Hopper: A True Life. Boston: John P. Jewett, 1853.

The Juvenile Souvenir. Edited with contributions by Child. Boston: Marsh & Capen, and John Putnam, 1828.

Ladies Family Library: The Biographies of Madame de Staël and Madame Roland. Boston: Carter & Hendee, 1832; *The Biographies of Lady Russell and Madame Guyon.* Boston: Carter & Hendee, 1832; *Good Wives.* Boston: Carter & Hendee, 1833; *The History of the Condition of Women in Various Ages and Nations*, 2 vols. Boston: John Allen, 1835.

Letters from New York. 1st ser., New York: C. S. Francis/ Boston: James Munroe, 1843; 2d ser., New York: C.S. Francis/ Boston: J. H. Francis, 1845.

Letters of Lydia Maria Child with a Biographical Introduction by John G. Whittier. Boston: Houghton Mifflin & Co., 1882.

The Little Girl's Own Book. Boston: Carter, Hendee & Babcock, 1831.

Looking Toward Sunset. Edited with contributions by Child. Boston: Ticknor & Fields, 1865.

Lydia Maria Child: Selected Letters, 1817–1880. Edited by Milton Meltzer and Patricia G. Holland. Amherst: University of Massachusetts Press, 1982.

"Mary French and Susan Easton." *Juvenile Miscellany.* 3d ser., 6 (May/June 1834): 186–201.

The Mother's Book. Boston: Carter, Hendee & Babcock, 1831.

The Oasis. Edited with contributions by Child. Boston: Allen and Ticknor, 1834.

The Patriarchal Institution, as Described by Members of its Own Family. Compiled by Child. New York: American Anti-Slavery Society, 1860.

Philothea: A Romance. Boston: Otis Broaders & Co., 1836.

The Progress of Religious Ideas through Successive Ages. 2 vols. New York: C. S. Francis, 1855.

The Rebels; or, Boston before the Revolution. Boston: Cummings, Hilliard & Co., 1825.

The Right Way, The Safe Way, Proved by Emancipation in the British West Indies, and Elsewhere. New York, 1860.

A Romance of the Republic. Boston: Ticknor and Fields, 1867.

Speeches on Political Questions, by George W. Julian. Introduction by Child. New York: Hurd and Houghton, 1871.

"Slavery's Pleasant Homes." In *The Liberty Bell.* Boston, 1843. Reprinted in *Wife or Spinster: Stories by Nineteenth Century Women.* Edited by Jessica Amanda Salmonson, et al. Camden, ME: Yankee Books, 1991.

"Willie Wharton." *Atlantic Monthly* 11 (March 1863): 324–45.

General Published Works

Books and Pamphlets

Adby, Edward S. *Journal of a Residence and Tour in the United States of North America.* London, 1835.

Ahlstrom, Sidney A. *A Religious History of the American People.* New Haven: Yale University Press, 1972.

Baer, Helene G. *The Heart is Like Heaven: The Life of Lydia Maria Child.* Philadelphia: University of Pennsylvania Press, 1964.

Barnes, Gilbert H., and Dwight L. Dumond, eds. *Letters of Theodore Dwight Weld, Angelina Grimké Weld, and Sarah Grimké, 1822–1844.* New York, 1934.

Baym, Nina K. *Women's Fiction: A Guide to Novels by and about Women in America, 1820–1870.* Ithaca: Cornell University Press, 1978.

Beach, Seth Curtis. *Daughters of the Puritans.* Boston: American Unitarian Association, 1905.

Blanchard, Paula. *Margaret Fuller: From Transcendentalism to Revolution.* New York: Delacorte Press, 1978.

Block, Marguerite Beck. *The New Church in the New World: A Study of Swedenborgianism in America.* New York: Henry Holt & Co., 1932.

Blumin, Stuart M. *The Emergence of the Middle Class: Social Experience in the American City, 1760–1900.* New York: Cambridge University Press, 1989.

Brooks, Van Wyck. *The Flowering of New England.* New York: E.P. Dutton & Co., 1936.

Brown, Arthur W. *Always Young for Liberty: Biography of William Ellery Channing.* Syracuse: Syracuse University Press, 1956.

Bruccoli, Matthew J. *The Profession of Authorship in America: The Papers of William Charvat.* Columbus: Ohio State University Press, 1968.

Buell, Lawrence. *New England Literary Culture: From Revolution through Renaissance.* Cambridge: Cambridge University Press, 1986.

Cameron, Kenneth W. *Philothea, or Plato against Epicurus: A Novel of the Transcendental Movement in New England.* Hartford, 1975.

Chambers-Schiller, Lee. *Liberty, a Better Husband: Single Women in America: The Generation of 1780–1840.* New Haven: Yale University Press, 1984.

Chapman, Maria Weston. *Right and Wrong in Boston.* Boston, 1836.

Chevigny, Beth Gale. *The Woman and the Myth: Margaret Fuller's Life and Writings.* Westbury, NY: The Feminist Press, 1976.

Child, David Lee. *Despotism of Freedom.* Boston, 1833.

Child, David Lee. *Oration in Honor of Universal Emancipation in the British Empire.* Boston, 1834.

Child, David Lee. *Rights and Duties of the United States Relative to Slavery Under the Laws of War.* New York: American Anti-Slavery Society, 1861.

Commager, Henry Steele. *Theodore Parker, Yankee Crusader.* Boston: Beacon Press, 1960.

Conrad, Susan Phinney. *Perish the Thought: Intellectual Women in Romantic America, 1830–1860.* New York: Oxford University Press, 1976.

Cott, Nancy. *The Bonds of Womanhood.* New Haven: Yale University Press, 1977.

Dillon, Merton L. *The Abolitionists: The Growth of A Dissenting Minority.* New York: Norton, 1974.

Emerson, Ralph Waldo. *Nature.* Boston: James Munroe & Co., 1836.

Foner, Eric. *Reconstruction: America's Unfinished Revolution.* New York: Harper & Row, 1988.

Formisano, Ronald P. *The Transformation of Political Culture: Massachusetts Parties, 1790s–1840s.* New York: Oxford University Press, 1983.

Friedman, Lawrence J. *Gregarious Saints: Self and Community in American Abolitionism, 1830–1870.* New York: Cambridge University Press, 1982.

Fuller, Margaret. *The Letters of Margaret Fuller.* Edited by Robert Hudspeth. Ithaca: Cornell University Press, 1987.

Fuller, Margaret. *Woman in the Nineteenth Century.* 1845. Reprint. New York: Norton, 1971.

Garrison, W. P., and Garrison, F. J. *William Lloyd Garrison: The Story of His Life as Told by His Children.* New York, 1885–1889.

Garrison, William Lloyd. *Letters of William Lloyd Garrison.* Edited by Walter M. Merrill. Cambridge: Harvard University Press, 1971–1981.

Gerteis, Louis S. *Morality & Utility in American Antislavery Reform.* Chapel Hill: University of North Carolina Press, 1987.

Greene, Lorenzo Johnson. *The Negro in Colonial New England, 1620–1776.* New York: Columbia University Press, 1942.

Gura, Philip F. *The Wisdom of Words: Language, Theology, and Literature in the New England Renaissance.* Middletown, CT: Wesleyan University Press, 1981.

Heilbrun, Carolyn G. *Writing a Woman's Life.* New York: Norton, 1988.

Hersh, Blanch Glassman. *The Slavery of Sex: Feminist-Abolitionists in America.* Urbana: University of Illinois Press, 1978.

Karcher, Carolyn, ed. *Hobomok & Other Writings on Indians by Lydia Maria Child.* New Brunswick: Rutgers University Press, 1986.

Kelley, Mary. *Private Woman, Public Stage.* New York: Oxford University Press, 1984.

Kerber, Linda. *Women of the Republic: Intellect and Ideology in Revolutionary America.* Chapel Hill: University of North Carolina Press, 1980.

Kraditor, Aileen S. *Means and Ends in American Abolitionism.* New York: Pantheon Books, 1969.

Lerner, Gerda. *The Grimké Sisters from South Carolina.* New York: Schocken Books, 1971.

Lesley, Susan Lyman. *Recollections of My Mother, Mrs. Anna Jean Lyman.* Boston: Houghton Mifflin & Co., 1899.

Litwack, Leon F. *North of Slavery: The Negro in the Free States, 1790–1860.* Chicago: University of Chicago Press, 1961.

Lowell, James Russell. *Fable for Critics.* Boston: Houghton Mifflin & Co., 1892.

Lutz, Alma. *Crusade for Freedom: Women of the Antislavery Movement.* Boston: Beacon Press, 1968.

Mabee, Carleton. *Black Freedom: The Nonviolent Abolitionists from 1830 through the Civil War.* New York: Macmillan, 1970.

Macleod, Anne Scott. *A Moral Tale: Children's Fiction and American Culture, 1820–1860.* Hamden, CT: Shoe String Press, 1975.

Martineau, Harriet. *The Martyr Age of the United States.* Boston: Weeks, Jordan & Co., 1839.

McPherson, James M. *The Struggle for Equality.* Princeton: Princeton University Press, 1964.

McPherson, James M. *Battle Cry of Freedom.* New York: Oxford University Press, 1988.

Melder, Keith. *The Beginnings of Sisterhood: The American Woman's Rights Movement, 1800–1850.* New York: Schocken Books, 1977.

Meltzer, Milton. *Tongue of Flame: The Life of Lydia Maria Child.* New York: Thomas Y. Crowell, 1965.

Merrill, Walter M. *Against Wind and Tide: A Biography of William Lloyd Garrison.* Cambridge: Harvard University Press, 1963.

Miller, Perry. *The Transcendentalists, An Anthology.* Cambridge: Harvard University Press, 1950.

Norton, Mary Beth. *Liberty's Daughters: The Revolutionary Experience of American Women.* Boston: Little, Brown, 1980.

Nye, Russell B. *William Lloyd Garrison and the Humanitarian Reformers.* Boston: Little, Brown, 1955.

O'Connor, Thomas H. *Lords of the Loom: The Cotton Whigs and the Coming of the Civil War.* New York: Charles Scribner's Sons, 1968.

Osborne, William S. *Lydia Maria Child.* Boston: Twayne Publishers, 1980.

Pease, Jane H., and Pease, William H. *Bound with Them in Chains: A Biographical History of the Antislavery Movement.* Westport, CT: Greenwood Press, 1972.

Proceedings of the Anti-Slavery Convention of American Women. New York: William S. Dorr, 1837.

Richards, Leonard L. *"Gentlemen of Property and Standing": Anti-Abolitionist Mobs in Jacksonian America.* New York: Oxford University Press, 1970.

Robinson, David. *The Unitarians and Universalists.* Westport, CT: Greenwood Press, 1985.

Rose, Anne C. *Transcendentalism as a Social Movement.* New Haven: Yale University Press, 1981.

Rossback, Jeffrey. *Ambivalent Conspirators: John Brown, The Secret Six, and A Theory of Slave Violence.* Philadelphia: University of Pennsylvania Press, 1982.

Schlesinger, Arthur M. *The Age of Jackson.* Boston: Little, Brown, 1945.

Simpson, Craig M. *A Good Southerner: The Life of Henry A. Wise of Virginia.* Chapel Hill: University of North Carolina Press, 1985.

Spann, Edward K. *The New Metropolis: New York City, 1840–1857.* New York: Columbia University Press, 1981.

Stearns, Frank Preston. *The Life and Public Services of George Luther Stearns.* Philadelphia, 1907.

Stewart, James Brewer. *Wendell Phillips: Liberty's Hero.* Baton Rouge: Louisiana State University Press, 1986.

Stewart, James Brewer. *Holy Warriors: The Abolitionists and American Slavery.* New York: Hill and Wang, 1976.

Thomas, John L. *The Liberator: William Lloyd Garrison.* Boston: Little, Brown, 1963.

Thompson, George. *Letters and Addresses by George Thompson During his Mission in the United States.* Boston: Isaac Knapp, 1837.

Thorp, Margaret Ferrand. *Female Persuasion: Six Strong-Minded Women.* New Haven: Yale University Press, 1949.

Tyack, David B. *George Ticknor and the Boston Brahmins.* Cambridge: Harvard University Press, 1967.

Walters, Ronald G. *The Antislavery Appeal.* Baltimore: The Johns Hopkins University Press, 1976.

Ward, Elizabeth Stuart Phelps. *Chapters from a Life.* Boston: Houghton Mifflin & Co., 1897.

Weld, Theodore. *American Slavery as It Is: Testimony of a Thousand Witnesses.* 1839. Reprint. New York: Arno Press, 1988.

Woloch, Nancy. *Women and the American Experience.* New York: Alfred A. Knopf, 1984.

Yellin, Jean Fagan. *Women & Sisters: The Antislavery Feminists in American Culture.* New Haven: Yale University Press, 1990.

Yellin, Jean Fagan, ed. *Incidents in the Life of a Slave Girl,* by Harriet A. Jacobs. Reprint. Cambridge: Harvard University Press, 1987.

Articles

Crapol, Edward P. "Lydia Maria Child: Abolitionist Critic of American Foreign Policy." In *Women and American Foreign Policy: Lobbyists, Critics, and Insiders*, edited by Edward P. Crapol, 1–17. Westport, CT: Greenwood Press, 1987.

Curtis, George Ticknor. "Reminiscences of N. P. Willis and Lydia Maria Child." *Harper's New Monthly Magazine* 81 (October 1890): 717–20.

Dall, Caroline. "Lydia Maria Child and Mary Russell Mitford." *Unitarian Review* 19 (June 1883): 519–31.

Emerson, Ralph Waldo. "Swedenborg; or the Mystic." In *Representative Men*, 91–146. Boston: Houghton Mifflin & Co., 1903.

Filler, Louis. "Lydia Maria Francis Child." In *Notable American Women*, edited by E.T. James et al., 330–33. Cambridge: Harvard University Press, 1971.

Hallowell, Anna D. "Lydia Maria Child," *Medford Historical Register* 3 (July 1900): 95–117.

Higginson, Thomas Wentworth. "Lydia Maria Child." In *Contemporaries*, 108–141. Boston: Houghton Mifflin & Co., 1899.

Higginson, Thomas Wentworth. "Lydia Maria Child." In *Eminent Women of the Age*, edited by James Parton, 38–65. Hartford, CT: S. M. Betts, 1868.

Holland, Patricia G. "Lydia Maria Child as a Nineteenth-Century Professional Author." *Studies in the American Renaissance* (1981): 157–67.

Holland, Patricia G. "Lydia Maria Child." *Legacy* 5 (Fall 1988): 45–52.

Holland, Patricia G., and Milton Meltzer. "Biography of Lydia Maria Child." In *Guide and Index* to *The Collected Correspondence of Lydia Maria Child*, 23–34. New York: Kraus Microform, 1980.

Hudson, Alfred Sereno. "The Home of Lydia Maria Child." *New England Magazine*, New ser., 2 (1890): 402–14.

Jaher, Frederic Cople. "Nineteenth Century Elites in Boston and New York." *Journal of Social History* (Fall 1972): 34–63.

Jeffrey, Kirk. "Marriage, Career, and Feminine Ideology in Nineteenth-Century America: Reconstructing the Marital Experience of Lydia Maria Child, 1828–1874." *Feminist Studies* 2 (1975): 113–30.

Karcher, Carolyn L. "Censorship American Style: The Case of Lydia Maria Child." *Studies in the American Renaissance* (1985): 283–303.

Karcher, Carolyn L. "From Pacifism to Armed Struggle: L. M. Child's 'The Kansas Immigrants.' " *Emerson Society Quarterly* 34 (1988): 141–58.

Karcher, Carolyn L. "Lydia Maria Child." In *Dictionary of Literary Biography*, 74:43–53.

Karcher, Carolyn L. "Lydia Maria Child's *A Romance of the Republic:* An Abolitionist Vision of America's Racial Destiny." In *Slavery and the Literary Imagination*, edited by Arnold Rampersad and Deborah E. McDowell, 81–103. Baltimore: Johns Hopkins University Press, 1988.

Karcher, Carolyn L. "Patriarchal Society and Matriarchal Family in Irving's 'Rip Van Winkle' and Child's 'Hilda Silfverling.' " *Legacy* 2 (Fall 1985): 31–44.

Karcher, Carolyn L. "Rape, Murder and Revenge in 'Slavery's Pleasant Homes': Lydia Maria Child's Antislavery Fiction and the Limits of Genre." *Women's Studies International Forum* 9 (1986): 323–32.

Kerber, Linda. "The Abolitionist Perception of the Indian." *Journal of American History* 62 (1975): 271–95.

Lerner, Gerda. "The Political Activities of Antislavery Women." In *The Majority Finds Its Past: Placing Women in History*, 111–28. New York: Oxford University Press, 1979.

Miller, Perry. "From Edwards to Emerson." In *Errand into the Wilderness*, 184–203. New York: Harper & Row, 1964.

Myerson, Joel. "Convers Francis and Emerson." *American Literature* (March 18, 1978): 17–36.

Newell, William. "Memoir of the Rev. Convers Francis." In *Proceedings of the Massachusetts Historical Society* (March 1865): 233–53.

Streeter, Robert. "Mrs. Child's 'Philothea': A Transcendental Novel?" *New England Quarterly* 16 (December 1943): 648–54.

Thorp, Margaret Ferand. "Dusting Mirrors: L. Maria Child." In *Female Persuasion: Six Strong-Minded Women*, 215–43. New Haven: Yale University Press, 1949.

Woodall, Guy R., ed. "The Journals of Convers Francis," parts 1 and 2. *Studies in the American Renaissance* (1981): 265–343, (1982): 227–84.

Periodicals and Newspapers

American Anti-Slavery Standard, New York
American Traveller, Boston
Courier, Boston
Juvenile Miscellany, edited by L.M. Child, Boston (1826–1834)
Liberator, Boston
The Liberty Bell, Boston
Massachusetts Journal, Boston
Massachusetts Daily Journal, Boston
Massachusetts Weekly Journal, Boston
Massachusetts Journal & Tribune, Boston
Woman's Journal, Boston

Unpublished Sources

Manuscript Collections

The bulk of Lydia Maria Child's correspondence can be found in microfiche in *The Collected Correspondence of Lydia Maria Child*, edited by Patricia

G. Holland, Milton Meltzer, and Francine Krasno. Millwood, NY: Kraus Microform, 1980. The following manuscript collections contain additional useful material.

Anti-Slavery Collection, Department of Rare Books and Manuscripts, Boston Public Library. Includes letters of David Child.
Child Family Papers, Milton Ross Collection, Corona del Mar, California.
Child Papers, Department of Rare Books and Manuscripts, Boston Public Library.
Child Papers, Department of Rare Books, Cornell University Library.
Child Papers, Manuscript Division, Library of Congress.
Child Papers, Massachusetts Historical Society. Includes letters of David Child.
Child Papers, Schlesinger Library, Radcliffe College.
Child Papers, Wayland Historical Society.
David Lee Child Papers, Department of Rare Books, Cornell University Library.
Loring Family Papers, Schlesinger Library, Radcliffe College.
Lydia Maria Child Papers, American Antiquarian Society, Worcester, Massachusetts.
Lydia Maria Child Papers, Department of Rare Books, Cornell University Library.
Lydia Maria Child Papers, Medford Historical Society.
Lydia Maria Child Papers, Schlesinger Library, Radcliffe College.
Lydia Maria Child Papers, Society for the Preservation of New England Antiquities.
Weston Family Papers, Department of Rare Books and Manuscripts, Boston Public Library.

Interviews

Elizabeth Miller of Norridgewock, Maine, May 1987.
Lydia Merrill of Oroville, California, October 1986.

Dissertations and Papers.

Bonham, Martha E. "A Critical and Biographical Study of Lydia Maria Child." Master's Thesis, Columbia University, 1926.
Clifford, Deborah Pickman. "Creating a Biography of Lydia Maria Child." Paper given at the American Studies Association annual meeting, 1988.
Cutting, Alfred W. "Childhood Memories." Unpublished paper, Wayland Historical Society.
Karcher, Carolyn L. "Woman of Letters as Political Activist: A Literary Approach to the Biography of Lydia Maria Child." Paper given at the American Studies Association annual meeting, 1988.

Kellow, Margaret. "Lydia Maria Child: Antebellum Woman as Political Activist." Paper given at the annual meeting of the Organization of American Historians, 1991.

Kellow, Margaret. "Must the Baby Go Out with the Bathwater? Psychohistory, Biography and Lydia Maria Child." Paper given at the American Studies Association annual meeting, 1988.

Ponder, Lisa Johnson. "The Legal Philosophy of Maria Child and Its Impact Upon her Law Reform Strategy." Paper given at the American Studies Association annual meeting, 1988.

Ponder, Lisa Johnson. "The Making of an Abolitionist: The Early Life Jurisprudential Development of L. Maria Child, 1802 to 1833." Master's Thesis, University of Oregon, 1987. University Microfilms, 1987.

Samuels, Shirley. "The Identity of Slavery." Paper given at the American Studies Association annual meeting, 1988.

Snay, Mitchell. "A World in Themselves and Each Other: Leadership in the New England Anti-Slavery Society." Seminar Paper, Brandeis University, 1976.

Taylor, Lloyd C., Jr. "To Make Men Free: An Interpretative Study of Lydia Maria Child." Dissertation, Lehigh University, 1956. University Microfilms, 1973.

Acknowledgments

I have lived with Lydia Maria Child for more than a decade, and, while my knowledge and understanding of this complex woman has come primarily from her writings, this portrait of her could not have been drawn without the advice and help of a great many people.

Credit for inspiring me to begin work on Child goes to Eva Moseley, curator of manuscripts at the Schlesinger Library. Pat Holland, principal editor of the microfiche edition of Child's letters, pointed the way to archives containing other Child manuscripts and to individuals who could provide further information.

Thanks to the microfiche edition of Child's letters and the availability of many of her books in the Abernethy Collection here at Middlebury College, I was able to do much of my research at or near home. Bob Buckeye, Kay Lauster, and Fleur Laslocky—all staff members of the Starr Library—went out of their way to be helpful.

Because Child spent most of her life in and around Boston, I did extensive research there. Over the course of the last decade I have spent many hours in the Rare Book Room of the Boston Public Library, which houses a major antislavery collection. I am very grateful to the staff there for their assistance. I spent nearly as much time at the Boston Athenaeum, where the reference librarians were always willing to help. My thanks go also to Lorna Condon, Librarian at the Society for the Preservation of New England Antiquities, who showed me a recently acquired collection of Child's letters to a Wayland neighbor, Alfred Cutting. Thanks are also due to the Watertown, Medford, Wayland, and West Boylston Public Libraries.

Joe Goesalt and Helen Emery, both members of the Wayland Historical Society, deserve special thanks for devoting the better part of a Sunday to showing Carolyn Karcher and me their Child holdings. We were also driven by the Childs' old house and given a tour of the graveyard where Maria and David are buried.

Farther afield was the Cornell Department of Rare Books and Manuscripts, where Lynn Farrington and other staff members went out of their way to be helpful. The American Antiquarian Society in Worcester, Massachusetts, which contains the most complete run of the *Massachusetts Journal*, also deserves my thanks. In addition I am grateful to Louise Woofenden for information about the early Swedenborgians in Boston.

The search for information on Child's early life took me first to Medford. My thanks go to Joseph Valeriani, President of the Medford Historical Society, for letting me see the Child collection there, and to Paul Bater for bringing me up to date on Medford history. In Norridgewock, Maine, Elizabeth Miller was an invaluable source of information on that town's early history.

Information on David Child came from various sources. I am particularly grateful to Milton Ross, a Child family descendant, who let me read the letters in his collection. Lydia Merrill, another Child family descendant, and Dorothy and Ormond Roberts of West Boylston, Massachusetts, were also helpful.

Mary Jackson, a most skillful and generous sleuth, was an invaluable research assistant for the years the Childs spent in Northampton. She also developed a great fondness for David and uncovered much useful information about him and his beet sugar business. Finally, Mary read the final manuscript and offered a number of helpful suggestions.

Such editorial assistance has been invaluable in leading me to a satisfactory understanding of this complex and elusive woman. Among others, I would like to express my gratitude to three fellow Child scholars: Carolyn L. Karcher, Margaret Kellow, and Lisa Ponder, all of whom shared their insights as well as their knowledge of Child. Carolyn has been especially generous both in sharing her ideas about Child and in offering to read the final manuscript.

Sally Brady's writing workshops on Naushon Island first taught me how to listen to Maria herself and not be overwhelmed by what others said about her. Brady's husband Upton deserves thanks not only for his skillful editing of the manuscript but more especially for helping me to understand the many paradoxes of this woman's life. My thanks also go to William B. Catton for his editorial help. Thanks also to Paul Mariani, who read some early chapters, and to Wendy Strothman, the director of Beacon Press.

Finally, this book would never have gone to press without the tireless help of my husband, Nicholas, who not only listened to hours of talk about Child and read the manuscript in various drafts, but who also helped me with the often frustrating complexities of printing the final version on the computer. In recent months he has often interrupted his own scholarly work to cries of anguish from my study upstairs.

Cornwall, Vermont
September 1991

Index

Abenaki, 27, 39
Abolitionists, 104, 243, 296; and
black suffrage, 274–77; Boston
Clique of, 110–11; and John
Brown, 236–37, 240, 241–42;
LMC joins, 92, 94–99, 104–7;
and Civil War, 257, 259; divi-
sion among, 146–51, 157, 164;
in Greenfield, MA, 143; and
Andrew Johnson, 274–75; last
meeting of, 287; and Lincoln,
247; organization of, 96–99,
108; and political action, 147–
48, 221, 247. *See also* Antiaboli-
tionists; Antislavery; Antislavery
societies
Adams, Hannah, 49
Adams, John Quincy, 63–64, 164
Alcott, Bronson, 184, 266, 286,
292–93
Alcott, Louisa May, 293
Alexander, Francis, 51
American Anti-Slavery Society
(AASS), 131, 155, 182; and

DLC's editorship of *Standard*,
183, 201–2, 230, 248; LMC
and, 158, 163–68, 201–3, 244;
and disunionism, 164–66; division within, 147–51, 157–58;
meetings of, 108, 147, 151, 156,
159, 161, 165–66
American Colonization Society:
abolitionists and, 92, 94, 97,
102, 104; DLC and, 94, 97;
LMC and, 100, 102
Antiabolitionists, 115–18, 120,
165, 246–51, 257
Antislavery: DLC's views on, 94,
96–97, 99, 257; petitions, 108,
133, 143, 164; receptions, 265–
66, 288. *See also* Abolitionists
Antislavery societies, 108; LMC
and, 109, 129, 163, 168, 186,
230, 234, 288; factionalism
within, 146–51, 159–60, 163–68;
in Northampton, 139, 141–43.
See also American Anti-Slavery
Society (AASS); Boston Female

359